RELIGIOUS PERSPECTIVES IN AMERICAN CULTURE

PRINCETON STUDIES

IN AMERICAN CIVILIZATION

NUMBER 5

VOLUME II

RELIGION IN AMERICAN LIFE

RELIGIOUS PERSPECTIVES IN AMERICAN CULTURE

EDITORS: JAMES WARD SMITH

AND A. LELAND JAMISON

PRINCETON, NEW JERSEY

PRINCETON, UNIVERSITY PRESS

1961

L. C. Card 61-5383

The Editors wish to express their gratitude
to the Carnegie Foundation
for a generous grant which made these four volumes possible,
and to Mrs. Helen Wright
for her continuous invaluable assistance in many ways.

Printed in the United States of America
by Vail-Ballou Press, Binghamton, New York

CONTENTS. VOLUME II

RELIGIOUS PERSPECTIVES IN AMERICAN CULTURE

INTRODUCTION

I

THIS is the second volume in a four volume series on the subject of religion in American life. The principles in terms of which the series has been conceived have been described in the introductory essay to the first volume of the series. The other essays in that volume dealt primarily with the historical development of American religious thought and institutions. It is hoped the essays in the present volume will be provocative as a selective cross-section of the kinds of study which can be made of the various ways in which religion influences contemporary American life.

Every one, we suppose, is aware in a general way that religious ideas and emotions can permeate the life of a people, providing norms and goals according to which, both consciously and unconsciously, they react to their daily concerns. When one tries to be specific in describing these influences, however, one is likely to be impressed both by their complexity and by their breadth of range. The influence of religious traditions is felt in classrooms, in law courts, and in the caucuses of politicians. It is at work in the political oratory one hears, the motion pictures and television shows one watches, the novels and the poetry one reads. In no single instance is the influence uniform or simple; it is almost always subtle, indirect, and puzzling. When we first conceived of the present volume of essays, we amassed a list of no less than thirty-five desirable topics, from which in the long run we were forced to be content with the selection of ten. We have settled on two groups of five essays: the first group includes perspectives in education, law, and political action; the second group includes a variety of perspectives in the arts. The third volume of our series is devoted to religion and economic thought.

The perspectives here are essentially contemporary rather than historical. Nonetheless, a good deal of history will be found in the present volume. Understanding the problem of religion and education as it exists in 1960 requires some grasp of its deep historical roots. Understanding the full impact of religious ideas in the contemporary novel requires a sense of the long and remarkable history of the religious novel. And so it is in all matters. But while the reader will find here much that is history—the history of education, of constitutional interpretation, of lobbying techniques, of the various art forms—our intention is to demonstrate the wide variety of ways in which religion engages the total life of the nation. We are concerned here primarily with influences felt outside the churches and the seminaries, hoping thereby to increase the reader's awareness of the impact of a religious tradition on his schooling, in his legal affairs, in his political action, and in the arts he creates and enjoys.

The essays, as we have said, fall into two groups. The first five call attention to several ways in which religion is involved in the social and political life of the nation. The problem of education, which recurs in a number of essays throughout the four volumes, is treated by Will Herberg. He concerns himself primarily with the complex matter of secondary education, places it in historical perspective, and shows how religion has tended over three centuries to lose its original status as the chief end of the educational process. He argues that the refusal, particularly by Roman Catholics, to subordinate the religious end to other cultural goals leads to conflict in regard to public financial support of church-affiliated schools. He suggests that a new formula is needed for sustaining universal education in a democratic, pluralistic, but non-discriminatory society. Wilber Katz mentions this same problem as one test-case of religious liberty under the Constitution, and maintains that carefully considered state support of parochial schools is essential to the achievement of full religious freedom. His essay is a defense of the "strict neutrality" interpretation of the constitutional guarantee of religious freedom, and he includes a discussion of the bearing of religious beliefs upon penal practice, especially capital punishment. Three essays treat problems that arise in the area of political behavior. In general, there are two ways in which religious belief and political action come together. On the one hand, Americans as individuals inject into political conflicts and debates innumerable shadings which are religious in character; on the other hand, the churches as organized institutions are important elements in the power structure of American political methods. William Lee Miller, Dayton D. McKean, and R. Morton Darrow examine with varying emphasis both of these aspects of the political dimension of American religion. Their findings indicate that the bearing of religion on political action has been highly ambiguous, seldom clearly defined, and never entirely effective. Here as elsewhere the tension between the ideal and the actual, between the intended and the achieved, is never quite resolved. It is possible that such tension is a continuing mark of the vitality of a civilized society.

The second group of five essays is devoted to the arts. The prose, the poetry, the music, and the architecture of America have seldom if ever achieved the heights of true greatness. We have produced no *Divine Comedy* or *Paradise Lost;* we have erected no Chartres Cathedral; we have given birth to no El Greco, to no Beethoven. Nonetheless, testimony to religious concern is amply evident in the works of art we have produced.

In the field of literature, Willard Thorp studies the peculiar genre of the religious novel with special reference to its phenomenal appeal to the reading public. The works he examines merit no prizes for literary excellence, but they have mirrored and perhaps shaped conventional folk piety in a way comparable, however vulgarized, to the medieval morality plays. Carlos Baker, considering works which are controlled by higher standards of excellence, documents the repeated use of Biblical themes and the continuous influence of the language of the King James Version of the Bible in the writings of the major novelists. Richard Blackmur strikes at dead center of the problem of defining the religious dimension of poetry. As for America, he has ignored the abundance of sometimes crudely pious verses which, like the religious best sellers, no doubt express something essential in our mass consciousness. At the same time, he shows that we have had our moments, and that, from time to time, the genuine spirit is present.

Americans have also sung songs and built churches. In music and architecture, as in theology, American religion has been derivative, mostly drawing on age-old traditions of Europe. Classical forms persist, repeatedly modified by new circumstances. In a panoramic survey of American religious music from the pre-Columbian Indians and the earliest Spanish missions to the sanctified syncopation of contemporary revivalism, Leonard Ellinwood delineates the blending of old and new into music wherein Americans have voiced their faiths, ideals, and hopes. This musical achievement has been surprisingly substantial, and the total Christian heritage has been enriched thereby. In church architecture, as in church music, basic traditional forms have been variously modified by different conceptions of the nature of the church and of worship as well as by the ready availability of particular building materials and by the requirements of climate. The tasteless and the imitative, along with a careless disregard of theological implications, have too often degraded American church architecture. Once again, however, there are brighter elements in a drab picture. Donald Egbert traces the history from the seventeenth century to the present, and with painstaking care supports the claim that the American house of worship has often expressed something deep and of lasting value in the spirit of man.

Throughout all these essays one senses the gropings of the religious consciousness toward appropriate expression and effective implementation of deeply held convictions, gropings which never quite find fulfillment, yet never despair of attaining "a city which hath foundations, whose builder and maker is God." True greatness may usually be lacking; the ideal may be constantly obscured or perverted by ignorance and self-interest; but in the last analysis Americans have probably been neither better nor worse than their counterparts anywhere. They have simply had other opportunities, obligations, and resources. They are what they are—these essays claim no more than to describe what has been and is.

II

We have noted that our ten perspectives are highly selective. It remains to mention some of the more important topics we have regretfully ignored.

The absence in the present volume of any essay which deals with religious factors in our economic thought is explained by the presence of Volume Three in the series. The reader is referred to Volume Three itself and to our account of its history in the introductory essay of Volume One. Among genuine gaps, the following may be mentioned:

There has been in recent years a significant flight of Protestantism from the cities. There is need for careful study of the role religion is playing—active as well as passive—as new forms of community life are developing in city and suburb. The Special Program in American Civilization at Princeton University, under whose auspices these volumes have been produced, is currently offering a senior seminar on developments in urban and suburban life. It is noteworthy that in numerous topics for research in this seminar, the religious question plays an important part.

Again, there is evidence on all sides that the pattern of the American family—the traditional seedbed of religious awareness—is significantly changing. The effects on American society of recent technological advances, the challenges to human dignity inherent in automation and in mass organization, have their influence upon religious feeling and religious practice. So too does the enforced idleness of a rapidly expanding older and "retired" population. As for the younger generation, even today's "beatniks" might have been a topic for a study in religious attitudes.

In several cases, a perspective here included has further ramifications which we have ignored. We include no essay which examines alternative views concerning the proper role of religion in higher education. Our essay on religion and the law selects only a few from an almost limitless range of possibilities. What, for example, are the moral and legal implications of marriages and adoptions across religious and racial boundaries? Or, again, to what extent are the sex-laws of the various states rooted in religious traditions; to what extent is our changing attitude toward these laws intertwined with our changing religious consciousness?

Such problems, and many others, we have left untouched. Many of them, though not all, receive constant attention in pulpit and press. We cite them as additional examples of an enormous range of perspectives from which we have had to select a mere handful. Certain topics, however, we have omitted for more positive reasons. These are the topics which we have considered too close to us, too much a matter of highly charged dispute at the moment, for scholarly objectivity to be achieved in 1960. We conclude with a few remarks about two such burning topics.

During the final stage of preparation of these volumes one of the major national political parties has, for the second time in our history, nominated a Roman Catholic for President of the United States. As we go to press it is impossible to say with any assurance how the American people will react, but it is certain that whatever happens during the campaign of 1960 will constitute an important phase in the evolution of our religious attitudes. One of the most persistent themes of these volumes concerns the thoroughly Protestant tone of America's past. There are, however, numerous references to the relatively recent but impressive growth of Catholicism in the nation. In early fall, 1960, the reaction to the nomination of Senator Kennedy as candidate for President seems to be twofold: first, there have been proclamations on all sides that we must act "maturely" and "keep religion out" of the campaign; second, possibly as a consequence of the foregoing, there have been confident predictions that there would be an enormous difference between the present situation and that confronted by Governor Alfred E. Smith in the campaign of 1928.

It has been conceded by all serious commentators—and not least vehemently by Senator Kennedy himself—that the American system has no place for ecclesiastical coercion in the political process; it has been further assumed that religious commitment in itself should not disqualify any candidate for high office. What is not so clear to many voters is the degree to which the official stand of the Roman Catholic hierarchy in the United States repudiates the traditional ecclesiastical claim to dominance over temporal affairs. Senator Kennedy has followed Governor Smith in the disavowal of any obligation to submit to ecclesiastical direction. Indeed, the candidate of 1960 has spelled out his adherence to the constitutional separation of church and state even more explicitly than did Smith in 1928. It remains to be seen whether or not the electorate will take the candidate at his word. In any case, the religious question may not be unambiguously resolved, inasmuch as secular issues may determine the final result of the election.

All intelligent men hope that irresponsible slander and canard will be kept out of the campaign of 1960; but a man would be unintelligent indeed if he failed to observe as closely as possible the important religious factor which is unquestionably part of the campaign of 1960. If this nation no longer cares about "the Catholic question," we have come a long way indeed since the times of Cotton Mather and of Thomas Jefferson. And as time passes, it is increasingly evident that 1960 will not be altogether different from 1928. Whether or not Senator Kennedy finally is elected, slander and canard seem at the moment to be growing, especially in that nebulous area called the "Protestant underground."

Temptation to include an essay concerning the problem of a Catholic in the White House has been great. We have decided, however, and we hope wisely, that an objective interpretation would be impossible during the excitement of the campaign. By the time these volumes are available, the results of this election will be a matter of history. We believe that the several essays here offered—those which discuss religious factors in the political traditions and practices of the nation—will be of more assistance to the reader who seeks a balanced appraisal of November 1960 than would any hasty and hazardous prophecies attempted before the event.

A second problem has seemed to us too current and too explosive to justify a scholarly essay at the present time: the role played by the churches in the present conflict both in the south and throughout the nation over the question of civil rights for the American Negro. In our initial planning for these volumes we wrote each author a letter in which we explained that, apart from a section of the bibliography, we did not intend to have an essay devoted solely to the problems of the American Negro. We therefore asked each author to include in his essay where possible some reference to those problems. Thus in Volume One the essay on Catholicism and the essay on special Protestant groups both discuss developments in which the Negro was involved. In the present volume the essay on music treats of the Negro Spiritual and the Negro is mentioned in a number of other contexts. On the other hand, the burning current question of civil rights for the Negro and its relation to the religious ethos of the nation is not discussed. We feel that the scholar performs a more valuable function if he examines for the reader the principles and traditions on the basis of which Americans individually are making their decisions on the controversial issues of today.

It has been a difficult but exciting task to plan and to edit the essays here offered. We hope that they will serve one purpose above all others: to stimulate the reader to an increased awareness of the complexity of the religious perspectives in American culture.

RELIGION AND EDUCATION IN AMERICA

WILL HERBERG

Religion and education have been related throughout American history in a most intimate way, yet also in a way often laden with tension and ambiguity. From the seventeenth century, when the two were closely identified in purpose and content, to the twentieth, when they have become separated and sometimes even hostile, the problem of the proper relation between the two has been one of the central concerns of both. It is not easy to say whether the shift of outlook over the centuries, or the continuing preoccupation with the problem in so many different historical contexts, is the more impressive. In any case, there is perhaps no better perspective from which to assess the place of religion in American culture than that which is afforded by the eventful story of its involvement with public education, that other all-absorbing interest of the American people.

No retelling of the story will be attempted here. What will be attempted is an analysis of the underlying patterns defining the changing relation between religion and education from the time of the Puritans to the present day. Perhaps something significant may emerge from such an account, especially since religion in public education has now once again become an urgent problem agitating the American people far beyond the narrow circle of educators and religious leaders.

If we scan the three centuries that separate the establishment of common schools in New England, where religion was the heart of the venture, from the current discussions over the "crisis" in education, where religion is one of the sharpest points of controversy, we may well ask what coherence there is to observe amidst so much change and confusion. Yet I think there is one generalization we can venture which may help give some measure of meaning to the story, and cast some light on its drift and direction. Roughly, we may say that, whereas in the first period of our history education was conceived as serving the ends of religion, and in the second the two were regarded as parallel but separate enterprises equally worthy of support, today the original relation has been reversed. Religion today, where it is most highly valued and most insistently recommended, is valued and recommended precisely for its contribution to education, the goals and ends of which are defined in other terms, in terms of the culture. Somewhere between the second and the third phases came the attempt to dispense with religion altogether in the educational enterprise; that experiment is now coming to an end, but its consequences are still with us, exerting a powerful influence upon our contemporary thinking on the question of religion and education.

I

The story begins in New England with the establishment of schools in Boston in 1635 and the passage of the celebrated act by the Massachusetts General Court twelve years later requiring towns within its jurisdiction to set up similar institutions for the education of children. Other New England settlements followed, and within a few decades the pattern was established—"public schools" set up by government authority, usually accessible to poor children without charge. Almost simultaneously, in 1636, Harvard College was founded, and at the opening of the next century (1701), Yale. On both levels, the animating purpose was emphatically religious: the schools were intended to form Christian men, Christian citizens, and Christian ministers, not as a by-product but directly. They were instruments of the church, which was, at least in the beginning, virtually coterminous with the community. Education was an enterprise undertaken primarily in the interests of religion, with religion of course defined in terms of the Calvinist orthodoxy then dominant in New England.

It was not entirely different in the other colonies, although the impetus there was generally not so strong. In the south, the initiative was taken largely by the English missionary societies, such as the Society for the Propagation of the Gospel in Foreign Parts, and many of the schools thus set up were under the jurisdiction of the Bishop of London. Nor was the New England precedent of government schools commonly followed; "public schools" in the south were more along the English model, schools set up by government authority indeed, but operated and managed under charter by some corporation or non-governmental agency. The pattern in the middle colonies was as variegated as were the colonies themselves; schools set up by the many sectarian groups, usually employing the ethnic tongue, flourished side by side with schools set up by the Society for Propagating Christian Knowledge Among the Germans in America, the purposes of which included instruction in the English language. Nor were schools and academies undertaken as private ventures by any means unknown. William Penn's original idea that "the Governor and Provincial Council shall erect and order all public schools" could not work out in a colony that became so pluralistic religiously as did Pennsylvania, and the situation was no different in the other middle colonies. Yet almost everywhere, and in almost every case, the avowed purpose of founding schools was religious: the schools were there to make Christians. On that there was agreement, although there was wide disagreement on what being a Christian meant. Aside from some of the private ventures, perhaps, there was here no essential difference in orientation between Puritan New England, on the one side, and the Anglican South or the multi-religious middle colonies, on the other—at least not in the beginning. The resolution of the Virginia Assembly in 1661, proposing that a college (later William and Mary) be established, illustrates this. "Whereas the want of able and faithful ministers deprives us of those great blessings and mercies that always attend upon the service of God," the Assembly declared, "be it enacted that for the advance of learning, education of youth, supply of the ministry, and promotion of piety, there be land taken up or purchased for a college and free school. . . ." Education was an enterprise understood and interpreted in terms of promoting Christian piety and undergirding the Christian life.

But from the beginning, in America, secularizing tendencies made themselves felt. Even Puritan orthodoxy was not quite singleminded in its educational outlook, for the Puritans were not only the apostles of the Reformation, but also the heirs of medieval scholasticism and the humanistic Renaissance. Harvard's first curriculum, drawn up in 1642, plainly shows the influence of four different, and sometimes divergent, traditions: (1) the liberal arts tradition of the medieval cathedral schools and universities; (2) the philosophical renascence of thirteenth-century Aristotelianism; (3) the classical-humanist "revival of letters" in the Renaissance; and (4) the Reformation conviction that the fundamental purpose of all human enterprises, including education, was to promote the Christian faith and advance the Christian life. In other colonies, but also before long in New England, the notion of "useful knowledge," often understood in very practical vocational terms, emerged to modify quite drastically the original religious idea informing education. John Winthrop had very early expressed his apprehension at the attention given to the pagan classics at Harvard, but was quickly reassured by the theologians that humanistic learning could be made to serve the Christian purpose. As the eighteenth century wore on, the secularization of educational purpose and program became increasingly evident, though the external religious framework remained virtually intact.

The Great Awakening of the 1730's revitalized the religious idea in education, as indeed it revitalized religiously most other aspects of American life. The revivalist fervor overflowed the narrower confines of religion and profoundly affected every facet of contemporary culture. New schools and colleges were founded, and the earlier religious dedication was reemphasized in warmer and more evangelical forms. But the dilemma of Christian education was not overcome; on the contrary, it was intensified and given a new dimension of Christian concern.

The Puritan problem, which so disturbed Winthrop, was: *what kind of education for religion?* Nothing is more striking than the fact that, whereas the purpose of Puritan education was Christian, its philosophy and psychology were humanistic, harking back to Athens rather than to Jerusalem. Philip Leon, in his brilliant inaugural address "The Professors," has well defined the difference. "Classical Antiquity," Leon points out, "made man's ideal, or good, self-realization in one form or another. To find this good, . . . we must look first for that function which differentiates man from the other species in the genus animal (his rationality or *logos*); then we must look for its *areté* (fitness, efficiency, or excellence); and after that we must live in accordance with that *areté*. This is what is meant by the 'humanism' and 'intellectualism' of ancient ethics. In this respect, Judaism and Christianity have introduced a profound and ineradicable difference which resists every attempt to return to this kind of humanism. According to Judaism and Christianity, man's proper good is to find and do the will of God. . . ."[1] Here precisely lay the problem. If man's good was the "life according to reason," as it was in the classical-humanistic ideal, then a liberal education along academic lines was obviously appropriate; but how appropriate was it, indeed what sense did it make, if man's good was what the Christian faith must hold it to be—to know and to do the will of God? How could the liberal arts, plus the classical philosophic and literary disciplines, serve to actualize the Christian life? Here, surely, it was Scripture and theology, rather than liberal learning, that must be looked to. Confronted with this problem—and it is a problem that confronts the Christian educator no matter what the content of a liberal education may be—Puritan thinkers sought for a solution in two directions, often simultaneously. On the one hand, they

[1] Philip Leon, *The Professors*, Leicester: University College, 1955, p. 5.

justified the liberal-humanistic disciplines (classical languages, philosophy, history) for the service they could render to the proper understanding of the Christian revelation; on the other hand, they defended these studies in terms of a thinly Christianized version of the Greek ideal of intellectual self-realization. If the former was rather unconvincing on its own account, as well as degrading to the liberal studies it strove to vindicate, the latter went far in dissolving the integral religious foundation of education upon which Puritan thought depended. In neither direction was there a real way out.

The dilemma was only compounded by the Great Awakening and subsequent revival movements. For if the Puritan problem was what kind of education was appropriate to foster religion, the problem projected by the Great Awakening was rather whether one could be educated into religion at all or, as the phrase ran, whether one could be "schooled into Christianity." To Jonathan Edwards, religion was what we today would call thoroughly existential. Anticipating Kierkegaard, he made a sharp distinction between "mere notional understanding" (objective conceptual knowledge) and the "sense of the heart" which constituted existential knowledge. It was the latter that was vital to religion. Edwards, says Perry Miller, "asserted the radical conception of man as an active, interested, passionate being, whose relation to objective reality is factual to the extent that he is concerned about it, whose anxieties and not his clear thinking make his destiny." [2] His entire religious philosophy, or perhaps in this context it is better to say his entire religious psychology, thus tended to "subordinate understanding to feeling" and to declare "the supremacy of passion." [3] The reason of religion was the Pascalian "reason of the heart," the reason of existential commitment. But if so, how could religion be taught through the familiar disciplines of liberal education, any more than love could be taught that way? Edwards had a profound under-

[2] Perry Miller, *Jonathan Edwards*, New York, 1949, p. 184.
[3] *ibid.*

standing of religious existence, and he also had a great respect for knowledge and learning. How to reconcile the two? Some such question is always lurking in the background of the celebrated controversy between Edwards and that champion of "sound reason," Charles Chauncy. Edwards was at his brilliant best in this controversy, yet at some points one cannot help feeling that he was seriously hampered by the older Puritan rationalism which he did not share but could not shake off. In the last year of his life, Edwards accepted the presidency of the College of New Jersey at Princeton, which itself was a product of the Great Awakening; but even his genius and capacity for "mediation" were not enough to reconcile the existential religion he understood so well and the intellectual disciplines he prized so highly. What Edwards could not do, later revivalism did not even attempt. Learning might help to cultivate the understanding of saints, but what could it do to save sinners? Every wave of revivalism through the eighteenth and nineteenth centuries brought with it its quota of schools, colleges, and academies, but the "divorce between reason and religion," which Edwards had vainly striven to avoid, became ever more notorious. Neither the dilemma of Puritan humanism, nor that of the Great Awakening, could be resolved, and this failure only speeded the progress of secularization.

Well-planned, deliberate programs for the secularization of education emerged early in the eighteenth century, throughout the colonies, but particularly in Pennsylvania and New York. Franklin's *Proposals Relating to the Education of Youth in Pennsylvania*, published in 1749, and Samuel Johnson's plan for King's College in New York, appearing five years later, are good examples of the trend that was gathering momentum. In these schemes, as in others like them, religion was not altogether ignored; it was merely relegated to the periphery as one of the minor items included. Classical, literary, scientific, and vocational studies, in varying proportions, formed the curriculum; religion was generally hardly mentioned, and then only as a kind of character training. These plans clearly reflected the "worldly," irreligious spirit that observers saw rampant in the colonies in the mid-eighteenth century; they also recommended themselves to those who were trying to achieve a "common" school system amidst unprecedented sectarian diversity. To reduce religion to a kind of "common-core" Protestantism, and to confine even that to a very secondary place in the curriculum, seemed the only way out. It was a way which the eighteenth century could not prevail upon itself to take; education was still too firmly anchored in its religious origins and too closely enmeshed with religious institutions. But it was a way that the nineteenth century was soon to follow, on the lower levels of education at least.

II

For all its "anti-intellectualistic" bias, the revival movement greatly advanced American education. Perhaps as many as 116 out of the 182 permanent colleges founded by 1861 were established by six religious groups, with Presbyterians, Methodists, and Baptists in the lead, with Congregationalists, Roman Catholics, and Episcopalians following close behind. Special educational agencies, such as the Society for the Promotion of Collegiate and Theological Education at the West (1843), were set up. Elementary and secondary education was immensely furthered; it was the great age of "academies." The Sunday School, introduced by the Methodists not long after the Revolution, flourished. The first part of the nineteenth century witnessed a tremendous upsurge of educational concern and educational activity. It also witnessed the emergence of the public school as a national institution.

The idea of a public school system, sponsored and operated by the governmental authorities of community or state, was not a new one. The New England system may be recalled, and other colonies made sporadic efforts along the same lines.

Jefferson had proposed a comprehensive scheme of public education from common school to university in Virginia at various times over a period of forty years. But when the public school finally came in the decades before the Civil War, it derived from other sources and embodied a very different idea.

The New England common school was a religious, one might almost say churchly, institution. Jefferson's "unitary state system of education" [4] came from the French Enlightenment, which took over and further developed the absolutist theory that it was the business of the state, and the state alone, to form the mind of the rising generation.[5] Neither of these influences was very significant in the nineteenth century. The Puritan conception had virtually disappeared by that time, while the Enlightenment doctrine, held enthusiastically for a while by a number of intellectuals, had been drowned out by wave after wave of revivalist evangelism. The great power behind the public school movement, so ably directed by Horace Mann, was the realization that became widespread in the early nineteenth century that "if elementary vernacular education was to become genuinely free for all and not just for the poor, . . . the free school would have to become a 'common' school under 'public,' i.e., government control, rather than under private, charitable, or religious control." [6] The need had been felt throughout the eighteenth century, but not very urgently. As the nineteenth century wore on, however, it became increasingly obvious that the older patterns of education were no longer adequate. Conditions were changing. Population, especially urban population, was growing by leaps and bounds; large numbers of people were coming into this country from Europe without any experience or tradition of

[4] R. Freeman Butts and Lawrence A. Cremin, *A History of Education in American Culture*, New York, 1953, p. 265.

[5] ". . . he [Fénélon] demands . . . education provided by law, because children belong to the State first, and to the family afterwards. . . ." Lord Acton, second lecture at Cambridge (Heralds of the French Revolution), in G. E. Fasnacht, *Acton's Political Philosophy*, New York, 1953, pp. 189–190.

[6] Butts and Cremin, p. 87.

popular education; and the established means of education that had served under less complex and demanding conditions were breaking down. It was growing plainer every day that if the great mass of people in America were to receive any kind of education at all, it could only be through schools established, financed, and maintained by the public authorities. The new appeal of the public school idea was the promise that it would provide all with the education that all, or almost all, felt to be necessary for the survival of "republicanism" (or what we today would call "democracy") under the new conditions.

The public school thus came to meet an urgent need of the developing American nation. And, despite a few setbacks here and there, it carried everything before it. Within a few decades, it had taken over elementary and secondary education (the Catholic parochial school system was still in its infancy), and seemed ready to absorb higher education as well. But here it failed. The Dartmouth case decision in 1819 blocked the efforts of state authorities to take over the older "private" colleges so as to incorporate them into a uniformitarian system of governmental education. The independent college survived, side by side with the state university and the land-grant college. On the upper level, at least, American education retained its earlier diversity. The arguments so cogent for elementary and secondary education obviously did not possess the same force here.

What was the place of religion in the emerging public school system? Here it is necessary to avoid two errors. The public school was "non-sectarian" from the very beginning, but this did not mean religionless, as so many latter-day secularists assume. On the other hand, we must not be misled into thinking that because religion was taken for granted in the life and work of the public school, it therefore possessed anything of the place it had enjoyed in earlier times. Religion was there in the public school, but it was there in a rather peculiar way.

There was never any intention whatever of excluding religion from the new public schools. No one could be more emphatic in affirming this than was Horace Mann, himself a Unitarian. "Horace Mann," Culver writes, "was opposed to sectarian doctrinal instruction in the schools, but he repeatedly urged the teaching of the elements of religion common to all the Christian sects. He took a firm stand against the idea of a purely secular education, and on one occasion said he was in favor of religious instruction 'to the extremest verge to which it can be carried without invading those rights of conscience which are established by the laws of God, and guaranteed by the constitution of the state.' At another time, he said that he regarded hostility to religion in the schools as the greatest crime he could commit. Lest his name go down in history as the one who had attempted to drive religious instruction from the schools [he was repeatedly accused of this by his opponents] he devoted several pages in his final report—the twelfth—to a statement in which he denied the charges of his enemies." [7]

The public school stood for "non-sectarianism" in religion; but "non-sectarian" did not then mean non-religious. It meant non-denominational religion, and in the America of that day, non-denominational religion meant a kind of generalized Protestantism. Horace Mann feared and detested the "sectarian" wrangling that had bedeviled education for so many years and had frustrated all attempts to establish a common school. In all sincerity, he proposed a "non-sectarian" way out, a way out that seemed to him fair to all, but which was obviously a Protestant way out. "That our public schools are not theological seminaries," he declared in his Twelfth Annual Report, "is admitted. . . . But our system earnestly inculcates all Christian morals; it founds its morals on the basis of religion; it welcomes the religion of the Bible; and, in receiving the Bible, it allows it to do what it is allowed to do

[7] Raymond B. Culver, *Horace Mann and Religion in the Massachusetts Public Schools*, New Haven, 1929, p. 235.

in no other system—*to speak for itself*." The Bible—the King James Version, obviously—speaking for itself without comment, explanation, or interpretation as the substance of religion, is, of course, a Protestant idea; but as long as the nation remained overwhelmingly Protestant, this Protestant idea naturally appealed to all, or almost all, as a reasonable and common-sense solution of the "sectarian" problem. Even the clergy agreed, although there were those who had their qualms and reservations.[8] Only when, in later decades, non-Protestants began to multiply into the millions, and to rise to power and influence in many parts of the country, did this "Protestant" solution cease to carry conviction. And then the public school faced another crisis.

In effect, the nineteenth-century solution was based on an unexpressed assumption that fundamentally religion and education were independent concerns, each of which should be allowed to develop in its own way, without involvement with the other. The minimum of religion included in the public school curriculum was interpreted as "character building" and was largely reduced to token Bible reading, hymn singing, and occasional holiday celebration. The business of the school was secular; religion was the business of the church and home. The former was concerned with instructing the youth in the common branches of knowledge, in the common elements of morality, and in the common principles of "republicanism" (that is, democracy); the latter's task was to inculcate Christian principles and to perpetuate the Christian religion. There was, of course, an area of overlapping since the school was concerned with "character," and American Protestantism largely interpreted its faith in practical, moralistic terms. But

[8] Thus the Episcopalian Rev. F. A. Newton insisted (in the columns of the *Christian Witness and Church Advocate*) that "a book upon politics, morals, or religion, containing no party or sectarian views, will be apt to contain no distinct views of any kind, and will be likely to leave the mind in a state of doubt and skepticism, much more to be deplored than any party or sectarian bias." But Mr. Newton "received little support either in church or secular newspapers. Even among his fellow Episcopalians his position did not find extensive favor." Butts and Cremin, p. 216.

this common ground was so obvious that it made little impression; the day was yet far distant when the public school would be stricken with a sense of moral failure. And so this rough and ready division of labor, so characteristic of American education and American religion in the nineteenth century, became enshrined as the American system of the "separation of church and state in education."

The public school was an immense success. It made popular education possible in a land of religious diversity and cultural heterogeneity. But more: in a way that Horace Mann could only dimly foresee, it became the primary engine of the Americanization of the millions of immigrants who kept pouring into this country from all parts of the old world. And now as we look back upon it, we can see that it accomplished this work incredibly well. It took the children of the immigrants just off the boat, and, in one or at most two generations, it made real Americans out of them. The immigrant parents were not slow to realize what the public school was doing, and were deeply grateful, for despite all reservations, what the immigrant parents wanted more than anything else was that their children become Americans and make their way up the ladder of American life. The public school became almost a sacred object to the American people; it was helping to create Americans, and nothing could be more important. Americanism—if that is the proper word with which to designate this deep desire to be an American—soon came to replace religion as the urgent concern of Americans, although this devaluation of religion was masked by the new conception of religion and education as parallel enterprises meeting only at infinity. In an altogether different context, Jefferson had foreshadowed this concept of parallel coexistence when in his plan for the University of Virginia (1822, 1824) he proposed, on the one hand, that theology (or "divinity") be excluded from the official curriculum (though he had included it in 1814), and on the other, that religious schools be founded by the denominations "on the confines of the university" with "convenient access" to university facilities. The coexistence was obviously to be a cooperative one, though neither party was to do the work of the other or interfere with it in any way. And so it continued through the nineteenth century.

Yet there were problems and difficulties, and as the century wore on, these problems and difficulties became more clamant. In the first place, what about the non-Protestants who were increasing in numbers every day? The public schools to which Catholic parents were required to send their children in the latter half of the nineteenth century were, as we have seen, to all intents and purposes Protestant schools, claiming to be "non-sectarian" because they were non-denominational within Protestantism. Obviously, no believing Catholic parent could send his children to such a school without violating his religious conscience; the fact that the Protestantism of the public school was only a shallow "common-core" Protestantism did not improve matters in the least. Not every Catholic parent was equally concerned, of course; many were ready to overlook the religious deficiencies of the public school for the sake of the marvelous work of Americanization it was performing. But the Catholic Church was deeply concerned, and so were many Catholic lay people. Parochial schools emerged to meet this challenge; they were designed to help preserve Catholic children in the faith, which was then generally expressed in the ethnic form in which it had been brought to this country by the immigrants. At about the same time, conservative Protestant groups, such as some of the German Lutherans, for whom a non-denominational "token" Protestantism was no Protestantism at all, set up religious schools of their own with very much the same double purpose. The emphasis on the ethnic culture declined as a new American generation appeared, but the religious urgency did not diminish. Jews, for reasons we shall examine more closely below, fell in readily with the emerging dualistic pattern of the "separation" of religion and education; Jews, also, perhaps more than any other immigrant group, cherished the public school as a vehicle of Americanization and advancement in American life.

For the time being, the Catholics could be ignored; they were building their own schools (thus once again proving their "clannishness"!), and their murmurs of discontent made no impression on the Protestant mind. But among the Protestants themselves certain misgivings began to arise. Was the secular-religious dualism upon which the "non-sectarian" public school was erected really viable? Would it not lead in the end to the total submergence of religion? Already the notion was becoming influential among educators that the government in its character and operations was obliged to be not merely "non-sectarian," but non-religious as well. In fact, to many minds "non-sectarian" was coming to mean "non-religious," and the constitutional ban on the "establishment of religion" was coming to imply a laic state on the European model. Madison had already foreshadowed this attitude when, in his later days, he expressed his qualms about the presence of chaplains in Congress as being a violation of the Constitution. Even earlier, in 1793, the Kentucky legislature, under the influence of the deist enlightenment, had dismissed its chaplain. But then came the Great Revival, taking fire in the very same Kentucky, and for some decades the evangelical movement swept everything before it. Now toward the end of the nineteenth century a new "separationist" mood began to emerge—this time, though, not merely among non-believers of Christianity, but among good conventional Christians as well. Under the Grant Administration, a constitutional amendment was sponsored to make the separation absolute, and though it failed of enactment, the support it mustered was not insignificant. Indeed, this kind of "separation" itself became a quasi-religious dogma, impervious to the criticism of fact or experience. "United with government," declared Ohio's Supreme Court in 1872, "religion never rises above the merest superstition; united with religion, government never rises above the merest despotism; and all history shows that the more widely and completely they are separated, the better it is for both." [9] Thus according to the learned judges, virtually all governments in existence at the time, aside from that of the United States, were "despotisms," and all religions except American Protestantism were "superstitions," merely because the American system of "separation," or what they took to be the American system of "separation," did not everywhere prevail. This system was presented as one of "complete separation," the more complete the better. The logic of this position was obviously the "religion-blind" state, hitherto hardly known in American experience. No wonder many educators and religious leaders began to have their sober second thoughts.

But for the time being, the movement of de-religionization continued apace. Thought was becoming explicitly secularistic, especially on the higher levels of education. The prevailing academic ideology was a naturalistic confidence in science, technology, and progress that seemed to render much of the earlier religion meaningless and irrelevant. The fateful split between thought and emotion that had come with the revival movement now began to tell heavily against religion. Religion was either reinterpreted as a new evolutionary deism, or else it was contemptuously relegated to the realm of private feeling. In the former case, science would do just as well, if not better; in the latter case, religion obviously had no place in the life of the mind. It was in this period that many of the state universities came into being or received their definitive character; it was in this period, too, that many of the older colleges abandoned their church connections and transformed themselves into secular institutions, in this respect indistinguishable from the state universities. The emancipation of education from religion seemed to be final and complete on the university level, and was rapidly gaining ground in the elementary and secondary schools as well. A new type of educator appeared, self-consciously secularistic, nourished on

[9] *Board of Education v. Minor*, 23 Ohio 211, 1872.

the new naturalistic educational philosophies that had already come to dominate the teachers colleges.

For public education on the elementary and secondary levels, the new secularist mood meant the systematic extrusion from the schools of even the token religion that had remained from earlier times, and with it the extrusion of all religion-based moral teaching. The rapidity with which this was achieved in the larger urban communities reflected the concurrence of a number of forces—the pressures of a multi-religious community; the new naturalistic ideology of many leading educational philosophers, policy-makers, and administrators; and the "separationist" mentality among teachers. It is not without its irony that this movement was speeded by Catholic protests against the residual Protestantism of the public schools, which Catholics, of course, found unacceptable. In exchange, they got the new secularism.

This picture, however, must be greatly modified if it is not to be misleading. What has been described was characteristic of the more modern urban centers; in the rural communities and small towns, especially where the population was overwhelmingly Protestant, the older patterns continued undisturbed. The schools remained "non-sectarian" in the non-denominational sense, and thus reflected the religious ethos of the community.

What did the balance sheet show as America entered the twentieth century and approached the First World War? For higher education, the secularization process meant a real gain in scholarship and intellectual substance, since many of the older church-connected colleges had not been particularly distinguished academically.[10] But it also meant a loss of unity,

[10] This was true for even the best of them. The Hopkins period (1836–1872) is generally regarded as the golden age of Dartmouth. Yet Frederick Rudolph tells us: "The absence of any overriding concern for the strengthening of standards during the Hopkins era was not accidental. The college, after all, was not preeminently interested in the intellect. As long as sound Christian influence could permeate the community, the college was almost ready to allow the mind to take care of itself. Certainly for many years, Mark Hopkins and his faculty cared more about the character of their students than

direction, and purpose, which higher education is now striving to retrieve. For the public elementary and secondary school, secularization meant that education was to become officially religionless. Even the older programs of religion-based moral education were eliminated in many institutions, and certainly were frowned upon in the most influential educational quarters. To some of the champions of the new trend, this meant that the schools were to be genuinely neutral in matters of religion, neutral, however, not merely as between the different brands of religion, but neutral also as between religion and no-religion. It soon became apparent, however, that the latter kind of neutrality was impossible, even more impossible than the former. As far back as the 1880's, when the idea of radical neutrality was first widely broached, the *Catholic World* had warned: "Secular education cannot be neutral. It will at least make men indifferent, and religion is a thing too important to have men indifferent about it." [11] Actually, when the older Protestantism was extruded from the schools, it was replaced, however unintentionally, by the substitute-religion of secularism, which may, I think, be accurately defined as the theory and practice of human life conceived as self-sufficient and unrelated to God. In the universities, the new "religion of no-religion" assumed the familiar forms of scientism, naturalism, and positivism. In the lower schools, however, something less philosophical, something more "down-to-earth," was required to serve as the underlying belief-system for public education. That was soon found in the American Way of Life.

III

In 1870, when the controversy over the public school had not yet died down, Samuel T. Spear reflected seriously on the

---

they did about their scholarship." *Mark Hopkins and the Log: Williams College, 1836–1872*, New Haven, 1957, p. 222.

[11] Quoted in Butts and Cremin, p. 386.

spiritual foundations of the new system of education. The common opinion that in a Christian nation public education should obviously be founded upon Christianity, upon "the elements of religion common to all the Christian sects," that is, upon a non-denominational Protestantism, did not satisfy him. "The state, being democratic in its constitution," he argued, "and consequently having no religion to which it does or can give any legal sanction, should not and cannot, except by manifest inconsistency, introduce either religious or irreligious teaching into a system of popular education which it authorizes, enforces, and for the support of which it taxes all the people in common."[12] But some spiritual foundation for so comprehensive an enterprise as education there must be. If not Christian, what then? Spear's reply was significant for the future. The American government, he said, was not a Christian government; it was rather a "republican" government, and "republicanism" rather than Christianity should be the foundation of the education offered and enforced by the government. What Mr. Spear called "republicanism" we today call "democracy," or the "democratic way of life." Spear was suggesting, in short, that "democracy," or the "democratic way of life," replace Christianity as the spiritual foundation of public education.

Samuel Spear was a Christian minister, a Presbyterian, and he no doubt had what he considered good Christian, as well as good American, reasons for advocating the thoroughgoing de-Christianization of the public schools in favor of a common "republican" ideology. As time went on, Spear's conviction became the conviction of increasing numbers of Americans who felt that everything of moral and spiritual value in the common-core Protestantism prevalent in the schools could be inculcated in a non-religious "democratic" context without the divisiveness that even the most "non-denominational" Christianity could not help but involve. In the "democratic way"—

[12] Samuel T. Spear, *The Bible in Public Schools,* New York, 1870, p. 76.

or, as it came increasingly to be denominated, in the American Way of Life—could be found the truly non-sectarian, truly all-inclusive spiritual foundation for public education.

The inherent pressures of American life made some such conviction almost inescapable, for where but in "democracy" could the heterogeneous multi-ethnic, multi-cultural, multi-lingual, and multi-religious America of the days of mass immigration find the unity it needed? Where but in the American Way of Life could it find the "common set of ideas, rituals, and symbols" which, sociologists tell us, every society must have to give it a sense of cohesion amidst tension and conflict? [13] "Democracy," or the American Way of Life, became the common creed of Americans, and as is the way with all common creeds, it became subject to multiple interpretation.

For our purposes, the crucial fact is that from its earliest days the American Way of Life functioned as the operative creed of the public school. The two were closely linked in the minds of the secularist philosophers who were becoming so influential in American education. Explicit formulations of this creed were not wanting, though none could claim to be official. In some versions, the new "Americanist" creed was regarded as superseding, at least for public purposes, an outworn Christianity; in other versions, however, it proved more generous and hospitable: any religion could find a place within the American Way provided it recognized its comprehensiveness and ultimacy. At the end of the period we are now discussing, the philosopher Horace Mann Kallen recommended the "democratic faith" in a persuasive article, significantly titled, "Democracy's True Religion." "For the communicants of the democratic faith," Mr. Kallen explained, "it is the religion *of* and *for* religion. For, being the religion of reli-

[13] "Every functioning society has, to an important degree, a common religion. The possession of a common set of ideas, rituals, and symbols can supply an overarching sense of unity even in a society otherwise riddled with conflicts." (Robin M. Williams Jr., *American Society: A Sociological Interpretation,* New York, 1951, p. 312.)

gions, all may freely come together in it." [14] Professor J. Paul Williams, himself a teacher of religion, at about the same time indicated the close connection between this "democratic faith" and public education:

"Americans must come to look upon the democratic ideal, though not necessarily the American practise of it, as the Will of God, or if they please, of Nature. . . . Americans must be brought to the conviction that democracy is the very Law of Life. . . . The state must be brought into the picture; governmental agencies must teach the democratic idea as *religion*. . . . Primary responsibility for teaching democracy might be given to the public school. . . . The churches deal effectively with but half the population; the government deals with all the population. The churches receive but voluntary attention; the government may require attention. . . . It is a misconception to equate separation of church and state with separation of religion and state." [15]

The establishment of the "democratic" religion as the civic religion of Americans, which Professor Williams was urging, had actually been achieved in the first decades of the twentieth century, though not quite in the official form he apparently desired. This was clearly seen by an eminent Christian thinker as he looked back upon the century of public education. "The religion of the American majority," Conrad Moehlman concluded in 1944, "is democracy. . . . In fact, the religion of public education is a more powerful factor in American life today than that of the churches. The only religion with which the great majority of American youth have ever come in contact is the religion of public education." [16]

[14] Horace M. Kallen, "Democracy's True Religion," *The Saturday Review*, July 28, 1951.

[15] J. Paul Williams, *What Americans Believe and How They Worship*, New York, 1952, pp. 368, 374, 78, 71.

[16] Conrad Moehlman, *School and Church: The American Way*, New York, 1944, pp. ix–x.

And so the religiously neutral education of the public school turned out to be a religious education after all—only the religion was no longer Christianity, but the "religion of democracy," the religion of the American Way. It was a religion that enjoyed the favor of the modern-minded educators, that appealed to the American people (though very few ever thought of it as a religion), and that therefore soon acquired the status of the unofficially established spiritual foundation of American education.

This development was not necessarily irreligious or antireligious in any explicit sense, for American Protestantism itself was rapidly undergoing a change in the same direction. "During the second half of the nineteenth century," Sidney E. Mead points out in a revealing article, "there occurred a virtual identification of the outlook of denominational Protestantism with 'Americanism' or 'the American way of life,' and . . . we are still living with some of the results of this ideological amalgamation of evangelical Protestantism with Americanism." [17] This syncretism, as Mr. Mead calls it, made it very easy for the Protestant mind to accept the emerging "Americanist" religion of public education without a sense of violence to its religious conscience. Protestant educators became some of the most enthusiastic proponents of the new spirituality.

In the beginning, Catholicism and Judaism, the two non-Protestant religions of America, were little affected by this

[17] Sidney E. Mead, "American Protestantism Since the Civil War: I. From Denominationalism to Americanism," *The Journal of Religion*, XXXVI, no. 1, January 1956. Mr. Mead goes on: "What was not so obvious at the time [in the second half of the nineteenth century] was that the United States, in effect, had two religions, or at least two different forms of the same religion, and that the prevailing Protestant ideology represented a syncretistic mingling of the two. The first was the religion of the denominations, which was commonly articulated in terms of scholastic Protestant orthodoxy and almost universally practised in terms of the experimental religion of pietistic revivalism. . . . The second was the religion of the American society and nation. This . . . was articulated in terms of the destiny of America, under God, to be fulfilled by perfecting the democratic way of life for the example and betterment of all mankind."

trend, since they were still foreign and therefore marginal to American life. Catholics were deeply suspicious of the public school on account first of its Protestant and then of its secularist character. The Catholic parochial school movement grew rapidly, though for a long time in most centers the majority of Catholic children were necessarily obliged to attend the public schools. With the Jews it was very different. Secularism found a welcome response among the younger Jewish immigrants, especially among the rising second generation; and the Americanizing work of the public school was prized above everything else. No immigrant group so cherished the public school and all it stood for as did the Jews of the great immigration. The Jewish "day school" movement was still a thing of the future, to arise and flourish under very different conditions.

Neither the Jews nor the Catholics remained foreign very long, although as long as mass immigration continued the ethnic groups which the immigrants formed continued to define the social and cultural context of their everyday lives. With the stoppage of immigration in the 1920's, and the restructuring of American society that followed, there emerged the "three-religion America" of today, organized in terms of the religious community (Protestant, Catholic, Jew) rather than in terms of ethnic-immigrant origin. The fusion of religion and the American Way that we have described began to characterize the outlook of the Catholic and Jew as well, as they moved toward the center of American life. What took place, and not in this respect alone, was the "Protestantization" of the non-Protestant religions of America.[18]

But this triumph of the American Way as the "common faith" of Americans, whether in explicit form or in syncretistic union with the "three great faiths" of contemporary America,

[18] For an account of this process of social transformation and religious change, see Will Herberg, *Protestant—Catholic—Jew: An Essay in American Religious Sociology*, rev. ed., New York, 1960, and Will Herberg, "The Making of a Pluralist Society," in Erich A. Walter, ed., *Religion and the State University*, Ann Arbor, 1958.

had its anomalous side. For the American Way was the "common faith" of a three-religion America in which men were becoming accustomed to define their social identities in religious rather than in ethnic terms. The religious community became a primary context of belonging, and religion once more became a "very important thing" for Americans, though in a way that would have greatly perplexed their grandfathers. The religionlessness of the public school, and the intolerant secularism of the state university, became a problem. A new crisis in public education was in the making.

IV

The new crisis involved two interrelated problems—the problem of the religious school, and the problem of religion in the public school. Both of these were old problems, but now they appeared in a new context characterized by a very different climate of opinion.

Until recently, the religious school—by which is meant not a school teaching religion or theology, but a school engaged in general education under religious auspices—was almost synonymous with the Catholic parochial school, and even today, when Protestant and Jewish schools are growing rapidly, it is still the Catholic school that figures largely in religious school statistics. We have seen how the Catholic school came into being, not in obedience to some master blueprint from abroad, but as part of the Catholic immigrant's adjustment to American reality. Through the nineteenth century, the public schools were in effect Protestant schools, as they still are in many parts of the country today. To preserve the immigrants and their children in the faith, the Catholic Church was impelled, in the face of almost insuperable difficulties, to establish its own schools, side by side with the public schools. In the new century, the prevailing ideology of the public schools, at least in the larger urban centers, became secularistic rather than Protestant, and "non-sectarian" came to mean simply non-religious. Religion now began to be systematically extruded from education, and American Catholics began to feel the need for their own schools more insistently than ever, because in their conviction no genuine education was possible unless it was religiously grounded and religiously oriented. Education from which religion had been eliminated, they believed, was not simply education without religion; it was, in fact, education based on the counter-religion of secularism.

In this conviction about the centrality of religion in education, Catholics were joined, in the years following the Second World War, by increasing numbers of Protestants and Jews, for whom, too, an education in principle religionless appeared utterly wrong, and who were therefore also beginning to look to the religious school as the only way out of an intolerable situation. Even the old-line defenders of the religionless public school had to take account of this wave of feeling. A good deal of the new sentiment for the religious school probably came from the deeper stirrings of faith that observers were noting among certain sections of the American people; a good deal, too, undoubtedly came from the new role that religion was beginning to play as a vehicle of heritage and context of belonging. But whatever the factors involved, and they were certainly more complex than appeared at first sight, the religious school was obviously enjoying a new favor among Americans. Protestant religious schools were growing in number and enrollment, and were being promoted by denominations hitherto hostile to the idea; while the Jewish "day school" movement was expanding rapidly and attracting increasing numbers of children from American Jewish families.

The religious school was not, however, the only alternative for people disturbed over the religionlessness of the public school. The majority of concerned Protestants, and even some Catholics and Jews, were turning not so much to the religious school as to renewed efforts to bring religion back to some sort of organic relation with public education, through "common core" curricula, through "teaching about" religion so as to overcome the appalling "religious illiteracy," through programs of moral and spiritual values, through efforts to create an atmosphere of "reverence for religion," and through released time schedules designed to coordinate public school work with outside religious instruction. Jews had always cherished the public school, and even Catholics were beginning to adopt a friendlier attitude toward it as they became more American in outlook, more involved in American community life, and more aware that, despite all their best efforts to build their own school system, an increasing proportion of Catholic children would have to attend the general public schools.[19] Concern with "reforming" the public school became urgent.

But both the religious school and the various programs of religion in the public schools raised the bitterly controversial question of church and state in education.

On the religious school question, two issues, quite distinct though often confused, were involved in the controversy: (1) the place of the independent school (that is, the non-governmental school engaged in general education) in the over-all system of American education; and (2) the public status of the religious school in view of the American tradition of the "separation of church and state."

The attack upon the independent school came from many quarters, but the burden of the argument was generally stated in terms of the Enlightenment conception of education as essentially the duty, and therefore properly the monopoly, of the state; a "unitary state system of education" (*l'école unique*) was their ideal. The people were the wards of the state, and forming the mind of the younger generation was felt to be one of the state's most important responsibilities and prerogatives; the state was in its nature a teaching in-

[19] In 1955, about half of Catholic children of elementary school age attended Catholic schools; within twenty years, it was widely predicted, the proportion would fall to 25 or 30 per cent, so great was the mounting pressure of school population upon resources that could not keep pace. For a recent survey of religious schools, see "Church-Related Elementary and Secondary Schools in Continental United States," *Information Service*, Bureau of Research and Survey, National Council of Churches of Christ, January 3, 1959.

stitution (*l'état enseignant*). From this point of view, private individuals and non-state institutions, even the parents of the children to be educated, really had no business to engage in education, which was intrinsically a function of the state. Under certain circumstances, they might have to be tolerated, but never of right, certainly not of prior right. In principle, non-governmental education should be suppressed for being divisive and for attempting to usurp the powers of the state over the public mind.

Despite the fact that it has its anticipations in the thinking of certain eminent Americans under the influence of the French Enlightenment, this statist theory is emphatically not the authentic English or American idea of public education, which is inexpugnably pluralistic. In the Anglo-American conception, as that emerged in the nineteenth century, the government was understood to engage in public education because experience had shown that this was the only way to provide educational opportunities for the great mass of the people under conditions of modern large-scale society. The governmental operation of education was thus conceived not as something inherent in the very notion of "republicanism" or "democracy," but rather as a function assumed by the government to meet a great and urgent public need where non-governmental efforts obviously did not suffice. But the government had not preempted the field, and had never been intended to preempt it. On the contrary, the parents (or whatever agency they might choose to represent them) retained their original prior right, since governmental intervention in education was fundamentally justified only because and to the degree that it was necessary to perform an essential public service not otherwise supplied by those whose first responsibility it was, that is, by the parents or their representatives.[20]

This pluralistic philosophy received its decisive vindication

[20] See Will Herberg, "Religion, Democracy, and Public Education," in John Cogley, ed., *Religion in America*, New York, 1958.

over against the statist doctrine in 1925, when the Supreme Court found an Oregon law requiring all children to attend public schools to be unconstitutional. The Supreme Court affirmed in the most explicit terms "the right of the parents to direct the rearing and education of their children, free from any general power of the state to standardize children by forcing them to accept instruction from public school teachers only."[21] This decision in 1925 came upon the appeal of a Catholic school; nineteen years later, in 1944, the Supreme Court handed down a decision on the appeal of a parent belonging to Jehovah's Witnesses. Denying the power of the state to prohibit parents from having their children below a certain age (the child in question was nine years old) distribute religious tracts, the Supreme Court declared, with a direct reference to the Oregon decision: "It is cardinal with us that the custody, care, and nurture of the child reside first in the parents, whose primary function and freedom include preparation for obligations the state can neither supply nor hinder."[22] The two decisions belong together as a charter of the rights of parents and the family over against the state. It is not without significance that these rights were explicitly grounded in the spiritual dimension of man's being that endows him with freedoms, duties, and responsibilities beyond the control and jurisdiction of the state.

These decisions proved highly unwelcome to those educators who had come to regard the public school as the government's indispensable agency for achieving "democratic unity" amidst the ethnic, religious, and cultural divisiveness of American life. Professor John L. Childs, of Teachers College, Columbia, argued that the Oregon decision needed reconsideration, and urged that all children be required to spend at least half their school lives in the public schools.[23] A similar

[21] *Pierce v. Society of Sisters*, 45 S. Ct. 571, 1925.
[22] *Prince v. Massachusetts*, 64 S. Ct. 438, 1944.
[23] John L. Childs, "American Democracy and the Common School System," *Jewish Education*, Vol. 21, 1949, pp. 32–57.

position was taken by James B. Conant, former president of Harvard.[24] But these protests were without effect, and they soon faded away. The Oregon decision became part of the American Way.

Under the doctrine of the Oregon decision, the religiously concerned parent obviously had the full right to educate his children according to his convictions, in religious schools if he so desired, provided the education there received met the specified standards of the community. Not only was the religiously concerned parent entitled to full freedom in setting up schools to give his children the kind of education that accorded with his religious convictions, but the schools thus set up, generally under church auspices, were plainly recognized as part of the nation's general educational establishment on a par with the public schools; their credits, diplomas, and certificates possessed exactly the same validity, in the eyes of the government as well as in the eyes of the public, as those issued by governmental institutions. They bore a very considerable share of the national educational budget, and in many places formed a substantial part of the educational system. Why should they not, it was asked, receive public support commensurate with their public service?

There was no denying that large numbers of Catholics felt a strong sense of grievance at what seemed to them a discriminatory situation in which they were compelled to bear a double burden—support of the public schools they could not use through the taxes they paid, and then again support of the schools which their children attended through tuition and other payments. Catholic spokesmen generally made no claim

[24] See *The Saturday Review of Literature*, May 3, 1952, p. 11. This is also the argument of Mr. Conant's influential book *Education and Liberty*, Cambridge, Mass., 1952, in which he says (p. 81): "The greater the proportion of our youth who fail to attend our public schools and who receive their education elsewhere, the greater the threat to our democratic unity. To use taxpayers' money to assist private schools is to suggest that American society use its own hands to destroy itself."

for public support of religious schools,[25] but there was a frequently expressed conviction that the Catholic schools were properly entitled to indirect and auxiliary aid from the state as well as from the federal government, under any federal school aid program that might be enacted.

Although these claims were meeting with increased understanding on the part of non-Catholics, especially among the younger men and women,[26] official Protestant and Jewish opinion was overwhelmingly opposed to the Catholic position as a gross violation of the "American principle of the separation of church and state" said to be enacted in the First Amendment. This issue became one of the focal centers of controversy in the exacerbating tension that characterized Protestant-Catholic relations after the war.

There was much contention as to exactly what the First Amendment did or did not mean in relation to education.[27] But one thing seemed clear: the American people had never intended to make this country into a laic state in a European sense, and the First Amendment did not do so. Neither in the minds of the Founding Fathers nor in the thinking of the American people through the nineteenth and into the twentieth century did the doctrine of the First Amendment ever imply an ironclad ban forbidding the government to take account of religion or to support its various activities. Nor did the practice of the government ever recognize such a ban.

[25] "A careful survey of expressions by Catholics on the rights to participate in federal aid will disclose no unanimity on the extent of federal aid to parochial schools. . . . I have discovered so far only one instance of a Catholic claim to full public support of religious schools." Joseph F. Costanzo, S.J., "Federal Aid to Education and Religious Liberty," *University of Detroit Law Journal*, XXXV, no. 1, October 1958. The reference is to an article in the April 1955 issue of *The Catholic World*.

[26] In reporting the results of a survey of public opinion on federal aid to church schools conducted in the middle of 1949, the American Institute of Public Opinion concluded: "The greatest acceptance of the Catholic argument in favor of federal aid to parochial schools was to be found among the young voters of all religions." *Public Opinion News Service*, August 17, 1949. Other evidence to the same effect could be cited.

[27] See, e.g., "Religion and the State," *Law and Contemporary Problems*, School of Law, Duke University, Vol. 14, no. 1, Winter 1949.

It was not difficult to point out that the federal government had for many decades been selecting, commissioning, and paying religious functionaries to carry on religious work —chaplains in the armed forces—and that the states were doing the same in the matter of chaplains in prisons and other public institutions. The federal government was constructing and maintaining, out of public funds, churches and other edifices for religious use (chapels at army posts and similar governmental establishments). The federal government was paying the tuition and expenses not only of students in church-related colleges, but even of theological students in ecclesiastical seminaries, under the G.I. Bill of Rights, where money followed the student wherever he went. The federal government, moreover, was imposing compulsory chapel attendance on the men at West Point, Annapolis, and the Air Academy.

This list of breaches in the "high and impregnable wall of separation between church and state," which Justice Black imagined to be enacted by the First Amendment, could be continued indefinitely. In the mind of the American people, and in the practice of the American government, the separation of church and state was never taken to mean forbidding the government to cooperate with, or even to assist, religion in certain of its activities. It did mean, of course, that there could be no "establishment of religion"; it did mean that whatever cooperation or assistance the government gave religion could not involve interference in the inner affairs of the churches, and could not be discriminatory; the government could not show partiality as among the various religious groups (in effect, among the "three great faiths"). And, above all, it could not go "too far."

How far was "too far"? To this, no general answer could be given. Had each of the breaches of the rigid separation of church and state listed above been put in the abstract—the government financing religious indoctrination and seminary study, the government building churches, and the like—most Americans would have been shocked and outraged. Confronted with the concrete cases, they were hardly aware that anything relating to the separation of church and state was involved. What was felt to be right and proper, and what was going too far, depended largely on how public opinion saw the case in the context of time, place, and circumstance, and could not be gauged by any general formula.

The treatment of the religious school was a good example of this curious situation that could not be defined by any abstract rules. In principle, there was no reason why the religious school should be denied governmental support because of what was said or implied in the First Amendment. And indeed it was receiving a considerable amount of governmental support in various ways, in the form of tax exemption and such "fringe" benefits as bus transportation, school lunches, health protection, and the like. But always the line was drawn at direct assistance; apparently that was as far as public opinion was ready to go under the existing conjuncture of circumstances. Beyond that, for the time being at least, was "too far."

This situation was well appreciated by those who were urging what they felt was a larger measure of justice for the religious school. There were those who believed that efforts would be most productive if they went along with the "grain of history" and pressed for more extensive indirect and auxiliary aid from state and federal government.[28] Others were of the opinion that a less fragmentary, more systematic approach was desirable. Rev. Virgil C. Blum, S.J., proposed, in a closely argued book, a "tax credit" plan that would permit genuine "freedom of choice in education," so that a parent could send his children to an independent school or a public school as he thought best, without being penalized if he chose the former.[29] These were not the only possibilities canvassed. It was clear that the religious school, and its relation to public education, was again a live issue.

28 See, e.g., Will Herberg, "Justice for Religious Schools," *America*, November 16, 1957.

29 Virgil C. Blum, S.J., *Freedom of Choice in Education*, New York, 1958.

Opposition to the religious school, whether on uniformitarian or "separationist" grounds, did not disappear by any means. On the contrary, it probably intensified, although it certainly affected narrower sections of the Protestant and Jewish groups than in earlier years. In both communities, the religious school was rising in favor, and public support did not seem quite so unreasonable as it had once appeared. Curiously enough, a sizable segment of Catholic opinion was cool to the idea of government aid to Catholic schools,[30] partly perhaps out of a certain dislike of such schools as "clannish" and "separatist," but largely out of the fear that governmental aid, particularly federal assistance, might well bring with it an unwelcome extension of governmental supervision and control.

Religion in the public schools was a parallel problem, with its own complexities and difficulties. There could be no doubt that the older attitudes varying from approval to indifference in the face of the religionless school were changing. One of the major sources of mounting dissatisfaction with the public school was precisely this religionlessness.[31] It was no longer taken for granted, even in advanced circles, that the American government should be religion-blind, neutral as between religion and no-religion, and therefore inherently incapacitated from doing anything to promote religion in its schools. On the contrary, the dictum of Justice Douglas speaking for the majority of the Supreme Court in the Zorach case in 1952,[32] "We are a religious people whose institutions pre-

[30] About 21 per cent of Catholics polled by the Gallup organization in 1949 did *not* favor federal aid to parochial schools on a par with public schools. *Public Opinion News Service,* August 17, 1949.

[31] Thus Butts and Cremin, in their account of the rising tide of criticism of the public school in the post-war years, gives "Religion" first place. "There were those who appealed to a religious orientation," these authors write (p. 539). "Catholic, Protestant, and Jewish alike, they argued that the paramount claims in education must rest upon religion. The development of religious faith, devotion to ethical principles, and concerns for moral character were the major elements determining their attitudes concerning whether education was serving its proper purposes or not." And they add: "Those of a religious orientation were deeply divided, however, as to just what role religion as such should play in the public schools."

[32] *Zorach v. Clauson,* 72 S. Ct. 679, 1952.

suppose a Supreme Being," clearly reflected the feelings of the mass of Americans in their pro-religious mood. There was general agreement that something had to be done to overcome the gross "religious illiteracy" in which the younger generation was growing up, but there was no agreement as to what could or should be done. Here, too, though in a rather different way, it was not the "separationist" ban in the First Amendment that stood in the way, but the fragmentation of religion in this country and the mutual hostility and suspicion so rife among the religious groups. The constitutional possibilities were broad enough. The McCollum decision (1948) forbade direct religious instruction of any kind on public school premises, but the Zorach decision (1952), four years later, permitted public schools to cooperate with religious authorities by adjusting schedules so as to make possible released-time religious instruction off school premises.[33] Moreover, though direct religious instruction in public schools was forbidden, there was nothing to prevent teachers and administrators from consciously working to create a genuinely religious atmosphere in the schools that was perhaps just as important in its own way as direct instruction. The Denver school system, for example, was able to develop a program of what they called "intergroup education" in which, through a variety of devices, the public school undertook to "teach that religion is sacred and that the only attitude to have toward it is one of reverence, remembering at the same time that we are talking *about* religion and not religious indoctrination." [34] This kind of pro-

[33] It may be worth while quoting the operative passage of the majority opinion: "We are a religious people whose institutions presuppose a Supreme Being. . . . When the state encourages instruction or cooperates with religious authorities by adjusting the schedule of religious events to sectarian needs, it follows the best of our traditions. For it then respects the religious nature of our people and accommodates the public service to their spiritual needs. To hold that it may not would be to find in the Constitution a requirement that the government show a callous indifference to religious groups. That would be preferring those who believe in no religion over those who do believe." (*Zorach v. Clauson*, 72 S. Ct. 679, 1952.)

[34] *December Festivals*, produced under the direction of the Department of Instruction, Denver Public Schools, 1955.

religious education in the public schools was quite in harmony with the doctrine of the separation of church and state as Americans understood it; it was, however, possible only where, as in Denver, the major religious groups were able to get together and agree upon a common program. Opinions as to what line to take in bringing religion back to the schools covered a wide range. Some placed their confidence in programs of "moral and spiritual values" with explicit religious reference. President Henry P. Van Dusen of Union Theological Seminary and former Dean Weigle of Yale Divinity School suggested a "common core" program of religious instruction, and a number of Catholic leaders proposed something very like it, a pedagogically appropriate version of natural theology and natural ethics. (Only now the "common core" would no longer be a generalized Protestantism, but rather what was common to American Jews and Christians for all their variety.) Others looked to various schemes of released or dismissed time to provide a partial remedy. I myself some years ago advanced the idea of combining pro-religious education in the public school with a greatly improved and extended system of released time for religious instruction, not one hour at the tag end of a week, but perhaps three or five hours a week on a par with other subjects in the curriculum.[35] There were obvious difficulties in the way of all these proposals, but they were not difficulties raised by the constitutional separation of church and state. They were rather difficulties stemming from the fragmentation, rivalries, and mutual suspicion that have long characterized American religious life, and have made it difficult for the religious concern of the American people in this area to come to institutional expression.

It is not without significance that the resource brochure *December Festivals*, used in the Denver public schools in connection with Christmas and Hanukkah, was produced with

[35] Will Herberg, "Religious Education and General Education: A Symposium," *Religious Education*, May–June 1953.

the assistance and support of the Anti-Defamation League of B'nai B'rith, the leading Jewish "defense" agency in the country. This participation of the Anti-Defamation League in the Denver program merely underlined the fact that even official Jewish opinion was no longer united behind a rigorous "keep religion out of the public school" policy as it once had been. The ultra-"separationism" of American Jewry could be traced to many sources. Perhaps most influential were the widespread secularism among second-generation Jews in this country, and the fear, shared by most Jews, secularist and religious alike, that if religion were to be permitted to return in any significant degree to public life, the Jew, because he was outside the bounds of the dominant religion, would once again be relegated to the margins of society, disfranchised culturally if not politically, shorn of his hard-won rights and opportunities. The greatest anxiety was felt about religion in the school, since every such intrusion would tend to isolate the relatively few Jewish children from their non-Jewish schoolmates, and thus render them more vulnerable to discrimination. That there was not a little validity to these considerations need not be questioned, but somehow they became less and less compelling as American Jews began to feel more secure and more American in the "three-religion" America that was emerging. There was not the same fear of isolation there had been, or the same sense of inferiority. On the other side, the old-fashioned secularism of the second generation was declining, and with it the older reluctance to stand out as Jewish. The ultra-"separationist" line still remained dominant among the official spokesmen of Jewish religious and community organizations, but even here there appeared strange doubts and qualms.[36] Among the rising third generation in

[36] These doubts and qualms may be gathered from the *New York Times* report of the 1958 annual gathering of the Central Conference of American Rabbis, the Reform rabbinical association. "CHICAGO, June 26—The Central Conference of American Rabbis affirmed today its rigid opposition to violations of the principle of the separation of church and state. But it left the door open for a more 'flexible' interpretation of the controversial subject.

the suburbs the older intransigence was rapidly losing whatever meaning it had once possessed. Even the community leaders had to take account of this new outlook.

A similar realignment was taking place within American Protestantism, but was running much deeper. The public school system had always been the peculiar care of American Protestantism, yet it was the American Protestants who were becoming the most deeply disturbed by the religionlessness of the public school. Where the public school was still largely a Protestant school, conducted along the old "non-denominational" Protestant lines, there was little to upset the Protestant mind, but this was no longer the case in most parts of the country. Protestant expressions of concern and protest were growing year by year, joining the many Catholic and the still few though multiplying Jewish voices that were being raised. It was a distinguished Protestant spokesman, President Van Dusen, who formulated the Protestant concern in a way that linked the two aspects of the school problem in their true relation. "Unless religious instruction can be included in the program of the public school," Mr. Van Dusen warned, "[Protestant] church leaders will be driven increasingly to the expedient of the church-sponsored school." [37] Outstanding Protestant theologians and church leaders took every opportunity to urge the necessity of unbiased, realistic thinking

---

A commission report approved by the 500 Reform, or liberal, rabbis, deplored what it described as an increasing effort to integrate religious education into the public schools and took sharp issue with such 'transgressions' as the installation of religious symbols on public property and distribution of Bibles to public school children. It acknowledged, however, the existence of a 'ground swell' of rabbinic opinion that viewed the conference's strict stand with some misgivings. . . . With this division in mind, the conference agreed to poll its 700 members by mail. On the basis of the response, recommendations will be brought to the next annual meeting of the body. Rabbi Arthur Gilbert of New York [an executive of the Anti-Defamation League] told the assembly that such practises as bus transportation of parochial school children, Bible reading in school, Christmas celebrations, and released time religious education, might not be violations of the church-state principle. . . ." *New York Times*, June 27, 1958.

[37] Henry P. Van Dusen, *God in Education*, New York, 1951, p. 119.

on the church-state question in education.[38] Clearly, new winds were blowing in the Protestant sector of the three-religion America.

Perhaps the most striking manifestation of the new time was the dramatic reversal in their attitude to religion on the part of leaders in state universities and other institutions of higher learning. Signs were multiplying that the cultural atmosphere on the campuses of this country was changing. The new generation was no longer living under the sign of modernity. The secularist philosophies of the nineteenth and early twentieth centuries were no longer so self-evident; to many of the rising generation these philosophies had become totally discredited, to almost all they had lost their earlier appeal. It was no longer self-evident, for example, that religion was simply emotion without intellectual content. On the contrary, the religious thinkers of the day—such men as Maritain, Berdyaev, Buber, Tillich, Niebuhr, and of course Kierkegaard—were enjoying a remarkable prestige as vanguard thinkers, not only among the "religionists," but particularly among those concerned with so-called secular interests—psychiatrists, historians, political scientists, poets, educators, and literary critics. Religion and theology were now recognized as having an important intellectual relevance, and no institution of higher learning could be said to live up to its responsibility if it did not take this fact into account.

The revival of interest in religion within the academic context of the major institutions of higher learning was noteworthy, and could be measured in part by the extraordinary increase in course offerings and programs of religious study. State universities managed in various ways to keep abreast of the times without violating constitutional prohibitions. Perhaps, indeed, the symbol of the present situation might be found in the great centenary celebration of religious work on

[38] See particularly "Statement on Church and State," signed by twenty-three Protestant theologians, church leaders, and educators, *Christianity and Crisis*, July 5, 1948.

the University of Michigan campus at Ann Arbor, held in 1958, with its lectures, symposia, and publications, in which the old and the new met in confrontation and dialogue.[39]

V

The place of religion in contemporary America is certainly very different from what one could have foreseen a generation ago. The older secularism is rapidly declining. Religion is enjoying a resurgence of impressive scope and proportions. Naturally, the relation between religion and education has undergone considerable change. It is no longer taken for granted that religion has no place in the serious business of educating the nation; on the contrary, the tide would seem to be running all the other way. The concern now is to bring back religion to some sort of significant relation with education, and this concern is felt in varying degrees by professional educators and the lay public, by those involved in government schools as well as by those working in independent institutions, by those responsible for elementary and secondary education as well as by those engaged in college and university education. Certainly, no one who remembers the barren and shallow secularism of a generation ago, contemptuous of everything that did not fit into its positivistic strait jacket, will fail to be grateful for this change, which makes it possible at least to try to reestablish some bond between the total educational enterprise and the deeper levels of human life and thought. Yet there is obviously another side to the story. The very resurgence of religious interest in education has brought with it certain new and pressing problems with which educator, religious leader, and concerned laymen alike will have to cope in the coming period.

(1) Sentiment is now running in favor of the religious school, certainly more so than at any time in the past century. But that only makes the problem of a balance between the

[39] See, especially, Erich A. Walter, ed., *Religion and the State University.*

public school and the religious school the more urgent. Each has its own values, the religious school as well as the public school, and the one should not be overlooked for the sake of the other. The public school remains the great instrument of achieving an over-all American unity in an ethnically, racially, and religiously heterogeneous society, a training in living together that even present-day America cannot altogether do without. The religious school, aside from its primary purpose of providing an education grounded in religion, contributes that element of diversity that an increasingly conformist society so sorely needs. These two types of schools, though united in their common "Americanness" and American outlook, obviously live in a certain tension. How to achieve creative cooperation within this tension, without sacrificing the one kind of school to the other, is one of the problems for the future.

(2) If the public school is to retain the support of the American people in the present period of religious upsurge, it cannot remain religionless. This would seem to be acknowledged, in one way or another, on all sides. But what kind of religion to bring back to the schools, and how to do it without going "too far" in the direction of church-state cooperation, remains a problem. The problem is really double: on the one hand, what can be done within the basic constitutional structure of the public school as a governmental institution; and on the other hand, what can be done without stultifying and corrupting the religious traditions of the American people by reducing them to a "common-denominator" religiosity. Perhaps some combination of "teaching about" religion and creating a pro-religious atmosphere in the schools with coordinated instruction in religion by outside religious bodies will have to be worked out, but the lines are by no means clear. There are those who despair of devising any practicable program to meet current requirements, but to do so is to despair of the public school. This we surely cannot afford to do.

(3) The challenge is not merely to the public school; it is

a challenge to the American religious consciousness. Informed observers testify that much of the contemporary "surge of piety in America" is distressingly superficial and consists largely of a religionization of the values of our culture as expressed in the American Way of Life.[40] The "syncretism" between traditional religion and the American Way which Sidney Mead sees emerging in the Protestantism of the latter half of the nineteenth century [41] has now apparently become universal in our emerging three-religion America. There is real danger that the "religion" that will be reintroduced into the schools under whatever form or guise, whether as a "common-core" program or as a program of "moral and spiritual values," will be little more than this syncretistic religion of religionized American democracy. The problem is a very real one for the independent school, even the church-sponsored school, as well as for the public school, since much of even denominational or "church" religion in this country is permeated through and through with the syncretistic spirit.[42] The change from religionlessness to religion would be little gain—some, indeed, would put it down as a loss—if it simply meant a change from a secularized version of the "religion of democracy" to a religionized version of the same "common American faith."

Beyond these problems is the basic perplexity that Puritanism and revivalism long ago raised: how can religion be taught, and conversely what does the enterprise of education mean in the perspective of an authentic Biblical faith? [43] But these questions carry us far beyond the present context of discussion.

[40] See A. Roy Eckardt, *The Surge of Piety in America*, Association Press, 1958; also Will Herberg, *Protestant—Catholic—Jew*, chs. V and XI, and Martin E. Marty, *The New Shape of American Religion*, New York, 1959.

[41] See n. 17.

[42] See Will Herberg, "A Religion or Religion? Some Comments on the Program of 'Moral and Religious Values' in the Schools," *Religion in the Schools*, no. 38, May 1956.

[43] See Will Herberg, "Towards Biblical Theology of Education," *The Christian Scholar*, XXXVI, no. 4, December 1953; also Otto Friedrich Bollnow, Ernst Lichtenstein, and Otto Weber, *Der Mensch in Theologie und Pedagogik*, Heidelberg, 1957.

RELIGION AND LAW IN AMERICA

WILBER G. KATZ

TO INTRODUCE law into a study of religion and American life is to suggest inquiry into the reciprocal influences of law and religion in American culture. The first area to which such an inquiry would direct attention is that of the law governing religious beliefs and practices and church-state relations. In considering this body of law, one would try to identify aspects and qualities of American religious life which have apparently developed under the influence of these legal rules. One would seek also for sources of the rules in the patterns of religious life in colonial America and in the century following the revolution. In the second part of such a general inquiry, the focus would be on religious doctrines and institutions, and the primary effort would be to determine their relevance in the understanding and criticism of general areas of American law. One would also inquire whether, in turn, these legal institutions have had any apparent effect upon American forms of religious thought and practice.

In this essay it would be impossible, of course, to go far in the pursuit of any of these inquiries. Nor does it seem useful to attempt a systematic outline or summary. Instead, I shall suggest, in the first section, a comprehensive legal principle with respect to religious activities, and shall examine the extent to which it is embodied in American constitutions and judicial decisions. This principle may not be the one most widely accepted, but it appears to me to be the soundest basis for American church-state relations, and I believe also that it represents the mature development of the central American tradition. When I turn, in the second section, to consider the bearing of religion upon American law, my effort must be limited by the fact that I am not a theologian or a sociologist or a historian. Instead of presenting a systematic account of religious doctrines relevant to law or an appraisal of the influence of such doctrines in the development of American law, I shall give a single illustration of my own search in religious ideas for criteria by which legal rules may be criticized and for deeper understanding of the meaning and purpose of law.[1]

I

My thesis in this section is that the basic American principle of church-state relations is neither separation of church and state nor impartial benevolence toward religion; it is the principle of religious liberty, which requires strict government neutrality with respect to religion.[2] Religion is to be kept free both from legal restraints and from government support or promotion.[3] This principle of religious liberty is incompatible with an absolute separation of church and state. Separation is not the primary principle. The separation required by the Constitution is the separation which promotes religious liberty. The Constitution does not shrink religious liberty to the liberty which is compatible with strict separation.

This principle of strict neutrality rules out government aid to religion, however impartial. But does the Federal Constitution prescribe such full neutrality or merely neutrality among religions? This question has been hotly debated in recent years and the answer is by no means clear. Both sides

[1] Contemporary interest in such inquiries is illustrated by two symposia: "Christian Faith and Human Law," *The Christian Scholar*, XL, September 1957, pp. 163–244, published also in *Vanderbilt Law Review*, X, August 1957, pp. 879–968; "Law and Christianity," *Oklahoma Law Review*, XII, May 1959, pp. 45–146.

[2] I have developed this "neutrality" position in "Freedom of Religion and State Neutrality," *University of Chicago Law Review*, XX, Spring 1953, pp. 426–440; "The Case for Religious Liberty," in John Cogley, ed., *Religion in America*, New York, 1958; "The Freedom to Believe," *Atlantic Monthly*, CXCII, September 1953, pp. 66–69.

[3] Canon Anson Phelps Stokes's voluminous work develops the interpretation that the United States has combined "entire Church separation with a definite attitude of friendliness toward the Churches." *Church and State in the United States*, New York, 1950, 3 vols., III, 694. Cf. Merrimon Cuninggim, *Freedom's Holy Light*, New York, 1955, ch. IV.

assume that Congress and state legislatures are forbidden to give preferential status to a particular church or religion. The controlling provision is that of the First Amendment: "Congress shall make no law respecting an establishment of religion, or prohibiting the free exercise thereof. . . ." While this prohibition applies in terms only to Congress, it has been held applicable to the states also by virtue of the due process clause of the Fourteenth Amendment. Verbally, the question thus turns on the meaning of the phrase "no law respecting an establishment of religion," but as we shall see, the controlling considerations have apparently been those of an expanding American conception of religious freedom.

The question of full neutrality toward religion was not faced by the Supreme Court until 1947. In that year, the court declared that the First Amendment forbids "laws which aid one religion, aid all religions, or prefer one religion over another."[4] The amendment "requires the state to be neutral in its relations with groups of religious believers and non-believers." The case in which this interpretation was made was *Everson v. Board of Education*, involving the action of a New Jersey township extending to pupils in parochial schools the benefits of a bus-fare reimbursement plan. The court was unanimous in accepting the principle of "no aid to all religions," but the majority held that the principle was not violated by the bus-fare reimbursement.

Vigorous challenge met this broad interpretation of the First Amendment proscription of laws "respecting an establishment of religion." It was insisted that the clause refers only to legislation giving a preferred status to a particular religion, that the prescribed neutrality is only neutrality among religions and not between religion and non-religion. This argument was strongly pressed upon the court the following year in the case involving the Champaign, Illinois program of "released time" religious education in public schools. Again, all the justices agreed that the amendment

[4] *Everson v. Board of Education*, 330 U.S. 1, 15 (1947).

forbids not only preferential aid but also "impartial government assistance of all religions,"[5] although Justice Reed dissented from the holding that the program under review constituted such forbidden assistance.[6]

In 1952, however, the court threw serious doubt upon the interpretation forbidding impartial aid to religion. The decision in *Zorach v. Clauson*[7] sustained the New York released time program, which differed from the Illinois only in that the classes in religion were not held in the public school buildings. Only the dissenting opinion of Mr. Justice Black spoke of complete neutrality and of equality between believers and non-believers. The majority said that "When the state encourages religious instruction . . . , it follows the best of our traditions." "We are a religious people whose institutions presuppose a Supreme Being."[8] To be sure, the opinion also emphasized that the Constitution "does not require the government to throw its weight against efforts to widen the effective scope of religious influence," language which is consistent with a rule of full neutrality.[9] But the opinion's only explicit reference to neutrality is the statement that "The government must be neutral when it comes to competition between sects."[10] Mr. Justice Black accused the majority of "legal exaltation of the orthodox" and "derogation of unbelievers."[11]

In this continuing controversy before the court and in legal journals, both sides have claimed to be following "the original meaning" of the establishment clause. The evidence, how-

[5] *McCollum v. Board of Education*, 333 U.S. 203, 211 (1948).

[6] For vigorous criticisms of the court's adherence to the "no aid to religion" rule, see Edward S. Corwin, "The Supreme Court as National School Board," *Law and Contemporary Problems*, XIV, Winter 1949, pp. 3–22; John Courtney Murray, "Law or Prepossessions?" in *ibid.*, pp. 22–43; Alexander Meiklejohn, "Educational Cooperation Between Church and State," in *ibid.*, pp. 61–72.

[7] 343 U.S. 306 (1952).

[8] *ibid.*, at pp. 313–314.

[9] *ibid.*, at p. 314.

[10] *ibid.*

[11] 343 U.S. at p. 319 (1952).

ever, is highly inconclusive. What the historical "studies" show primarily is that in this field of law, as in religion itself, controversy becomes so charged with emotion that objectivity is difficult to maintain.[12]

In the first Congress, which framed the amendments incorporating the Bill of Rights, several of the early drafts of the "establishment" clause forbade only laws establishing a particular church. The version adopted by the Senate was of this type,[13] although the draft approved in the House had been more general, covering laws "establishing religion." [14] There is little evidence of the intention of the conference committee which reported the final language: "no law respecting an establishment of religion," although this language was apparently insisted upon by members of the House.[15] Those who support the broad interpretation of this language usually argue that it was intended to incorporate the views expressed by James Madison in 1785 in his "Memorial and Remonstrance Against Religious Assessments." [16] This document was an elaborately reasoned argument against a bill in the Virginia legislature to levy a tax for the support of "Teachers of the Christian Religion." Taxpayers were to have the privilege of designating the particular "society of Christians" to which this tax should be paid, and for those who

[12] Professor Howe has characterized the historical studies of some who are fearful of the power of churches as attempts to "safeguard the citadels of suspicion with a Maginot line of spurious history." Mark DeWolfe Howe, "The Constitutional Question" in *Religion and the Free Society*, The Fund for the Republic, New York, 1958, p. 57. Compare Leo Pfeffer, "Church and State: Something Less than Separation," *University of Chicago Law Review*, XIX, Autumn 1951, pp. 1–29, with J. M. O'Neill, *Religion and Education Under the Constitution*, New York, 1949. Mr. Pfeffer criticizes Professor O'Neill for ignoring action in the Senate rejecting versions of the First Amendment which forbade only preferential establishment, but Pfeffer himself ignores the fact that the version later passed in the Senate was of the same kind. See footnote 13.

[13] *Journal of the First Session of the Senate*, New York, 1789, p. 129.

[14] *ibid.*, p. 104.

[15] *ibid.*, p. 145; *Journal of the House of Representatives*, New York, 1789, p. 152.

[16] Gaillard Hunt, ed., *The Writings of James Madison*, New York, 1901–1910, 9 vols., II, 183–191.

preferred to make no such designation the tax proceeds were to be applied by the legislature "for the encouragement of seminaries of learning." This important document and the bill to which it was addressed were incorporated in full in appendices to Mr. Justice Rutledge's opinion in the New Jersey bus case.[17]

Madison's Remonstrance eloquently defended the position that religion should be entirely free from state aid. It is by no means clear, however, that Madison himself urged that this principle should be incorporated in the Federal Bill of Rights. The draft amendment introduced by Madison used the language "nor shall any national religion be established. . . ."[18] At the time at least five of the states still gave preferential status to particular churches,[19] and it seems clear that Congress was to have neither the power to choose among them nor the power to abolish such "establishments." This may, indeed, be the only intention reflected in the choice of the language "no law respecting an establishment of religion." This is the view taken by Justice Story in his *Commentaries on the Constitution* published in 1833.[20]

As already noted, the First Amendment limitations upon congressional power have been held extended to the states by the Fourteenth Amendment provision that no person shall be deprived of liberty without due process of law.[21] It is understandable that the court should have subsumed under the term "liberty" the freedoms of speech, press, assembly, and petition covered by the First Amendment and also the "free exercise of religion." However, the court might well have found more difficulty in thus "incorporating" in the due process clause the prohibition of laws "respecting an estab-

17 *Everson v. Board of Education*, 330 U.S. at pp. 63–74.

18 United States Congress, *Annals*, Washington, 1834, I, 434.

19 See Edward S. Corwin, pp. 3, 12; R. Freeman Butts, *The American Tradition in Religion and Education*, Boston, 1950, pp. 26–38.

20 Joseph Story, *Commentaries on the Constitution*, Boston, 1833, 3 vols., III, §§1871–1873.

21 *Cantwell v. Connecticut*, 310 U.S. 296 (1940).

lishment of religion."[22] It is paradoxical that a clause the terms of which protected state-established churches from congressional action should come to mean that no state may have an established church.[23] On the other hand, when the Fourteenth Amendment was adopted, no established churches, in the ordinary sense, remained, although some states still had provisions discriminating against non-Christians. The liberty protected by the Fourteenth Amendment might then have been understood as including freedom from church establishment, but it could hardly have been understood more broadly as making religion free from all discrimination and even from non-discriminatory state aid.

The American conception of religious freedom has continued to expand, however, and in many areas the Supreme Court has given expanding scope to constitutional liberties. It would not, therefore, be surprising if the mature American concept of religious liberty should come to preclude not only preferential treatment of a particular religion, but all exertion of government influence in favor of religion, however impartial. Religious liberty would thus include freedom to doubt on a full parity with freedom to believe.[24]

Much of the opposition to this view apparently springs from a fear that strict government neutrality would mean, in effect, hostility to religion. This is because strict neutrality is often confused with strict separation of church and state. It is important to keep these concepts separate and to see

[22] See Alfred W. Meyer, "The Blaine Amendment and the Bill of Rights," *Harvard Law Review*, LXIV, April 1951, pp. 939–945.

[23] Professor Howe has suggested that the states are forbidden to aid religion only when the aid would significantly affect religious liberties. He has suggested also that the "no establishment" clause of the First Amendment may impose broader limitations on Congress, since it may embody a political principle of limited federal government as well as a principle of individual liberty.

[24] Cf. Wilfred Parsons, *The First Freedom*, New York, 1948, p. 79: "As for those who profess no religion, or who repudiate religion, it is difficult to conceive that they can appeal to the First Amendment, since this document was solely concerned with religion itself, not its denial."

neutrality as the controlling concept. If the state is to be neutral, it cannot be insulated from contact with religion. Many types of government provision for religion are necessary under the strict neutrality principle in order to avoid unintended restraints upon religious freedom. For example, provision for voluntary worship in the armed forces is constitutional, not because government policy may properly favor religion, but because, in the absence of some provision for worship, the government would be exercising its military powers in a manner hostile to religious freedom. The government is not required to abandon neutrality in an effort to maintain strict separation.[25]

As government activity is extended, instances multiply where strict separation would limit religious freedom and where action which might appear as government aid is only the result of an effort to maintain full neutrality. A recent instance is furnished by the urban renewal project for the Lincoln Square area in New York. In the plan two blocks were set aside for educational purposes, and Fordham University was permitted to acquire this property from the city at $7 per square foot, less than half of the estimated cost. Objections that this constituted aid to sectarian education were overruled.[26] Justice McGivern said, "To hold, under the instant circumstances, that a denominational school may not be afforded the same opportunity to contract as any other private institution or corporation, would be to convert the constitutional safeguards into a sword against the freedoms which they were intended to shield." [27]

[25] Wilber G. Katz, "Freedom of Religion and State Neutrality," *University of Chicago Law Review*, XX, Spring 1953, pp. 426, 429–433.

[26] *64th St. Residences v. City of New York*, 173 N.Y.S.2d 700 (1957), 4 N.Y.2d 268 (1958). In *Berman v. Parker*, 348 U.S. 26, 34–35 (1954), the Supreme Court had referred without comment to inclusion of churches in a slum clearance project for Washington, D.C.

[27] 173 N.Y.S.2d at p. 703. Compare the language of the Court of Appeals: "Special Term pointed out, probably correctly, that Fordham would be deprived of constitutional rights if it alone were excluded from the bidding.

The exemptions from property taxation usually granted to churches and religious charities are often cited as showing that non-discriminatory aid to religion is permissible.[28] Such exemptions, furthermore, have been opposed by advocates of the "no aid" principle.[29] The typical exemptions, however, apply not only to religious bodies but to a general class of non-profit organizations including non-religious schools and charities. Inclusion of religious bodies in such a general exemption is defensible as an effort to maintain neutrality and avoid discrimination against religion. Only if churches were singled out for a special exemption would the question of the propriety of affirmative aid to religion be squarely presented.

Some writers have supported "cooperation" between church and state, using language which seems to suggest more freedom for state aid than strict neutrality would permit. Thus Alexander Meiklejohn has urged that the state and the churches have a community of interest in education which requires active cooperation.[30] He insists that a democracy is concerned that its citizens find living roots for democratic attitudes and for faith in the possibility of responsible self-government. Since "40 or 50 or 60 per cent of our people" find in religious beliefs the ultimate moral ground for democratic institutions, a democracy should give to religious belief a "positive status in the public planning of education." [31] But this positive status he asks equally for non-religious efforts to

---

Perhaps this is only another way of saying that, since this sale is an exchange of considerations and not a gift or subsidy, no 'aid to religion' is involved . . ." 4 N.Y.2d at 276.

[28] See, for example, Alexander Meiklejohn, "Educational Cooperation Between Church and State," *Law and Contemporary Problems*, XIV, Winter 1949, p. 64. Cf. John C. Bennett, *Christians and the State*, New York, 1958, pp. 234–235. On the general problem, see Monrad G. Paulson, "Preferment of Religious Institutions in Tax and Labor Legislation," *Law and Contemporary Problems*, XIV, Winter 1949, pp. 144–159.

[29] Editorial, "Churches Should Pay Taxes," *Christian Century*, LXIV, April 5, 1947, p. 454.

[30] "Educational Cooperation Between Church and State."

[31] *ibid.*, pp. 62, 67.

teach respect for the human spirit and its freedom. Thus the cooperation which Meiklejohn approves is the cooperation of a positive neutrality which is careful to avoid undermining the effective freedom of religious teaching.

Similarly, John C. Bennett distinguishes between aid to all religions for their own sake ("multiple establishment") and the "cooperation" or aid which is necessary to the "free exercise" of religion. Where "the state finds itself involved in activities, such as education, in which the churches have a special stake . . . it may . . . seek to arrive at some adjustment that limits the injury to the interests for which the churches stand." [32]

The competition between the principles of separation and neutrality is most sharply illustrated in the hotly debated issue of the application of tax funds to educational costs in parochial schools. The general subject of religion and education is considered in another chapter, but this aspect raises serious legal questions. The central question, as it relates to the power of Congress, may be considered in the context of a section of the United States Code which is seldom noticed. This is the provision made by Congress for the education of the pages who serve in the houses of Congress and in the Supreme Court.[33] Funds are appropriated to the school authorities of the District of Columbia to cover the cost of instruction of the pages attending the public schools. For those choosing to attend a parochial or private school, payment is directed to be made to the school chosen (but at a rate no higher than that paid for public school education). This statute was apparently enacted without opposition. Is it open to constitutional attack as a "law respecting an establishment of religion"? Could Congress make similar provision for other children living in the District? Would it be permissible for a state to divide tax money on a similar principle between patrons of public and private schools?

[32] *Christians and the State*, p. 233.

[33] U.S. Code, Title 2, §88(a).

In discussions of such questions, it is usually agreed that parents may not be required to send their children to public schools. This was decided unanimously by the Supreme Court in 1925 in *Pierce v. Society of Sisters.*[34] The Oregon statute under review was held to deprive parents and children of "liberty" in violation of the Fourteenth Amendment. Since the case was decided before the court had come to speak of the Fourteenth Amendment as "incorporating" the First, no reference was made to the First Amendment guaranty of "free exercise of religion." Very rarely is it urged that this decision should be overruled, but as one reads discussions of the tax-support problem, one gets the impression that many people concede only reluctantly that the Constitution protects in this way the freedom to combine secular and religious education.

The defense of the type of financial provision illustrated in the page-boy statute is based explicitly on the *Pierce* case. If parents have a right to choose a parochial school, presumably this choice should be free from discriminatory burdens.[35] At least it should be permissible for the government to arrange its tax and school policies so as to avoid such discrimination. This is the theory on which, in many states, parochial school pupils are included in arrangements for free bus transportation. In sustaining the validity of such inclusion, Mr. Justice Black said for the majority of the court: ". . . we must be careful in protecting the citizens of New Jersey against state-established churches, to be sure that we do not inadvertently prohibit New Jersey from extending its general State law benefits to all its citizens without regard to their religious beliefs."[36]

The classic statement of the strict separation position is that

[34] 268 U.S. 510 (1925).

[35] William Gorman, "A Case of Distributive Justice" in *Religion and the Schools*, The Fund for the Republic, New York, 1959, p. 50: "Certainly, in the school case, where an antecedent personal right is involved, what cannot be rightly coerced cannot be rightly solicited by the use of a coercive burden."

[36] *Everson v. Board of Education,* 330 U.S. 1, 16 (1947).

of Mr. Justice Rutledge's dissenting opinion in this case. He used the arresting metaphor of a price exacted by the Constitution for religious liberty. "Like St. Paul's freedom, religious liberty with a great price must be bought. And for those who exercise it most fully, by insisting upon religious education for their children mixed with secular, by the terms of our Constitution the price is greater than for others." [37] The "price" includes surrender of any share in the tax funds applied to educational costs or to "fringe" items such as bus transportation. This price tag Mr. Justice Rutledge found in the phrase "no law respecting an establishment of religion" which he construed as requiring a complete and permanent separation of religious activity and civil authority.

This reasoning would make invalid the page-boy statute and also the veterans' education provisions of the G.I. Bill of Rights.[38] Under these provisions, veterans might choose to have the payments applied to tuition in church-related colleges or even in sectarian schools for training of ministers. This precedent is not to be distinguished as dealing merely with compensation for services rendered the government. It does not involve compensation which the recipient is free to spend for purposes other than education. When the question relates to educational costs awarded to government employees as additional compensation, there is no greater justification for abandoning church-state separation and permitting the government to respect religious preferences than where the question relates to educational costs for citizens generally.

I have contended that the basic principle embodied in the religion clauses of the First Amendment is the principle of strict neutrality, leaving religion free from government discrimination against it or in its favor. In my opinion, this principle supports not only measures like the G.I. Bill, the page-boy statute, and non-discriminatory school bus plans, but also inclusion of parochial schools in the application of

[37] *Everson v. Board of Education*, 330 U.S. 28, 59 (1947).

[38] Servicemen's Readjustment Act of 1944, 58 Stat. 284 (1944), Title II.

tax funds to the cost of instruction in secular subjects. The almost universal rejection of this view by non-Catholics represents a denial of full religious liberty and reflects hostility to parochial schools and perhaps fear of the extension of the political influence of a clerical hierarchy.[39]

Such a curtailment of religious liberty would be expected if one were to accept the suggestion of Professor Howe that the American doctrine of religious liberty has theological presuppositions which are inconsistent with full neutrality among religious groups. He says that we shall not reach the heart of our constitutional problem until we ask "whether the objective of freedom and separation is not so intimately related to an article of religious faith as to make the state a religious partisan when it seeks to attain that objective." [40] "Those who support the thesis that each man should be left free by government to follow the faith which his mind and heart prefer, very generally, if not invariably, have in religion, abandoned the belief that an ultimate truth has been revealed for all and, as truth, is binding on all. The political conviction that religious liberty is of profound importance generally bespeaks a Protestant, and very frequently a skeptical attitude towards the 'truths' of religion. Behind our constitutional provisions there may lie, therefore, an attitude, if not a religious faith itself, which is predominantly Protestant in spirit." [41]

Howe concludes that "It is unlikely that the equality which results from liberty will be attained by any church which is

[39] William Gorman, p. 53: "A majority of a ruling people [distrustful of particular religious beliefs or a particular church] . . . might in fact consider itself justified in some special vigilance, based upon an expectation that such beliefs and such an institution might produce actions harmful to the common good. But whatever its posture regarding possible *actions*, the majority of a mature free people, constitutionally committed to freedom of religion, would not think it right to put a price on the religious *beliefs* of any parent-citizens. A free people would know that to attach a burdensome inequality, under a civic law, to an article of faith was to abridge the freedom of religion."

[40] Mark DeWolfe Howe, Review of Anson Phelps Stokes, *Church and State in the United States*, *Harvard Law Review*, LXIV, November 1950, pp. 170, 175.

[41] *ibid.*, p. 172.

committed, or seems to the bulk of the community to be committed, to the doctrine not only that all men are obligated to seek and follow the truth, but that the truth is to be found in its faith only. This is not because civil government as such is unwilling to perform the political promise contained in constitutions but because performance would entail the violation of religious presuppositions in which the promise is grounded." [42]

This is an interpretation of the Constitution which I would have the greatest reluctance to accept. It is reminiscent of the late pressures to deny freedom of speech and assembly to those whose ideas are hostile to basic American liberties.[43] Notwithstanding these pressures, the courts have usually heeded Mr. Justice Holmes's reminder that freedom of thought includes "freedom for the thought that we hate." [44]

So far we have dealt with the problem as though only the Federal Constitution were involved. In many states, however, the state constitution provides an additional obstacle. This is in the form of an explicit provision forbidding (in varying language) any use of tax funds for the support of sectarian schools. A few state courts have given such provisions a narrow construction. Thus, in Illinois, payments to sectarian industrial schools in amounts not exceeding the cost of the service furnished have been held not "grants" to the schools.[45] This reasoning, however, if applied to ordinary parochial schools, would leave little scope to such prohibitions. In view of the history of their adoption during the nineteenth-century controversies over parochial schools, the general application of this narrow construction would seem unwarranted. In many states, furthermore, the provisions have been broadly construed from the outset. Even if the future should see the disappearance of hostility to parochial schools, the abolition of financial discrimination against their

[42] *ibid.*, pp. 172–173.
[43] *Terminiello v. City of Chicago*, 337 U.S. 1 (1949).
[44] *United States v. Schwimmer*, 279 U.S. 644, 655 (1929).
[45] *Dunn v. Chicago Industrial School*, 280 Ill. 613 (1917).

patrons would in many states have to await amendment of the state constitution. Under provisions as specific as these, there is less room for evolution of constitutional law by judicial interpretation than in the case of vague words such as "liberty" and "establishment."

American religious freedom is subject, of course, to many other limitations. Legislation may validly forbid some types of conduct which a particular religion deems obligatory, or may prescribe action forbidden by religious law. Some such limitations are obviously necessary to protect the interests of citizens who do not share the particular faith. This justification may cover measures such as compulsory vaccination [46] and isolation of victims of contagious disease.[47] The restrictions, however, are often more broadly defined and seem designed to give to the faithful themselves a protection they do not wish. Thus prohibitions of ceremonial use of poisonous snakes are not limited to their use in services which are attended by outsiders.[48] Sometimes a legal requirement is made applicable only to children, overruling religious convictions of parents, such as those against blood transfusion [49] or against medical treatment in general.[50]

Limitations on the free exercise of religion are not lightly to be imposed, however; they can be justified only in terms of "grave and immediate danger to interests which the state may lawfully protect" [51] (language quoted from the opinion holding that children of Jehovah's Witnesses must be excused from a compulsory flag salute regulation).

As one reflects upon the limits of constitutional religious liberty, it may be suggestive to contrast our permissive policy

[46] *Zucht v. King,* 260 U.S. 174 (1922).

[47] *Moore v. Draper,* 57 So.2d 648 (Fla., 1952).

[48] *State v. Massay,* 229 N.C. 734, appeal dismissed sub. nom. *Bunn v. North Carolina,* 336 U.S. 942 (1949).

[49] *People ex rel. Wallace v. Labrenz,* 411 Ill. 618, cert. denied 344 U.S. 824 (1952).

[50] *People v. Pierson,* 176 N.Y. 201 (1903).

[51] *West Virginia Board of Education v. Barnette,* 319 U.S. 624, 639 (1943).

toward conscientious objectors with our strict prohibition of plural marriage. Congress is not constitutionally required to respect religious scruples as to military service,[52] and the exemption of conscientious objectors is widely hailed as showing the strength of American traditions of freedom. On the other hand, our historic policy of suppression of Mormon marriage institutions [53] is almost taken for granted. Perhaps we should at least ask whether the compulsion is applied for the good of the saints themselves or whether it is the public peace or the stability of gentile monogamy which would be threatened by a toleration of deviant marriage customs. In any event we must remember this chapter of our continuing history lest we claim too wide a scope for American religious liberty.

II

In the foregoing section I have been writing as a lawyer, surveying the area of American law which protects—and limits—the free exercise of religion. In this second section, however, I write as a citizen personally concerned with the bearing of religious ethics on controversial problems of legal policy. For an illustration, I have chosen the problem of capital punishment. This is an issue on which there have been sharp disagreements among spokesmen for religion as well as among secular writers. It is a problem which provides a critical test for general theories as to purposes and justification of punishment.

Discussions of criminal sanctions have usually distinguished three purposes which penalties may serve: protection of society through preventing crime, retribution for wrongdoing, and rehabilitation of the offender. Perhaps dominant in American secular thought is the view which rejects retribu-

[52] *United States v. Macintosh,* 283 U.S. 605, 624 (1931).

[53] *Reynolds v. United States,* 98 U.S. 145 (1878); *Davis v. Beason,* 133 U.S. 333 (1890).

tion, makes crime prevention the primary purpose, and assigns to rehabilitation a secondary role.[54] Under this view, penalties are primarily imposed to incapacitate the offender (temporarily or permanently) or to deter him and other potential offenders. (Statistics of crime are often cited as showing the absurdity of deterrence theories. Actual crimes do mark the extent of the law's failure as a deterrent, but they cannot refute its claim to success. For the principal deterrent function of the law may be in reinforcing the internal restraints of "law abiding" citizens, a function in which the law may be an outstanding success.) [55]

Sometimes the prevention theory is presented as entirely divorced from notions of moral wrong. This was true, for example, in Holmes's lectures on *The Common Law*,[56] in which the basic justification of punishment was put on no higher ground than that of the "natural" self-preference of shipwrecked men who push others from the piece of wreckage which cannot keep all of them afloat. In many other writers, however, the moral quality of the act and the actor's moral responsibility are emphasized.[57]

Under the prevention theory, it would seem clear that penalties should be only so severe as will contribute to the checking of crime. But even writers who retain retribution as a purpose of the criminal law do not usually determine the maximum extent of penalties on the basis of retribution. Usually concern for rehabilitation or other considerations

[54] Jerome Michael and Herbert Wechsler, *Criminal Law and Its Administration*, Chicago, 1940, pp. 4–17; also the same authors' "A Rationale of the Law of Homicide II," *Columbia Law Review*, XXXVII, December 1937, pp. 1261–1325.

[55] "The chief use of punishment in the State is to frighten the majority of citizens from behaving as they wish to behave, and as a minority *do* behave." Charles Williams, *He Came Down from Heaven*, London, 1956, p. 174. (The "wishes" referred to may, of course, be largely unconscious.)

[56] Oliver Wendell Holmes, *The Common Law*, Boston, 1881, Lect. II.

[57] Joel Prentiss Bishop, *Criminal Law*, 9th ed., Chicago, 1923, 2 vols., I, pp. 139–140: ". . . though [punishment] is merited, it will not be inflicted by the governmental powers, which do not assume the full corrective functions of the Deity, unless it will presumably contribute to the public good."

lead them to support penalties no more severe than would be required for purposes of prevention.[58]

In relation to capital punishment, these non-religious approaches make the issue turn primarily on a question of fact, the question of whether the death penalty adds (or would add) substantially to the deterrent force of the law. We shall be inquiring whether this question of fact is crucial also in religious approaches, or whether there are religious writers who defend or reject capital punishment regardless of its utility as a deterrent.[59]

We may begin with the recent declaration of the General Assembly of the United Presbyterian Church:[60]

> Recognizing the responsibility of the state to protect its citizens and to promote justice and freedom in society,
>
> Recognizing that one of the means by which the state has sought to exercise this responsibility has been the imposition of the death penalty,
>
> Realizing that in Western Europe only France and Great Britain retain the death penalty and that in our country eight states have abolished it,
>
> Knowing that studies have shown that the retention or abolition of the death penalty has no observable effect on homicide rates, that justice sometimes miscarries because of human fallibility in the judicial process, and that enlightened penal practice seeks both to protect society and to reform and rehabilitate guilty persons, and
>
> Believing that capital punishment cannot be condoned by an interpretation of the Bible based upon the revelation of

[58] Jerome Hall, *General Principles of Criminal Law*, Indianapolis, 1947; Francis Wharton, *Criminal Law*, 12th ed., Rochester, 1932, 3 vols., I, ch. 1; William L. Clark and William L. Marshall, *A Treatise on the Law of Crimes*, 6th ed., Chicago, 1958, § 2.00.

[59] We shall be sampling chiefly the arguments of contemporary religious writers. Some of those active in the nineteenth century are cited in Louis Filler, "Movements to Abolish the Death Penalty in the United States," *Annals of the American Academy of Political and Social Science*, CCLXXXIV, November 1952, pp. 124–136.

[60] *Social Progress*, XLIX, July 1959, pp. 18–20.

> God's love in Jesus Christ, that as Christians we must seek the redemption of evil doers and not their death, and that the use of the death penalty tends to brutalize the society that condones it,
>
> The 171st General Assembly
>
> Declares its opposition to capital punishment. . . .

For the authors of this statement, the sociological studies (which report that the death penalty has no apparent effect on homicide rates) may be the crucial factor. Concern for the offender and his redemption requires rejection of the death penalty in the absence of evidence of its special utility in crime prevention. But does this declaration imply a belief that the use of capital punishment would be justified if this penalty were shown to be uniquely effective in preventing homicide? A negative answer is suggested by one of the "background papers" distributed with the declaration,[61] but the authors of the declaration itself seem carefully to have avoided giving a definite answer.

Roman Catholic statements usually begin with the proposition that natural law permits the state to kill, but only to protect society from future crimes.[62] There are wide differences, however, in the way individual Roman Catholics approach the question of utility. The natural law principle just stated would seem to place the burden upon those who support the death penalty. Some Roman Catholic spokesmen recognize this presumption against capital punishment and

[61] "[We should see penology] not in the concept of every man according to his due, but to every man according to his need. This would surely mean that some men would need to spend the rest of their natural lives in prison, because freedom is too great a burden for them and their presence is too great a danger to their fellow men. The case of each would have to be seen in the context of his potential for redemption, which in this case is personal renewal. . . . Death is the one penalty that seems not to be allowable, for it actually prevents the redemptive process from its fullness, not allowing man the full use of his years for overcoming this brokenness and achieving wholeness." Gordon Jackson, quoted in *Social Progress*, XLIX, July 1929, p. 18.

[62] J. D. Nicola, "The Case Against the Death Penalty," *Information*, June 1959; pamphlet reprint of N.Y. Institute of Criminology.

support abolition on the ground that the available evidence fails to establish its unique deterrent effect.[63]

For other Roman Catholics, however, the deterrent effect of the death sentence is treated as almost axiomatic, requiring only a reference to the human instinct of self-preservation. A vigorous expression of this position is the recent minority report of the Massachusetts Special Commission on capital punishment, signed by the Rt. Rev. Msgr. Thomas J. Riley. The report concedes that execution can be justified "only if it serves as a deterrent . . . and only if less drastic measures towards the same end will not be sufficiently effective."[64] However, the sociological studies of the incidence of crime are dismissed on the ground that "It does not seem logical to say that the death penalty should be abolished because statistics prove that it is not a deterrent. . . . If we admit that the State has, in principle, the right to inflict it, we should admit likewise a corresponding obligation on the part of the State to make it effective and we should not urge failure to do this as a proof that the death penalty itself is not necessary."

Another possible religious position is one which would justify capital punishment on retributive or other religious grounds, entirely apart from its usefulness as a deterrent. Religious writers often urge retribution as a justification of punishment in general. Thus the Rev. Washington Gladden, in his Beecher Lectures at the Yale Divinity School, started from the Pauline premise that the civil magistrate "is a minister of God, an avenger for wrath to him that doeth evil." "[L]aws and penalties ought to express the divine displeasure against wrong-doing; they ought to be regarded as a solemn testimony of the moral sense of the nation. . . ."[65]

[63] *ibid.* See also Robert Hovda, "The Death Penalty," *Commonweal*, LXX, July 1959, pp. 367–368.

[64] Special Commission Established for the Purpose of Investigating and Studying the Abolition of the Death Penalty in Capital Cases, *Report and Recommendations, December 30, 1958*, Boston, 1959, pp. 64–74.

[65] Washington Gladden, *Social Salvation*, Boston, 1902, ch. IV, pp. 103, 104.

This view of the function of penalties implies that their severity should be graduated according to the seriousness of the offense. "There is no computing the enormity of the guilt of murder," wrote the Rev. George B. Cheever in 1843. Therefore, "There ought to be such a penalty, high, awful, distinctive, to mark this crime in its *retribution*, as it stands in its *guilt*, paramount to every other." [66] This argument (together with scriptural injunction) [67] seems to be urged as requiring capital punishment quite apart from consideration of utility. But Cheever then proceeded: "it being granted that the murderer deserves to die, and that society have the right in some cases to inflict the punishment of death, the question of expediency before us is simply whether punishment by death operates more effectually to prevent the crime of murder than any other penalty." [68]

As in the case of this example, retributive defenses of capital punishment are usually coupled with utilitarian arguments. I have been unable to find an American religious writer who clearly urges retributive penalties more severe than he would defend in terms of prevention. However, a recent poll of Illinois clergymen did disclose a few who defend capital punishment on this simple retributive ground.

In the British debate, the Archbishop of Canterbury supported the death penalty on the ground of its usefulness in promoting eleventh-hour conversion and repentance.[69] So far as I know, this argument is not advanced by American theologians, although I recently heard it urged in a debate by a Roman Catholic prosecuting attorney.[70] Under the United

[66] George B. Cheever, *Capital Punishment* (argument in reply to J. L. O'Sullivan, Esq., in the Broadway Tabernacle), New York, 1843, p. 42.

[67] Genesis 9:6: "Whoso sheddeth man's blood, by man shall his blood be shed."

[68] Cheever, p. 43.

[69] *Parliamentary Debates*, House of Lords, CXCVIII, London, 1956, p. 746.

[70] The contrary view was recently taken by Robert Hovda, "The Death Penalty," *Commonweal*, LXX, July 1959, p. 367: ". . . it is much too easy to say that, knowing the time of his death, the prisoner has ample opportunity to prepare. A state of shock is not fertile ground for faith. Nor can the external pressure of death row . . . be conceived as encouraging the disposi-

States Constitution, however, this argument raises a serious question. May the state kill for the purpose of promoting spiritual rehabilitation for a future life? This would be a use of state power for a religious end quite inconsistent with the American tradition discussed in the first half of this essay.

A third religious position is one which would reject capital punishment even if it were shown uniquely useful in preventing crime. Some American religious groups oppose the death penalty on simple and absolute grounds. "Killing is inherently wrong, . . . regardless of the victim's guilt, regardless of social or penological considerations. The gift of human life is from the Almighty; we dare not impinge on His domain by taking the life of another. . . . Present-day penology does not put its emphasis on retribution, or even on deterrence, but on rehabilitation." [71] This quotation is from the statement of a spokesman for the Church of the Brethren before a committee of the Maryland legislature.

Similar emphasis on rehabilitation is the basis of the declaration of the Methodist Social Creed: "We stand for the application of the redemptive principle to the treatment of offenders against the law, to reform of penal and correctional methods, and to criminal court procedure. For this reason we deplore the use of capital punishment." [72] These unqualified statements raise the question whether no exception would be recognized where conditions of unusual social disintegration suggest the need of unusual severity, and where lives might be saved by the use of capital punishment. Would the Methodist Board recognize a tragic dilemma in such a situation and the necessity of a choice between evils?

These contemporary religious statements on capital punish-

---

tions necessary to fruitful reception of the sacraments. Those who advance this argument suffer from a view of the holy signs that is as outdated as it is mechanical."

[71] Testimony of the Rev. Clyde R. Shallenberger, *Brethren Service News*, June 1958 (reprint distributed by Brethren General Offices, Elgin, Illinois).

[72] Leaflet distributed by Methodist Board of Social and Economic Relations, Chicago.

ment are disappointing in their failure to deal adequately with what seems to me the most troublesome aspect of the problem. Most of the writers seem unconcerned with the morality of using a condemned criminal to deter others. Immanuel Kant declared most emphatically that such use is immoral and insisted that punishment is justified only as retribution.[73] Whether or not one accepts this justification, the problem Kant raised cannot be avoided. It is peculiarly acute in relation to the death penalty. Other penalties may be defended as directed primarily against the risk of further harm from the offender himself. Self-defense may therefore be invoked as a justification for appropriate measures to incapacitate the offender or to deter him from further crime. The fact that such measures are incidentally useful in deterring others does not undermine this justification. But non-parolable life imprisonment would incapacitate an offender just as effectively as his execution (apart from the minor risks of ill-advised pardon, escape, or violence in the penitentiary). The death penalty is used primarily to check the risk from *other* potential criminals, and the problem of the use of men as instruments is therefore directly involved.

For Holmes, this aspect of capital punishment apparently presented no problem. Writing to Harold Laski, he calmly explained: "If I were having a philosophical talk with a man I was going to have hanged (or electrocuted) I should say, I don't doubt that your act was inevitable for you but to make it more avoidable by others we propose to sacrifice you to the common good. You may regard yourself as a soldier dying for your country if you like. But the law must keep its promises."[74] This justification is somehow unsatisfying, at least if the issue is to be faced as one of religious ethics.

As we have already noted, the religious justification of punishment in general is usually stated in terms of the of-

[73] Immanuel Kant, *The Philosophy of Law*, W. Hastie, tr., Edinburgh, 1887, pp. 194–204.

[74] Mark DeWolfe Howe, *Holmes-Laski Letters*, Cambridge, 1953, p. 806.

fender's "fault"—moral guilt which makes punishment "deserved," even though the limit of the penalty may be set by considerations of utility. In modern American religious thought, the assertion that punishment is deserved is usually associated with belief in the offender's freedom of choice. For example, Msgr. Riley's minority report in Massachusetts was based upon an explicit premise that man is "capable of self-determined activity" and therefore responsible.[75] Modern writers have sometimes criticized this view as inconsistent with a "scientific" approach. Thus Harry Elmer Barnes charged that religious belief in freedom of the will has led to a doctrine of responsibility which blocks rational approaches to the crime problem. The criminal law, he asserted, "will remain hopelessly archaic" until we are able "to destroy root and branch the free moral agent doctrine in criminal responsibility." [76]

The view that punishment is deserved, however, is not always associated with belief in free will. Early American Calvinism is an obvious example. Barnes's own studies of colonial penal codes should have led him to question whether penal harshness is simply to be traced to belief in free will.[77] Compared with the codes written under Quaker influence, the Puritan laws were much harsher, particularly in their

[75] Special Commission, p. 64.

[76] Harry Elmer Barnes, *The Twilight of Christianity*, New York, 1929, pp. 72–73. Today scientists are not so likely to insist that criminals should be dealt with on strict deterministic assumptions. At a recent discussion of "Determinism and Responsibility in Law and Ethics," Percy W. Bridgman protested against this approach: ". . . the insistence that punishment is unjustified can lead only to social catastrophe. At present the only technique we have for dealing with our fellows is to act as if they were the same sort of creatures as we ourselves. We disregard determinism when dealing with ourselves—we have to disregard it, within reason, in our everyday contacts with others. Too many of us take our [scientific] verbal structures with a deadly seriousness—a certain tough-mindedness and small sense of humor might provide an antidote." *Determinism and Freedom in the Age of Modern Science*, Sidney Hook, ed., New York, 1958, pp. 144–145.

[77] Harry Elmer Barnes, *The Evolution of Penology in Pennsylvania*, Indianapolis, 1927, pp. 27ff.; *A History of the Penal, Reformatory and Correctional Institutions of the State of New Jersey*, Trenton, 1918, pp. 27ff.

indiscriminate use of capital punishment. No one could attribute to Jonathan Edwards a belief that men (in Barnes's phrase) are "perfectly free to choose law-abiding modes of conduct." But a student of the theology of Edwards reports that "The punitive justice of God was not mere abstract theory with these Calvinists as the history of their treatment of wrongdoers will show. The stern and inevitable justice of God to his subjects certainly gave support and direction to a penology which was stern and severe towards the citizen-subjects of the earthly theocracy." [78]

Modern religious theories of man's nature usually emphasize the limits of his freedom. In the theology of Paul Tillich, for example, man's finite freedom stands in "correlation" with his "destiny"—the sum-total of his inheritance, his character, and his environment.[79] Man's freedom is a limited (but indeterminate) capacity to mold his destiny. Tillich does not speak of responsibility as the consequence of freedom; he says rather that "freedom is experienced as deliberation, decision, and responsibility." Nor is the concept of responsibility central in his treatment of justice.

Legal justice, for Tillich, is "tributive," i.e., proportional to the individual's "power of being." "Distributive justice gives to any being the proportion of goods which is due him; retributive justice does the same, but in negative terms, in terms of deprivation of goods or active punishment." [80] Tillich adds, however, that there are exceptions to this "tributive" view of legal justice, and they point to another level of justice, which is "transforming or creative." Creative justice operates by "listening, giving, forgiving." [81] In creative justice it is love that recognizes what justice demands; in

[78] George Noel Mayhew, *The Relation of the Theology of Jonathan Edwards to Contemporary Penological Theory and Practice*, Chicago, 1932 (Thesis in Library of University of Chicago), p. 69.

[79] Paul Tillich, *Systematic Theology*, Chicago, 1951, 1957, 2 vols. I, 184–185; II, 42, 56–57.

[80] Paul Tillich, *Love, Power, and Justice*, New York, 1954, pp. 63–64.

[81] *ibid.*, p. 64.

creative justice love effects reconciliation, "reuniting those who are estranged by guilt." [82]

In this theological structure, the first question as to a proposed penalty would seem to be whether it is "due" in a retributive sense, not whether its imposition would be useful. However, if the law is to "point to" the level of transforming justice, presumably no unnecessary harshness must be shown, since on that level justice operates through "giving and forgiving." But harshness is necessary: "Love, in order to exercise its proper works, namely charity and forgiveness, must provide for a place on which this can be done, through its strange work of judging and punishing." [83] Nor, apparently, is capital punishment ruled out, for Tillich says that the "strange work" of love includes "bitterness, killing, and condemnation."

My difficulty with this analysis relates to the initial retributive premise. I would prefer to start by asserting that legal judgments are not attempts to adjudicate "real" responsibility or to impose penalties which are ontologically "due." Legal judgments—and human moral judgments as well—have a quite different function. They call upon men to *take* responsibility for their acts. The emphasis is not on freedom and responsibility as characterizing the act of wrongdoing, but on the God-given freedom in virtue of which the actor can take responsibility. The law declares that responsibility is not to be evaded; the law imposes responsibility and does what it can to promote its voluntary acceptance.

What does it mean to take responsibility? Taking responsibility for a criminal act includes seeking to make restitution; it means recognizing that one's act has added to the world's evil and wishing to do something to neutralize that effect. In a world where most men need deterrent examples to reinforce their moral restraints, a repentant offender willingly accepts useful punishment as an appropriate act of restitution.

[82] *ibid.*, p. 86.
[83] *ibid.*, p. 49.

And while the law seeks to promote such voluntary acceptance of responsibility, it cannot leave the offender free to refuse. The law imposes as a penalty what it may ask the offender to accept as his just contribution to the maintenance of social order.[84]

Such a restitutionary interpretation, however, justifies the imposition of penalties only if the state is doing what it can to help the offender to accept responsibility. This means that forgiveness cannot be foreign to the law.[85] Mr. Justice Douglas has said (albeit in a dissenting opinion) that "the principle of forgiveness and the doctrine of redemption are too deep in our philosophy to admit that there is no return for those who have once erred."[86] At the least, the law's procedures should avoid the rhetoric and symbols of personal rejection. They should be designed not only for the protection of society but in most cases also to facilitate the offender's reintegration into the community. A redemptive approach would mean, of course, a shouldering by the community of costs of careful diagnostic procedures, well-staffed institutions with varying degrees of security precautions, and the like. It would mean also, in many cases, the acceptance of a degree of risk in the use of probation, parole, and suspended sentence.

Does this "restitutionary" view of criminal justice have any place for capital punishment? Clearly not, in the absence of showing that the death penalty would reduce the rate of homicide. In twentieth-century America, capital punishment is primarily a symbol of the unforgiving defensiveness of "law-abiding" citizens. Its principal effects may be those which it has within our penitentiaries, widespread effects in reinforcing unrepentant hostility and in blocking acceptance

[84] See Albert Eglash, "Creative Restitution," *Journal of Criminal Law, Criminology and Police Science*, XLVIII, March–April 1958, pp. 619–622.

[85] "Forgiveness goes before punishment and so makes punishment efficient." "Forgiveness is the self-defense of the Law under attack. It puts forth new and creative powers. . . . The will of the offender, with all his offenses, is caught up within the superior, the redeeming will." Henry Sylvester Nash, *The Atoning Life*, New York, 1950, p. 90.

[86] *Harisiades v. Shaughnessy*, 342 U.S. 580, 595 (1952).

of responsibility. But what of a situation in which capital punishment might seem to be necessary to check violence? One example of such a situation was described to me by a psychiatrist who was usually uncompromising in his opposition to severe penalties. He had been acting as adviser to the military commander of a front line sector which had been under long and heavy attack. Increasingly serious breaches of discipline and crimes of violence were showing a dangerous weakening of morale. In this situation, he felt he had to advise the use of maximum penalties to check further disintegration.

What of the situation where abolition of the death penalty is followed by lynchings which the authorities seem unable to prevent? [87] Here the restoration of capital punishment might restore due process of law and prevent the lynching of innocent men. What is appropriate restitution under such conditions? Might a repentant murderer be willing to accept death in order thus to save the lives of others? And does it follow that the penalty might justly be imposed? I have to answer "yes," but with reluctance and with hope that today nowhere in the United States would sober inquiry rebut the general presumption against legalized killing.

Under "normal" conditions, the case against capital punishment is compelling. It may be true, as my colleague Malcolm Sharp suggests, that the death penalty "seems to get some of its support as a result of religious views of sin, crime, retribution, and vengeance." [88] But it is true also that much of the strength of the current movement for abolition comes from religious groups.

[87] In Colorado, the death penalty was restored in 1901 after a four year period in which three lynchings took place. J. E. Cutler, "Capital Punishment and Lynching," *Annals of the American Academy of Political and Social Science*, XXIX, June 1907, pp. 183–184.

[88] Malcolm Sharp, Review of Arthur Koestler, *Reflections on Hanging*, *University of Chicago Law Review*, XXV, Spring 1958, p. 561.

AMERICAN RELIGION AND AMERICAN POLITICAL ATTITUDES

WILLIAM LEE MILLER

Rising to an election eve peroration, Dwight Eisenhower quoted a "wise philosopher" from abroad who answered, many years ago, the question "wherein lie the greatness and the goodness of America?" It was not in "her harbors and rivers," or her "fertile fields and boundless forests," he said in Boston in 1952; it was not in her "rich mines and vast world commerce," nor even her "democratic congress and her matchless constitution." Where, then, was it? "Not until I went into the churches of America and heard her pulpits flame with righteousness did I understand the secret of her genius and power."

For those who have gone into the churches of America but still not grasped that secret the quotation may not mean much; it may seem to be just another example of the routine obeisance an American politician pays to God or religion as he draws near the end of his speech. But the fact that American politicians still pay such obeisance is worth noting. There is in America a kind of public semi-secular national religion that appears on state occasions, that fuses patriotic themes with antiseptic references to religion, and that Presidential candidates had better refer to.

But more important, there really is something expressive of the politics of the nation—some "secret," as the quotation says—exhibited in the churches. The phrase about "righteousness" serves to suggest what it might be. The American religious tradition has been hortatory and moral in its appeal, suffused with emotion, applied—although sometimes vaguely—to the affairs of the practical world and, above all, fervently addressed to the moral decision of the individual will. This "righteous," idealistic, active, individualistic spirit, this "flame," has burnt its way into the national consciousness; it still affects the national temper, and is important in the way people deal with politics.

Does the pulpit flaming with righteousness symbolize America's political "genius and power"? Yes, maybe so, but her weakness, too. It is worthwhile noting both.

I

We want to examine the effect of religion in America upon the political attitudes of that mysterious entity, "the American public." To do so is to make many assumptions, of which we mention briefly three.

(1) We assume that religion does have an important influence upon American culture. William Warren Sweet, who has most prolifically pursued American religious history, once quoted with understandable approval an address of J. Franklin Jameson before the American Historical Association: "Of all the means of estimating American character . . . ," Mr. Jameson had said, "the pursuit of religious history is the most complete." "Millions have felt an interest in religion," continued Mr. Sweet, paraphrasing, "where thousands have felt an interest in literature or philosophy or music or art . . . no view can be a truthful one that neglects a consideration of the ideals which animated and actuated the toiling millions and the thoughts concerning the universe and man which informed their minds." [1] Mr. Sweet goes on to say that all this applies with special strength to America, because here, far more than elsewhere, the churches have been managed by laymen: religious history is not a history of ecclesiastics or a "priestly caste" but of the people.

If we reject this last, because it is too simple and antichurchly a view of distinctions between Catholic and Protestant countries, and if we also have doubts about the test of sheer numbers to decide what is culturally determinative,

[1] William Warren Sweet, *Religion in the Development of American Culture,* New York, 1952, pp. vii–viii.

still we may accept the general point, softened a bit: religion is an important, perhaps an indispensable, clue to what America is like.

(2) We assume also that there is an effect of religion upon the nation's politics that goes beyond the direct and visible manifestations that the political scientist and journalist ordinarily treat, and that the politician ordinarily thinks about. Religious groups lobby against an Ambassador to the Vatican, for aid to Israel, for and against federal aid to religious schools. They fight for prohibition or legislation against birth control. Some Protestants vote against Al Smith; political parties in big cities must be careful to "balance the ticket" among Protestants, Catholics, and Jews; religious affiliation is one "variable" in the politics of the citizens of Erie County, Ohio, which social scientists can correlate with the voters' party affiliation, among other things. The religious groups, like groups of veterans, landlords, or shipbuilders, have organizations to promote their own interests and ideas in government; even more, in various "social action," "social welfare," and "social progress" organizations they educate their constituency about political matters. Clergymen preach about "social issues." These direct effects of religion on politics have a significance ranging from that of small nuisance to a significant social force. But there is also a still more important, if less measurable, *indirect* and long-term effect of the religious tradition upon the nation's politics. This is the impact of ways of thinking, believing, and acting in religious matters upon the shape of the mind, which impact affects the way other fields, like politics, are understood. Such effects, seeping down into the national character, may be discernible not only in clergymen and church people but in members of the society at large.

(3) We assume, thirdly, that the religion in America that has an important indirect effect upon political attitudes does have a certain unity and shape despite the variety that appears at first glance. It is true that the United States contains an

enormous number—some 268 at last count—of what yearbooks call "religious bodies," and that none of them can claim any official priority or preference. But to conclude, as do some bewildered visitors from lands with more orderly religious arrangements, that here we have nothing but diversity, is to miss the fact that America has a particular, and peculiar, religious tradition of its own.

Even considered quantitatively, American religion is not quite as unmanageably diverse as is sometimes suggested. Nearly two-thirds of the church members in America are members of three large religious families; more than two-thirds of the Protestants are members of four religious families; 205 of the religious groups which fill the pages of the *Yearbook of Churches*, comprise together only 3.6 per cent of the religious population.

But the more important point is that the quantitative and organizational view is not the best way to understand American religion. The main currents of American religion have not stayed within the banks of denominations or even "faith groups"; the organizational multiplicities have not been as important as the "spiritual" unities; the superficial variety has masked deeper common strands. Viewed negatively, the underlying problem of American religion is not the number of organizations but the singleness of point-of-view of a popular culture-religion that tends simply to be a moralized version of Americanism. Viewed positively, the main current of American religious thought, the marrow of American divinity, has been a unique free church spirit and tradition that arises out of the Protestant past and in some ways is reinforced by the pluralistic present.

Before examining its politics, we make a brief, general summary of relevant aspects of this main religious tradition.

II

Some of the characteristics of religion in America come from (1) the nature of all Protestantism; this, in turn, is changed and intensified by (2) the *kind* of Protestantism that develops in the American nation.

(1) PROTESTANTISM IN THE PLACE OF CATHOLICISM. H. Richard Niebuhr described America as the land of "constructive Protestantism." Here, almost uniquely, the Protestant movement was not in protest against a present or a past Catholicism, but had a culture to build, afresh, of its own.[2] Louis Hartz's treatment of De Tocqueville's observation that America is born free, and did not have to become so, suggests a related fact: America is born Protestant, and does not have to become so.[3] America was already Protestant at birth, and had to endure no reformation, counter-reformation, and religious war. As there is no feudalism in our past, and hence no left-over aristocracy, no remnant of feudal classes, traditions, unities, and servilities, so also there is no Catholicism in our background, and hence no left-over national church, no remnant of Catholic authority, sacrament, order, hierarchy of higher and lower ways, little memory-ridden clericalism and anti-clericalism. When Dean Sperry was describing to an English audience the difference between American religion and their own, he fastened first and most importantly upon the absence here of anything like their Establishment.[4] But that negative institutional fact may be taken to indicate a whole cluster of other, related facts that distinguish religion in America even from the tradition it is closest to, the English: one tradition takes over from a Catholic past, retains its geographical parish system and its connection with the state and the national culture and has something of its communal social thought and ethic; the other is a traditionless tradition that, not having had these, starts fresh with Protestant principles.

But how does "constructive Protestantism" construct? That is the problem, the religious form of the general American problem: how do the liberating, dynamic, anti-traditional,

[2] H. Richard Niebuhr, *The Kingdom of God in America*, Chicago, 1937, ch. I.

[3] Louis Hartz, *The Liberal Tradition in America*, New York, 1955.

[4] Willard L. Sperry, *Religion in America*, New York, 1945, p. 6.

individualistic movements that shape this society develop constructive communal standards, goals, and structures? Dr. Niebuhr described the Protestant problem thus:

"The dilemma of Protestantism lay . . . in these factors: it had no will to power and in view of its positive principle could have none, for supreme power belonged only to God . . . ; it had no definite idea of the end toward which it was traveling and could have none, since the future lay with the free God; . . . As a theory of *divine* construction the Protestant movement was hard put to it to provide principles for human construction."[5]

One might say that Protestantism as a whole lacks the structural equipment for *explicitly* shaping a whole culture in the way that—in theory at least—the Catholic apparatus provides. The content which Christianity claims to transcend individual opinion and cultural ethos is not fastened solidly to an infallibly interpreted doctrinal truth; the grace of God is not mediated in objective sacraments, efficacious of themselves, but is "free," received alone by the faith of the believer; the objective indelible office of the priest, independent of the character of the man, is erased, and every man becomes his own priest, and the priestly office has no objective sacrament to administer, no objective authority to invoke.

The Roman Catholic version of Christianity may build on the foundation of an authoritarian church, an objective means of grace, an indelible priesthood, a Thomistic philosophy, and a doctrine of natural law, a structure in which all the parts of cultural life, each in its proper place, can—in theory at least—be contained, each retaining its own integrity but related ultimately to the framework of church and doctrine. In natural law it has a principle by which all the forms and parts and culture may be related ultimately to Christian truth. Protestantism does not have such a clear basis, sociological,

[5] H. R. Niebuhr, p. 30.

theological, or philosophical, for building itself into an explicit relationship to the broader elements of culture. Max Weber's Protestant "monk in the world" has no monastery and no outer monastic discipline, and that is an important difference. A great part of Protestantism has forgotten or explicitly rejected any notion of natural law. The doctrines of justification by faith alone and the priesthood of all believers are in considerable part to be understood against the Catholic background which they reject, and the "works-righteousness" and the priesthood they reject represent the externals that fastened Catholicism into the surrounding culture. These Protestant doctrines are doctrines of liberation more than of construction, doctrines for the "freedom of the Christian man" more than the building of the Christian society.

The constructive impact of Protestantism therefore depends upon how the Christian man uses his freedom. It is more volatile, and perhaps more dynamic than its Catholic counterpart. Release from the historical anchor meant a new creative dynamism, free from the static and traditional, and the possibility of a new kind of penetration of the culture; it also meant a danger that, when the dynamism of Protestant Christianity is spent, its dependence upon the will (and opinion and desire) of the individual believer will leave its version of the distinctive content of Christian faith at the mercy of dynamic forces arising elsewhere.

America's Protestantism has entered into the common creed in something of the way that, in Mr. Hartz's view, political liberalism has done: as an unchallenged set of assumptions that are not argued, but taken for granted as self-evident. The implicit religious ethic which affects American politics not only has an anti-authoritarian, anti-traditional, anti-corporate strand in it; this strand is an almost universal, unchallenged, unexamined axiom.

(2) Sects with the Power of Churches. The nature of American religion results in part from its birthright of

Protestantism and the absence of an indigenous Catholicism to take over from, to remember, and to be in face-to-face rebellion against. But it results also from the *kind* of Protestantism that came here, and then that developed here. The most important part of this is what James Hastings Nichols calls "Puritan Protestantism":

". . . the common ethos of that family of Anglo-American denominations whose best known representatives are the Congregationalists, Baptists, Presbyterians, Methodists, Unitarians, Quakers, Disciples, Salvation Army, and the evangelical party within the Anglican communion. These groups are often more pre-occupied with their differences than with their common inheritance from the Puritan Revolution in seventeenth century England, but from a historical and sociological perspective they constitute a collective unity of religious and ethical attitude. Historically they represent a fusion of Calvinism, Spiritualism, and the Baptist sect movement, and may be called 'neo-Calvinism' in contrast to the aristocratic and authoritarian Calvinism of the sixteenth century. Ethically and sociologically they share the orientation that Troeltsch indicated by the terms 'ascetic Protestantism' and 'individualistic-activistic Protestantism.' "[6]

The Calvinist element of this ethos has in it a drive to build and to dominate a culture that goes well beyond even what Roman Catholicism intends, because it wants to "order all under God" directly and without gradations, relative autonomies, or intermediaries. The full impact of that drive was felt, for a moment, in seventeenth-century New England. But out of this religious background there developed a religious spirit, and a relation of religion to culture, that was different from what the Puritans at first intended. The more Calvinistic denominations, the Presbyterians and Congregationalists, numerically dominant at the time of the Revolu-

[6] James Hastings Nichols, *Democracy and the Churches*, Philadelphia, 1951, p. 10.

tionary War, were outdistanced by the freer churches, the Baptists and Methodists, by the time of the Civil War; the more evangelical spirit gained the initiative. Timothy Smith's study of *Revivalism and Social Reform* makes clear that the rigid old "Calvinism," which social historians love to denounce, was very much subordinated by the first half of the nineteenth century to a perfectionist, revivalistic Christianity.[7]

Something remained of the remarkable Puritan vision, of a practical world built on the direct rule of God, but the range of practical life to which the rule of God was to be directly applied was narrowed, partly because the way that world was to be built was changed. That way became the voluntary way, the individual way, and therefore the rule of God was applied especially to individual morality and to those aspects of society in which voluntary action was most relevant and "moral" distinctions most evident. The focus changed from the Godly community to the converted individual, from the righteous society to the "interfering spirit of righteousness" that has characterized American religion and American society.

Sidney Mead has listed five characteristics of American Protestantism in the period he calls the formative one, the early nineteenth century: "historylessness"; the voluntary principle; the mission enterprise; revivalism; pietism.[8] It is notable that each of these characteristics emphasizes the free decision of the individual will. Christianity in America has emphasized these expressions of a change of heart and of the conversion of the individual: the pious practice of the believer, the revival in the society, and the missionary effort to the unconverted. Fundamental to all of this is a fresh grasp on a free and inward decision of the spirit as essential to real religion, and a corresponding rejection of any coercion in religious belief.

[7] Timothy L. Smith, *Revivalism and Social Reform,* Nashville, 1957, pp. 32–33.

[8] Sidney Mead, "Denominationalism: The Shape of Protestantism in America," *Church History,* December, 1954.

As to "historylessness," the most typical American religious groups—like, say, the Disciples—tended to leap from nineteenth-century America straight back to New Testament times, and to regard everything in between as sort of a mistake. And as, in their view, history dropped away leaving an unencumbered present, so also society dropped away, leaving an unencumbered individual.

The idea of the "voluntary principle" in religion, which Winthrop Hudson calls the "great tradition of the American Church," applies primarily to the nature of the church itself, and from that to the absence of an institutional connection between the church and the government.[9] It describes a form of the church, free, gathered, separated from civil power. Its best-known corollary, the separation of church and state, is not solely the inadvertent result of the multiplicity of religious groups in the colonies, nor is it the result simply of indifference to religion. It is in considerable measure the product of theological convictions about the sovereign power of God and the freedom of man. A large part of American Christianity affirms the voluntary principle in religion not in spite of, but *because* of, what it believes. This affirmation has been helped along by a liberal and democratic environment, but the religious spirit helped in turn to create that environment.

The voluntary principle, however, extended beyond a conception of the separation of church and state, of religion as uncoerced, and of the church as gathered in freedom; it also involved a conception of the whole relation of religion to the surrounding culture. The Calvinist will to order the society, under God, became the revivalist's attempt at converting the society by individual and voluntary means. The assumption of this free church religion is that the personal religious convictions of individuals, freely gathered in churches and acting in voluntary associations, will permeate the society by

[9] Winthrop Hudson, *The Great Tradition of the American Churches*, New York, 1953.

persuasion and example. That is the most central American understanding of religion and culture.

Neither "sect" nor "church" describes the unusual relation of religion to culture favored by the "denominations" in America. As with the sect, there are sharp and simple moral lines drawn for the individual's behavior, and an emphasis upon the *pure* community and the condemnation of the instrumentalities of coercion and of power and of compromise with the world. But at the same time that some elements of a sectarian morality persist, the denominations that embody that ethic not only are not withdrawn from the world, but very much related to and interfering in it—even, at times, aggressively oriented toward making it over. The intent is *not* to withdraw from the society into a separated, pure community; quite the contrary—the Puritan intent to remake the larger society is still very much present. But the sectarian attachment to a pure, non-coercive, unstained morality remains. How can these two be combined? How can religion both be pure and yet mold the society? By using only example, persuasion, voluntary means; by changing the individuals who will then change the society. The "sect" withdraws from the "world" and its powers in order to retain purity. The "church" embraces the world to order it within a universal framework, compromising with it in order to domesticate its powers by churchly influence. But the remarkable image one gets of the American Protestant enterprise is that of an intention to embrace the world, yet without compromise; to be a sect, and yet to mold the whole culture; to reject power, and yet be powerful.

Winthrop Hudson is eloquent in describing the positive cultural results of this voluntary principle: "Cut loose to stand or fall by their own efforts, to 'that moral coercion which makes men work,' the churches were roused from their lethargy, compelled to assume responsibility both for their own institutional life and for the moral and spiritual life of their society, and were able to exert by voluntary efforts, societies, missions, and revivals, a deeper influence than ever before."[10]

Out of this free church idea in the nineteenth century came the great energy of revivals, of the missionary enterprise spreading Christianity over the nation and the world, and of the immense profusion of voluntary associations for reform which resulted in a remarkable penetration of the total culture by evangelical Christianity.

But voluntary Christianity, for all its virtues, had its limits as a social force. Those limits appear whenever the problem of power appears. The voluntary principle tends to become not only part of the essence of religion; not only a theory of the relation of religion to society; it is also, at least in implication, a social philosophy, with distinct limitations in dealing with politics.

III

To describe this social philosophy, which is partly explicit but partly implicit in the religious experience in America, we would have to use some very familiar words, words like moralistic, individualistic, voluntaristic, idealistic. These familiar words come to the fore because the way religious Americans look at society is of course very much like the way other Americans look at society. Certain aspects of the broader common view, however, are held with particular intensity within the religious community, and are the parts that the religious community has brought into the broader American view with particular force.

First among these would be the moral and moralistic element. "Authoritative observers from De Tocqueville, through Bryce, Siegfried and others, down to such recent studies as those of Vernon L. Parrington, Margaret Mead, Gunnar Myrdal, and Harold Laski, have agreed on at least one point: Americans tend to 'see the world in moral terms.' "[11] When,

[10] *ibid.*, p. 79.

[11] Robin M. Williams, Jr., *American Society*, New York, 1951, pp. 396–397.

for example, during the war Margaret Mead turned from her research elsewhere to examine the "national character" of her own land, she wrote in her introduction:

"As America has a moral culture—that is, a culture which accepts right and wrong as important—any discussion of Americans must simply bristle with words like *good* and *bad*. Any discussion of Samoans would bristle with terms for awkward and graceful. . . . If I were writing about the way in which the Germans or the Japanese, the Burmese or the Javanese would have to act if they were to win the war, I would not need to use so many moral terms. For none of these peoples think of life in habitually moral terms as do Americans." [12]

The kind of religion that has predominated in America is obviously a chief source of this emphasis on moral consideration. America's religious groups have been mightily concerned with the "moral," with "principle," with "ideals," with "right and wrong." The distinctiveness of this emphasis can be seen when it is set in contrast to the other elements of religion more prominent in other societies. For example, the contemplative aspect of religion is very much subordinated in American experience. H. Richard Niebuhr's interpretation of American Protestantism begins with the distinction between the medieval and Catholic emphasis upon the perfection of God and man's contemplation, and the reformers' emphasis upon the sovereignty of God and man's service and activity. The stress was upon the dynamic will of God rather than His static perfection, upon the kingdom of God rather than the vision of God, upon action rather than upon contemplation.

In the same way one can see the subordination of the mystical element in religion; though there have been mystics around the edges of American society, in the main there have not been many flights from the Alone to the Alone. There is

[12] Margaret Mead, *And Keep Your Powder Dry*, New York, 1942, pp. 10–11.

similar subordination of the sacramental sense that appears in the religion of more churchly countries, and with the sense of awe before what is holy, and with the awareness of mystery and of tragic elements in life. Perry Miller says that the American Puritans really had too little rather than too much sense of tragedy, and if they did not have it, certainly their heirs did not.

The communal and traditional elements of religion, as in Judaism, of familial acts hallowed by the group's life through centuries, is very subordinate in American religion. Dean Sperry told his English audience that in American religion "there never has been and there is not now, that felt distinction between the sacred and the secular which is a commonplace in most religious circles."[13] Finally, the intellectual, theological element, though prominent in Puritan Christianity, came with the growth of the churches of the common man and the triumph of pietism to be neglected in American religion. "It is scarcely an exaggeration to say," wrote Henry Steele Commager, "that during the nineteenth century and well into the twentieth, religion flourished while theology slowly went bankrupt. From Edwards to Royce, America did not produce a first rate religious philosopher."[14]

In the main drift of religion in America the theological and liturgical and mystical and contemplative move into the background; the hierarchical and communal give place to the individualistic, the traditional to the immediate, the authoritative to the freely decided, the appeal to the mind and the aesthetic sense to the appeal to the will, the awareness of the ultimate to the concern with the practical life. The penumbra of beyondness, absoluteness, and mystery fades away, and leaves—as the core of what Americans think religion to be—the moral.

The different strands of religion in America would join in

[13] Sperry, p. 146.

[14] Henry Steele Commager, *The American Mind*, New Haven, 1950, p. 165.

asserting the centrality of ethics. The Puritan and the revivalist, the orthodox and the liberal, the fundamentalist and the modernist, the social gospel advocate and the conservative, each in his own way, shares a strong moral emphasis. The deistic and rationalistic strand which furnishes a continuing opposition to the main thread of American religion also emphasized ethics as the heart of religion; its simplifying and rationalizing largely meant dropping away non-moral elements.

But what has this moral emphasis to do with *social* philosophy? Just this: these moral distinctions, primarily drawn from the experience of individuals, are fully applied to collective life. Its complexities are continually interpreted in rather simple dichotomies between good and bad, purity and evil. One cause of this is a fundamental failure to distinguish individual from collective life; the force, reality, and peculiar characteristics of the latter are overlooked, and great social and historical phenomena are interpreted in individualistic terms. American "individualism" has many facets, but surely one of the more prominent and enduring is just the factual part, the assumption that the human world is a collection of more or less discrete individuals. This descriptive part is felt to be a necessary foundation for the normative part, and perhaps that is the error. In order to hold to a high view of the "dignity" and "worth" of the individual, it is felt, one must also hold to a large view of his importance in making himself, mastering nature, and determining history. Similarly, it is felt that in order to protect and promote freedom as a goal, one must hold to a very large view of freedom as a fact; in order to encourage individual initiative and moral responsibility, one must hold to very large estimates of the difference such initiative and responsibility in fact can make. The American, and especially the American in church, resists much emphasis on social conditioning, on the limits on human freedom, on the power of historical forces, on the place of the communal and organic forms of life; he sees in every hint of determinism a threat to individual moral responsibility. Implicit in the ideas of gathered churches, adult baptisms, congregational politics, and homiletical services, was the image of the powerful role of the free decision of the individual, and that image carried over into society at large.

All this is to emphasize again the "voluntariness" of the American outlook, but then to add an emphasis on one individualistic dimension of it. There is here little Jacobin voluntarism of a collective kind, seeing one great entity, a people or folk, imposing a single will on history; neither is there much of a Nietzschean voluntarism of a superior few, imposing their strong will on the passive many. Instead, the American emphasis on human "will" is liberal, democratic, individualist, seeing many separate and more or less equal individuals exercising diverse initiatives, pursuing many careers, "cooperating" maybe in "teamwork," but fundamentally separate.

These separate individuals can, by force of will, have a great influence upon their own destiny; they can also, joined together, have a great influence upon the society. In the secularized version, they individually can become self-made men, and together they can create what might be called a self-made society.

All of this was implicit in the "voluntary principle" of the free churches. The decisive importance of conversion in the evangelical work of the church is extended to become the decisive importance of the change of will in social action. The voluntary principle saw an individual's free response to God as the heart of religion, and a voluntary gathering of converted individuals as the nature of the church; it also saw the church extending its influence out into society by voluntary, persuasive means. The combination of the perfectionist, individualist ethic of the sect, with the inclusiveness and power of the church, is possible if one assumes that one can alter society by changing individuals, first, from within, and that one can make that change by persuasive appeals to the will.

The prevailing American idea of the relation of religion to culture, we said, was that religion dealt with the individual heart and will, a voluntary change which produced automatically a changed society. This idea is represented, perhaps in caricature, by familiar American slogans like these: religion deals with the individual, not with society; religion is a private matter; religion deals with spiritual matters, not with materialistic matters; religion does not "mix" and should not "meddle" with politics. If it treats of social affairs, religion should proclaim the "principles," the "ideals," which individual Christians can then "apply on their own." "If we would each one follow Jesus, then social problems would take care of themselves." "If we would each be converted, one by one, then social problems would take care of themselves." A streak of sentimentality and naïveté runs plainly through the whole tradition, but behind that streak there is an authentic position on questions of social change. As between the respective roles of the social environment on the one hand, and of the will and conscience of the individual on the other, in shaping and changing human history, this religious tradition is heavily committed to a major emphasis on the latter. The important matters have to do with men's *ideals* ("The world is *run* by its ideals," said Woodrow Wilson; "only a fool thinks otherwise").[15] The important field of action is the individual conscience. This inner, moral, ideal realm is the decisive one, and the details of outward social arrangements seem quite secondary in relation to it. This view—centered around the homiletical art, the perfectionist ethic, and the voluntary principle—reserves a very high place for persuasion, example, and exhortation, and sees little need for, and much

[15] Quoted in Raymond B. Fosdick, "Personal Recollections of Woodrow Wilson," in Earl Latham, ed., *The Philosophy and Policies of Woodrow Wilson*, Chicago, 1958, p. 44.

harm in, the other means of power, especially organized pressure and physical force. If ideals are not achieved, then the failure must be in an inadequate proclamation of the ideal and in an inadequate rousing of energy to fulfill it.

The expectation that great things can be done by voluntary means is then extended from the individual to the society. William Jennings Bryan wrote: "A man can be born again; the springs of life can be cleansed instantly. If this be true of one, it can be true of any number. Thus, a nation can be born in a day if the ideals of the people can be changed." [16]

IV

This way of looking at society does not come only from religion in America; something like it is encouraged by almost every aspect of America's history and culture. It has been helped along by America's social structure and dominant philosophy; by the country's relative peace, relative wealth, and relative isolation; by the winning of wars, overcoming of depressions, and living long years in the great spaces and resources of a separate continent. Most of all, it has been created by her fundamental liberalism—liberalism both economic and political, both as a set of ideas and as an existing social fact. America's popular social philosophy is as lopsided as it is because the forces bearing upon it have turned in the same direction.

Religion in America has had a peculiarly vague and hospitable relation to the resulting national creed, partly because it helped to make the creed and was compatible with it; partly because the creed was very powerful; partly because the nature of religion in America, as we have said, left it open to heavy influence by the surrounding culture. Here liberal Protestantism and political liberalism, democratic religion and democratic politics, American faith and Christian faith, pene-

[16] Quoted in Richard Hofstadter, *The American Political Tradition*, New York, 1954, p. 186.

trated each other and exerted a profound influence upon each other. Sidney Mead has indicated that during the second half of the nineteenth century ". . . there occurred a virtual identification of the outlook of . . . denominational Protestantism with 'Americanism' or 'the American way of life' and . . . we are still living with some of the results of this ideological amalgamation. . . ." [17]

One religion of nineteenth-century America, Protestant evangelicalism, Mr. Mead says, "was commonly articulated in terms of scholastic Protestant orthodoxy and almost universally practiced in terms of the experimental religion of pietistic revivalism." [18]

The other was "the religion of the democratic society and nation. This was rooted in the rationalism of the Enlightenment . . . and was articulated in terms of the destiny of America, under God, to be fulfilled by perfecting the democratic way of life for the example and betterment of all mankind." [19]

The amalgamation of the two with which Mr. Mead is primarily concerned is that which justified classical economics in religious terms. But his own discussion makes clear that this is only one facet of a deeper and broader amalgamation. Not only the economics of laissez faire, but also the progressive social reform that challenged it, were informed by an American creed that mingled evangelical Protestantism with democratic ideology.

In the United States a distinction is difficult to draw between Christian and other influences, between a religious and a secular ethos. The content of religion is much affected by and devoted to "democracy" and the "American way of life" and the prevailing morality; the national, democratic ideology, however, has real and obvious roots in, and would

[17] Sidney E. Mead, "From Denominationalism to Americanism," *The Journal of Religion*, January, 1956, p. 1.

[18] *ibid.*, p. 2.

[19] *ibid.*

include some deference to, the religious heritage. In between, connecting the two, there is a peculiar kind of semi-secular religion or semi-religious secularism.

The mutual influence and mutual support between this kind of religion and "Americanism" are deeper than rhetoric or religiosity. It has long been a feature of American democracy, noted for example by De Tocqueville and Bryce, that its people widely regard religion as essential to democratic institutions. The religious ingredient that is essential, however, is not any item of doctrine or worship, but the conviction that there is a moral order—the conviction that Ralph Gabriel makes the first affirmation of the "democratic faith," and for which he finds a chief source to be our religious heritage. Religion mostly means morality, and morality of an individualistic kind. The argument often would be: democracy requires morality, and morality requires religion. "You cannot otherwise explain our government," says President Eisenhower, "except on the basis of a deeply felt religious faith."

The other faiths in America have come to share many of the emphases that the Protestant, free church tradition has developed. Catholicism in America, for example, has had a "puritan" streak in it—an emphasis on activity and on the individual and on morality in a narrow and legal sense—that is not wholly derived from the influence of Irish Catholicism, but comes also, no doubt, from the American environment. The appeal of a Bishop Sheen as a "personality" ("those eyes"), quite apart from his priestly office, a personality preaching not Roman Catholicism but just "religion," is an obvious American development; the theme of the Christopher movement about not cursing the darkness but lighting the world by each one lighting a candle, is straight out of the ethos of an American Protestant summer camp. Judaism in America, too, being American, is also heavily influenced by Protestantism. At the same time, the presence and growing importance of these other major faiths may be one of the causes which—inadvertently, as it were—produce the effect of a kind of generalizing and secularizing of the old amalgam of evangelical Protestantism and Americanism into a contemporary public, patriotic religiosity.

At any event, the ethic inherited from the Protestant past is partly reinforced, but partly qualified and made secular, by the powerful force of an American ideology.

V

The ideas about society that spring from religion in America have, of course, a close tie to some of the best attributes of the American nation, at the same time that they lead to some of her political faults. One praiseworthy aspect of American life that can be connected to these ideas, no doubt, is a large supply of ordinary human friendliness. Gunnar Myrdal wrote, "Competent and sympathetic foreign observers have always noted the generosity and helpfulness of Americans. . . . I cannot help feeling that the Christian neighborliness of the common American reflects . . . an influence from the churches . . . it shows up in the American's readiness to make financial sacrifices for charitable purposes. No country has so many cheerful givers as America." [20]

But the contributions go beyond the obvious merits of charitable giving and friendly face-to-face relationships to the whole spirit and tradition of humanitarian social reform. This spirit, popularly overrated, may be academically underrated. Richard Hofstadter, writing about the low historical reputation of abolitionist Wendell Phillips, says that "historians in condemning men like Phillips have used a double standard of morality. . . . Somehow the same historians who have been indulgent with men who exaggerated because they wanted to be elected have been extremely severe with men who exaggerated because they wanted to free the slaves." [21]

Perhaps these historians, and also some theologians, diplo-

[20] Gunnar Myrdal, *An American Dilemma,* New York, 1944, p. 11.
[21] Hofstadter, p. 137.

matists, and ethicists, are over-reacting to an opposite inclination in the society at large, where the sins accompanying a single-minded moral passion would surely be forgiven long before those accompanying political work. Contemporary American academics reacting against the naïveté and sentimentality that infected this tradition, may sometimes reverse that imbalance. In the "righteous" American environment it is hard to get the balance right in evaluating American "righteousness." But surely, if it comes down to it, it *is* better to act to free slaves than to get elected, and if one were pressed by critics of America, a chief defense against the charge that we are just a materialistic technocracy would be this element of social idealism in the American people.

The merits of this heritage appear where there is a clear, humanitarian issue; but then the faults appear more prominently where issues are complex and "political," and it is the political part that we are considering here.

This American religious tradition has had its own particular way of affecting American politics. The characteristic effects of religion upon politics in general may be said to spring from its dimension of beyondness: the sense of the absolute, of mystery, of the ultimate questions. From such a sense come certain characteristic contributions, and also harmful results; the contributions are those associated with a deeper view of the complex workings of history, and a more elevated commitment in their midst. The harmful effects are those that come when the absoluteness of religion is brought into the political arena without maintaining the distance between the ultimate questions to which it applies and the immediate questions with which politics deals. Religion may encourage men to ignore politics, because from the peak of the religious aspect of eternity the hills and valleys way down in the temporal world are dwarfed into insignificance. But much worse, religion may sanctify and make more dangerous some particular political persuasion: it lends a sense of the absoluteness, of the will of

God, to the status quo, and thus encourages quiescent acceptance, passivity and pessimism, in the face of injustice; or, on the other hand, it may so sanctify the energies of causes, crusades, and holy wars as to make them more self-righteous and fanatical. Such characteristic contributions and dangers of religion in politics are by no means missing in the American experience. However, they are not the central ones. The sense of the beyond, the ultimate, from which they derive is just the dimension which American religion characteristically loses. The charge that religion will lead to an "other-worldly" neglect of practical life is rather ludicrously wide of the mark so far as much of American religion is concerned; a religious culture that can produce books with subjects like "Pray Your Weight Away" can hardly be accused of giving insufficient attention to the concerns of the flesh. The characteristic virtues and vices of the politics of American religion are of a different order. They are not so much those of other-worldly elevation as those of a confidence in the worldly efficacy of a converted individual. The characteristic contribution of American religion to American politics therefore has been—not perspective, wisdom, depth of insight—but the rousing of the sentiments and energies of charity, generosity, and social reform; the characteristic vices have been those of a tremendous oversimplification and sentimentalization of politics.

It is exactly the domain of politics that this social philosophy ignores, denies, and denounces, and which therefore it is inclined to misunderstand, and to deal with in inadequate ways. The view of the social world in the religious groups in America, and particularly in those of the central strand, is almost by definition unpolitical or anti-political. If we would list the defining elements of "politics" they would be almost precisely the opposite of what these religious communities have emphasized.

Politics deals with collective man—with nations, classes,

parties, interest groups. But the American religious tradition is inclined to ignore the collective, and to see instead the unencumbered individual.

Politics deals with power—with the overt and covert restraint of man over man through law, physical force, psychological pressure, economic control. But the American religious tradition is inclined to overlook the facts and problems of power, and to see instead a world marked by the voluntary response of reason and conscience to moral persuasion.

Politics deals with the fundamental human conflicts—with the clash of ideologies, purposes, and (most of all) interests. But the American religious tradition characteristically underestimates the role of interests, and overestimates their possible harmony.

Politics deals with the possible—with what the limitations of a particular situation will allow. But the religious tradition is inclined to neglect limits and proclaim ideals as immediately realizable.

Understanding politics requires a sense of "ideology"—of the way ideas and values are affected by the underlying interest of groups. Acting in politics requires a sense of political organization—of compromise, of party, of planned seeking for power. But Americans generally, and religious Americans in particular, ordinarily lack just this sense of ideology, of party, of the possible. They are inclined to take moral claims of dominant social groups at face value, to deprecate those forms of organization (political parties, pressure groups, alliance systems) which are overtly concerned with power, and to insist optimistically that "the impossible takes a little longer."

Whom are we describing? Probably most of all, Anglo-Saxon, middle class Protestants, let us say from smaller towns of the middle west. But this is not just one group among many; it has a normative and symbolic place for all Americans, and the ideas found in quintessence in it are influential for all Americans. These unpolitical attitudes may be most intense in the religious community, and in the Protestant community in particular, but they are found throughout the society.

They root in the heritage we have tried to describe: in a pervasive liberalism influenced and supported by a "voluntary" Christianity.

VI

We can illustrate and corroborate what we have said by noting some standard American attitudes in and toward politics, attitudes that are most likely to appear in the churches:

(1) "Dirty Politics." The first such attitude would simply be the deprecation of politics as such, the deprecation reflected in the derogatory flavor of the word and of its cognates "politician" and "political." This disdain implies that, somehow, politics itself is an unnecessary intrusion into the harmonies of life, an intrusion that is evil in its essence. "Politics" is looked upon as bad and unnecessary, because it is the realm in which conflict, the collective base of life, the grip of self-interest, and the pervasiveness of power, all come out into the open. For those whose philosophy inadequately grants the constant and omnipresent existence of these realities, "politics" appears, then, as a separate, negative realm, which one can evade and repudiate by an act of will. "Politician" is an invidious term, because the man engaged in that activity is peculiarly prone to compromise moral ideals, and to create conflict, because of his traffic with a "dirty" part of life. To be "political" is to be self-promoting, power-seeking, and compromising; it is a pejorative word. For an American political candidate to be able to say, as for example Eisenhower could, "I am not a politician," does not hurt him in American politics; on the contrary, it helps him. The case of Eisenhower brings to mind another, related, conception, that of being "above politics." To be "above politics" means, primarily, to be untouched by the contention of factions and (particularly)

parties, and to be "above politics" is regarded, in American politics, as a good thing. The belief in an unsullied and accessible realm above politics reflects, in part, the bourgeois and technological element in the culture, which looks at the insoluble conflicts of value as though they were soluble problems of technique and administration, requiring only the energetic application of "best brains," "know-how," and "business-in-government." But the belief also and more importantly reflects the culture's moral-voluntary ingredient, springing from the religious heritage, that we have been describing. This element contributes the feeling that all activity touched by the factional contention over power is unnecessary and nasty, and that there is an achievable realm of universal, ideal life above and apart from all of that nastiness. Voluntary associations for persuasion are all right, in this view, but political parties are suspect; the UN and the League are good, but alliances and pacts are dubious; the cooperative is worthwhile, but the labor union is not. Charity and humanitarian action should be pure and separated from political action: for example, "point four" technical assistance and other "foreign aid" should be set off from the nation's political purposes. These views are common among the religious social idealists. There is a somewhat different set of views among the religious social conservatives, but they share the rejection of politics that springs from the very nature of the religious background of Americans.

(2) "The Good Man." The realm of moral ideals "above politics" is inhabited by the "good man"; one of the main ways one may rise "above politics" is to look, not at factions and their interests, but at an individual and his character. The cliché "I vote for the *man* and not the party" is a reflection of this treatment of politics in personal-moral terms; it contains the plain implication that looking at politics in this way is morally superior to the views that deal in groups, parties, interests, and policies. A great deal of the feeling that being an "independent" is more praiseworthy than being a party

man roots in this conviction that the real solution to political problems is to get "good" men in office, men of character and "integrity." Those who look at the world in this way do not ordinarily ask "integrity to what?" They do not see that the political views of "good" men may be as much a simple uncriticized reflection of the interests and limitations of their group as that of "bad" men, or that "good" individuals can do evil politically, and vice versa. Character, motive, integrity —these are decisive; policy, interest, group allegiance, the consequences of lines of action—these are more or less overlooked. The emphasis on the efficacy of the good man and his good motives is of course implicit in the social ethic of the religious tradition we have described, for in order to believe in the religious and moral penetration of the culture by voluntary, inward, individual, hortatory means, one must believe then in the powerful effect of the individual brought from badness to goodness by such means. One must believe that the *main* thing is for public men to be of worthy character; the specific, outward social arrangements then are thought to be quite secondary. Such a belief is of course widespread in the churches, especially the Protestant ones. A recent study said: "This concern for personal purity, this attempt to make political judgements in terms of the good will and intent of the politician rather than in terms of the consequences of action, is a strong motif throughout Protestant political ethics. Protestant leaders have a strong belief that personal conviction and purity of motive can overcome limits imposed by group interests and institutional structures. The Christian ideal can be achieved by the spontaneous and free acts of love, kindness, and honesty." [22]

(3) The "Moral Issue." The flight to a realm "above politics" also may head for an "issue" on which clear moral lines can be drawn. At its simplest, this may be combined with the

[22] Kenneth Wilson Underwood, *Protestant and Catholic*, Boston, 1957, p. 364.

"good man" theme, choosing as the test of his goodness some "issue" of the individual morality to which a sectarian heritage is particularly attuned. Many Protestant folk opposed Franklin Roosevelt because he "repealed prohibition," and Adlai Stevenson because of his divorce.

In slightly broader form, this impulse may fasten on the issue of "corruption." Americans are known to be peculiarly excitable on the subject of bribery and influence, deep freezes, mink coats, and oriental rugs; they are peculiarly prone to make great political decisions on the basis of this issue.

"Corruption" is a conveniently one-sided, clear "moral" issue—one that fits the feeling that all politics is dirty, anyway, and one that gives a satisfying feeling that in opposing it one is on the right side. It is clear, it is simple, it is moral; it does evoke social passion, but it does not involve social change. This problem is not lost in a maze of impersonal, social forces, but is the plain result of the work of bad men, of a different sort and separate from the moral opponents. "Deep freeze and minks, and all those pinks," sang Texans for Eisenhower, "you bet they're not from Texas."

An interpretation that would attribute widespread corruption to social, "structural" causes would not be very appealing to those schooled in the ethic of evangelical religion.

Richard Hofstadter, writing about one expression of American morality in politics, the "progressive impulse" of the early part of the century, suggests both the breadth of feeling of moral responsibility and the shallowness of social analysis: ". . . the middleclass citizen received quite earnestly the exhortations that charged him with personal responsibility for all kinds of social ills. It was his business to do something about them. . . . But what would he do? He was too substantial a fellow to want to make any basic changes in a society in which he was typically a prosperous and respectable figure. What he needed, therefore, was a *feeling* that action was taking place, a sense that the moral tone of things was being improved and that he had a part in this improvement. Corruption thus became a particularly fine issue for the moral energies of the Progressive."[23] It was, obviously, still a particularly fine issue three or four decades later. Foreign policy, and high finance, are hard to understand and hard to relate to the conscience and will, but on bribery a stand is easy to take.

At another level, the "moral issue" may have to do with social policy, but with policy about matters defined by the individualist ethic—matters like local option, dog racing, and bingo. The fight over bingo suggests another dimension to these issues: they may involve, along with differing ethics, the clash of the institutional interests of churches.

Or the "moral issue" in politics may just be legislation exacting particular precise moral convictions of particular religious groups into law, making what one group regards a "sin" into a crime for all as in the case of legislation against birth control in Massachusetts and Connecticut, for example, or the prohibition amendment. But the search for issues that are clearly moral has not stayed solely on this level; the "moral" frame of reference applies also to some major matters of public policy. For the conservative, the image of classically proper fiscal behavior is filled with moral content, certain "natural laws" of the economics of the free market being a reflection of a transcendent and immutable moral order: balanced budgets are morally right, subsidies to farmers are morally wrong. For the nationalist, certain issues of foreign policy (recognition of Communist China) are "moral" issues, because of the criminality of particular regimes. The liberal and internationalist has also a set of moral issues, drawn less from a fixed, legalistic moral scheme than from humanitarian and idealistic passions: economic aid abroad, disarmament, a UN collective security system (all conceived in humanitarian rather than "political" terms) are "moral" matters. Racial segregation is a moral issue. Economic "justice" is a moral issue, where the human effects are clear enough. Civil liberties

[23] Richard Hofstadter, *The Age of Reform*, New York, 1955, p. 210.

matters can be "moral" when, as in the McCarthy period, they are plain and dramatic.

That is the point: the approach to politics by way of "moral issues" tends to select items for attention on the basis of their simplicity, their human drama, their connection with a preconception of certain moral laws and principles, rather than on the basis of their historical importance or their social-political meaning. The issues are fitted, that is, to the free church outlook we have described: to a clear-cut pattern of right against wrong and to an appeal to the individual's will and conscience.

(4) The "Change of Heart." At the center of all these themes, and of the tradition from which they spring, is the image of an inner turning, of a change of heart, of a conversion within. Politics is dirty because it deals with the sordid outer world of powers and interests, leaving the inward man untouched; the good man is the solution because it is only from within a man, becoming good, that goodness can come; the issues that deserve to be treated are the *moral* issues, because they lay a claim upon the moral sense within; and the way to deal with politics is through the crusade, because it sounds a call to the heart of men.

The social philosophy of free church Christianity in America, we noted, tends to say that "changed individuals will change society," that if we begin with the individual then social problems will take care of themselves, that the persuasion of individuals to be good will permeate the society with goodness. This outlook not only exalts the role of individual-moral change; it correspondingly deprecates structural-political change. On the problems of racial relations, for example, there has come to be a standard position that change must come through "a slow process of education," *rather than* the force of law or political action. "You can't legislate against prejudice," it is often said. The change must be voluntary and inward. President Eisenhower, for example, has approached many questions from this point of view, particularly the question of racial relations. "What I'm working for here," he would say, in the middle of the Little Rock crisis in 1957, "is a change of heart."[24]

(5) The "Crusade." When the "moral issue," "above politics," is defined, by a "good man," appealing to the heart to change, then there may be a "crusade." The sectarian-puritan heritage has not quietly debated its "moral issues," but rather has wanted to respond with zealous action. The prevalence of the word "crusade" in American public life needs no comment at the time of this writing, in the middle of the second Eisenhower administration. It would not require much comment at any earlier period of American history, either, from the day of the crusades for prison reform, women's rights, temperance, poor relief, and care of the insane, that grew out of "freedom's ferment" in the 1830's and 1840's, provoked Emerson's address on "New England Reformers," and spilled over into all sorts of Utopian communities and experiments, through the great abolition crusade that grew out of the Finney revivals, through the manifold crusades of the Social Gospel movement and the progressive era, through the international crusades of the Spanish war and World War I, through the pacifist and prohibitionist crusades of the interwar period, through the rather more chastened crusades for Four Freedoms in World War II, on down to the nostalgic echo of this history in the "Great Moral Crusade" of 1952. America has continually sounded this morally expansive note. As a young abolitionist wrote, "However terrible the strain, we rejoice that we are doing our part toward the moral conquest of the world."

The "morality" that the American religious tradition pro-

[24] Dwight Eisenhower is reported to have said that what he really is is a preacher. One of his favorite predecessors had the same bent. Owen Wister wrote of Theodore Roosevelt: "If they treated Theodore as they deal with certain composite substances in chemistry, and melted him down, it's not a statesman they'd find, or a hunter, or a historian, or a naturalist: they'd find a preacher militant." Quoted in Henry F. Pringle, *Theodore Roosevelt*, New York, 1956, p. 334.

duces has not been any cool, calm ethic of a Confucius or of wisdom literature; it has rather been passionate, zealous, full of fervor. It has been surcharged with emotion and filled with the drama of conversion and revival. The underlying expectation is that a sufficiently "bold, new" program, with dramatic rousing of energies, will resolve the dilemmas of history. The discussion of public affairs in American religious groups regularly features an underlying impatience with the mixed, problematical, and prosaic, and yearns instead for a show of proclamatory fervor. There is a kind of politics of sermon endings—of high, pure, uncomplicated, ideal causes—that is dissatisfied with a treatment of world problems that is not rousing and final.

The crusade is the march of the pure against an evil. America knows the sectarian attitude of withdrawal, which pretends to look down upon the world of power and conflict from a realm of moral perfection above it, but it usually turns it into something else—an aggressive effort to make over or eliminate the evil by crusaders who still retain their purity. The "crusade" of this kind thus is a characteristic expression of the effort of voluntary religion to "permeate" the society. To do so it must select the subjects for crusading with care, or interpret the world carefully to fit the pattern, with clearly identifiable evils. The history of American religion's response to society has been that of endless forays against such evils: against Demon Rum, Sunday mail, slavery, the sweatshops, and war; against slave owners, saloon keepers, and warmongers. No call is so familiar or attractive as the call to the crusade.

The subordinate layer of pugnacity underneath the liberal-idealist surface may break through, in American public affairs, when the techniques of persuasion and exhortation fail, and conflicts of interest are made plain. The outlook we have described is philosophically unprepared for such conflicts. When confronted with them, it tends to fall back upon sharp moral distinctions, finding the fault to be not in differences of social structure, interest, power, and perspective, but in the evil will of some particular persons, who refuse to have a change of heart and be good men, who are on the wrong side of a moral issue, and who therefore are fit objects for the crusader's wrath.

VII

Another way to illustrate and to substantiate the points made here is to show their effect in one particular area of public affairs—foreign policy. In the relations among nations, the elements of politics show themselves most plainly, and therefore it is in relation to international affairs that the nonpolitical aspect of the American ethos has been most evident.

We may illustrate this by American popular attitudes toward war. The critique of those attitudes that is common now among writers on international and military affairs goes something like this: Americans treat war as a phenomenon wholly discontinuous with the rest of human experience, a horrid intrusion into normal life, a parenthesis in history's paragraphs. We have, it is said, "the faulty habit of mind that regards war as a thing in itself rather than a continuation of political intercourse." [25] Again, "war as something to abolish, war as something to get over as quickly as possible, war as a means of punishing the enemy who dared to disturb the peace, war as a crusade—these conceptions are all compatible with the American outlook." But not "war as an instrument for attaining limited, concrete objectives." [26]

We Americans can be forgiven, or even praised, for rejecting such a Clauswitzian view of war as an "instrument" if it means the instruments are morally indistinguishable—sometimes one uses negotiation, sometimes war—and there may sometimes be, in the presuppositions of the "realistic" critics

[25] Robert Endicott Osgood, *Limited War: The Challenge to American Strategy*, Chicago, 1957, p. 30.
[26] *ibid.*

of American opinion, an amorality that needs a little of America's moralism or idealism as a corrective. But that is not the usual situation, for, ironically, it is the moralistic view that characteristically makes war the most terrible and amoral, because it leaves it a separate, unlimited thing, discontinuous from the ordinary life that is governed by ordinary moral rules, in a world of its own with rules of its own. War is holistically avoided and repudiated by an isolationist nation —until it comes, and then it is holistically entered upon, without restraint: the only thing to do now is to "give them hell"; in war there is "no substitute for victory." The idea that war is fought for specific, limited political objectives, although seeming immoral to the American idealist, may have less destructive results than the idealist's view, because it subordinates military to political considerations and hence limits war. On the other hand, the moralist-idealist view—springing from the religious ethic in large part, and dominant at least until recently in America—draws such a sharp line between normal life and war, looks on the pursuit of political objectives through war with such utter repugnance, that when war comes it is wholly abandoned to its own military logic, without restraint from political aims. More than that, the idealist view may not only abandon war to an unlimited destructiveness; it may *encourage* that development: ". . . if moral sensibilities forbid the use of war as an instrument of national policy, they do not prevent the use of war as an instrument of ideology, once war has become unavoidable. In a sense they encourage this; for tender consciences find in broader, more exalted goals a kind of moral compensation for the enormity of war and a rational justification for their contamination with evil. . . . An aversion to violence is transmuted into an exaltation of violence. Nothing defeats political limitation and control of military power like the transformation of war into an ideological contest." [27]

[27] *ibid.*, p. 33.

If the isolationist period before World War II and the response to Pearl Harbor provided one illustration of this mind set, the Korean War provides another and different illustration. The tremendous public impatience with the latter war shows the American's repugnance at a limited, unresolved situation, particularly where war is involved: "Let's win it, or let's get out!"

This attitude toward military power is only the extreme case of an attitude toward power in general, an attitude that appears throughout America's foreign as well as domestic policy. The analysts of America's response to the world political scene point to the fluctuation of mood,[28] and to the assumption that there is a normal harmony of international interests, from which all calculations of power and all conflicts of interest are an abnormal deviation, which is one attitude lying behind that fluctuation in mood.

The most notable condemnation of such an American outlook was that penned by George Kennan. After surveying the past fifty years of American diplomacy he wrote: "I see the most serious fault . . . to lie in: . . . the legalistic-moralistic approach to international problems . . . [which] runs like a red skein through our foreign policy of the last fifty years. . . . It is the belief that it should be possible to suppress the chaotic and dangerous aspirations of governments in the international field by the acceptance of some system of legal rules and restraints." Then there is "the inevitable association of legalistic ideas with moralistic ones: the carrying into the affairs of states of the concepts of right and wrong . . . whoever says there is a law must of course be indignant against the lawbreaker and feel a moral superiority to him. And when such indignation spills over into military contest,

[28] This is a main theme of Gabriel Almond's *The American People and Foreign Policy*, New York, 1950. Almond attributes this "mood" response to world affairs on the part of American public opinion primarily to the absorption in private careers, to which public affairs, and particularly world affairs, contribute.

it knows no bounds short of reduction of the lawbreaker to the point of complete submissiveness—namely, unconditional surrender." [29]

The *bête noire* of the realistic critics of an idealistic American foreign policy is Woodrow Wilson, and he serves as perhaps the best symbol of the strengths and weaknesses of the whole tradition of social ethics that develops from American religion. As to the weakness, John Maynard Keynes's observations on Wilson, when he went to Europe in 1919, may serve as one more summary, this one making clear the essential detachment of abstract ideals from concrete political reality that plagues the whole tradition.

Keynes described as follows the disappointment some Europeans felt when they actually encountered the Woodrow Wilson for whom they had the highest hopes: "But if the President was not the philosopher-king, what was he? . . . The clue, once found, was illuminating. The President was like a Nonconformist minister, perhaps a Presbyterian. His thought and his temperament were essentially theological, not intellectual, with all the strength and weakness of that manner of thought, feeling, and expression. It is a type of which there are not now in England and Scotland such magnificent specimens as formerly. . . . The President's programme for the world, as set forth in his speeches and his Notes, had displayed a spirit and a purpose so admirable that the last desire of his sympathizers was to criticize details—the details, they felt, were quite rightly not filled in at present, but would be in due course. . . . But in fact the President had thought out nothing; when it came to practice, his ideas were nebulous and incomplete. He had no plan, no scheme, no constructive ideas whatever for clothing with the flesh of life the commandments he had thundered from the White House. He could have preached a sermon on any of them, or have addressed a stately prayer to the Almighty for their

[29] George F. Kennan, *American Diplomacy 1900–1950*, Chicago, 1951, pp. 95, 100.

fulfillment, but he could not frame their concrete application to the actual state of Europe." [30]

VIII

In these paragraphs we have not dwelt on the qualifications to the central theme, or on the differing evaluations of it that might be given. Not all of American religion fits the nonpolitical picture drawn here, and being "nonpolitical" is not entirely bad. To complete the picture one would have to note, for example, that American Protestantism was somehow able to produce, as an authentic representative and not as a maverick, a social ethicist whose career could be said to be built on a vigorous repudiation of all that we have described here as typical of that Protestantism. Reinhold Niebuhr, arising out of this nonpolitical ethos, has been above all a "political" thinker, aware of and forcing upon the attention of America and Christendom exactly those political truths and aspects of life that we said America, and American religion in particular, overlooked. One would have to say again, also, that the implicit criticism in the foregoing description of nonpolitical attitudes does not sufficiently expand upon the merits there are in such attitudes. There is much to be said for the voluntaristic and "moral" and individualistic alternative; if one had to choose, certainly it is better for a society to be overbalanced in this direction than in the opposite deterministic and collectivist one.

For all that is mistaken in it, then, and for all the sentimentality involved in quoting words about it in a political campaign, it is not entirely wrong to say that the "flame" of "righteousness" in the churches is a secret of America's "genius and power." The point is just that that flame needs to cast a new, more realistic and political light. It is not that we need to discard our idealism, but that, as Reinhold Niebuhr has

[30] John Maynard Keynes, *Essays and Sketches in Biography*, New York, 1956, pp. 266–267.

said, we need a "reorientation of the whole structure of our idealism." [31] Religion in America, which helped mightily to produce the idealism, may also help to provide the reorientation.

[31] Reinhold Niebuhr, *The Irony of American History*, New York, 1952, p. 133.

THE STATE, THE CHURCH, AND THE LOBBY

DAYTON D. MCKEAN

THE social resolutions adopted in 1956 at a meeting of the General Council of the Congregational Christian Churches make up a pamphlet of twenty printed pages. The political issues on which the church took a stand were international, national, state, and local; topically, they ranged from statehood for Alaska to racial integration in public schools.[1] Some of the issues, such as the control of alcoholism, have a religious aspect; others, such as support for the General Agreement on Tariffs and Trade, seem to have the most remote (if any) association with religious beliefs.

But this wide-ranging interest of the Congregationalists in public affairs is typical of religious organizations. Of the many other examples that might be cited, one more may suffice. In what the *New York Times* called "one of the most solemn statements of his pontificate," Pope Pius XII, speaking to 25 cardinals and 150 archbishops and bishops, said that "the belief that 'the Church's authority is limited to purely religious matters' is an error, and Roman Catholics 'must take an open and firm stand' against it."[2]

A leading student of the political activities of religious groups, Luke E. Ebersole, wrote that "There are no signs that the churches are withdrawing from the ranks of political protagonists; on the contrary, their participation is increasing. . . . The churches have moved far from mere opposition to 'liquor, war, and sin.'"[3] Presidents, secretaries of state, senators, governors, mayors—public officials from the Chief Justice of the Supreme Court to the members of a township school

[1] The Council for Social Action, *Social Resolutions Adopted by the General Council of the Congregational Christian Churches*, New York, 1956, pp. 20ff.

[2] *New York Times*, November 4, 1954.

[3] Luke E. Ebersole, *Church Lobbying in the Nation's Capital*, New York, 1951, p. 176.

board—must take account of the political interests of organized religious bodies. In the breadth of their concern with public affairs churches are unusual in the political process: the tendency of most organized groups is to narrow their scope to one or a few objectives, the welfare of Negroes, the business of railroading, or the profession of dentistry, for examples. The religious associations are not unique, however, in the wide variety of issues in which they are interested; in American politics there are other organizations, such as the United States Chamber of Commerce, the American Legion, and the League of Women Voters, that take positions on many current public problems.

The English language does not, unfortunately, possess a word that adequately covers the political activities of organized, nonpartisan groups; the word *lobby* used in the title of this chapter is the best available, but it is far too narrow. It seems to imply that the groups are interested in legislation only, whereas administrative and judicial decisions may be far more important to many of them than statutes to the attainment or preservation of their objectives. In the words of the Buchanan Committee, "Wherever the power of government is exercised, there lobbying is to be found. . . . Wherever government has power to act, efforts to influence this action are inevitable."[4] This is the position of the present writer: that lobbying is widespread and inevitable. It is part of the political process, and it is good, or bad, or mixed good and bad, depending upon the agreement of the observer with the objectives or the methods of the group or groups under consideration.

An appraisal of the political effectiveness, current or potential, of any organization may begin with an examination of the social characteristics of the group, such as its size, its regional distribution, the coherence of its membership, its relationship to the political parties, and similar factors. No

[4] House Select Committee on Lobbying Activities, 81st Congress, 2d Session, *General Interim Report*, Washington, 1950, p. 46.

statistics on religious bodies in the United States appear to be satisfactory, because the churches use different criteria in assembling their figures. For our purposes, a series of surveys by the American Institute of Public Opinion (the Gallup Poll) is revealing. In 1954 the question "Are you a member of a church?" was asked to a sample of 3,000 adults.[5] The results, projected to the total population of persons over 21, showed that about 81,000,000 were church members; 21,000,000 were not. There are, of course, many persons under 21 who are members, but the number of adults (who are voters or potential voters) is important in any political analysis. The potential voting strength of church members is thus enormous. Not even the American Legion—commonly used as a measurement, because it is regarded by students of lobbying as the most powerful group in American politics—approaches the possible political power of organized religion.

The same Gallup poll showed the percentages of church members and non-members in various categories:

Church Members

	Yes	*No*
NATIONAL	79%	21%
Men	75%	25%
Women	83	17
21–29 years	78%	22%
30–49 years	80	20
50 years and over	78	22
College	83%	17%
High School	81	19
Grade School	73	27

[5] Release of July 21, 1954. A sampling error of plus or minus four percentage points may fairly be assumed in all surveys.

Church Members (continued)

	Yes	*No*
Professional & Business	83%	17%
White-Collar	82	18
Farmers	77	23
Manual Workers	77	23
New England	85%	15%
Mid-Atlantic	80	20
East Central	75	25
West Central	82	18
South	85	15
Far West	65	35
Cities over 50,000	73%	27%
100,000–500,000	84	16
10,000–100,000	83	17
Under 10,000	78	22
Farm	77	23

It is common knowledge that more women than men are interested in church work, but the disparity of eight percentage points is greater than many observers, perhaps, would expect. Since other evidence indicates that men are politically more active than women, the lower membership of men would be expected to reduce somewhat the political effectiveness of churches. The presence of a large proportion of older people in Sunday services would lead one to generalize that church membership increases with age; but no significant difference appears from these figures. The common allegation that education, and especially college education, causes a loss of faith is not borne out by this study; on the contrary, church membership among persons who did not get beyond grade school is ten percentage points below that of people who attended college. Another significant difference is that apparent among sections of the country; the disparity between 85 per cent membership in New England and the South, on the one hand, and 65 per cent in the Far West is striking. Such a difference, other factors being equal, might lead a congressman from New England to respond to pressures from religious groups, when his colleague across the aisle, coming from a state in the Far West, would feel safe in resisting them. Finally, the common generalization that the people in big cities are less religious than the people in small towns and on farms is borne out by these statistics, but the difference is not great; and perhaps somewhat surprisingly, people in the large cities (100,000 to 500,000) show the highest church membership.

Church (or synagogue) attendance may be a better index than total membership to the political potential of religious bodies, for it tends to show the degree of interest, and it also reveals the number of persons who may be exposed to political or quasi-political arguments in sermons and who may receive the printed matter often distributed at church services. What proportion of the 81,000,000 members attend church on a typical Sabbath? A series of Gallup polls has found that attendance had risen markedly since World War II to 49,600,000 in 1955, but this all-time high fell off to 47,500,000 in 1956. The differences in attendance by faiths and other factors are significant:[6]

Church Attendance During Sample Weeks, 1955

Men	43%
Women	54
Catholics	74%
Protestants	42
Jews	27

[6] Release of January 1, 1956.

Church Attendance During Sample Weeks, 1955 (continued)

21–29 years	47%
30–49 years	52
50 years and older	45
Attended college	53%
High school only	49
Grade school only	47
East	52%
Midwest	49
South	51
Far West	38

These percentages are compatible with those on church membership; for example, men attend less faithfully than women, and attendance in the Far West is notably below that in the East and South. The most startling facts are the low attendance of Jews and the high attendance of Catholics. A low degree of group cohesion and discipline among Jews may be inferred from this and other evidence.[7] A high degree of cohesion and discipline may be inferred from the high attendance of Catholics.[8] Although 96 per cent of Americans say that they believe in God,[9] this near-unanimity does not take them to church in the same proportion; if it did, the church buildings would be far from adequate. Nor does the high level of belief accompany a high level of information about religion; for example, 51 per cent could not name the first book of the

[7] Cf. Lawrence H. Fuchs, *The Political Behavior of American Jews*, Glencoe, Illinois, 1956, passim.

[8] The general concept of group cohesiveness is a highly complex one. Jews with little sense of group discipline may nonetheless have a high degree of sense of a common bond. Similarly, Irish and Italian Catholics, while sharing a high degree of discipline, may have little sense of common bond.

[9] Gallup Poll, release of December 18, 1954. The survey did not attempt to explore what the respondents' conception of God was.

Bible, 60 per cent could not give the names of the Holy Trinity, 66 per cent did not know who delivered the Sermon on the Mount, and 79 per cent could not name one prophet mentioned in the Old Testament.[10]

The political effectiveness of any group is, of course, adversely affected by organizational disunity. There are about 255 religious bodies in the United States. The highest degree of sectarianism is characteristic of the Protestants, not only in that there is no single Protestant church, but the principal denominations are split into many separately organized bodies; thus, there are 27 varieties of Baptists, 21 kinds of Methodists, 9 types of Presbyterians, and so on. There are even five Mormon sects.[11] The National Council of Churches of Christ in the U.S.A. was formed in 1950 by 25 Protestant and four Eastern Orthodox bodies, but it has no control over the political positions of the member organizations; indeed, we may well doubt that one-half of one per cent of the Protestants ever heard of it. By contrast, the Roman Catholic Church with its world-wide organization headed by the Pope has a high degree of unity, and, other factors being equal, could be expected to have a higher percentage of successes in its political objectives than a less unified organization with equal membership.

As has been noted, statistics of religious bodies in the United States are far from satisfactory, but roughly there are 2,600,000 Eastern Orthodox; 5,500,000 Jews; 36,000,000 Roman Catholics; and 79,000,000 Protestants, according to the National Council of Churches. About 40 per cent of the population of the United States are not members.

At this point we may turn to the political issues that cause religious groups to engage in lobbying at various levels and before different governmental agencies. The number of issues is very great, but they may be assembled into a few categories. The principal differences among religious bodies on these matters may also be considered.

[10] Release of December 20, 1954.
[11] *World Almanac*, 1959, pp. 711–718.

The separation of church and state versus their union, an issue with scores of sub-issues, is a most persistent and formidable problem in this and in other western nation-states. The dispute has led to religious wars, and it is far from being settled today. This controversy is so big and of such long standing that a considerable number of books has been written about it, and the periodical literature is enormous.[12] Only the chief points may be considered here.

The union of church and state means the establishment of and support by the state of a preferred or required religion. There are degrees of establishment, all the way from the recognition of one church merely for purposes of public ceremonies to the use of the powers of the state to stamp out all religious movements but the approved one. Contemporary examples will occur to the reader from the nations of the world today. A majority of the thirteen American colonies had some sort of established religion at one time or another, and some of the New England colonies were most intolerant of nonconformists. Cotton Mather, for instance, favored the union of church and state with civil punishments for persons who failed to observe Puritan church law and ceremony.[13] Protestant thought in the United States today, however, is almost unanimously opposed to establishment.

The Roman Catholic Church, on the other hand, has always favored the union of church and state, provided it is the church recognized by the state. In a textbook widely used in Catholic schools, Monsignor John A. Ryan printed the Encyclical Letter

[12] See Paul Blanshard, *American Freedom and Catholic Power*, Boston, 1951; Robert A. Horn, *Groups and the Constitution*, Stanford, 1956; Alvin W. Johnson and Frank H. Yost, *Separation of State and Church in the United States*, Minneapolis, 1948; Charles C. Marshall, *The Roman Catholic Church in the Modern State*, New York, 1931; Conrad Moehlman, *The Wall of Separation between Church and State*, Boston, 1951; John A. Ryan and M. X. Millar, *The State and the Church*, New York, 1922; Anson Phelps Stokes, *Church and State in the United States*, New York, 1950; W. S. Torpey, *Judicial Doctrines of Religious Rights in America*, Chapel Hill, 1948.

[13] Charles E. Merriam, *A History of American Political Theories*, New York, 1926, pp. 12–15.

Immortale Dei (1885) of Leo XIII, and in commenting upon it, wrote, "In governments which profess absolute neutrality toward religion, the actual policy is one of hostility." [14] The state, said Leo XIII, must make a "public profession of religion." "But Pope Leo goes further," wrote Monsignor Ryan, "He declares that the state must not only 'have care for religion,' but recognize the *true* religion. This means the form of religion professed by the Catholic Church." [15] Under such a union of church and state other religions must logically be suppressed, for, as Monsignor Ryan wrote, error does not have the same rights as truth, and he raised the question, "Should such [non-Catholic] persons be permitted to practice their own form of worship?" He answered it, "If these are carried on within the family, or in such an inconspicuous manner as to be an occasion neither of scandal nor of perversion of the faithful, they may properly be tolerated by the state." [16] Such a public policy is approximately what is followed in Italy and Spain today, but it is obviously incompatible with the First Amendment to the Constitution of the United States.[17]

At the time the Constitution was adopted, several states, as has been noted, had official churches; and Congress wrote the amendment that was the first to be ratified by the states so as to permit these establishments to continue—as that in Massachusetts did for forty years—while forbidding Congress to establish a national church: "Congress shall make no law respecting an establishment of religion, or prohibiting the free exercise thereof. . . ." Freedom of religion is the first free-

[14] Ryan and Millar, p. 30. This book bears both the "Nihil Obstat" of the Censor of Books, Arthur J. Scanlon, and the "Imprimatur" of Patrick Cardinal Hayes, and may therefore be taken to represent an official commentary upon and translation of Catholic documents.

[15] *ibid.*, p. 32. Italics in the original.

[16] *ibid.*, p. 35. See also Theodore Maynard, *The Story of American Catholicism*, New York, 1941, p. 152.

[17] For several perspectives on this question see *Catholics in America*, published as a special issue by the *New Republic*, January 25, 1960 to March 21, 1960.

dom in the Bill of Rights, but it was for generations a freedom against Congress only. In 1833 John Marshall for the Supreme Court laid down the rule that the first ten "amendments contain no expression indicating an intention to apply them to the states. This Court cannot so apply them." [18] No case to determine what is an establishment of religion or what is the free exercise thereof reached the Supreme Court until *Reynolds v. United States*, decided in 1879.[19] This case arose from the territory of Utah and turned upon the constitutional power of Congress to govern the territories. The Court held that Congress could constitutionally prohibit polygamy in a territory without violating the First Amendment.[20] Over the years no act of Congress has been successfully challenged as infringing the religious provisions of the First Amendment.

In 1868, however, the Fourteenth Amendment was ratified by the states. It is one of the longest amendments, but only one sentence in it is important to us here: "No state shall make or enforce any law which shall abridge the privileges or immunities of citizens of the United States, nor shall any state deprive any person of life, liberty, or property without due process of law, nor deny to any person within its jurisdiction the equal protection of the laws." Did this amendment forbid the states to establish churches, to infringe upon religious liberty, and so on? For nearly sixty years the Supreme Court refused to use the Fourteenth Amendment to make the Bill of Rights applicable to the states, but in 1925 it did so.[21] The

[18] *Barron v. Baltimore*, 7 Peters 243 (1833). This case was not concerned with religion.

[19] 98 U.S. 145 (1879). For other cases involving Mormons see *Davis v. Beason*, 133 U.S. 333 (1890); *Church of Jesus Christ of Latter Day Saints v. United States*, 136 U.S. 1 (1890); and *Cleveland v. United States*, 329 U.S. 14 (1946).

[20] For a discussion of the political and constitutional theory involved see Horn, pp. 24–27.

[21] In *Gitlow v. New York*, 268 U.S. 652 (1925), a case involving freedom of speech and press. The principle was affirmed and extended in *Near v. Minnesota*, 283 U.S. 697 (1931) and *Powell v. Alabama*, 287 U.S. 45 (1943). But the Court has refused to extend every right mentioned in the Bill of Rights to cover state action—double jeopardy, for instance: *Palko v. Connecticut*, 302 U.S. 319 (1937).

way was then opened for religious organizations such as Jehovah's Witnesses to challenge in the federal courts state laws affecting them, and for individuals such as A. R. Everson or Vashti McCollum to plead the First Amendment against certain state laws on schools. When in 1948 an organization was formed with the ponderous title "Protestants and Other Americans United for Separation of Church and State" (hereafter referred to as POAU), it announced in its manifesto that one of its immediate objectives would be "to invoke the aid of the courts in maintaining the integrity of the Constitution with respect to the separation of church and state, wherever and in whatever form the issue arises. . . ."[22] The bitterest enemy of POAU could not say with truth that it has failed to carry out this objective to the best of its ability. We may observe in passing that this use of the judicial process is common among organizations of all sorts: when they cannot stop a bill from being passed and approved by the executive, or when they find in the statutes laws they do not like, the next recourse is usually to the courts.

When the New Jersey bus case reached the Supreme Court it was argued for the plaintiff that the state law to reimburse parents for bus fares paid to send children to parochial schools was a violation of the establishment of religion clause of the First Amendment, made applicable to the states by the Fourteenth.[23] Four of the nine justices agreed with this view, but

[22] Protestants and Other Americans United for Separation of Church and State, *A Manifesto*, Washington, D.C., 1948, p. 11. John E. Swift, Supreme Knight of the Knights of Columbus, issued a statement reprinted in full in the *New York Times* January 13, 1948, in which he said that POAU "questions the patriotism of any citizen, Catholic, Jew, Protestant, or nonbeliever who dares to disagree with the organization's biased and inaccurate interpretation of the First Amendment." The present writer, who has read the entire manifesto fully and carefully, is unable to find in it this questioning of patriotism. Mr. Swift predicted that POAU would "fall of its own weight" because "it is loaded with intolerance," and he concluded that the executives of the new organization "irresistibly remind us of 'wolves in sheep's clothing.'" Violent rhetoric is not unique to partisan politics.

[23] *Everson v. Board of Education of Ewing Township*, 330 U.S. 1 (1947). But in *Cochran v. Louisiana Board of Education*, 281 U.S. 370 (1930) the public payment for textbooks in parochial schools was upheld.

five did not. The majority, however, in an opinion by Justice Black, commented in words that have since been much quoted on the meaning of the phrase "an establishment of religion" in the First Amendment:

"The 'establishment of religion' clause of the First Amendment means at least this: Neither a state nor the Federal Government can set up a church. Neither can pass laws which aid one religion, aid all religions, or prefer one religion over another. Neither can force or influence a person to go to or remain away from church against his will or force him to profess a belief or disbelief in any religion. No person can be punished for entertaining or professing religious beliefs or disbeliefs, for church attendance or non-attendance. No tax in any amount, large or small, can be levied to support any religious activities or institutions, whatever they may be called, or whatever form they may adopt to teach or practice religion. Neither a state nor the Federal Government can, openly or secretly, participate in the affairs of any religious organizations or groups and *vice versa*. In the words of Jefferson, the clause against establishment was intended to erect a 'wall of separation between church and state.'"

Far from settling the matter, this opinion raises many new questions and opens the lobby door for much new agitation. If only one religious order is engaged in distilling brandy from grapes, and if religious orders are exempt from paying taxes, including the tax on distilling liquor, is not such an act in fact an aid to one religion? Indeed, are not the tax exemptions on church property laws that "aid all religions"? When the adherents of one sect are excused from military service, is not this a preference of "one religion over another"? When men in military academies and establishments are marched to church services, is not this forcing or influencing a person to go to church? Does the prohibition upon any tax, large or small, being levied "to support any religious activities" forbid only a tax specifically levied for such a purpose? Or does the limitation extend to the use of funds raised from broad and general taxes, such as those on sales and incomes, when some of the money is used to pay the salaries or fees of chaplains for legislative bodies, military camps, public institutions, and so on? Does this prohibition extend to building and maintaining chapels at military posts and academies? If government may neither participate in the affairs of religious organizations nor religious organizations in the affairs of state, does the First Amendment forbid lobbying by religious groups, the sending of an ambassador to the Vatican, the determination by courts of the disputes over property that may arise when a sect breaks off from a parent church?

The Jeffersonian metaphor quoted with approval by the Court (and much quoted since the Everson decision) "betrays the whole case," wrote Dr. Robert A. Horn:

"It suggests that churches and the state are different societies; each exists on its own territory with its own population, and between them there is a wall. . . . [But] how can the state ignore churches that exist in the same society? True, it might leave them to maintain their own fire departments, employ their own guards, and provide many other services at their own expense. . . . If the state withheld what it alone can provide, it would deprive churches not only of their liberty, but their life. A state which refused to give churches certain minimal public aid would in fact be passing upon them the dread sentence of outlawry. So to interpret the freedom from religion that the First Amendment guarantees would pervert it from its object of strengthening freedom for religion to destroying that freedom."[24]

Not only is the definition of an establishment of religion still in the area of argument, but we have scarcely got into the more difficult determination of what constitutes "prohibiting

[24] Horn, p. 52.

the free exercise" of religion in the First Amendment. Religious groups commonly make announcements concerning freedom of religious practice that are couched in the most sweeping terms. For example: "We believe that the New Testament teaches us to obey God rather than man. Loyalty to God takes precedence over the claims of the state. The government must not interfere with the freedom of an individual to obey God and to act according to conscience." [25]

Taken at its face value, this statement would mean that a believer should be free to exercise any religious rites or follow any religious practices his conscience may permit or direct. But we have already noted that the United States long ago prohibited polygamy in the territories, as all of the states prohibit it today; and no plea of conscience sufficed to stay the judicial hand from enforcing the law. As late as 1946 the Mann Act (which forbids the transportation of women for immoral purposes across state lines) was upheld as no violation of the First Amendment when it was enforced against a Mormon who took his wives over a state line.[26] In a series of raids on Mormon settlements in northern Arizona a few years ago the state police, led by the state attorney general, arrested and later sent to prison the men who were heads of plural-marriage households. The men, aside from their determination to follow what they regarded as God's law and Old Testament example on marriage, were said to be fine fathers and law-abiding citizens before their convictions, and model prisoners after. As some have been released when they served their sentences, they have been reported to be unrepentant and unconvinced that they should obey the attorney general of Arizona rather than God.

The police of Arizona, Colorado, and New Mexico around every Easter season seek to stop the rites of the Pentitentes, a sect that practices mutual flagellation with long leather straps in which cactus spines have been embedded. With one

[25] Council for Social Action, p. 5.
[26] *Cleveland v. United States*, 329 U.S. 14 (1946).

of their members who is supposed to be particularly virtuous, they enact the crucifixion, although not usually to the point of death.[27] When a county sheriff hears about one of these Easter rites and arrives with his deputies to clap the participants in jail, is he not interfering with the free exercise of religion?

The religious body called Jehovah's Witnesses should go down in our history as the most litigious group on religious matters ever to arise in this country. They have done more than all other sects combined to induce the Supreme Court to interpret the First Amendment. Jehovah's Witnesses are prone to practice their religion in public places, such as parks, street corners, sidewalks. Without asking the police for a permit, they staged a parade in downtown Manchester, New Hampshire, on a Saturday night, disorganizing traffic. When the leaders were arrested and fined, did the action of the police constitute an unconstitutional interference with the free exercise of religion? The Supreme Court thought not,[28] but in other cases the Witnesses had better luck; their use of sound trucks was sustained,[29] as well as their use of parks for religious services,[30] and their right to distribute handbills on streetcorners.[31] They have been involved in other cases and will doubtless be involved in many more, for city councils are striving (so far without success) to draft an ordinance that will be at once constitutional and capable of protecting non-Witnesses from the advocacy of this religion in their homes, on their doorsteps, or over their telephones.

Clearly, the question of what is the practice of religion that cannot constitutionally be prohibited is far from determination. Here church and state face each other squarely; each

[27] The father of the present writer, from a hiding place, witnessed one of these ceremonies.

[28] *Cox v. New Hampshire*, 312 U.S. 569 (1941). See also Hollis W. Barber, "Religious Liberty v. Police Power," *American Political Science Review*, Vol. 41, April 1947, pp. 226–247.

[29] *Saia v. New York*, 334 U.S. 558 (1948).

[30] *Fowler v. Rhode Island*, 345 U.S. 67 (1953).

[31] *Lovell v. City of Griffin*, 303 U.S. 444 (1938).

claims the right to decide. No census, no poll, no majority rule is going to satisfy the religious groups, no matter how reasonable the law may seem to those who make and enforce it, for the sects get their beliefs not from man, but from God's word as they interpret it. No argument that certain of their practices are annoying to non-members is persuasive to them. In one such case Mr. Justice Fishburne for the Supreme Court of South Carolina considered the practices of a sect known as the House of Prayer: [32]

"The evidence shows that the plaintiffs dance in the church, and, in the course of the meeting, give forth weird and unearthly outcries. There is loud shouting, clapping of hands in unison, and stamping of feet. The incessant use of drums, timbrels, trombones, horns, scrubbing boards, and wash tubs adds to the general clamor. Some of the votaries are moved to testify; others enter into an hypnotic trance. The central pillars of the church are padded to protect them from injury during their transports. The tumult can be heard for many blocks . . . [and] residents who live in the vicinity testified that life is made unbearable by the continual din, which deprives them of all peace and tranquility, and makes sleep impossible. . . .

"It is, however, evident from the testimony of the plaintiffs themselves that their form of worship is inseparably connected with and accompanied by unrestrained noise and consequent public disturbance. . . . That the nuisance will continue is very plainly and clearly indicated in the testimony of W. M. Morison, the pastor in charge of the House of Prayer, who in his testimony gave Biblical citations for the clapping of hands, shouting, making a joyful noise, and the worship of the Lord both morning and evening. . . .

[32] *Morison et al. v. Rawlinson, Chief of Police, et al.*, 193 S.C. 25, 7 S.E. (2d) 635 (1940). In this case the court affirmed a lower court's denial of an injunction against the chief of police of Columbia, S.C., who was ordered by the city council forthwith to "abate the nuisance, and to close and keep closed The House of Prayer. The order was immediately carried into effect by the police department."

"It is not a question here of prohibiting the free exercise of religious worship in any constitutional sense. It is a question of peace and public order in a thickly settled community. . . ."

In instances of this kind, as well as in those where religious practices endanger the lives or safety of non-members (such as using live rattlesnakes in religious services) the question of church *versus* state is likely to be resolved, under some formula or other, in favor of the state. Backed by the majority of the people, the state may indeed, as in the House of Prayer Case, use its force first and construct a formula afterward.

The most tolerant government may be caught between religious pressures when those groups that observe the first day of the week as their Sabbath demand laws to force the closing of places of business and amusement on that day, whereas those sects that observe the seventh day demand the right to do business on the first day. The Seventh Day Baptists, Seventh Day Adventists, and other such groups allege that Sunday closing laws and other laws invalidating certain business transactions if made on Sundays work a hardship on them, besides violating the will of God as they see it; they claim that their work week is against their will reduced to five days. What appears to happen in most American jurisdictions is that governments respond to the pressure exerted by the greatest number, usually the observers of the first day of the week, and they pass statutes to restrict Sunday business; these are upheld by the state courts, even though none seems to have reached the Supreme Court; and finally, police and other administrative officials wink at violations when the heat goes off. Thus, a part of the harm that good men do may lie in their inducing the uneven enforcement of the laws.

More important, no doubt, is the conflict for some sects between nationalism and religion, not only in America, but in many other nation-states. This conflict breaks out in various ways, for love of country and love of one's church are both deep loyalties, each with many aspects. That the cross-pressures and conflicts of loyalties are not an exclusively American phenomenon was revealed in a short dispatch in the *New York Times*, November 2, 1956, from Rotterdam, the Netherlands. There a Judge A. Dirkzwager sought to have the Dutch nationality of Monsignor M. A. Janseus canceled under the Dutch nationality act of 1892 when he took the oath as a Catholic bishop; the judge alleged that the bishop could not serve the "head of the sovereign Vatican City" without losing his Dutch nationality.[33] Similarly, Paul Blanshard, an American author and lawyer, petitioned the State Department in 1953 to revoke, under the McCarran Act, the American citizenship of Archbishop Gerald P. O'Hara, papal nuncio to Ireland, on grounds that he had taken an oath of allegiance to, and was serving in the diplomatic corps of, a foreign state. Nation-states today commonly cancel, or threaten to cancel, the citizenship of their nationals if one of them takes an oath of allegiance to a foreign power or voluntarily enters its service. In this particular problem of loyalties the American Protestant argument runs somewhat as follows: either the Holy See is a sovereign state or it is not. If it is, then an American who enters its foreign service or takes an oath of allegiance to its sovereign, the Pope, as all bishops must do, should under the McCarran Act forfeit his American citizenship. If, on the other hand, the Holy See (or Vatican City) is not a sovereign state, then the Catholic demand that the United States send an ambassador to it is absurd and contrary to international law and practice. Blanshard, however, received only an equivocal reply from the State Department.

The concern of many Jews in the United States with the defense and development of the State of Israel has led to comparable arguments about dual nationality. For example, the columnist Dorothy Thompson, addressing the Phila-

[33] The *Times* never reported how the case came out.

delphia chapter of the American Council for Judaism, said that no one can be a member of the "American nation and the Jewish nation at the same time," and that Jews cannot "allow a system to develop whereby a foreign state in effect levies taxes upon citizens of other states which they regard as, somehow, Diaspora nationals." [34] The American Council for Judaism to which she spoke, founded by Lessing J. Rosenwald, is anti-Zionist; it takes the monistic view of nationality, insisting that Judaism should be regarded as a religion only. At its 1955 convention it adopted a resolution that read in part, "Nationality and religion are separate and distinct . . . our nationality is American, our religion Judaism. . . ." In another resolution the conference "rededicated itself" to an "increasing national, civic, and social integration of Americans of Jewish faith." These resolutions were immediately denounced as "insinuations of divided loyalty" by Rabbi Irving Miller, chairman of the American Zionist Council, and he added that they were "a slanderous attack by a tiny, embittered minority." [35] His statement, as quoted in the press, did not really answer the dual nationality allegations made by his coreligionists.

The phenomenon of cross-pressures is a familiar one in our complex society: a public school principal, for example, may desire a higher salary, but he is aware that an increase in salary will result in higher taxes on his home. He would doubtless resolve this conflict by supporting the higher salary, knowing that other taxpayers will assist in carrying the increased cost, but it is an oversimplification of human motivation to assume that in these situations economic motives will always prevail. The fundamentalist Mormon wishes to be loyal to his country and obedient to its laws, but at the same time he wishes to be loyal to the teachings and practice of his sect on plural marriage. The Catholic judge who finds that canon law and civil law conflict in a case before him has

[34] *New York Times,* November 2, 1949.
[35] *ibid.,* March 21, 1955.

an unhappy choice to make: if he ignores the civil law and applies canon law, he violates his oath and renders himself liable to impeachment. Yet he knows that as recently as 1949 the Pope, addressing jurists throughout the world, laid down strict rules for his behavior in this dilemma, among them that a judge "cannot shirk responsibility for his decisions and place the blame on the law and its authors," and that he can never hand down a decision "which would oblige those affected by it to perform an intrinsically immoral act; that is, an act which in itself is contrary to the law of God and of the Church." [36] Whenever a Catholic is nominated to the Supreme Court he is likely to have someone on the Judiciary Committee of the Senate quiz him about this possible conflict of loyalties; a recent instance was William J. Brennan. Senator Joseph O'Mahoney asked him this long question: "You are bound by your religion to follow the pronouncements of the Pope on all matters of faith and morals. There may be some controversies which involve matters of faith and morals and also matters of law and justice. But in matters of law and justice you are bound by your oath to follow not Papal decrees and doctrines, but the laws and precedents of this nation. If you should be faced with such a mixed issue, would you be able to follow the requirements of your oath, or would you be bound by your religious obligations?"

The committee was satisfied when Justice Brennan replied, "There isn't any obligation of our faith superior to that oath." [37] The answer was not fully responsive to the question; it is reminiscent of Governor Smith's reply to the questions raised by Charles C. Marshall when Smith sought the presidency. Smith said, "I recognize no power in the institutions of my church to interfere with the operations of the Constitution." [38]

Proposed legislation or administrative action that involves

[36] *ibid.*, November 8, 1949; see also October 31, 1952.
[37] Associated Press dispatch, February 27, 1957.
[38] *The Atlantic Monthly*, Vol. 139, April 1927, p. 721.

moral values will arouse the church lobby as almost nothing else—except, perhaps, education—will do. "Moral values," wrote Charles E. Merriam, "may be conjured up against Galileo, or against Darwin, or against the dissection of the dead, or against vaccination, or against birth control or sterilization, or against an amendment to a constitution, or against a form of tax which may be found 'immoral.' "[39] Among other current issues that may be mentioned are: the use and sale of tobacco and liquor; the definition of crimes and modes of punishment; the regulation of marriage, divorce, annulment, and the adoption of children; the suppression of certain types of sexual behavior; the censorship of plays, books, magazines, moving pictures, and television programs; euthanasia; cremation; gambling; compulsory insurance; the celebration of religious holidays, such as Thanksgiving and Christmas; medical practice in public hospitals; and many others. All of these cannot be discussed here. Only some illustrative examples can be mentioned, particularly those that show the characteristic divisions among the religious bodies.

Politics, it is said, produces strange bedfellows; but surely no stranger bedfellows were ever produced than the American Medical Association and the Christian Science Church, both opposing compulsory health insurance during the Truman Administration.[40] The Christian Scientists believe that "spiritual healing without drugs, manipulations, or appliances is an integral part of the Christian Science religion," as one of them wrote.[41] With such beliefs they suffer endless violations of their religious code: they are taxed to support medical schools and public hospitals which teach and practice a theory of health and disease contrary to theirs; they must oppose hospitalization and medical payments provisions in social security, workmen's compensation, and disability legislation

39 *Systematic Politics*, Chicago, 1945, p. 328.
40 See Ebersole, p. 156.
41 *ibid.*, p. 157.

—or at least seek amendments to exempt Christian Scientists. They have always to enter their objections to what they call compulsory medication—among public employees, the armed forces, the schools. Currently they are engaged in scores of towns and cities in lobbying city councils to prevent the flouridation of public water supplies, which is intended to prevent tooth decay. Since it is impracticable for Christian Scientists to be provided with a separate water system, they cannot obtain, as they have in some other legislation, separate treatment in the ordinance; instead, they must seek to impose their religious code upon others. In the lobbying presently conducted, they have had ranged against them the American Dental Association and the American Medical Association; each side has won some battles and lost others.

Many Protestant and some Jewish bodies seem to be on one side in the current issue of euthanasia, the Catholic Church on the other. In the struggle to obtain laws to permit voluntary euthanasia, the Euthanasia Society of America acts as a bridge among the sects. The issue, like some others in the area where religious groups contend, brings forth violent language. In 1949, for example, 379 Protestant and Jewish clergymen and religious leaders signed a petition to the New York Legislature urging a law to permit voluntary euthanasia when authorized by a court of record upon receipt of a signed petition from the sufferer, and after investigation of the case by a medical committee designated by the court. The moral issue was also discussed, in part as follows:

> "We no longer believe that God wills the prolongation of physical torture for the benefit of the soul of the sufferer. . . . We believe that such a sufferer has the right to die, and that society should grant this right, showing the same mercy to human beings as to the sub-human animal kingdom. 'Blessed are the merciful.' "[42]

[42] *New York Times*, January 6, 1949.

The Catholic response came the following Sunday. According to the *New York Times:*

"Msgr. John S. Middleton, education secretary for the Roman Catholic Archdiocese of New York, yesterday condemned 'mercy killings' as 'murder.' Preaching at solemn mass at St. Patrick's Cathedral, at which Cardinal Spellman presided, Msgr. Middleton declared that the 379 Protestant and Jewish clergymen who recently called on the state legislature to enact a law permitting voluntary euthanasia were disobedient to the law of God. . . . It is an 'inhuman humanism' that calls murder 'mercy,' he held." [43]

It is perhaps needless to add that the Legislature of New York did not pass the law the 379 petitioners sought; in general, legislatures tend not to act at all when they are subject to cross-pressures such as this.

Protestant denominations commonly regard gambling as sinful. In 1951 the House of Bishops of the Protestant Episcopal Church denounced gambling "in all its forms." In 1954, when a proposed amendment to the Colorado constitution was put on the ballot to authorize slot machines, the Colorado Council of Churches circulated a leaflet to the voters, entitled "Slot Machines Lead to Crime." A headline in the leaflet urged "One Thousand Sermons Against Gambling" before the election. Whether they were delivered or not, the amendment was defeated. Until the Great Depression the Protestant groups had largely succeeded in obtaining legislation that forbade gambling, but the depression demands upon the legislatures for new and greater sources of revenue to meet the rising need for welfare funds led one state after another to permit pari-mutuel betting on horse and dog racing, which the states taxed, until today their total revenue from such gambling exceeds a quarter of a billion dollars a year.

[43] *ibid.,* January 10, 1949.

Every dog- and horse-track operating may, however, be regarded as a legislative defeat for certain Protestant groups.

The Catholic Church, however, does not regard gambling as necessarily sinful, and many Catholic charitable and educational enterprises are, as is well known, assisted from the proceeds of raffles, bingo, and other games of chance, where these operations are permitted. When attempts are made to liberalize state gambling laws or local ordinances the Knights of Columbus will often do the lobbying for their church.

The Prohibition movement, which attained a victory with the ratification of the Eighteenth Amendment in 1920, was largely Protestant.[44] The two leading organizations, the Anti-Saloon League (which changed its name in 1948 to the Temperance League of America) and the Woman's Christian Temperance Union were predominantly Protestant in membership. The Methodists and Baptists were leading supporters, but the Episcopalians were indifferent or even hostile. The repeal of the amendment may be regarded as a defeat for many Protestant organizations. Since repeal, the temperance groups, although never despairing of one day re-establishing national prohibition, have concentrated on winning local option elections, until it is estimated that more than half of the land area of the United States is legally dry. The dry forces also seek legislation limiting liquor advertising on radio and television and the sale or use of liquor in or near military camps. Their representatives appear before city councils to object to the issuance of more tavern and other liquor licenses, or to urge higher license fees. In 1953 President Eisenhower received Dr. Caradine R. Hooten, executive secretary of the Methodist Board of Temperance, who told the press afterward that he had surprised the President by informing him that there were 2,411 licensed drinking places in Washington, D.C., the city with the highest

[44] See Peter Odegard, *Pressure Politics; the Story of the Anti-Saloon League,* New York, 1928, especially Chapter 1, "The Church in Action Against the Saloon."

per capita consumption of alcohol in the country. He also expressed his disapproval of the Capitol Hill Club, established by Republican members of Congress near the Capitol, which has a bar and a cocktail lounge.[45] Meanwhile, sentiment for the return of prohibition, reported biennially by Gallup, reached an all-time low of 26 per cent.[46]

While some organizations dominated by Protestants would, if they could, bar to persons of all faiths the use of alcoholic beverages, the Catholics seem more interested in barring moving pictures from being shown when these are, like *The Miracle*, regarded as sacrilegious, or like *Martin Luther* hostile to the Catholic Church or inaccurate, or like *The Moon is Blue* and *Baby Doll* too frank or unorthodox about sex or marriage. The lobbying in these cases is commonly done through the Legion of Decency, upon state boards of censorship, or upon television stations or theaters that may show the pictures—whatever is appropriate. On occasion Catholic organizations have picketed theaters in New York and elsewhere that have shown disapproved films. The Catholic Church has had for centuries its *Index of Prohibited Books* (*Index Librorum Prohibitorum*), a list of books the faithful are forbidden to read, but perhaps in view of the freedom of the press provision of the First Amendment, no attempts have been made to bar publication or sale in the United States of books on the *Index*. Protestant organizations occasionally object to some of the books (especially certain paperbacks) and magazines sold on newsstands, usually on grounds of salaciousness.

International relations in this generation are, as every newspaper reader knows, in a turmoil unequaled since the close of the Napoleonic wars. Religious bodies appear to believe that international affairs are of particular importance to them, in part, perhaps, because many American churches are branches of international churches or affiliated with re-

[45] *New York Times*, February 18, 1953.
[46] Release of March 31, 1957.

ligious bodies in other countries, and in part because many theologies teach that all men are brothers and their duty to God precedes their duty to their countries. For example: "Mankind is, under God, one family, and this unity is more fundamental than the existence of nations, distinctive social systems, and differing stages of social development. . . ."[47] It seems a plausible, if unprovable, generalization that since World War I the churches have taken an increasing interest in world politics; at any rate, the number of issues on which they take positions runs into the scores, and almost every church convention or assembly adds to the number.

On a few issues in international politics the major religious groups appear to be in substantial agreement. Among these may be mentioned: the undesirability of war as a means of settling international disputes; support for the United Nations; foreign aid programs, particularly nonmilitary aid; disarmament; and opposition to communism. Many religious groups have long had their American headquarters in Washington. With the establishment of the United Nations headquarters in New York they have had to establish another set of offices somewhere near it.

Even though the churches may agree on the desirability of ending war, they do not agree on what to do when war comes. The great majority of the faiths offer no opposition to the state in its war efforts, but instead send (at public expense) ministers, priests, and rabbis to serve as chaplains with the armed forces. Certain sects, such as the Quakers, have long opposed all war to the point of refusing military service, although individual Quakers usually seek noncombatant war work. Jehovah's Witnesses, however, usually refuse all military duty and service, and refuse to salute the flag. They regard the flag salute as a violation of the First Commandment and a bowing down to graven images.[48] Although they have aroused bitter opposition from the American Legion,

[47] Council for Social Action, p. 10.
[48] Barber, p. 227.

the conscription laws of the United States have dealt gently with them, whereas Hitler sent several thousands of them to the gas chambers. Whatever else may be said about the Witnesses—and much has been said—the intensity of their devotion to their faith disproves the frequent allegation that modern Western man is incapable of strong religious feelings, as well as the Marxian hypothesis that man is moved primarily by his economic interests.

In a world containing millions of displaced persons the immigration law of the United States has produced acute problems in our foreign relations and has aroused many church groups to lobby Congress for amendments. The immigration acts of 1921 and 1924 unquestionably favored the northern European (and Protestant) countries and cut the immigration from southern European (and Catholic) countries. Thus, the quota from Italy for 1959 was 5,645; for Great Britain and Northern Ireland, 65,361; for Spain it was 250; for Sweden 3,295.[49] The McCarran Act of 1952 preserved the quota system.

Pope Pius XII himself may be said, if newspaper reports are correct, to have engaged in lobbying for an easing of the United States immigration law. On October 22, 1949, in a speech to a group of United States congressmen whom he had received in audience, he said, "Is the present immigration policy as liberal as the natural resources permit in a country [the United States] so lavishly blessed by the Creator and as the challenging needs of other countries would seem to demand?"[50] But Samuel Cardinal Stritch of Chicago was more specific; presiding over a meeting of the National Catholic Resettlement Council which "has brought about 125,000 displaced persons here from Europe since 1947," he advocated the immediate "entry of at least 100,000 of Italy's surplus manpower population."[51] Protestant groups have

[49] *World Almanac*, 1959, p. 644.
[50] *New York Times*, October 23, 1949.
[51] *ibid.*, October 10, 1951.

not insisted upon the maintenance of the quota system as presently effective but instead have urged the liberalization of the McCarran Act.

In the general area of foreign affairs the most bitter dispute between American Catholics and Protestants has been over the sending of an ambassador to the Vatican, a dispute already noticed in this chapter. To the student of pressure politics what may be called the case of General Mark Clark is instructive, because it showed that the multitude of Protestant denominations can, on an appropriate issue, unite quickly and act most vigorously. It also revealed the methods of pressure and lobbying they use.

The first diplomatic relations with the Vatican were established by President Polk, when in 1848 he sent Jacob L. Martin as chargé d'affaires.[52] Relations continued until 1867, when Congress cut off funds for the mission, and the American minister, Rufus King, returned home in 1868. The United States was then without formal representation at the Vatican until 1939, when President Franklin D. Roosevelt sent Myron C. Taylor as his personal representative. This appointment was protested by various Protestant groups, but it continued for eleven years, until Mr. Taylor resigned because of age and ill health. The Taylor mission was one of the events that led to the formation of Protestants and Other Americans United for Separation of Church and State. The third of the "immediate objectives" in their manifesto was "to demand the immediate discontinuance of the ambassadorship to the papal head of the Roman Catholic Church." According to a statement made in 1951, representatives of the National Council of Churches of Christ called upon President Truman on June 5, 1946, and on November 14, 1947, urging him to terminate Taylor's appointment and were told by him that it was temporary and would end with the establishment

[52] It should be pointed out that in 1848 the Pope was a temporal as well as a spiritual ruler.

of full peace.[53] For nearly two years after Taylor's retirement the President made no move to replace him, and then, on October 20, 1951, he nominated General Mark Clark as ambassador. Congress, however, adjourned without acting on the nomination or on the accompanying legislation that was necessary.

The anonymous "seasoned observers" that newspapers like to quote were reported to be "amazed" at the violent Protestant reaction to the nomination. Presiding Bishop Henry Knox Sherrill of the Protestant Episcopal Church called an emergency meeting of the National Council of Churches of Christ, of which he was then president, which issued a statement. Hundreds of other statements followed from Protestant leaders, day by day. Reformation Sunday, October 28, 1951, was chosen by the National Association of Evangelicals to obtain a nation-wide denunciation of the nomination from Protestant pulpits, and, according to the *New York Times*, the "Protestants across the country took the occasion of the observance of Reformation Sunday yesterday to protest the appointment by President Truman of a United States ambassador to the Vatican. . . . Ministers in many churches spoke against the action, and petitions that will be sent to Washington were signed on church steps. . . ." In approximately 2,000 words the *Times* summarized some of the sermons and estimated the audiences; it reported that in St. Louis the federation of churches had prepared 10,000 post cards to be sent to Washington after a night mass meeting. Half a million dollars for radio time, contributed by laymen, was used on that Sunday.[54] The barrage of criticism continued through November and December. *Time* reported that the first week after the nomination 21,000 letters and telegrams, six to one against it, were received at the White House, more than had been produced by any issue of recent

[53] *New York Times*, October 31, 1951.
[54] *ibid.*, October 29, 1951.

years except the dismissal of General MacArthur.[55] As denominational meetings and conventions occurred, more resolutions were adopted and petitions signed. No doubt many national legislators, home from Washington and facing a campaign year, heard from their constituents, for news accounts began to express doubt that General Clark could be confirmed. In mid-December the Executive Committee of the Southern Baptist Convention authorized a letter to every pastor of every church in its jurisdiction, asking them to urge members to write or wire members of Congress opposing the appointment.[56] A Gallup poll indicated that 60 per cent of the voters had heard or read about the nomination, a very high proportion for a public issue; the vote among the 60 per cent on whether the Senate should or should not approve was:

Should	19%
Should not	29
No opinion	12
	60%

Catholics approved, 3½ to 1; Protestants disapproved, 3 to 1.[57] When Congress reconvened, statements by various senators indicated that the cause was hopeless, and on January 13 General Clark withdrew. President Truman announced that he would find another nominee, but he never did. The anti-ambassador drive had, however, developed so much momentum that a week later "A thousand banner-waving church members gathered in Washington . . . to put heat to the controversy about whether the U.S. should send an ambassador to the Vatican. They were on a 'pilgrimage' sponsored by the American Council of Christian Churches. . . ."[58] President Truman refused to receive them or their

[55] *Time*, Vol. 58, no. 12, November 2, 1951, p. 21.

[56] *New York Times*, December 14, 1951.

[57] Release of December 9, 1951.

[58] *Time*, Vol. 59, no. 5, February 4, 1952, p. 9. *Time* carried a picture of the crowd, with their placards.

leader, so they took their petitions (which were said to bear 50,000 signatures) to Senator Tom Connally, then chairman of the Senate Committee on Foreign Relations.

The issue is now with us and will remain for years. As the 1952 campaign began, the Associated Press asked each of the men they then thought were the leading candidates for the presidential nominations—Kefauver, Stassen, Warren, and Taft—whether he favored sending an ambassador to the Vatican. All four avoided giving an answer.[59] When a reporter asked Adlai Stevenson for his views at a press conference on September 16, he said he would not propose an ambassador. General Eisenhower never made any statement, but after his election the National Lutheran Council, representing eight Lutheran bodies with four million members, adopted a resolution urging him not to appoint any representative, "personal or otherwise," warning that if he did, "we should be bound by conscience to oppose the appointment with all possible vigor."[60] In 1959, the Catholic Senator John Kennedy of Massachusetts, seeking the 1960 Democratic nomination for President, several times announced that he would not, if elected, send an envoy to the Vatican.

Another old issue that we may expect to be around for a long time to come is that of religion and education. It may be traced to the dawn of history, for religions have always recognized the importance of the training of the young in the faith, knowing that beliefs instilled early in life are likely to persist to the end of it. Many churches have therefore set up their own schools and colleges to see that only the true doctrine, pure and undefiled, is taught to their youth. When schisms have occurred, sometimes the first step for the dissident sect has been to build a new meeting house, the second, a new school.

And religious schools and politics are always getting involved with each other. For example, G. G. Van Deusen has

[59] *New York Times,* January 27, 1952.
[60] *ibid.,* February 7, 1953.

said of William H. Seward, governor of New York more than a century ago:

"It is evident that he wanted to give part of the state's common school fund to the Catholic Church for its parochial schools, an idea that had a very strong appeal for [Catholic] Bishop John Hughes and his parishioners, but this proposal raised a perfect storm among all those with leanings toward Native Americanism. Two years of controversy ensued. . . . It was futile as a means of luring immigrants into a party [the Whigs] in which their enemies were firmly ensconced." [61]

Public financial aid to sectarian schools or to students in such schools is an issue today, and not only in the United States but in many other countries as well. The majority doctrine in the Everson case seems to be that public aid to religious schools is unconstitutional, but financial aid to the students who attend such schools or to their parents is permissible. To POAU and to various Protestant bodies this is a distinction without a difference, for they allege that when the aid is channeled to the students it has the same ultimate effect as direct aid to the schools they attend in relieving the schools of the necessity of providing bus service, school books, supplies, scholarships, and other assistance. Consequently, they oppose bills, such as that which passed the Minnesota legislature in 1956, to permit income tax deductions for tuition paid by parents whose children attend religious schools. There is continuing agitation to amend the federal income tax laws to permit such deductions. Many religious bodies in the United States maintain schools or colleges, but the Protestant churches that do, notably the Lutherans, do not seek tax support for the schools or the students who attend them. In 1952, however, the Catholic Bishops of the United States joined in a statement asserting

[61] G. G. Van Deusen, *Thurlow Weed: Wizard of the Lobby*, Boston, 1947, p. 117.

that financial aid to students attending parochial schools was a constitutional "right."

Attempts since World War II to obtain federal aid for schools have kept the religious lobby in continual action. Proposals that federal aid be extended to the states on a basis of their total school population, to be distributed by the states as their own laws may permit, have aroused the opposition of Protestant groups, who see such plans as devices by which federal funds could be paid to parochial schools or to parents of students attending them. In 1949 the issue broke out in a bitter controversy when H.R. 4645, introduced by Representative Graham A. Barden of North Carolina, would have authorized $300,000,000 federal aid, but only for "tax-supported grade schools and high schools which are under public supervision and control." Francis Cardinal Spellman, speaking at a Eucharistic rally at Fordham University, denounced Representative Barden as a "new apostle of bigotry" and asserted that "the Catholic school is . . . equal in right with the public school." [62] When Mrs. Franklin D. Roosevelt in her newspaper column "My Day" rather vaguely approved of the Barden Bill, which she wrote that she had not read, Cardinal Spellman made public a long letter to her denouncing her stand in sharp language and concluding "whatever you may say in the future, your record of anti-Catholicism stands for all to see—a record which you yourself wrote on the pages of history which cannot be recalled—documents of discrimination unworthy of an American Mother!" [63] From this and other statements by officials of the Catholic Church, it appears that opposition to public aid to Catholic schools is now equated by them with opposition to the church itself.

Ceremonies in public schools that have any religious significance stir up religious groups. The flag salute cases, already cited, went clear to the Supreme Court, which finally held

[62] *New York Times*, June 20, 1949.

[63] *ibid.*, July 23, 1949. This issue reprinted in full Mrs. Roosevelt's columns, Cardinal Spellman's letter, and the Barden Bill.

that students could not be required to salute. Opening of a school day with prayer, the singing of hymns or Christmas carols, or the observance of religious holidays have in some school systems produced so much friction that school boards or school officials have stopped them all. In New York City, for instance, an assistant superintendent of schools issued the following order: "Christmas, and other similar occasions, may be celebrated only as seasonal, pre-vacation occurrences. There must not be any reference in dramatizations, songs, or other aspects of the occasion to any religious significance involved. Christmas carols with reference to the Nativity may not be sung, nor any decorations include religious symbols of any faith."[64] The New York Society for Ethical Culture has even objected to the singing of the fourth stanza of the song "America" by school children because its words form a prayer.[65] Acting on a protest by Monsignor Edward V. Dargin of Croton Falls against high school baccalaureate services that contained non-Catholic songs and prayers, Dr. Lewis A. Wilson, New York State Commissioner of Education, banned all baccalaureate exercises from all public school buildings.[66] Although New York City and State possibly have more religious friction in and about their public school systems than most areas of the country, still the response of these school officials to religious pressures is probably typical: if some church or officer of a religious organization objects to an observance, in the interest of impartiality stop the whole thing. The religious groups are, however, then able to point with disapproval to the "godless" public schools.

[64] *ibid.*, December 5, 1947.

[65] *ibid.*, November 3, 1952.

[66] *ibid.*, June 14, 1951. As further evidence that religious feelings can arouse violent reactions, the same account reported: "At Somers 125 residents stormed a regular meeting of the Board of Education last night and demanded that the Somers Central School hold the baccalaureate service for the 24 graduating high school students Sunday night as scheduled. They suggested that the board proceed with the planned service until a court injunction was served or that the group go to court to authorize the service."

Attempts to teach religion in the public schools have led to endless disputes. In the famous McCollum case the Supreme Court, with only one dissent, held unconstitutional a "released time" plan in use in Illinois and other states by which public school students were given a choice between attending study hall and attending religious classes held in the schools.[67] The Court objected not only to the use of school property for religious purposes, but also to the "use of the state's compulsory public school machinery" to enforce attendance. The decision was not well received by many religious groups:

"Many gentlemen of the cloth forgot their Christian charity for an erring sinner in their denunciations of the Court. Even worse, many of the two thousand communities which had released-time programs went on a sit-down strike against the decision. Finding trivial distinctions between their programs and that condemned in the McCollum case, they kept their pupils sitting down to religious instruction." [68]

Perhaps the Supreme Court not only follows the election returns, in Mr. Dooley's famous aphorism, but it also follows the religious press. At any rate, by 1952, with several justices switching sides or modifying their positions, the Court upheld a New York released-time scheme that differed from the Illinois plan only in that the students left the school buildings to attend religious classes in churches, synagogues, or other meeting places.[69] Public school teachers and administrators, who will rarely permit themselves to be quoted, seem generally to oppose all released-time schemes on grounds that they disrupt the school day, that there are always a few students whose faiths have no local representative, that the teaching of religion should occur on Saturday or Sunday, and

[67] *Illinois ex rel. McCollum v. Board of Education,* 33 U.S. 203 (1948).
[68] Horn, p. 65.
[69] *Zorach v. Clauson,* 343 U.S. 306 (1952).

that the coercive powers of the state should not be used to check up on and enforce attendance at religious classes. The controversy may be expected to continue.

What constitutes religious teaching may be almost as difficult a problem as what constitutes religious practice. The New Jersey Supreme Court unanimously forbade the free distribution in schools of the King James version of the Bible by the Gideons in a case brought by a Jewish and a Catholic parent jointly, holding that it is a sectarian document.[70] Having the Ten Commandments posted on the walls of classrooms in public schools has produced objections, but apparently no adjudication. In 1950 Christian Scientists got a bill through the New York legislature, which Governor Dewey signed in spite of an appeal for a veto from the New York Academy of Medicine, excusing Christian Science students from a course—until then compulsory in New York high schools—on health and hygiene. The chief objection of the Christian Scientists was that the course taught the germ theory of disease; but, because after passage of the law some students had to be excused from the course, the Board of Regents decided that no questions on the state-wide regents' examinations could thereafter involve the germ theory of disease. The Academy of Medicine issued a statement against the statute, saying that it "disrupts the orderly teaching of biology and hygiene, the basis of modern sanitation and public health." [71] The wearing of religious garb by persons teaching in the public schools has been alleged to be teaching religion by example; in 1952 the voters of North Dakota adopted an amendment to their state constitution forbidding it.

When public schools and church schools are engaged in building schools at the same time, there is apt to be a political contest. Few such conflicts attract more than local notice. A state-wide one occurred in New Jersey in 1954 when the state university, Rutgers, sought a bond issue to build

[70] *New York Times*, December 7, 1953.
[71] *ibid.*, March 13, 14, 1950, and December 12, 16, 1951.

medical and dental schools at the same time that Seton Hall University, a Catholic institution, had announced plans for a medical-dental school in the Jersey City Medical Center, built by public funds in the regime of Mayor Frank Hague. In the words of the *New York Times:*

"Roman Catholic voters in New Jersey were urged yesterday by official diocesan publications to oppose plans for a $25,000,000 state medical-dental school and health center. A proposal to authorize bonds in that amount will be voted upon in a state wide referendum next Tuesday. . . .

"The appeal to voters to turn down the proposal was contained in *The Advocate,* official organ of the Newark archdiocese, *The Catholic Star-Herald* of the Camden diocese, and *The Monitor* of the Trenton diocese." [72]

Although the proposal was supported by the CIO, the medical and dental societies, even by the New Jersey Taxpayers' Association, it was defeated.[73]

Any organization seeking political objectives is naturally desirous to see its members elected or appointed to public office, for it can ordinarily expect a sympathetic hearing at the least and devoted allegiance at the most. Of all groups in American society the legal profession has fared best.[74] When an association has in a legislative body a number of faithful adherents, these members are sometimes called the "inside lobby." Unfortunately, we have only fragmentary statistics on the religious membership of American legislators. For three recent Congresses Donald R. Matthews has summarized the evidence:

"Protestant denominations with congregations of high social status (Congregational, Presbyterian, Episcopal, Unitarian)

[72] October 30, 1954.

[73] *National Municipal Review,* Vol. 48, no. 11, December, 1954, p. 589.

[74] Donald R. Matthews, *The Social Background of Political Decision-Makers,* Garden City, New York, 1954, p. 30.

possess about twice the number of Representatives and Senators they would have if Congressmen were completely representative in their religions. The Methodists, Lutherans, and Baptists have about the right number. On the other hand, Roman Catholics have only one-half to one-third, and Jews one-sixth the number of Congressmen they should have if the Congress is to be a religious cross-section of the nation. As far as the Senate and House are concerned, then, a Protestant has better than average opportunities, while Catholics and Jews have more limited ones." [75]

We do not have any general systematic study of the voting behavior of legislators in relation to the religious issues that come before them; to make such a study would be an enormous undertaking. In the meantime we can only assume that religious groups have better access to and more influence upon coreligionists in legislatures than they can have upon others, but we can only guess at the dimensions of that influence.

The chief prize of American politics for any interest is the presidency. Not only does the office carry world-wide prestige, but the constitutional powers of the President are also great; for example, during his term a President is able to fill the vacancies that occur in the federal judiciary, and under our doctrine of judicial review a constitutional amendment may be necessary to overcome one of their decisions. The appointment of a single justice to the Supreme Court may tip the balance one way or the other. As we have noted, more and more cases involving religious groups seem to be going to the Supreme Court. Again, the veto power of the President is so great that it is likely to be futile to work a bill through Congress if it is to meet a veto; few interests can obtain the necessary two-thirds in each house to overcome it. The President, moreover, has large control over foreign affairs, even if his power is not complete. This authority is important to religious groups with

[75] *ibid.*, p. 26. Matthews also presents a table showing membership by principal sects.

their world-wide interests and affiliations, and one reason that Protestants have opposed an ambassador to the Vatican is that the papal nuncio who would be sent to the United States by the Pope would have, under international law, personal access to the President, a status that would not be available to representatives of other religious groups.

As every one knows, no Catholic has been elected President; indeed, only one, Alfred E. Smith, has been nominated by a major party. His religion was an issue in the campaign of 1928, and although Herbert Hoover would probably have won anyhow, probably he cracked the then Solid South only because Smith was a Catholic. There is still enough opposition to a Catholic President so that any party convention would have to conclude that a Catholic candidate would begin his campaign under a heavy handicap. Three times the Gallup Poll has asked the question, "If your party nominated a generally well-qualified man for President, and he happened to be a Catholic, would you vote for him?"[76] The results have been:

	1959	*1956*	*1940*
Yes, would	68%	73%	62%
No, would not	24	22	31
No opinion	8	5	7

Even though opposition has diminished since 1940, a 24 per cent disadvantage (35 per cent in the South) is more than most candidates in our close elections could overcome; in 1956, to take the latest presidential election, the Eisenhower majority was only 7.8 per cent of the two-party vote. The opposition, moreover, is still vocal. According to a United Press dispatch of April 30, 1959, the General Assembly of the American Council of Christian Churches unanimously adopted a resolution that "To nominate a Roman Catholic would precipitate

[76] Release of June 24, 1956. The greatest opposition is among older people and in the states of the South.

a religious conflict of major proportions . . . [which] would seriously divide the United States. . . ." The organization claims to represent 1,500,000 members of seventeen Protestant denominations.

This is no place for a party history of the United States. We may summarize it by noting that religion has been an interest in politics since colonial days; that it formed the principal base of one minor party, the Know-Nothing party; that the Federalist-Whig-Republican succession has been dominated by Protestants; and that until the 1956 election a majority of Catholics have, in national elections, voted Democratic. Little empirical evidence for voting behavior by religious adherence was available until the development of public opinion survey techniques. Even now different polls are conducted on different plans, so that the results are not strictly comparable. For the elections of 1948 and 1952 the Survey Research Center of the University of Michigan reported on voting by religious affiliation thus, not separating the Jewish vote:[77]

	Protestant		Catholic	
Voted for:	*1948*	*1952*	*1948*	*1952*
Democrat	25%	26%	49%	43%
Republican	28	45	25	41
Did not vote	43	29	20	15
Not ascertained, voted other, etc.	4	*	6	1
	100%	100%	100%	100%

* Less than one-half of one per cent

The Gallup Poll figures on major party voting only, expressed as a percentage of members of three principal faiths voting Democratic, were:[78]

[77] Angus Campbell, Gerald Gurin, and Warren E. Miller, "Political Issues and the Vote," *American Political Science Review*, Vol. 47, no. 2, June, 1953, p. 381.

[78] Release of January 23, 1957.

	1952	*1956*
Catholic	56%	51%
Jewish	77	75
Protestant	37	37

The political methods used by religious groups in America have been mentioned only in passing. They are considered in detail in another essay in this volume. Religious bodies commonly depend upon the voting strength of their memberships as the ultimate sanction. The strength of this sanction varies, of course, from state to state: the wishes of the Mormons would be critical in Utah, unimportant in Rhode Island; Roman Catholic desires are likely to be attained in any New England state, unlikely in any southern state; Jewish influence is more important in New York than anywhere else; and wherever the Protestant sects can unite upon an issue their strength will vary from being significant to being overwhelming.

The future of the church in politics is the future of the church in American life: if church membership and religious interest continue to increase as they have since World War II, then the religious lobby will become more important; if, on the other hand, there is a decline comparable to that which occurred between the wars, the influence of religious groups will decline, too.

THE CHURCH AND TECHNIQUES OF POLITICAL ACTION

R. MORTON DARROW

CHURCHES in a pluralistic society face a fundamental problem in the conflict between their goals and values and the practices of society, including politics. Theoretically, the church can choose between striving to change society to conform to creedal ideals, or rationalizing the differences between its creed and society's behavior. The first choice may call either for complete withdrawal from, or a declaration of war against, major social institutions—a war in which denunciation would abound. The latter choice calls for a high degree of tolerance, or else places the church group in a position submissive to other institutions. Few churches are to be found at either of these extremes. Depending upon the nature of their goals, their perspective, their membership, their leadership, and the society in which they find themselves, most church groups choose an intermediate position and moderate their ideologies accordingly.

The Roman Catholic Church has made such adaptation, resulting in great diversity under the universal panoply. In this organization paradoxical elements of permanence and resistance to large historical trends are coupled with broad cooperation with all sorts of secular agents. A Roman Catholic *Weltanschauung* that views the world as sinful and inferior includes a theory of change that is not revolutionary. Denying the foreseeable possibility of a Utopia on this earth, the Church does not aim to change fundamentally human nature or human institutions. Dogma is maintained as rigidly as is humanly possible, but flexibility in more mundane matters is permitted.

The Church does not retreat into an other-worldliness which would render it solely a moral symbol, condemned to permanent ineffectuality in large affairs. Never forgetting its goal of universal proselytizing, the Catholic Church strives to achieve a dominant position in secular society, counteracting, insofar as possible, inevitable sinfulness. This striving takes many shapes, ranging from ultra-conservative authoritarian political and social movements in Spain and Portugal to ultra-liberal labor movements in France, Australia, and the United States. Competing with other churches or secular institutions, the Catholic Church finds itself forced to employ the manipulative tools and techniques of secular society as well as those unique to religious groups.

Protestant churches, too, have been concerned with possible conflict between the goal of individual salvation and perfection and the goal of making this a better world to live in by influencing other institutions. Their concern that the primary goal of individual salvation will be diluted by the infusion of secular aims resulting from power conflicts is augmented in America by the doctrine of separation of church and state. Whatever else the doctrine of the "wall of separation" has done, it has thrown a shadow of guilt upon church participation in political affairs. Churches, however, are an integral part of the institutional fabric of American society and few have been able to resist the ever-increasing pressure to participate in the political process. Although individual Protestant clergymen had been active throughout the nineteenth century in humanitarian political movements such as prison reform, abolition, and industrial reform, the strong American Protestant tradition of emphasis on individual redemption long served as a conservative force slowing down the impulse to project broad political and social programs. As the struggle within the Episcopal and Lutheran churches during the 1930's attests, the achievement of broad social and political programs as the official position of the majority of the large Protestant denominations was not won until well into the twentieth century.[1]

Official doctrine, theology, and political theory may help set the framework of values in which the individual clergy-

[1] Anson Phelps Stokes, *Church and State in the United States,* New York, 1950, Vol. 3, pp. 454–552.

man will operate, but his entrance into politics usually occurs in a rather casual, mundane fashion. The young clergyman, arriving fresh from seminary or apprenticeship for his first real assignment, will not be vitally concerned with the great issues of the "church in politics"—foreign aid, military alliances, federal aid to education. Somehow, to a great extent, these issues will be decided without him. His real baptism into political waters will usually take place, seemingly without regard for his church's official stand on separation of church and state, as the result of parishioners' needs. Housing difficulties will mean a visit to the local Housing Authority; a boy in trouble, a visit to the county Probation Officer or the Parole Board; the breadwinner unemployed, a visit to the local patronage dispenser. These initial trips across the "wall of separation" pave the way for his future greater involvement.

With time, the clergyman may find himself a member of the local Housing Authority; he may be on the Advisory Council to the Probation Office; he may be consulted regarding public works projects. As he advances in the ranks of his church either to ministries of greater responsibility or to episcopal rank, his political involvement may be broadened past local and state levels to reach national influence.

How and why do churches differ in degree, method, and efficacy of political participation? Ranging widely over the past to select illustrative incidents (since much political activity is episodic, motivated by a current burning issue), we shall suggest some reasons for the differences, at the same time placing minimal stress on issues, which are the usual focus of any discussion of the church in politics. We shall deliberately avoid attempting to portray, in all their subtleties, the individual positions taken by churches on various social and political questions.

Aggregate statistics of church membership showing relative strengths are considered elsewhere in this volume. In a federal system of government, the distribution of membership—geographically, socially, and economically—is of equal importance with size. We have seen historic patterns of church concentration changed by shifts of population—witness the present-day dominance in many parts of the south of Methodists and Baptists; the concentration of Catholics and Jews in large urban areas; the dominance of Mormons in Utah; and other areas of concentrated denominational strength. In the northeast and in several American cities, Catholics form either a majority or are the largest single religious group. Clusters of Lutherans in the northwest create local majorities for that denomination.

There are over 300,000 local churches in the United States and few are not readily identifiable by denomination, national origin, or class. A foreign observer would have as little difficulty in a southern city discovering differences between the membership of the Episcopal church up on the hill and the Evangelical church down by the river, as he would in New England discovering differences between the membership of an old disestablished church and the membership of a Roman Catholic parish. Depending upon the community, a local clergyman will find his political role spelled out for him. He may alter that role by strength of personality and by other personal attributes he brings to the job, but his constituency sets the basic framework.

It is difficult to generalize about 300,000 local situations, but some patterns are clear. If the clergyman "represents" a dominant majority in the electoral unit—be it ward, county, or congressional district—it is likely that he will find its political representatives to be of his religious faith, regardless of party lines.[2] He will further find himself, in this circumstance, to be a sharer in political power rather than a protester against its use. In New York City, one of the forms this sharing takes is the exercise of a veto by the archbishop of the New York archdiocese over appointments of the allotted number of Catholics to the Board of Higher Education.

Having its members in public office is an extremely valuable

[2] Madge E. McKinney, "Religion and Elections," *Public Opinion Quarterly*, Vol. 8, Spring 1944, pp. 110–114, offers statistical proof for congressmen.

asset for a church. It comes as no shock when the minister of a fundamentalist, evangelical sect has difficulty getting a police permit from a Methodist police commissioner or Methodist mayor in a small southern city while the minister of the largest Methodist church has no difficulty changing the site of the new public school. Nor would it be surprising to find a Presbyterian minister in the same town using the services of a communicant with "good connections downtown" to attain political ends. In brief, the basic resource of the church is its members—considered in terms of their geographical distribution, their position in the community, their class and status, and their accessibility to political leaders.

Another politically relevant attribute of church membership is the degree of its group cohesiveness. There is tremendous variation between and within churches in willingness of individuals to identify themselves with group values and goals.

At one end, we have the immigrant churches where the number of values held and shared by group members is so extensive as to warrant labeling the group a sub-culture. At the other end, we have churches where the bonds of commonly held values are extremely thin. A relatively large number of values held and shared by church members leads to ease of sharing additional political goals, enabling individuals to integrate them into their framework of values. Since a large part of the recognition by political leaders of a clergyman's political influence lies in the recognition of his ability to have church members follow his cue, group loyalty is a factor of enduring importance.

This recognition of group cohesiveness leads to a certain degree of stability in political life. Churches have established their power in American society over a long period of time by a series of battles. Political leaders know church positions on certain issues, know what churches can do if aroused, and give churches their due as part of the ordinary political process of adjustment. Without such peaceful adjustment, political battles would easily degenerate into violence. Thus what has often been described as "pressure" in the political process should be thought of not merely in terms of precipitous acts, but also in the sense of political "atmospheric pressure." No suit of mail has yet been devised that will permit a skillful political leader to take on directly the Baptist Church in Birmingham or the Roman Catholic Church in Chicago or the Methodist Church in Mobile.

A second resource with political relevance for churches is material wealth. Direct use of wealth is relatively rare. One notable instance of direct use was the large contributions made by the Methodist and Baptist churches to the operation of the Anti-Saloon League during its heyday.[3] By and large, however, material wealth has only indirect bearing. Money may be used to maintain a permanent staff for lobbying in the state and national capitals; or more indirectly, used to maintain a widespread communications network including such things as religious magazines, newspapers, and radio stations.[4] Another source of potential political power involving material wealth is the financial ability to create and maintain auxiliary lay societies.

Experienced leaders and knowledge of political tactics also influence the effectiveness of church participation in politics. The Anti-Saloon League and the Catholic Church have deservedly received credit for possessing political sophistication. Both have familiar strategies for solving recurring problems in political areas and have employed specialists to do the job. Noteworthy political specialists—Monsignor Robert F. Keegan, liaison agent for Cardinal Hayes in New York; Monsignor York, liaison agent for Bishop Molloy in Brooklyn; the Reverend Maurice F. Sheehy, liaison agent for Bishop Curley of Baltimore—developed an enviable store of knowledge and personal relationships during their lengthy service.[5]

[3] Peter H. Odegard, *Pressure Politics; the Story of the Anti-Saloon League*, New York, 1928, passim.

[4] Peter M. H. Wynhoven, ed., *Swim—or Sink*, Marrero, La., 1939, passim.

[5] Interview with Adolph A. Berle, New York City, June 1950. *Hyde Park Papers*, Letter from Father Sheehy to Miss Le Hand, April 10, 1937. Interview with James A. Farley, New York City, September 1950.

Besides differences in degree of specialized services, there seem to be great differences among churches in the degree to which their political concern is historical and traditional. Jewish clerical leaders on the Palestine question, and Irish Catholic clerical leaders on the Irish question, maintained a high level of political activity for many years.[6] From these groups emerged new clergymen and future leaders of their churches, men to whom political activity is hardly alien.

Beyond differences in psychological preparation, there are other important differences among churches in the educational preparation of their clergymen, in the administrative climate in which the clergymen work, and in their possibilities for advancement. Self-criticism by the churches of the theological seminary education and the preparation students undergo before ordination indicates that thorough grounding in fundamentals of government and political participation is received by few. In general, the best of both Catholic and Protestant seminaries are on a par in giving sound professional training, but the low educational requirement for the ministry in some Protestant denominations serves to bring the average level below that of the Catholic Church.[7] The importance in politics of the educational backgrounds of clergymen will vary, depending on local conditions.

Two somewhat paradoxical sources of increased clerical political activity are contained in the basic church structure. On the one hand, the rough-and-tumble of internal church politics of organizations such as the episcopal one equips some clergymen with great insight into the personal relationships and personalities involved in governmental politics. In the case of the Catholic Church, there is the suggestion that the kinds of leaders rising in that organization often resemble closely those who rise in the urban political machines, a parallel

[6] Theodore Maynard, *The Story of American Catholicism*, New York, 1941, pp. 506–507, and Stokes, Vol. 2, pp. 414–421.

[7] Benson Y. Landis, "Religion," in J. F. Dewhurst et al., *America's Needs and Resources*, New York, 1955, pp. 414–429.

also maintained in respect to the ethnic, educational, and economic backgrounds of the two groups of leaders. Similarity of temperament and background lead to good rapport between church leaders and political leaders.[8]

On the other hand, there is evidence that political genius will not be contained by organizational structures. For those whose political appetites are not completely satisfied by the opportunities for a political role offered by church politics, the secular political area holds many attractions. Three Presbyterian ministers who were politically active while holding pastorates are notable illustrations: the Reverend Charles H. Parkhurst, who scored sensational victories over Tammany Hall in the 1890's; the Reverend Norman Thomas, who was active in municipal reform in New York City before going on to the national scene; and the Reverend Lester H. Clee, who

[8] The following local or generalized works offer fragmentary evidence: Robert S. Allen, ed., *Our Fair City,* New York, 1947, pp. 25–28, 186–187; Robert S. Allen, ed., *Our Sovereign State,* New York, 1949, pp. 53–55; Harold F. Gosnell, *Machine Politics: Chicago Model,* Chicago, 1937, pp. 39, 45, 64, 102; John Gunther, *Inside U.S.A.*, New York, 1947, pp. 77, 89, 157, 222, 351, 465, 500, 648, 805, 834, 904; Edward J. Flynn, *You're the Boss,* New York, 1947, pp. 145–146; Paul F. Lazarsfeld, Bernard Berelson, and Hazel Gaudet, *The People's Choice,* New York, 1944, pp. 21–27; Dayton D. McKean, *The Boss, the Hague Machine in Action,* Boston, 1940, pp. 13, 61, 126–127, 150, 161–165; Charles E. Merriam, *Chicago: A More Intimate View of Urban Politics,* New York, 1949, pp. 134–151; Warren Moscow, *Politics in the Empire State,* New York, 1948, pp. 44–47, 139–142; Peter H. Odegard and E. Allen Helms, *American Politics,* 2nd ed., New York, 1947, pp. 324–359; Roy V. Peel, *The Political Clubs of New York City,* New York, 1935, pp. 251–267; Charles W. Van Devander, *The Big Bosses,* New York, 1944; Harold Zink, *City Bosses in the United States,* Durham, 1930; George Seldes, *The Catholic Crisis,* New York, 1939, pp. 155–183; Madge E. McKinney, "Constitutional Amendment in New York State," *Public Opinion Quarterly,* Vol. 3, October 1938, pp. 635–645.

These fragments about Catholic political power and Catholic political leaders were compared with material derived from Joseph Bernhart, *The Vatican as a World Power,* New York, 1939; Paul Blanshard, *American Freedom and Catholic Power,* Boston, 1949; F. R. Hoare, *The Papacy and the Modern State,* London, 1940; Francis E. McMahon, *A Catholic Looks at the World,* New York, 1945; Theodore Maynard, *The Story of American Catholicism,* New York, 1941; William Teeling, *The Pope in Politics,* London, 1937; Michael Williams, *The Catholic Church in Action,* New York, 1935; Henry Morton Robinson, *The Cardinal,* New York, 1950; Edwin O'Connor, *The Last Hurrah,* Boston, 1956.

served as Speaker of the New Jersey Assembly and was an unsuccessful candidate for governor. Clee is no rarity among Protestant clergymen. One will usually find a number of congressmen who are Protestant clergymen—from north and south, colored and white. The most notable current clerical-political leader is the Reverend Adam Clayton Powell, pastor of the Abyssinian Baptist Church in New York City.

Methodist Bishop G. Bromley Oxnam, Archbishop John Ireland, Rabbi Stephen S. Wise, and James Cardinal Gibbons are outstanding examples of how strong personalities with tremendous political skills may influence their parent church organizations. In the case of Jehovah's Witnesses, we have seen a brilliant and talented man of law, Judge Joseph F. Rutherford, lead the group into the forefront of advocacy of civil liberties. In the case of the Reverend Martin Luther King we have seen a militancy imparted to the role of southern Negro minister that is a marked departure from the traditional role of supporter of the status quo, relied upon by state and local political leaders to keep trouble from brewing. Nor should one forget the role and skill shown by Father Charles Coughlin in helping defeat the World Court proposal and in leading his Social Justice movement.

Having reviewed the goals, values, and resources of churches relevant to political activity, let us now turn to the organizations and activities themselves. Although it is true that in America's multifarious society there is a vast subsurface of unorganized interests which exert great influence in creating "rules of the game" of politics, major power struggles are carried on by the organized ones. American society, particularly during the nineteenth century, was marked by a casualness of structure which permitted the individual great freedom of choice in selecting his associations. Individuals were free to remain relatively aloof from organized groups, maintaining a great deal of direction over the course of their lives because of the large areas of life which were casually ordered. The tendency in modern times, however, has been to reduce individual choice with progressively wider activities of organized groups. The struggle for power by these groups has not been limited to political or economic spheres but encompasses almost all of the social structure.

Churches have shared in this organizing trend, as evidenced by the proliferation of auxiliary societies—men's discussion groups, Knights of Columbus, women's leagues, youth groups, and the like. These groups can form the core for both discussion and positive action. In 1951 when President Truman nominated General Mark Clark as ambassador to the Vatican, Methodist, Baptist, and Presbyterian discussion groups throughout the country were used to collect and send petitions to Congress protesting the action. Most clergymen were convinced a long time ago that appeals to the laity to be "politically active" without affording them the means for doing so are likely to be ineffectual. These means are largely organized efforts.

The high degree of centralized authority in the Catholic Church has often caused it to be used by envious Protestants as a model of efficiency for political purposes. In a nation dedicated to a business way of life, episcopal structures offer many attractions. American individualism, however, penetrates all institutions. At a time when the Catholic bishop of Detroit was encouraging Father Coughlin in his political activities, a neighboring Catholic bishop declared his own Hatch Act, forbidding priests in his diocese to engage in any overt political activity.[9] It has also been traditional to believe that a strong episcopal organization limits the freedom of the individual clergyman at the local level. To some degree this is true, but there is another side to that coin. As we have seen in the south recently, the segregationist sentiments of Protestant congregations have forced silence upon many a minister whose own feelings coincided with a national church position in favor of integration. These pressures by local majorities for clergy-

[9] Stokes, Vol. 3, pp. 470–471, quotes a letter to his clergy by Archbishop John Murray of St. Paul.

men to abstain from support of school integration were felt in Protestant, Jewish, and Catholic churches throughout the south. Under these circumstances, some clergymen have been less than enthusiastic about the appearance, in vestry control of their living, of the democratic principle of majority rule. Some have spoken with envy of the forthright positions taken by clergymen who could not be removed by the local vestry.[10]

The unwillingness of white southerners to follow the leadership of their clergy in the school integration issue is a good example of some of the limitations on church political action. In a pluralistic society where loyalties are divided, individuals must see that issues are relevant to the group, or group cohesiveness must be intense, for loyalty to prevail under competitive conditions. We know that consciousness of belonging to a group is strongly affected by historical events—a war, a wave of intolerance, a campaign with religio-political connotations, or an era of good feeling.

Churches are particularly sensitive about the need for showing members the relevance of their group's participating in the political scene. One result is that religious leaders feel pressure to state political issues in moral (religious) terms in order to validate political activity to members and to mobilize their support. Churches have found that muted appeals to members are generally canceled out by discordant appeals of other groups. On large issues, therefore, churches have found loud clarion calls to be particularly effective when a defensive stance is taken. Group survival becomes the issue and one hears the call to "beat back the threat."

Church direction of political activity takes many forms. In 1928, many Methodist and Baptist ministers were to be found as key figures in local Anti-Smith Democrats committees.[11] In the Knights of Columbus and the Holy Name Societies we see another form of leadership. Many of the members of such

[10] "The Southern Churches and the Race Question," *Christianity and Crisis*, Vol. 18, no. 3, March 3, 1958, pp. 17–28.

[11] Rembart G. Smith, *Politics in a Protestant Church*, Atlanta, 1930.

auxiliary groups are members who care only for the opportunity of fraternizing, taking little interest in other activities, content to let their lay leaders speak for them. These leaders speak often at the behest of members of the hierarchy who wish to express views on political and other secular activities from a platform other than the pulpit, through other, less-than-official voices. Conversely, in practically all dioceses, it is the custom to get clearance from the hierarchy before the Knights make pronouncements on secular subjects; only rarely does one find the policies of the Knights at variance with the stated policies of the Catholic Church. Illustrative of this relationship is an incident reported by Catholic Bishop Noll of Fort Wayne regarding a statement made by the *Chicago Tribune* about certain Catholic practices: "I asked him [the editor] to make a correction, but he didn't do that. So I published in the *Sunday Visitor* my letter to him, along with what the *Tribune* carried, and merely noted that the Catholic group in Chicago, constituting more than a million, might find it more profitable to patronize one of the other papers for the news. Then I wrote to the head of the United Holy Name Society in Chicago and asked him to make a protest in the name of 200,000 Holy Name men. He did it. Then I received a letter from the editor of the *Tribune* and he wanted an appointment. He came down to see me and apologized. . . ." [12]

Stirring up lay groups to political action is not entirely without risk for attainment of a church's goals. Many public officials have a distinct aversion to "do-gooders." As one state legislator stated the case shortly after receiving a group of prominent Protestant laymen who were advocating an anti-gambling measure, "I hate do-gooders. They are the biggest ingrates you can run across in political life. They have no understanding that politics is the art of compromise. If they only get 99 per cent of what they ask for, you are accused of

[12] National Catholic Welfare Conference, *Proceedings of the Meeting of Diocesan Directors Bureau of Information NCWC*, Washington, 1938, p. 11. Hereafter cited as *Proceedings*.

having sold out the cause. Do-gooders are idealogues who don't care who gets hurt as long as they get what they are asking for."[13] In addition, the violent language engendered by partisan religious passions frequently backfires. In one incident, Senator Elbert Thomas of Utah, a devout Mormon, took a position that was interpreted by Catholic groups as anti-Church. The resulting flood of letters, containing such vituperative terms as "atheist" and "communist" only served to stiffen his determination to maintain his original point of view.[14]

Another means of influencing political decisions is the use of the pulpit as a political rostrum. From the pulpit Jews have been urged to write to the State Department condemning the policy of shipping arms to Arab countries; Protestants have been urged to write or wire their congressmen to support the United Nations; and Catholics have been asked to vote "No" on a child-labor amendment to a state constitution. On occasion, following the great precedent of the Reverend Henry Ward Beecher's invitation to Abraham Lincoln to speak in the First Plymouth Church of Brooklyn (the famous address that was ultimately given at Cooper Union), politicians have been invited to use the pulpit for partisan addresses.

The religious press, maintained by all important denominations, has played an important role in influencing the political behavior of church members, and therefore, indirectly the behavior of office holders. Churches publish newspapers, periodicals, and pamphlets. Although the Catholic press gives a great deal of coverage to the issues of artificial birth control, aid to parochial schools, artificial insemination, mixed marriages, divorce, sterilization, and euthanasia, the Protestant press pursues a broader range of political interests and advocates many more measures. Another distinguishing characteristic between Catholic and Protestant efforts to influence political opinion through media of mass communications is the

[13] Witnessed by the author on the floor of the New Jersey State Legislature, Trenton, April 1955.

[14] Interview with Senator Thomas, Washington, June 1950.

greater Catholic vigilance over the content of the secular press. A century that saw the Know-Nothings, Nativists, A.P.A.'ers, K.K.K.'ers, and the campaign of 1928, did not bear strange fruit in producing an embattled Catholic group who were extremely sensitive at being a minority. As a result, the Catholic Church maintains ceaseless, unremitting pressure on the secular press to obtain what it feels is a fair deal. Over the course of years it has in general been successful. Open conflicts usually arise only during periods of special stress, such as the years following the 1928 presidential campaign.

Richard Reid, a prominent Catholic layman, has described a plan he helped to develop during this period to deal with misrepresentations in the secular press in Georgia: "We copied voting lists from various counties and we got telephone lists, and whenever a newspaper down there refused our material, we would prepare special material and send it out to all the people in that territory. We found, however, that that was rather expensive. We did it regardless of the expense, but we felt it could be done better through a newspaper. We thought we ought to have an organ of our own, and therefore we established our own publication. It was first a quarterly and then it became a monthly newspaper. A monthly newspaper is rather an anomaly, but nevertheless it is the best we can do down there, and we find it very effective. If an editor were to refuse to publish matter we sent in, we would put it in our paper and circulate it in his county." [15]

We should add that Jewish groups are no less vigilant in protesting remarks in the secular press that they interpret as misrepresentations of the Jewish point of view. The best illustration of similar steady pressure by Protestant groups is the continuous activity by temperance organizations to ban the channels of mass communications to the liquor industry.

Few churches try to limit their political messages to members only; most seek to broaden the base of support from outside groups. The moralistic tone of the formulation of political

[15] *Proceedings*, pp. 40–41.

issues by churches, forced upon them by the shadow of the wall of separation and the need for proving group relevance, frequently causes embarrassment in the search for allies. Presbyterians, Methodists, and Baptists have historically taken the leadership in well-organized groups seeking strict Sunday observance. Sixty years ago, these groups were isolating "swing" congressional districts (those in which the margin of victory was narrow) and sending incumbents harsh petitions. On the issue of forcing the Chicago World's Fair of 1893 to close on Sundays, one Protestant church resolved in a message to Congress: "We do hereby pledge ourselves and each other that we will from this time henceforth refuse to vote for or support for any office or position of trust any member of Congress, either Senator or Representative, who shall vote for any further aid of any kind of the World's Fair except on conditions named in these resolutions." [16] Today, similar Protestant groups proposing stricter Sunday observance laws at the local and state levels find themselves uncomfortably allied with downtown merchants fighting for economic survival with highway discount stores and shopping centers.

During the political controversy surrounding the Spanish Civil War, Catholic organizations sought Protestant allies to support the pro-Franco position. It was a source of embarrassment to many Catholics that Protestants were so difficult to recruit that refuge had to be taken in such anti-democratic disreputables as Joseph P. Kamp of the Constitutional Educational League, Clarence M. Penfield of the American Defenders Society, Merwin K. Hart of the New York State Economic Council, and Allen Zoll of the American Patriots.[17] Negro church groups fighting for civil rights have similarly been embarrassed on occasion by unwelcome alliances from far left groups.

There are many other aspects of church organization that

[16] Stokes, Vol. 2, pp. 153–176.

[17] *New York Times*, November 25, 1938. Interview with Edward J. Heffron, then secretary of the Keep the Spanish Embargo Committee, New York City, August 1950.

deserve at least passing mention. Churches vary in their coordinating skills—their abilities to bring together organizational resources in the most efficient manner. High tribute has been paid to both the Catholic Church and prohibition movements in regard to this skill. Another aspect is the varying ability of churches to adapt to changing conditions. Unless there are free lines of communication within churches that provide channels for bringing pertinent data to bear on the formulation of policies, strategies, and tactics for political activity, leaders will find themselves beating dead horses or struggling ineffectually to use techniques that should have been discarded years before.

This same organizational ability to adjust is important in maintaining a balance between various church goals. Viewed broadly, it would seem that Protestant churches with their preoccupation with prohibition and the Catholic Church with its preoccupation with anti-Communism suffered from imbalances. In the case of the former, it took many years before other moral issues were raised to the level of the great crusade.[18]

Paralleling political organization, churches are banded together on intradenominational, interdenominational, and interfaith bases in town and city councils, state and regional groups, and national councils. As might be expected, the national groups try to give leadership and guidance to affiliated units. How they do this, besides influencing national government, is the next part of this story.

Located in Washington, the American Catholic hierarchy's national organization is the National Catholic Welfare Conference (NCWC). In a nation lacking a Primate, this group serves as a coordinating body for the entire hierarchy. NCWC grew out of a Catholic coordinating council set up during the First World War. At the annual meetings of NCWC, Ameri-

[18] Paul A. Carter, *The Decline and Revival of the Social Gospel: Social and Political Liberalism in American Protestant Churches 1920–1940*, Ithaca, 1956, p. 129.

can bishops gather to discuss common problems and lay plans requiring interdiocesan cooperation. There, the Administrative Board of sixteen archbishops and bishops is elected by the hierarchy, the various activities of NCWC are reviewed, and plans laid for the next year. These activities cover such diverse fields as are suggested by some of the Department titles: Education, Press, Executive, Social Action, Legal, and Lay Organizations.[19]

NCWC engages in activities similar to other pressure groups in the nation's capital. Records of legislation passed and pending are maintained, and appropriate representations made to the branches of government on behalf of the Church. These representations take the shape of formal statements and appearances before legislative committees and administrative bodies, as well as informal conferences with public officials.[20] Since the total staff of NCWC, numbering over two hundred, is engaged in many other nonpolitical activities, sheer number is not indicative of the extent of political activity. On the other hand, the single individual, a member of the Legal Department, formerly registered as lobbyist for NCWC, is not an accurate reflection of resources either (NCWC has recently followed the lead of many of the Protestant groups in not registering anyone as a lobbyist).[21]

The Spanish Civil War controversy provides a good illustration of the interaction between NCWC, Congress, and the laity.[22] In January 1938, a group of Loyalist sympathizers went about the halls of Congress trying to get signatures to the following petition:

[19] *Catholic Action* (official journal of NCWC), December 1936. Stokes, Vol. 3, pp. 11–17.

[20] Luke Ebersole, *Church Lobbying in the Nation's Capital*, New York, 1950, pp. 106–113.

[21] Paul Blanshard, *God and Man in Washington*, Boston, 1960, pp. 100–102.

[22] Unless otherwise cited, the information regarding this particular incident comes from an *NCWC News Service Release*, February 4, 1938 by Burke Walsh and the author's interview with Mr. Walsh, Washington, D.C., June 1950.

"To the members of the Spanish Parliament, meeting in Barcelona, February 1, 1938:

"We the undersigned members of the Congress of the United States, are happy to send our greetings and good wishes to the Spanish parliament on the occasion of its regular session convened in accordance with the provisions of the constitution of 1931. For you to meet again in the face of the trying and tragic circumstances of the present, demonstrates that the Spanish people and their representatives stand firm in their faith in democratic government.

"We, who cherish freedom and democracy, above all else, realize the significance of your heroic and determined fight to save the democratic institutions of your young Republic from its enemies both within and without Spain. Your struggle is a stirring example to all democratic people."

Those circulating the petition avoided pro-Franco and stalwart Catholic legislators, "warming up" the petition by getting signatures of those known to be friendly to the Loyalists. Other Congressmen were informally approached and asked to sign. Reluctant legislators met with the argument that "This is just like the greeting sent to the Irish parliament a short time ago." When a legislator who was considered a likely prospect refused to sign, further effort was expended and appeals were made through intermediaries such as pro-Loyalist friends. Some legislators were asked to sign as often as three times, and signed on the third.[23]

The apparently final result of these efforts was a front-page story in the *New York Times* of January 31: twenty-six Senators and thirty-four Representatives had signed the greeting. Senatorial signatures represented all shades of political thought and party, including six Republicans and one Progressive in addition to the Democrats. Among the Representatives, only two Republicans and three Farmer-Laborites signed. Pro-Loyalists were jubilant about the public commitment of sixty

[23] Interview with Senator Elbert Thomas of Utah, June 1950.

members of the American legislature to sympathy with Republican Spain. Their joy was short-lived.

The very next day, Monsignor Michael J. Ready, general secretary of NCWC, condemned the message and expressed amazement at expressions of sympathy with a Communist regime which had committed grave crimes against the Church.[24] Throughout the Catholic press, the signers of the message were depicted as anti-Catholic. Catholic organizations like the National Catholic Alumni Federation joined the attack.[25] When, a week later, newspapers carried stories of legislators retracting their signatures or disavowing the use to which the message had been put, it appeared as if the Church had once more shown its political power.[26] Pro-Loyalist papers attacked this example of the tremendous pressure which the Church could exert, and students of the political scene could not fail to be impressed by a political power which could procure such seemingly abject apologies as that of Senator Prentiss M. Brown of Michigan who had "signed it without reading it . . . decided it was a mistake for me to do so . . . did not have sufficient knowledge of the situation in Spain to form any judgment." His colleague, Senator Clyde L. Herring of Iowa, retracted his signature because, "I had a misunderstanding when I signed it." Observers could only guess at the strength of the pressure which had brought about such reversals.

Although lacking in drama, what actually took place was highly enlightening. A correspondent from the NCWC News Service, Burke Walsh, had gone over to the Capitol and retraced the steps the Loyalist sympathizers had trod obtaining signatures. Walsh read Monsignor Ready's statement to the signers and asked each if he realized he was committing such a grave offense against millions of Catholic Americans. Each

[24] *Catholic Action*, February 1938, p. 5. *New York Times*, February 1, 1938.

[25] *New York Times*, February 4, 1938.

[26] *The Nation*, Vol. 146, February 12, 1938, p. 170.

was now squarely faced with a consideration of the consequences of his signing: sympathy for the Loyalists had to be weighed against very probable Catholic attacks. More than half of the signers recanted. Knowing the political power of the Church and having little intensity of feeling for Loyalist Spain, these recanting legislators made a practical decision. Senator Brown was not groveling when he made his statement; ingenuously, he merely stated the truth when he said that he had signed without reading. Others had signed with as little reflection, glancing through the message and seeing only safe symbols, or looking at the names of those who had already signed and following suit. Those who had signed in emulation of the Irish message were as quick to emulate the large group who disavowed any intention of favoring the Loyalists. Within a week, there were four retractions and twenty-six disavowals, with four more claiming that the message was intended only as a greeting to democracy. Seventeen repeated their sympathy for the Loyalists, five were inconclusive in their comments, and four had nothing to say.

Besides throwing light upon the loose way in which Congressmen formerly signed petitions, the disavowals show a distinct respect for the Church. Over and over, members of both Houses repeated that they had no idea the Church would be offended, and they would do nothing to cause the Church any offense. Some went out of their way to attack the Loyalists, and others denounced the menace of Communism as well. The full story was circulated by the NCWC News Service to the hundreds of Catholic publications where it was reprinted, and served as a focal point for the activities of thousands of auxiliary groups.

Seventeen Loyalist sympathizers were left to bear the brunt of Catholic ire. Led by members of the hierarchy and Catholic lay organizations, many thousands of protests were soon received by the seventeen from Catholics throughout the country and particularly from their constituencies. Signatories from districts where there were relatively few Catholics, such as

Senator Elbert Thomas of Utah, were upbraided by Catholic clergy outside the state.[27] Elsewhere, although Senator Claude Pepper of Florida had told Burke Walsh that he did not intend his signing to be taken as choosing sides, he was still attacked for having signed it in the first place. The bishop in St. Augustine lashed out at Senator Pepper and the heaviest protest mail came from that region.[28] Representative Fred H. Hildebrandt of South Dakota had made a declaration similar to Pepper's. Continued Catholic attack forced him to enter a further apology in the *Congressional Record*. He pointed out how he, as were many others in Congress, was being called upon by "certain groups in our constituencies" to explain his having signed the greeting. Representative Hildebrandt apologized for having signed and attacked the promoters of the greeting for alleged duplicity. He claimed that the second paragraph of the greeting had been added after he signed, without anyone's informing him of the change. Hildebrandt expressed regret that offense had been given those whose interest in Spain was greater than his own.[29]

Another entry in the *Congressional Record* reveals the weight of the pressure brought against the seventeen. Representative Usher L. Burdick of North Dakota, the seventh to retract his signature, had originally told Burke Walsh unequivocally, "I signed it. I knew what it was when I signed it, and I meant it that way." One month and many headaches later, Representative Burdick said, "I have signed nothing in Congress or out of it that has stirred up the ill-feeling that this petition caused. I heard from almost every State in the Union, and for the first time in three years, heard from North Dakota." Much of the pressure came in the form of protesting letters from personal friends. Representative Burdick was made to see the "religious nature of the struggle in Spain," and that by signing, "we were apt to start a religious controversy in

[27] Interview with Senator Thomas.

[28] Interview with Senator Pepper, Washington, D.C., June 1950.

[29] March 10, 1938, p. 959. *NCWC News Service Release*, March 12, 1938.

this country, and, in fact, that was the result that did follow." [30]

A final example will suffice as testimonial to the pervasiveness of Catholic influence in this incident. More than three months after the initial publication of the greeting, Senator Gerald P. Nye of North Dakota still felt called upon to explain his having signed, "To the extent that some have read into the statement an expressed sympathy for the cause of Communism, or against a religious faith, I repudiate my signature to it." [31]

Today, NCWC has a significant advantage in its ability to utilize special skills and talents over a sustained period. Experienced clergymen have worked alongside government officials for so long that a rapport is created out of common experience. When the Church has *ad hoc* opposition, its adversaries are often overwhelmed by the first-name relationship the clergyman has with key government officials such as legislative committee chairmen. Although Catholics will continue to be under-represented in Congress as long as agrarian areas are over-represented, there is always a sizable group within both Houses. In recent years, leadership on matters of interest to the Church was exercised in the House by Representative John W. McCormack of Massachusetts and in the Senate by Senator Joseph C. O'Mahoney of Wyoming. These men could usually be relied upon to give authentic versions of the Church position on controversial issues to fellow legislators, Catholic and non-Catholic, desiring these views.

Despite the heavy concentration of Catholics within the Democratic party and the role of Irish Catholics as leaders in Democratic urban machines, NCWC has maintained a remarkable freedom from partisan affiliation.[32] It has not escaped, however, charges of being a pawn in international politics, a tool of the Vatican. As we shall see, this internation-

[30] February 28, 1938, p. 800. *NCWC News Service Release,* March 1, 1938.

[31] *NCWC News Service Release,* May 9, 1938.

[32] Blanshard, *God and Man in Washington,* pp. 100–102.

alist charge has also been leveled at Protestant and Jewish groups. The origins of NCWC, however, give an ironic ring to these charges, for it was organized at a time (1919) when it seems to have been Papal policy to avoid the creation of strong national Church feelings among Catholics in this country. Coupled with the failure to appoint a Primate was an apparent Papal desire to see NCWC discontinue its activity after World War I. NCWC was permitted to continue, but only on a voluntary basis to make clear that there was no intention of constituting another authority between the bishops and the Vatican.[33]

The first Protestant lobby, according to the claim of its founder, Dr. Wilbur Fisk Crafts, was the International Reform Bureau. Started in 1895 with strong support from Methodists, Baptists, and certain Presbyterians, this organization was located in Washington, D.C., to represent vigorously "the attitude of conservative evangelical Christians toward current social problems" through acting as a self-styled "Christian lobby." Over the years, dozens of offices in Washington have been added by Protestant denominations. With typical Protestant diversity, they have ranged in the past from highly effective pressure-group operations to ineffectual information bureaus; from promoters of a host of social and economic measures to single-purpose advocates.

Leaving aside for the moment the single-purpose advocates, among the political offices maintained by major Protestant denominations have been, to name a few, the Council on Christian Social Progress of the Northern Baptist Convention, the Congregational Christian Council for Social Action, the Department of Social Welfare of the Disciples of Christ, the Friends Committee on National Legislation, the Division of Public Relations of the National Lutheran Council, the Women's Division of Christian Service of the Methodist

[33] Msgr. John A. Ryan, *Social Doctrine in Action*, New York, 1941, pp. 151–153. Teeling, *The Pope in Politics*, p. 150.

Church, the Christian Education Department of the African Methodist Episcopal Zion Church, and the Division of Social Education and Action of the Presbyterian Church in the United States of America. However much they may have differed in the past, the most striking feature of these non-fundamentalist organizations today is their similarity. Viewed broadly, their statements of goals and stands on major national issues show remarkable affinities; their central staff groups are comparable in being small; their operating methods are parallel.

As one might expect, size of denomination is directly related to church effort to influence national legislation. In 1947, three-fourths of the denominations with over one million members made organized efforts to influence legislation; in the denominations with five thousand to one hundred thousand members, only one-third did so.[34] What might not be expected, however, is the relative homogeneity of the positions taken on issues by participating denominations. The traditions of these churches regarding separation of church and state and the importance of individual redemption were such that most had taken no official position on broad social and economic problems (with the exception of the temperance issue) until well into the twentieth century. Other factors contributing to churches' avoiding social and economic programs were middle-class orientation in political attitudes and upper-class domination of church administration. In church after church, movements for social and economic reform led by individual clergymen or laymen were squelched by vestrymen or their equivalents, who, viewing society from a lofty perch of affluence and high status, could see no need for drastic changes. Nor can it be said that there was any loud clamor for active participation from the members of these churches—largely middle class in the white, Protestant churches outside the south.[35]

[34] Stokes, Vol. 3, p. 83.
[35] Carter, passim.

Today, after two world wars and a great economic depression, we witness general assemblies and general councils of churches adopting broad programs of social and economic reform almost identical in intent, urging disarmament, support of the United Nations, end of racial discrimination, extension of social security, provision for better housing, and so on. Against the resistance of tradition and vested interests, churches have been swept along by seemingly irresistible social, economic, and intellectual forces into abandoning their conservative positions. Even the staunchest resisters, the Lutherans—the last major Protestant denomination to remain aloof—have been caught up by the tide and are urging active political support of social measures.

The small size of central staffs for political activities in Washington offices of Protestant denominations—ranging from one person working part time to a half-dozen people working full time, including secretarial assistants—represents the concept of the job to be done rather than the extent of denominational resources. The Friends, with less than a hundred thousand members, maintain one of the largest staff groups—the Friends Committee on National Legislation—with three registered lobbyists. The Presbyterian Church of the United States of America, with over two million members, long operated with one part-time lobbyist.

The political sophistication of the staff members, however, varies greatly. Some are hardboiled veterans of temperance and pacifist crusades whose tenure in Washington exceeds that of most Congressmen and top-level administrators. Others are social workers chosen for their availability or ministers chosen because their church is located in the District of Columbia.[36] There is little evidence of any organized Protestant effort to recruit, select, and train personnel for political work at the national level. This is in sharp contrast to the personnel policies of NCWC.

Like NCWC and unlike industry and labor groups, Protes-

[36] Ebersole, pp. 24–42.

tant representatives do not usually put direct political pressure on Congressmen or administrators. Their emphasis is on mutual exchange of information—telling the church's position on issues and finding out and publicizing the stand of public officials. The telling may be done through the appearance of witnesses or the reading of statements at legislative and administrative hearings, or through the press and personal interviews. Finding out official views may be accomplished through analyzing the press and the *Congressional Record,* supplemented by personal interviews.[37]

The dissemination of this information through church periodicals, news letters, and talks to local, regional, and national groups, becomes a major function of political activity. Even if there is no specific call for pressure to be brought by church members on public officials, there is a continuous process of trying to shape attitudes and to modify political beliefs. In large measure, much of the activity of the national groups can be considered either as "purposeless" educating of the public or as keeping up the political "atmospheric pressure." In the latter sense, despite the avowed action program of many national groups, they seem charged largely with mobilization. These operating bureaucracies lay the organizational and ideological foundation for rapid mobilization of the members during crises or self-proclaimed emergencies. Without this prior preparation, the type of mobilization reported by Luke Ebersole as occurring during the struggle in 1948 over universal military training would not be possible. Presbyterians and other opponents of universal military training were hard at work to keep the legislation bottled up in committee when the alarm was sounded. A Republican strategy meeting was to be held shortly and a rough head count showed that the proponents of universal military training would probably succeed in bringing the bill out of committee. Previous work by church groups had revealed Representative Ross Rizley of Oklahoma to be a key man in

[37] Ebersole, pp. 74–113.

the situation. The operating bureaucracy went into action. The legislative secretary of the Presbyterian Division of Social Education and Action telephoned local division officers in Oklahoma. Springing to work, the local officials telephoned influential persons in Representative Rizley's district. Over the weekend he heard directly from them and their message was quite clear. As a result, the Republican strategy meeting was never held and the bill remained in committee.[38] It is safe to conclude that, without the years of indoctrination and public education about universal military training conducted by the Presbyterian Division of Social Education and Action, such rapid mobilization would not have been possible.

The efficiency displayed in this isolated mobilization incident by Presbyterians was the hallmark of the most powerful of the single purpose groups, the Anti-Saloon League. Resolute in their single-minded purpose, the Methodists and Baptists, with assistance from other Protestant groups, fashioned the League into a formidable political machine. For twenty years, more than fifteen per cent of all local churches in the United States were affiliated with the League in a tremendous grass-roots organization, administered at local, county, district, state, and national levels. Effective authority was centralized in the board of directors and executive committee. In a brutal struggle, with the liquor industry fighting for survival, the League perfected tactics to emerge triumphant. Publishing their own temperance material, they flooded the country with reams of effective propaganda. Their lobbyists prowled the halls of state legislatures and Congress, cajoling, coaxing, threatening. The chief threat of the League, one which they succeeded in making good on numerous occasions, was to alert its constituents to action at the polls. Disregarding party lines or record of performance in other governmental areas, a "wet" incumbent in Protestant areas was marked for removal from public life. With ample funds provided by the churches, and with use of churches as

[38] Ebersole, p. 89.

rallying points for political activity, the League was able to maintain a veto power over candidates in constituencies where the balance of power was held by the dry bloc.[39]

Another temperance group whose effectiveness was owing to the combination of zeal and organizational structure was the Methodist Board of Temperance, Prohibition, and Public Morals. Founded in 1916, the Board of Temperance paralleled the episcopal organization of the Methodist Church. The Board of Managers had representatives from each Episcopal area who could be relied upon to mobilize local churches. Although there was no official connection between the Board of Temperance and the Anti-Saloon League, the Methodists leading both groups have received major credit for achieving the high point of the temperance movement, passage of the Eighteenth Amendment to the Constitution.[40]

Symbolic of the Protestant advance from preoccupation with temperance to concern with scores of social and economic issues is the National Council of Churches of Christ. After fifteen years of planning, the National Council was formed in 1950 through the integration of twelve interdenominational organizations including the Federal Council of Churches. Represented in this new coordinative body were twenty-eight Protestant and Eastern Orthodox denominations, each retaining its power of independent action.[41] The National Council continues many of the activities of the Federal Council, including the Washington office that had been started in 1945. Today this office still serves as an information bureau for the National Council located in New York City. The Washington staff of three executives and three secretaries operates within the original proscription not "to make decisions regarding policy for the Churches." The staff issues legislative summaries without editorializing and serves as a guide "to interested persons of proper channels

39 Odegard, passim.
40 Stokes, Vol. 2, pp. 328–344.
41 Landis, p. 427.

for contacts in Washington and furnishing facilities for effecting such contacts when desired." The direct political activities of the National Council, therefore, are minimal.[42]

Indirectly, however, the National Council contributes to the political scene through what one opponent has decried as "the taking of sides in controversial political, economic and social issues." The importance of National Council pronouncements is derived largely from its massive base, a Council denominational membership of thirty-eight million persons. Despite the need for finding a common denominational denominator acceptable to constituent bodies, the National Council has succeeded in developing a broad social program similar to that previously described as common to most major Protestant denominations. In addition, the National Council has worked with the World Council of Churches as part of the ecumenical movement.

Both the domestic and international policies of the National Council have resulted in sharp, continuous attacks from interdenominational, fundamentalist groups originally established as anti-Federal Council bodies. Groups such as the American Council of Christian Churches, the National Association of Evangelicals, and the International Council of Christian Churches have frequently used political platforms to oppose the National Council, appearing at congressional committee hearings to attack the National Council's integrity or to support measures opposed by the Council and vice versa.[43]

In 1960 the ferocity of the fundamentalist attack and their willingness to use political tools were laid bare by a rather bizarre episode. Discovery was made that an official Air Force training manual contained allegations that the National Council had been infiltrated by Communists, citing as evidence the charge that thirty of ninety-five ministers involved in the drafting of a new Bible text had subversive or Com-

[42] Stokes, Vol. 3, pp. 10–11.
[43] Ebersole, pp. 43–47.

munist leanings. Further investigation revealed that much of the controversial material in the training manual came from the pen of an Oklahoma evangelist, Billy James Hargis. Extracts had been taken from two pamphlets written by Hargis, the tenor of which is shown by their titles: *The National Council of Churches Indicts Itself in Fifty Counts of Treason against God and Country*, and *Is the National Council of Churches Subversive?* The question raised by the last tract was answered with a resounding "Yes" by all three fundamentalist groups in the controversy in the press that followed for weeks.[44]

Although there are, undoubtedly, theological issues in the dispute between the modernist National Council and the fundamentalist groups, political issues play a prominent role. In defense of the National Council, the Reverend Edwin T. Dahlberg, President, charged that any prominent clergyman taking a stand on race, disarmament, halting nuclear bomb tests, or "even on strengthening the United Nations runs the risk of being called soft on Communism."[45]

It should be mentioned that within the major Protestant denominations, similar charges of pro-Communism have been leveled by vociferous minorities. The Reverend Dahlberg's statement has wider application than the limited controversy over the misbegotten Air Force training manual.

Jews constitute an ethnic-religious minority in a predominantly Protestant society. While Judaism has succeeded in placing its imprint in varying degrees upon the spirit and values of the Jewish group in America, non-religious factors have also been extremely significant. Minority consciousness, national origin, philosophic traditions (admittedly with a religious foundation), and historical heritage have tended to outweigh and overshadow any political activity directed by the synagogues for national associations of clergymen. So

[44] *New York Times*, February 19, 1960.
[45] *New York Times*, February 26, 1960.

deep are the shadows that it was possible in 1956 for an acute scholar, Lawrence H. Fuchs, to write a book, *The Political Behavior of American Jews*, a historical account of the political behavior of American Jews since colonial times, with an intensive study of Jewish voting in recent elections, that gives practically no mention of any church participation.[46]

On the other hand, there is no absence of Jewish national religious organizations—Orthodox, Conservative, and Reform—and they are as open as Protestant groups in taking positions on national issues. They do not maintain Washington offices on a permanent basis, but with such articulate spokesmen as Representative Emanuel Celler of New York, their views are heard. Although Zionism in its infancy faced opposition from the Right of orthodoxy and the Left of reform and labor, the period after World War I saw Zionism providing a coalescing political issue as the growing movement encompassed greater numbers of clergy and laymen. By the end of World War II, developments in Europe had united clergymen and laymen in virtual unanimity regarding Zionism for, as Oscar Handlin reported: "These developments induced the Jewish labor movement in America to espouse Zionism, pushed the reform wing of Judaism into a position of official neutrality and unofficial support, and strengthened orthodox approval. After 1945, American Jews stood almost solidly behind the Zionists. Only a relatively small group in the American Council for Judaism thereafter remained apart."[47] Also active in political affairs are such groups as the American Jewish Committee, the American Jewish Congress, and the Anti-Defamation League of B'nai B'rith.[48]

[46] Lawrence H. Fuchs, *The Political Behavior of American Jews*, Glencoe, Ill., 1956.

[47] Oscar Handlin, *Adventure in Freedom*, New York, 1954, pp. 168–171, 216–219. Abraham G. Duker, "The Impact of Zionism on American Jewry," in Theodore Friedman and Robert Gordis, eds., *Jewish Life in America*, New York, 1955, pp. 301–321.

[48] Blanshard, *God and Man in Washington*, pp. 43–44.

Having set out to trace the form of church participation in politics, we must now face some of the problems raised by this participation. It should be apparent from the existing diffusion of political power and the stalemates resulting from groups exercising veto power (witness the fifteen-year deadlock over federal aid to education) that the formal problem of separation of church and state (in the sense of an established church) has long been settled and is no real problem today. Further, there is no compelling necessity for defining the extent to which churches should engage in political activity. Cultural autonomy allows churches to determine their own limits of political action.

Churches, however, should realize that political activity incurs certain responsibilities and limitations. A church should be willing to be identified with its political program and face political opposition without seeking religious immunity by uttering cries of bigotry and persecution. A church engaging in political activity should consider the consequences of injecting a highly charged and dogmatic religious atmosphere into the more compromising sphere of political dealings. A church runs the risk of bringing about the defeat of its political program, regardless of merit, because its participation in politics may arouse the great irrational residue of antagonism among religious groups that slumbers in American society.

Considering the events of the last century, people who expect church participation in politics to bring about the millennium must be bitterly disappointed. Political action by churches has had about the same influence as has woman suffrage on bringing society closer to perfection. Utopians may still hope that churches will achieve social transformation through political action, but this seems unrealistic in the light of exploding nuclear weapons. If ever there was a complex social issue with moral overtones tailor-made for churches, it has been the use of atomic energy. In the fifteen years following Hiroshima, churches have proved no more effective than other social institutions in keeping society from marching closer to the brink of extinction.

We may expect churches to continue to participate in the political process in order to protect themselves from detrimental governmental action, to advance their own interests, and to promote general welfare measures. Churches may well develop more expertness and perfect new techniques of participation. They are caught, however, in the complex web of being but one among many social institutions, which renders their political influence less effective.

THE RELIGIOUS NOVEL AS BEST SELLER IN AMERICA

WILLARD THORP

FOR well over a century religious fiction has been a staple of the book trade in this country. Nearly every fall and spring list has contained at least one best seller, telling over again, with variations, the life of Christ or presenting dramatic episodes from the Old or New Testament or describing the woes and rewards of Christian's journey through this sinful world.[1] For many Americans, even for those who

[1] The terms "religious" and "best seller" need to be defined. By "religious novel" I intend any piece of fiction whose *main* concern is to present a sermon in the guise of a story (mere piety is not enough). The action must turn on the effect the Christian message has on the lives of the characters. Actually, among the scores of novels which qualify under this definition two main types have persisted: those which deal with the fervor and excitement of the early days of Christianity (or the great moments of Jewish history which prefigure the coming of the Messiah), and those which show what it means to be a Christian in modern times. There is an insatiable desire to hear the Christ-story told over and over again, with the theological coloring best suited to the new generation of readers. Of course, much more variety has been possible in the other type of novel. In the middle of the last century the hero or heroine struggles to resolve his doubts about the question of Calvinistic orthodoxy *vs.* the religion of love; by 1900 he or she was worrying about how one might put the teachings of Christ into practice. Could the Social Gospel be made to work? What would Christ do if He came to Chicago?

Defining "best seller" or "better seller" for the purpose of this chapter is an easier matter. In the main I have used the lists compiled by Frank Luther Mott in the Appendix to his *Golden Multitudes. The Story of Best Sellers in the United States*, New York, 1947. Each book in his list of best sellers "is believed to have had a total sale equal to one per cent of the population of continental United States . . . for the decade in which it was published." Mott's better sellers "are the runners-up believed not to have reached the total sales required for the over-all best sellers." I have also had recourse to the list of books "most widely read in America" drawn up by James D. Hart in his *The Popular Book. A History of America's Literary Taste*, New York, 1950.

Strangely enough, the best seller limitation of this chapter excludes one kind of religious novel which flourished in the 1850's and 1860's, the sectarian novel. These novels which defend and propagandize for Methodism or Unitarianism, the anti-Catholic novels (of which there were many), and the attempts made by Catholic writers to parry these attacks, though they were numerous, did not become best sellers. The explanation is probably simple enough. The Catholics did not read the Methodist novels and the have never read one of these novels, the titles of the most successful produce some kind of reverberation when they are named. In 1942, *The Robe;* in 1913, *The Inside of the Cup;* in 1897, *In His Steps;* in 1888, *John Ward, Preacher;* in 1880, *Ben-Hur;* in 1873, *Barriers Burned Away;* in 1868, *The Gates Ajar;* in 1855, *The Prince of the House of David.* These and scores besides have gone up attic, but they still crowd the shelves in secondhand bookshops and public libraries. Very few of them achieved distinction in plot, theme, or style. In some the actions of the characters are preposterous; in others there are pages of undigested moralizing or theologizing. But we must remember that they were best sellers for a reason: they brought light and comfort to an untold number of readers. The piety in them is genuine. Many of them were written by clergymen who were converting their most dramatic sermons into novels. Even those Americans who still believed, late in the nineteenth century, that novel-reading was a frivolous and possibly debilitating pastime felt perfectly safe with the Rev. E. P. Roe's *Barriers Burned Away* or the Rev. Charles M. Sheldon's *In His Steps.*

As the religious novels gained in popularity, and some of them proved to be fantastically successful, the novelists evolved new themes to suit each new generation, or remade old ones. A discernible pattern of development through the nineteenth and well into the twentieth century can be made out. It is this pattern which I shall try to trace in my discussion of the novels themselves.

I. The Early Christians in a Pagan World

The first religious novel to qualify as a best seller would seem to be the Rev. William Ware's *Letters of Lucius M. Piso, from Palmyra to his Friend Marcus Curtius at Rome,* published in 1837. A second edition, retitled *Zenobia; or,*

Unitarians didn't read the Catholic novels. To become a best seller a religious novel had to possess a generalized and not a sectarian piety.

The Fall of Palmyra, was required in 1838. By 1850 there had been eight editions.

Ware (1797–1852) was the son of the Hollis Professor of Divinity at Harvard and was himself ordained as a Unitarian minister in 1821. His first pastorate was that of the newly established Unitarian church in New York City. Finding himself temperamentally unsuited for the ministry—he later suffered from epilepsy—Ware looked about for another profession. In the year he left the church, 1836, he began contributing to the *Knickerbocker Magazine* installments of his first novel. *Zenobia* purports to be a series of letters from a high-born Roman, Lucius M. Piso, to his friend Marcus Curtius in Rome. He has traveled to the wealthy and beautiful city of Palmyra, where Queen Zenobia reigns on sufferance of the Emperor Aurelian, in search of a captive brother who is thought to be still alive. In no time at all Lucius is a member of the court circle where he falls under the spell of the great Queen, renowned for her charm, her interest in philosophy and religion, and her cultivation of the arts. Zenobia's daughter Julia has begun to take instruction in Christian doctrine from the Bishop of Antioch and from a holy hermit who talks like a Unitarian saint. She argues at great length with the philosopher Longinus who would like to believe in the immortality of the soul but, tolerant though he is, can scarcely bring himself to listen to Julia's defense of the Christian revelation. To Longinus' objection that there is no clear voice from Christianity and that Christians are already disputing among themselves, Julia offers irrefutable Unitarian replies.

These religious debates are interrupted by Aurelian's march on Palmyra (Zenobia has been taking too much power to herself). We live through her capture and the sack of the city, then move on to Rome to witness Aurelian's triumph.[2] But

[2] Ware agrees with Gibbon that this is the most magnificent triumph Rome had ever seen. And well he might, since he is using Gibbon's account of it in *The Decline and Fall* for many of his details.

all's well in the end. Aurelian bestows a magnificent villa on Zenobia. The love affair between Lucius and Julia prospers, and a Christian wedding for them is in the offing.

In *Probus; or, Rome in the Third Century,* the sequel to *Zenobia* which followed in 1838, Lucius Piso keeps on with his incessant letter-writing, this time with correspondents in Palmyra. The Christian Pisos prosper for a while, spending much of their time trying to convert their Roman friends to abolitionism and democracy as well as Christianity. But the capricious Aurelian turns cruel again and under Fronto the persecution of the Christians begins. Their leader, Probus, who had been permitted to deliver a twenty-five page sermon before Aurelian, is condemned to be devoured by lions. Three in succession refuse to eat him and "an hundred fierce tenants of the vivaria" have to be let loose to finish the job. Aurelian had promised that no harm would come to the Pisos but when he is absent, Fronto arrests them and Julia narrowly escapes the rack. Aurelian, fortunately, is murdered and the gentle Tacitus succeeds him.

II. The Christ Appears

With his third, and last, novel, *Julian; or, Scenes in Judea* (1841), Ware found the plot which was to become perennial with the religious novelists—the unbeliever who hears about Christ's disturbing presence among the Jews, then comes to Judea to converse with those who have seen Him perform miracles, and, finally, in the climactic moment, beholds the Christ. This—the "greatest story ever told"—will, so it seems, bear retelling indefinitely. Ware had found what was to be the best formula of all.

His hero is Julian, a Jew who has been brought up in Rome as a Roman. On a visit to Judea he discovers that he is a Jew at heart and joins his people. He hears much of John the Baptist and of Jesus. Hoping for a sight of the new prophet, he goes to the Sea of Galilee. Jesus has left the region but

Julian talks with fishermen who were companions of the disciples. Most of them feel that Jesus is sent of God but cannot be the Messiah since he preaches peace. Julian finally sees Jesus during the entry into Jerusalem. Here is Ware's climactic scene, how many times to be repeated with variations!

"I cannot well describe my sensations as Jesus drew nigh, so that I could with distinctness observe his countenance and form, but they were such as I never before experienced in the presence of a mortal; and it could not well be otherwise, as I doubted not that I looked upon one within whom were lodged the very power and wisdom of Jehovah. Awe and dread were therefore the feelings that would have alone prevailed, were it not that, however wonderfully I felt he was united to God, I saw that the language of his countenance was not that of an angel, nor of a God, but of a man, bound like myself, by the closest ties to every one of the multitudes who thronged him. Its expression was mild and pitiful; but at the same time of one who, if full of regard and compassion for each and for all, also possessed the energies and the will to do for those whom he loved whatsoever should be needful for their advantage or redemption. Strength and power were lodged in the lines and forms of the face, not any less than benevolence, giving ample assurance that there were inward forces of intellect and will, equal to every work that might be given to him to do. . . . While the innumerable multitude of those who encompassed him, and hailed him King and Deliverer, and could find no words of joy in which to give vent to the hopes that were within, he rejoiced not, but was evidently sad. The sight of the city with its populace all awaiting him and the sounds of their tumultuous cries as they were borne to us from afar, and the waving of their hands in token of welcome, seemed to awaken no feeling of triumph in his heart, but, instead, drew forth tears. I confess that I was also astonished; and could only say, the whole of this man is mysterious and impenetrable—we know him not—we do not comprehend what he is, nor what he has come to do."

Though Julian is deeply moved by what he has seen and later by the accounts of the Crucifixion and the Resurrection, he remains faithful to Judaism. The signs and wonders doubtless proved Jesus to be "a messenger and prophet of God, at the same time that they failed to prove him the Messiah who had been foretold, for whom Israel had waited so long, and still waits."

Ware's *Julian* pointed the way to future success with the Christ-story in novel form but his Unitarianism held him back from a full-organ use of the theme. Fourteen years later another clergyman, the Rev. Joseph Holt Ingraham, showed what a devout believer in the divinity of Christ, who was also a professional novelist, could make of it. His *The Prince of the House of David* (1855) is one of America's fabulously best-selling novels. After the copyright expired in the 1880's many cheap editions came on the market, including the Street and Smith edition at ten cents. It was a great favorite in Sunday School libraries and as a gift book.

Ingraham (1809–1860) led a life which was almost as full of adventure as that of any of his heroes. He went to sea when he was still a boy and is said to have played a part in a South American revolution. It is possible that he graduated from Bowdoin College, though the record is not clear. He early found that he could support himself by turning out sensation novels at an incredible rate of speed. By the end of 1851 he had written more than eighty, with such indicative titles as *Captain Kyd; or, The Wizard of the Sea; Frank Rivers; or, The Dangers of the Town. A Story of Temptation, Trial, and Crime;* and *Lafitte; the Pirate of the Gulf* (one of his earliest and most successful).[3] At the age of forty-two Ingraham be-

[3] Longfellow recorded this in his journal, under the date of April 6, 1846. "In the afternoon, Ingraham the novelist called. A young, dark man, with soft voice. He says he has written eighty novels, and of these twenty during

came an Episcopal clergyman. He settled finally in Holly Springs, Mississippi, as rector of Christ Church. The urge to write fiction would not down, but after his ordination he changed course decidedly. His principal later production was a group of three religious novels, the aim of which was "to draw the attention of those who seldom open the Bible to that sacred volume, by unfolding to them the beauty, riches, eloquence, and grandeur of the Holy Scriptures." The first in the series was *The Prince of the House of David; or, Three Years in the Holy City*. The two which followed are: *The Pillar of Fire; or, Israel in Bondage* (1859) and *The Throne of David, from the Consecration of the Shepherd of Bethlehem, to the Rebellion of Prince Absalom* (1860). Ingraham's grandson reported that the novelist-turned-priest spent much time and money trying to buy up the copyrights of his earlier novels in order to stop their republication.

No wonder Sunday School readers were entranced by *The Prince of the House of David*. Its glimpses of the lives of the followers of Jesus are irresistible. Adina, a young Jewess from Cairo on a visit to Jerusalem, reports in letters to her father the events of Jesus' life from the time of his Baptism to the Ascension. She certainly gets around! An intimate of the house of Mary and Martha, she has her ears open to all the pious gossip about Christ's acts and words. She is always on the edge of the crowds which follow Him and she takes a front seat on such spectacular occasions as the raising of Lazarus and the Crucifixion. We wait, with mounting excitement, for the expected moment when Adina first sees Jesus. She tells her father in Letter VII (her trembling fingers scarcely able to hold the light reed with which she writes) that "Messias has come! I have seen Him! I have heard His

---

the last year; till it has grown to be merely mechanical with him. These novels are published in the newspapers. They pay him something more than three thousand dollars a year." *Life of Henry Wadsworth Longfellow. With Extracts from his Journals and Correspondence*, edited by Samuel Longfellow, Boston, 1886, Vol. II, p. 35.

voice." But we must read on through two letters extending to thirty pages before the moment is revealed. Adina witnesses the baptism of Jesus and hears John cry out, "Behold Him who taketh away the transgressions of men." Having set the stage, Ingraham brings on his purple prose.

"No sooner did the baptized stranger go up out of the water, than there was heard above all our heads a noise as of rolling thunder, although the sky was cloudless; and when in great fear we looked up, we beheld a dazzling glory far brighter than the sun; and from the midst of this celestial splendor there darted with arrowy velocity a ray of light which descended and lit upon the head of the Christ. Some of the people said it thundered! and others that it lightened! but judge the amazement and admiration of all, the dread awe that shook every soul when, amid the glory above His head, was seen the form of a dove of fire, with outspread wings overshadowing Him as it were; and from the heavens what was supposed to be thunder, shaped itself into a voice, which uttered these words in the hearing of every ear:

" 'THIS IS MY BELOVED SON IN WHOM I AM WELL PLEASED.' "

In spite of her father's cautionary advice, Adina becomes an ardent Christian and she is soon at work trying to convert him. Surely he will doubt no longer when he understands the true meaning of Christ's last days on earth. If anything He spoke were not true, "either concerning the Father or concerning Himself, He would not have received such a welcome back to the heavenly abodes."

"Doubt, then, no longer, dearest father! Jesus, the *son of Mary* in his human nature, was the SON OF GOD in his Divine nature; an incomprehensible and mysterious union, whereby He has brought together in harmony the two natures, separated far apart by sin, by sacrificing his own body as a sin-offering, to reconcile both in *one* Immaculate body upon the cross. There is now no more condemnation to them who believe in Him and accept Him; for in his body He took our sins, and with his precious blood, as that of a lamb without blemish, cleansed them forever away."

One can scarcely imagine that any later novelist could surpass Ingraham's *The Prince of the House of David* in presenting the Christ-story with all the resources of sentiment, pathos, and melodrama. But General Lew Wallace (1827–1905), also a professional novelist, accomplished this in 1880 with *Ben-Hur, A Tale of the Christ.* No religious novel has ever equaled it in popularity.[4] By 1936, so Wallace's biographer Irving McKee reports, it had "earned the greatest material reward ever meted out to the owner of an American novel."

Wallace had shrewdly imagined that the Christ-story needed a world setting to bring out its full possibilities in fiction. His hero is a young Jewish patrician who is wrongly accused by Messala of trying to kill the Roman governor Gratus by "flinging a tile upon his head from the roof of a palace." So off to the galleys with him. He escapes to Rome where he is adopted by the tribune Arrius as his son. At last his chance for revenge on Messala arrives when they are pitted against each other in the chariot race in the Circus at Antioch. Everyone knows how the crowds shouted for their favorite, how the betting rose higher and higher, how Ben-Hur's Arab steeds carried him closer and closer to the winning Messala. Then the crash of wheel on axle. Messala is trampled by the Arabs. Ben-Hur is the winner.

The chariot race finished off (five chapters are needed to

[4] The primary source of information about the origins of *Ben-Hur* and the circumstances of its publication is *Lew Wallace. An Autobiography,* New York, 1906. The chapter on the novel in Irving McKee's *"Ben-Hur" Wallace. The Life of General Lew Wallace,* Berkeley, 1947, is very detailed and is especially valuable for its full account of the remarkable course of the stage-version of *Ben-Hur.* For all one knows there may still be some road company barnstorming in the provinces with the five chariots which were first introduced in the 1906–1907 season.

get in all the details), Wallace turned his attention to Jesus and His share in Ben-Hur's life. (We have been getting news of Him intermittently from the beginning.) Once again the climactic moment when the hero beholds the Lord Jesus is the Baptism.

"In this time, it should be remembered, Ben-Hur was studying the face of the stranger, though with an interest entirely different [from Balthazar's]. He was not insensible to its purity of feature, and its thoughtfulness, tenderness, humility, and holiness; but just then there was room in his mind for but one thought—Who is this man? And what? Messiah or king? Never was apparition more unroyal. Nay, looking at that calm, benignant countenance, the very idea of war and conquest, and lust of dominion, smote him like a profanation."

Ben-Hur suddenly realizes that he has seen this face before.

"Faintly at first, at last a clear light, a burst of sunshine, the scene by the well at Nazareth that time the Roman guard was dragging him to the galleys returned, and all his being thrilled. Those hands had helped him when he was perishing. The face was one of the pictures he had carried in mind ever since. In the effusion of feeling excited, the explanation of the preacher was lost by him, all but the words—words so marvellous that the world yet rings with them:

" '*—this is the* SON OF GOD!' "

Ben-Hur has need of Christ's ministrations. His mother and sister have become lepers, but their affliction is cured by an unrecorded miracle. Ben-Hur is privileged to be an eyewitness of the Crucifixion. By this time, inevitably, he has become a Christian. His estate is returned to him and he later devotes it to all kinds of Christian good works, including the embellishment of the Catacomb of San Calixto, from which "vast tomb Christianity issued to supersede the Caesars."

Trying to give a synopsis of *Ben-Hur* is like trying to condense an encyclopedia. This brief review cannot suggest the varieties of life presented—Jewish, Roman, Antiochan, Christian—the hordes of people who crowd in from every part of the ancient world, the clash of characters and the opposed religious arguments, the descriptions of cities renowned in antiquity, the exotic rooms, gardens, terraces, streets, lakes, arenas, palaces—and above all the Holy Places with which General Wallace furnished his novel. Later users of the Christ-story in fiction must have hesitated, remembering the competition *Ben-Hur* would give them. Certainly Elizabeth Stuart Phelps Ward and Herbert D. Ward in *Come Forth* (1890)—the Lazarus story—Sholem Asch in *The Nazarene* (1939), though they were successful with the theme, did not attempt the all-inclusiveness of Wallace's novel. Two recent novels, Lloyd Douglas' *The Robe* (1942) and Taylor Caldwell's *Dear and Glorious Physician* (1959), imitate the *Ben-Hur* all-the-world formula but they lack the skill of the master in controlling masses of detail.

When the General began *Ben-Hur* he was merely in search of a sure subject. (Wasn't the Bible the best seller of all times?) He seems to have been converted by the scenes he created, for he later declared in print that the writing of *Ben-Hur* brought him a "conviction amounting to absolute belief in God and the divinity of Christ." The immediate impulse was a conversation with Robert G. Ingersoll in 1876, in which the celebrated atheist surpassed himself in a "pungent excoriation of believers in God, Christ, and Heaven." Wallace resolved to answer Ingersoll by means of the novel about a young patrician Jew on which he was at work.

Ben-Hur was completed in 1880, seven years after it was begun. The sales were not immediately encouraging. Perhaps Mr. Joseph Henry Harper's fears lest the bold introduction of the Savior might be too indelicate were going to be realized. In the first seven months only 2,800 copies were sold. Then came a decline. By the end of 1882 sales were up to

300 a month and increasing. Up and up they went, until, by the end of 1889, 400,000 copies had been sold. In 1911 the one million mark was passed and the novel had been pirated in at least a dozen foreign countries. In 1944 Harpers estimated that at least 2,500,000 copies had been sold but there was, of course, no way of computing the actual total. Possibly the strongest testimony to the power of *Ben-Hur*, aside from these staggering sales figures, is the line of imitations it touched off. At least eight appeared between 1891 and 1906, including three that were famous in their own right: Whyte-Melville's *The Gladiators* (1893), Marie Corelli's *Titus, a Comrade of the Cross* (1900), and Florence Kingsley's *Paul of Tarsus* (1902).[5] Possibly the strangest tribute *Ben-Hur* received was the edition put out by Professor Henry Salvadori, honorary chaplain to Pope Leo XIII. The Professor had to introduce "various modifications of ideas into the work in the interests of piety" but his Holiness commended him for his labors.[6] The most gratifying tribute was Sears, Roebuck's print order, in 1913, for a million copies to sell at 39 cents each. *Books in Print, 1958* lists eight editions of *Ben-Hur* as still available.

III. Practical Piety, with Some Conversions

During the 1850's and 1860's an avalanche of pious novels descended on the American public. Though piety is persistent

[5] McKee, p. 175.

[6] *Lew Wallace. An Autobiography*, II, 941.

As this essay was being completed (February, 1960) William Wyler's production of the newest *Ben-Hur* was just beginning to reap the millions it is supposed to return for the $15,000,000 Metro-Goldwyn-Mayer spent on the production. Other millions have gone into one of the most expensive promotion campaigns in the history of Hollywood. There are Roman armor kits, "scooter-type" chariots, Ben-Hur T-shirts, chocolates, bathrobes, footwear, ladies' handbags, and costume jewelry sold in the theaters and other outlets—something for every age and taste. Hollywood intends that this *Ben-Hur*, seven years in the making, shall be the most popular movie ever made. As the reviews appear, it begins to look as if the critics may agree that it is also the best of all the Bible-fiction pictures.

—and usually triumphant—in them, not many qualify as religious novels as I am using the term; that is to say, the crux of the action is not the effect which the Christian message has on the lives of the characters.[7] For example, Maria S. Cummins' *The Lamplighter*, which was a best seller in 1854, suggests in its opening chapters that religion will be the theme throughout. Little Gerty is rescued from the slums by the kind-hearted lamplighter, Trueman Flint, and is taken, after his death, into the home of a benevolent lady who had been accidently blinded in her youth. Gerty has learned from Uncle True how to be a Christian. "Perhaps, in his practice of Christian virtues, and especially in his obedience to the great law of Christian charity, he more nearly approached to the spirit of his Divine Master than many who by daily reading and study are far more familiar with Christian doctrine." When we read this on page 55, we feel certain that something momentous will come of Uncle True's teachings. Will Gerty's piety become a force in the world? Will she marry a minister and become a comfort to his flock, healing the sick and praying at deathbeds? Far from it. *The Lamplighter* turns out to be a middle class success story. We are even introduced to wealth and fashion in the end. But the interspersed piety must have helped the sales to climb to 40,000 in eight weeks.

At least two able writers of the day expressed their abhorrence of this goody-goody fiction. Hawthorne wrote to his publisher in 1855 that he had decided to stay in Europe. One of his reasons is his disgust with the American reading public.

"America is now wholly given to a d—d mob of scribbling women, and I should have no chance of success while the public is occupied with their trash—and should be ashamed of myself if I did succeed. What is the mystery of these innumerable

[7] There is an excellent discussion of these pious novels in Herbert Ross Brown's *The Sentimental Novel in America, 1789–1860*, Durham, 1940, ch. v, "Stepping Heavenward."

editions of the 'Lamplighter,' and other books neither better nor worse?—worse they could not be, and better they need not be, when they sell by the 100,000." [8]

When Charles Kingsley wrote *Water-Babies*, in 1863, he made Tom see in the course of his journey

"all the little people in the world, writing all the little books in the world, about all the other little people in the world; probably because they had no great people to write about: and if the names of the books were not Squeeky, nor the Pumplighter, nor the Narrow Narrow World, nor the Hills of the Chattermuch, nor the Children's Twaddeday, why then they were something else. And all the rest of the little people in the world read the books, and thought themselves each as good as the President; and perhaps they were right, for every one knows his own business best. But Tom thought he would sooner have a jolly good fairy tale, about Jack the Giant-killer or Beauty and the Beast, which taught him something that he didn't know already." [9]

A few of the best sellers in this group of novels can, however, be called religious. Two, especially, fall neatly into place, one at the beginning of this season of piety, the other at the end: Susan Warner's *The Wide, Wide World* (1851)

[8] Caroline Ticknor, *Hawthorne and His Publisher*, Boston, 1913, pp. 140–141.

[9] The passage needs a gloss. Kingsley is alluding to several of the novels written by the "damned mob of scribbling women." "Squeeky" is Susan Warner's *Queechy* (1852), popular in England as well as America. The "Pumplighter" is, of course, *The Lamplighter*. The "Narrow Narrow World" is Miss Warner's *The Wide, Wide World* (1851) and the "Hills of the Chattermuch" is *The Hills of the Shatemuc* (1856), also by Susan Warner. "Children's Twaddeday" must be Kingsley's invention.

Kingsley also wrote to *his* publisher about these lady novelists, saying he could not abide them because of "their execrable goody-goody-ness,—the insipid respectability (utterly untrue to life) of their personages, who make up for want of character and want of action by endless analysis of little dirty commonplace motives." C. L. Graves, *Life and Letters of Alexander Macmillan*, London, 1910, p. 93.

and Mrs. Elizabeth Payson Prentiss' *Stepping Heavenward* (1870).

Susan Warner (1819–1885) and her sister Anna, also a novelist, were faithful attendants at the Mercer Street Presbyterian Church in New York. Later, when they were living on Constitution Island, opposite West Point, Miss Susan's Sunday Bible class for privileged cadets was the great event in their lives at the Point. One of "Miss Warner's boys" has left a record of the sessions.

"After each of the boys had read a Bible verse Miss Warner, choosing her subject from some New Testament text, talked to them for perhaps half an hour until her enthusiasm and interest had obviously almost exhausted her small strength. Her English was the best and purest I have ever heard, and as she went on and her interest grew her eyes shone like stars and her voice became rich and warm. There was never any cant or sectarianism, and she always gave to the boys the brightest and most optimistic side of the faith she loved so well."

When Miss Susan finished her talk, Miss Anna "came down from the house with the rare treat of the whole week, tea and homemade gingerbread." [10]

Mr. Warner had had reverses and the sisters felt obliged to help out in some way. Aunt Fanny suggested that Susan write a story. (The sisters never referred to their books as novels.) And so *The Wide, Wide World* was begun, Anna giving the story its name.

Of plot there is almost none. Little Ellen Montgomery, soon to be an orphan, is forced to go live in the country with her unfeeling, work-obsessed aunt. But her miserable life is soon brightened by the kindness and Christian love of a minister's daughter and her brother who is a divinity student.

[10] Olivia Egleston Phelps Stokes, *Letters and Memories of Susan and Anna Bartlett Warner*, New York, 1925, pp. 37–38.

Ellen is not a very good little girl when we first meet her and she needs constant instruction from dear Alice. Here is a sample of Alice's pedagogical method.

> "O! were the world but full of the right kind of example, the kingdom of darkness could not stand. 'Arise, shine!' is a word that every Christian ought to take home."
>
> "But how can I shine?" asked Ellen.
>
> "My dear Ellen!—in the faithful, patient, self-denying performance of every duty as it comes to hand—'whatsoever thy hand findeth to do, do it with thy might.' "
>
> "It is very little that *I* can do," said Ellen.
>
> "Perhaps more than you think, but never mind that. All are not great stars in the church; you may be only a little rushlight;—see you burn well!"

By such steps does Ellen climb heavenward.

Alice has to die, of course, and a finer Christian death has never been died. Ellen is eventually packed off to Scotland to live with her grandmother. Her Christian ways and words are not highly thought of in the household but she has thoroughly learned what is expected of her and persists in her piety. Just what is going to happen to Ellen is not clear when the novel ends, but we know she will ever bear witness to Christ's saving word, wherever she may find herself in the wide, wide world.

The Wide, Wide World only barely got born. When Harpers returned the manuscript, someone had written "Fudge" across the first page. G. P. Putnam also nearly turned it down, but when he asked his mother to look it over, she said it must be published, adding, "Providence will aid its sale." And Providence did, with the help of tearful readers everywhere. In 1853 it earned $4,500 in one semi-annual royalty payment. In two years' time thirteen editions were required. Eventually over a half-million copies were sold in this country.[11]

[11] Again we are dealing with a novel which was written out of the most fervent piety. Anna B. Warner, in her biography of her more famous sister (*Susan Warner*, New York, 1909, p. 264), testifies to this. "It was written in closest reliance upon God: for thoughts, for power, and for words. Not the mere vague wish to write a book that should do service to her Master:

The life of Katy Mortimer, in Mrs. Prentiss' *Stepping Heavenward,* is even less eventful than Ellen Montgomery's but her piety is—eventually—greater, probably because, once she gets going, she works at it every hour of the day. Not one to blink at her own sinfulness, she fills her journal with accounts of her failures to follow her mother's teaching. Gradually she finds there is joy in visiting the poor and sick and teaching a Bible class. In the first years of her marriage to Ernest, a doctor, she is still too selfish to be pleasing in her own sight. But Ernest's patience and a fair number of deaths of loved ones bring her around. When she writes the last entry in her journal, she is able to say that she will henceforth spend her writing time "in praying for all men; for all sufferers, for all who are out of the way, for all whom I love. And their name is Legion, for I love every body."

"Yes, I love every body! That crowning joy has come to me at last. Christ is in my soul; He is mine; I am as conscious of it as that my husband and children are mine; and His Spirit flows forth from mine in the calm peace of a river, whose banks are green with grass, and glad with flowers. If I die, it will be to leave a wearied and worn body, and a sinful soul, to go joyfully to be with Christ, to weary and to sin no more. If I live, I shall find much blessed work to do for Him. So living or dying, I shall be the Lord's."

We know from her husband's memoir—*The Life and Letters of Elizabeth Prentiss* (New York, 1882)—that Mrs. Prentiss (1818–1878) was one of the most pious of women. She also suffered a great deal from ill health and the death of children, but bore her afflictions like a Christian. She wrote her stories—most of them were for children—in order "to

but a vivid, constant looking to him for guidance and help: the writer and her work both laid humbly at the Lord's feet. In that sense, the book was written upon her knees: and the Lord's blessing has followed it down to this day. How many of whom even I have heard, trace their heart conversion straight to that blessing on the pages of the 'Wide, Wide World.' "

help others to know and love Christ and His truth." Of *Stepping Heavenward*, she told a friend, "Every word of that book was a prayer, and seemed to come of itself." The novel took hold wonderfully, though not with the reviewers. (Mrs. Prentiss was a mite resentful of this neglect.) What the Rev. Marvin Vincent said of the book in his "Memorial Discourse" (*Life and Letters*, p. 281) is undoubtedly true:

"The response to 'Stepping Heavenward' was instant and general. Others of her books were enjoyed, praised, laughed over, but this one was taken by tired hands into secret places, pored over by eyes dim with tears, and its lessons prayed out at many a Jabbok. It was one of those books which sorrowing, Mary-like women read to each other, and which lured many a bustling Martha from the fretting of her care-cumbered life to ponder the new lesson of rest in toil. It was one of those books of which people kept a lending copy, that they might enjoy the uninterrupted companionship of their own."

Some of the writers of pious domestic novels soon discovered that a conversion to Christianity would supply enough incidents along the way to make up the entire plot. The doubts, the retreats from the inevitable giving of oneself to Christ, the conversations over doctrine, the quoting from dogmatical works (and from dangerous, modern heretical ones as well), the slow turning of the sinner from his sin or the atheist from his scoffing; what a treasure horde such episodes provided. Mrs. Augusta Evans Wilson and the Rev. E. P. Roe specialized in conversions.

Augusta Jane Evans (1835–1909)—she became Mrs. Wilson in 1868—will have to be called a phenomenon. Born in Columbus, Georgia, and brought up in various parts of the South, including Texas, she was the Southern answer to Mrs. Stowe. Her most famous novel, *St. Elmo* (1867), was ridiculed by the literary for its melodrama, its parade of learning, and its maudlin piety, but it sold over a million copies. This record puts it in third place among best-sellers, just after *Uncle Tom's Cabin* and *Ben-Hur.* Mrs. Wilson's biographer reports that steamboats and railway coaches were named St. Elmo. "Many Southern towns had 'St. Elmo Hotels' and at least two villages were named for the book. There was a 'St. Elmo' punch, a very strong 'St. Elmo' cigar, and several blue-ribboned dogs named 'St. Elmo.'" Many unfortunate children were christened Edna Earl, for the heroine, or St. Elmo, for the hero.[12] One tribute to the novel's popularity must have displeased Augusta Evans—a parody by Charles Henry Webb ("John Paul") entitled *St. Twel'mo; or, The Cuneiform Cyclopedist of Chattanooga* (New York, 1867). Webb hit off very well the novel's inflated style and Edna's staggering erudition.

Mrs. Wilson published her first novel, *Inez: A Tale of the Alamo* (1855), when she was twenty. It is violently anti-Catholic, and though it did well enough it never made the grade as even a better seller.[13] She found a more successful formula with *Beulah* (1859), which was a kind of trial run for *St. Elmo.* We begin with the sufferings of the inevitable orphan (this time—trust Augusta Jane Evans for the added touch—she is an orphan in an *asylum*). Beulah is eventually taken into the household of Dr. Hartwell who faintly resembles Charlotte Brontë's Mr. Rochester. The Doctor is an unbeliever and he warns Beulah away from some of the dangerous books in his library. She has been a pretty fair Christian up to this time and she resents his words of caution: "Christianity has triumphed over the subtleties of infidelity for eighteen hundred years; what have I to fear?" Dr. Hartwell still dreads what may happen, and adds a clincher to his argument.

[12] William Perry Fidler, *Augusta Evans Wilson, 1835–1909, A Biography,* University, Alabama, 1951, pp. 128–129.

[13] *Inez* may get up there yet. There have been many editions of it and it was still in print in 1951.

" 'Beulah, do you want to be just what I am? Without belief in any creed! hopeless of eternity as of life! Do you want to be like me? If not, keep your hands off my books! Good night. It is time for you to be asleep.' "

Alas! Dr. Hartwell was right. Though Beulah becomes a learned lady and eventually a successful writer, by reading Emerson, Carlyle, Goethe, and "plunging into the gulf of German speculation," what a price she pays! "The landmarks of earlier years were swept away; the beacon light of Calvary had sunk below the horizon." She tries to pray her way out of doubt, but to whom or what can she pray? "To nature? to heroes? These were the new deities. She could not pray; all grew dark . . . 'Satan' had effectually blindfolded her."

Slowly and painfully, Beulah reconverts herself and when Dr. Hartwell comes back from a five-year tramp in the Orient and for the second time asks her to marry him, she accepts. He is now ripe for conversion, and by the time we reach the last page, we are convinced that Beulah will manage. Who could resist a wife who argues so cogently?

> "Yet I believe the day is dawning, when scientific data will not only cease to be antagonistic to scriptural accounts, but will deepen the impress of Divinity on the pages of holy writ; when the 'torch shall be taken out of the hand of the infidel, and set to burn in the temple of the living God'; when Science and Religion shall link hands. Human thought subserves many useful, nay, noble ends; the Creator gave it, as a powerful instrument, to improve man's temporal condition; but oh, sir, I speak of what I know, when I say: alas, for that soul who forsakes the divine ark, and embarks on the gilded toys of man's invention, hoping to breast the billows of life, and be anchored safely in the harbor of eternal rest! The heathens, 'having no law, are a law unto themselves;' but for such as deliberately reject the given light, only bitter darkness remains. I know it; for I, too, once groped, wailing for help."

Some may wish to argue that *St. Elmo* is not a religious novel. Certainly there are many secular thrills in it, induced by Edna's plight as an orphan, by a blind girl, a crippled boy, a deaf-mute, a train wreck, Edna's nearly fatal illness, a duel (fought by St. Elmo when he is a student at Yale), several incidental deaths, and some of the most rococo descriptions of grounds and buildings to be found in fiction. But Augusta Jane Evans, stout Methodist that she was, intended it to have a message. She wrote appreciatively to a friend who had found the novel inspiring: "Indeed my dear Sir, I am inexpressibly gratified that you esteem *St. Elmo* so highly; and I trust that with the blessing of God, my 'labor will not be in vain', and that I may be the humble instrument of doing some good, of leading some soul safely to Christ." [14]

Essentially *St. Elmo* is *Beulah* magnified a thousand times. Edna Earl is the orphan this time. Unlike Beulah she never loses her faith, but like her she becomes a successful writer of a pious Miss Lonelyhearts kind. St. Elmo is Dr. Hartwell in Byronic dress, passionate, moody, and wicked. (We can only guess at some of his sins.) Edna has to reject him as a husband though his pitiful plea is: "Edna, as you value my soul, my eternal welfare, give yourself to me! Give your pure sinless life to purify mine." Edna rebounds from his unwelcome embrace and tells him what he must do.

" 'Look yonder to Jesus, weeping, bleeding! Only his blood and tears can wash away your guilt. Mr. Murray, I can never be your wife. I have no confidence in you. Knowing how systematically you have deceived others, how devoid of conscientious scruples you are, I should never be sure that I too was not the victim of your heartless machinations. Beside, I—'

" 'Hush! hush! To your keeping I commit my conscience and my heart.'

" 'No! no! I am no vice regent of an outraged and insulted God! I put no faith in any man, whose conscience another keeps. From the species of fascination which you exert, I shrink with unconquerable dread and aversion, and would almost as

[14] Fidler, p. 137.

soon entertain the thought of marrying Lucifer himself. Oh! your perverted nature shocks, repels, astonishes, grieves me. I can neither respect nor trust you. Mr. Murray, have mercy upon yourself! Go yonder to Jesus. He only can save and purify you.' "

They must go their lonely ways: Edna to fame and St. Elmo Murray—have you guessed it?—to a Christian conversion and ordination as a clergyman. When Edna receives the news from his ghostly confessor, her cry of joy rings through the room.

" 'Saved—purified—consecrated henceforth to God's holy work? A minister of Christ? O most merciful God! I thank thee! My prayers are answered with a blessing I never dared to hope for, or even to dream of! Can I ever be grateful enough? A pastor, holding up pure hands! Thank God! my sorrows are all ended now; there is no more grief for me. Ah! what a glory breaks upon the future! What though I never see his face in this world? I can be patient indeed; for now I know, oh! I know that I shall surely see it yonder!' "

After a decent interval St. Elmo tries again. This time his proposal is accepted. Edna will give up her career as a writer and help him in his holy work. The marriage takes place. The novel ends with an appropriate quotation from Tennyson's *Princess:*

> My wife, my life. Oh! we will walk this world
> Yoked in all exercise of noble end.

In the religious novels of the Rev. E. P. Roe (1838–1888)—a late comer to the ranks—the conversion theme stands out clearly almost from the first page. In an article in *Lippincott's Monthly Magazine*, Roe remarked that "the day of prolix, fine, flowery writing" was over and that what was needed in its place was "simplicity, lucidity, strength." [15] His plots are not cluttered up with the digressions or long sermons disguised as dialogue one finds in Mrs. Wilson's novels. He is plain and straightforward. He gets to work at once and does not leave off until the unbeliever or the sinner is safely in the fold. The one luxury he permits himself is a calamitous event of some kind, needed to precipitate the conversion.

Roe attended Williams College for a time. He was ordained as a Presbyterian minister in 1862 and served as an army chaplain with the Second New York Light Cavalry during the Civil War. He got his first taste of the pleasures of authorship while acting as weekly correspondent for the New York *Evangelist.* There is good writing in his dispatches and they have the virtue of being informative about aspects of army life which were not much written about.[16] Roe was minister of the Presbyterian church in Highland Falls, New York, when, in 1871, the turning point of his life arrived. As soon as he heard the news of the great fire in Chicago he felt "a passionate desire to see its houseless, homeless condition." He got to Chicago while the wreckage was still smoking and "spent several days among the ruins and people, who found refuge wherever they could. I wandered around night and day, taking notes of all I saw, and there the plot of my story was vaguely formed." [17] *Barriers Burned Away* (1872) was first serialized in the New York *Evangelist* and then issued by Dodd, Mead.

The plot which Roe found among the smoldering ruins could scarcely be simpler. A fine Christian lad comes to Chi-

[15] Quoted in Alexander Cowie, *The Rise of the American Novel,* New York, 1948, p. 441.

[16] Some of these letters are reprinted in *E. P. Roe. Reminiscences of His Life,* 1889, written by his sister, Mary A. Roe. The edition I have used appears in *The Works of E. P. Roe,* XIX, issued by P. F. Cellier, New York, 1900.

[17] *E. P. Roe. Reminiscences of His Life,* p. 218.

cago from the country. He begins to make his way in business, never for one moment compromising with his religion. He falls in love with a frivolous society young lady who mocks his piety and humiliates him. Then comes the fire. Of course Mr. Dennis Fleet saves Miss Christine Ludolph. With the city in flames behind them, she is ready for conversion. Dennis' first try ends in failure. He urges her to pray but she cannot pray. He tells her to "wait the King's time." Two pages later the "King's time" arrives.

"Then Dennis saw her start up and glance around in a strange bewildered manner. Suddenly she clasped her hands and looked up with an ecstatic thrilling cry:

" 'There is! there is! [a God] God lives and loves me, I feel, I know, and therefore I may hope and live.' Turning to the still raging flames, she exclaimed: 'Burn on with your fiery billows, I do not fear you now! I am safe, safe for ever! Oh, how can I ever love and praise thee enough!'

"Then springing to Dennis's side, she took both his hands in hers, and said: 'Mr. Fleet, you have saved my life again and again, and I am, oh, how grateful; but in leading me to this knowledge you have made me your debtor for evermore. God does live, and I believe now He loves even me.'

"As the glare of the fire fell on her face, he was awed and speechless at its expression. From its ecstatic joy and purity it seemed that the light of heaven, instead of her burning home, was illumining it.

"At last he said brokenly: 'Thank God! thank God! my many, many, prayers are answered.' "

Though *Barriers Burned Away* was instantly a success, Roe was not yet certain he was called to be a novelist. He would venture further before making the decision. By the time he published his fourth book, *Opening a Chestnut Burr* (1874), also a best seller, he was convinced that he should abandon the ministry and write his sermons in the form of fiction. How could he resist longer when had received so many assurances that his novels were "sources not only of pleasure, but also of help and benefit"? ("Preface" to *Opening a Chestnut Burr.*)

The only change in his formula Roe made in *Opening a Chestnut Burr* was to reverse the roles played by the sexes. Here Walter Gregory, an unbeliever, "who has sinned against the clearest light, a gambler, a libertine, an embodiment of selfishness" (his own words about himself), is the lost one standing in need of conversion. Annie Walton is fit and ready for the job of penetrating Walter's prickly, burr-like skepticism. Actually he is not the sinner he thinks he is and he is already on the road to salvation. He confesses to Annie that he does believe in a "Supreme Being,—a great First Cause." The trouble is that He hides Himself behind the stars and is lost to Walter "in His vast universe." If only one could believe "in a personal God who thought about us and cared for us." The doctrine of predestination is also troublesome. Annie's steadfast faith gradually prepares Walter for conversion but there is no sudden moment of illumination as in *Barriers Burned Away*. Various near-catastrophes occur in which Walter proves himself a hero. But not even the shipwreck in which he saves the life of his enemy approaches the spectacularity of the Chicago fire. Still, the shipwreck is useful because as Annie and Walter believe they are about to be drowned, Walter comes 'round.

> "Both father and mother are awaiting us—and, Annie," he whispered, tenderly, "you, too, will soon be there. So courage! 'Good neighbors,' soon."

Year in, year out the Rev. E. P. Roe could count on an annual royalty check of $15,000 as contrasted with the $200 average for a book earned at that time by most authors.[18] He took no great pride in authorship and was genuinely content with the comfort his novels brought to thousands of

[18] These figures are given by James D. Hart, *The Popular Book*, p. 121.

readers. As a man he was generous, unpretentious, and outgoing. His fellow-members of the Authors Club in New York liked and respected him. He was sincere in his belief that since a passion for novel-reading had seized the American public, Christian writers should come to terms with the situation and teach in parables, as Christ had done. In his "Preface" to *From Jest to Earnest* he argues his case well. Young people are going to read novels, in stealth, if they have to. The craving for truth in narrative form is too deeply embedded to be eradicated. Ask the librarians of Sabbath-school and public libraries if this is not so. What, then, is to be done? The answer was obvious.

"If millions in the impressible period of youth, in spite of all that any can do, will read fiction, then it would appear a sacred duty in those who love their kind, to make this food of the forming character healthful, bracing, and ennobling in its nature. Earnest men and women, who hold and would transmit the truth, must speak in a way that will secure a hearing." [19]

In offering this, his newest novel, Roe did not think he had "abandoned the ministry." It was a sermon "as truly as if I stood up and preached it; and if the audience will take home its teaching, I am content to be neither seen nor thought of." While his Christian heroes and heroines were busy bringing lost souls to Christ, the Rev. E. P. Roe was effectively converting American readers to his belief that a single novel could be more useful to the Christian cause than a thousand sermons.

IV. The Old Law and the New

The mid-century ferment in the churches caused by new liberal views in theology was bound to make itself felt in the

[19] *From Jest to Earnest* is also a religious novel on the conversion theme. It was a better seller in 1875.

religious novels. The older orthodoxy, based on Calvinism, was gradually giving way and the religion of love moved in to take its place. The questions were many which sprang up to trouble thoughtful Christians. What would be the effect of Darwinian evolution and of the higher criticism of the Bible on true believers? Would such modern heresies as Unitarianism, Transcendentalism, and Universalism undermine the orthodox churches? Could one any longer believe in the resurrection of the body and a personal immortality? Were there not great dangers lurking in the Transcendentalists' trust in conscience as the guide to life and in their extravagant reverence for Nature? Though there were scores of novels published between 1850 and 1900 which debate such questions as these, only a very few of them became best sellers.[20] Why they were not more popular may be ascribed to their lack of drama. A novelist could hardly make a *Ben-Hur* or a *St. Elmo* out of a debate over predestination *vs.* free will. Toward the end of the century several novels which advocated the practice of the Social Gospel reached a wide public but since they stand in a group by themselves and represent a change in the evolving pattern of the religious best seller, they will be discussed in the next section.

One of the best treatments in fiction of the conflict between orthodoxy and the new liberal views is to be found in *The Minister's Wooing* (1859) by Harriet Beecher Stowe (1811–1896). Many critics think it her greatest artistic success. After *Uncle Tom's Cabin* it is probably her best-remembered work. The setting is Newport at the end of the eighteenth century. One of the chief characters is Dr. Samuel Hopkins, an actual historical personage, a friend and follower of Jonathan Edwards and one of the last great upholders of the older orthodoxy. The leading fictional characters are Mrs. Scudder, an ardent admirer of the Doctor; Mary, her daughter; James

[20] Herbert Ross Brown deals with the appearance of these questions in fiction in a work already cited, *The Sentimental Novel in America, 1789–1860*, pp. 323–357.

Marvyn, a young seaman, who is in love with Mary; and his devoted mother. Mary refuses James's love because he is not a true believer, though he takes her Bible to sea with him and promises to try to be worthy of salvation. As he writes Mary, "If through your prayers, your Bible, your friendship, you can bring me to your state, I am willing to be brought there,—nay, desirous." James's trouble is that Dr. Hopkins' "system" seems so unsuited to the world one lives in. "Much of his preaching about men is as like live men as Chinese pictures of trees and rocks and gardens,—no nearer reality than that. All I can say is, 'It isn't so; and you'd know it, Sir, if you knew men.'" Months later the news comes that James has perished at sea. His mother nearly goes insane with grief and in her wild sorrow denies her God. Brought up to believe in the damnation of the unregenerate, Mary is in anguish over James's soul. "If he were among the lost, in what age of eternity could she ever be blessed? Could Christ be happy, if those who were one with Him were sinful and accursed?"[21] Gradually Mrs. Marvyn and Mary find it possible to discuss their terrible doubts. Prompted by the simple faith of her Negro servant, Mrs. Marvyn begins to find a way out.

> "There is a world of comfort to me in the words, 'He that spared not his own Son, but delivered him up for us all, how shall he not with him also freely give us all things'? These words speak to my heart. I can interpret them by my own nature, and I rest on them. If there is a fathomless mystery of sin and sorrow, there is a deeper mystery of God's love. So, Mary, I try Candace's way,—I look at Christ,—I pray

[21] Mrs. Marvyn's grief over James's death is conveyed with great poignancy. It undoubtedly reflects Mrs. Stowe's sorrow over the drowning of her son Henry while he was a student at Dartmouth. Mary's great fear lest James has been condemned to utter damnation is based on Mrs. Stowe's fears for her unconverted son and on the experience of her sister, Catharine Beecher, whose lover, a brilliant young Yale professor, was lost at sea. Because he had never experienced conversion, Catharine's Calvinistic father, the Rev. Lyman Beecher, could hold out no hope for his salvation.

to Him. If he that hath seen Him hath seen the Father, it is enough. I rest there,—I wait. What I know not now I shall know hereafter."

Of course James hasn't been lost at sea. He returns, with a fair fortune, in time to prevent the marriage of Mary and Dr. Hopkins, who yields as soon as he knows of their early love. James has found a way to believe. His reading in the Bible has convinced him that the men of the Old Testament had tried to obey God and find out God's will in all they did and that their "experiment" worked. "I began to feel a trembling faith that *Somebody* was guiding me, and that the events of my life were not happening by accident, but working themselves out by His will." James is ready, now, to accept the even higher truth of Christ's teaching. At last he understands what met him in the very first of Matthew: "Thou shalt call his name Jesus, for he shall save his people from their sins." What saves is not Dr. Hopkins' system, so full of contradictions and unfathomable mysteries, but one's simple faith in Jesus as redeemer.

Nearly thirty years later Margaret Deland (1857–1945) could still make a popular novel out of this theme of the opposition between the Old Law and the New. In *John Ward, Preacher* (1888), her first novel, she is not so gentle with her Calvinist—John Ward—as Mrs. Stowe had been with Dr. Hopkins. The novel is unrelenting, and one is surprised that it appealed to so many readers.[22] In his private life John Ward is gentle and courageous; as a preacher the doctrine of reprobation is all important to him. In his eyes

[22] One should remember that in this year, 1888, Mrs. Humphrey Ward's *Robert Elsmere* was a sensation in both England and America. The hero of Mrs. Ward's novel is driven to relinquish orthodoxy. He leaves the Church of England to found a social-religious settlement in London. His doubts are resolved when he comes to love Christ as the most nearly divine of men. The two novels were naturally often compared. Gladstone, who disapproved in print of the heresies in *Robert Elsmere*, wrote the English publishers of *John Ward, Preacher* (Longmans) that it contained, so far as he could see, no attack on Christianity.

his wife Mary is not yet a convinced Christian. He had been sure that, once married, he might save her soul. But Mary, deeply as she loves him, will not compromise. Presently it becomes common knowledge that she holds heretical views and the Presbyterian session wishes to summon her so that it may remonstrate with her. This John Ward refuses to permit. But he soon decides that they must live apart until she can learn by suffering to believe as he believes. When John is dying, he sends for Mary, still hoping and expecting that she will yield.

"He knew that death was near, but there was an exultant look in his fading eyes, and sometimes his lips moved in grateful prayer. Perhaps his physical extremity had dulled his fears for his wife's salvation into a conviction that his death was to be the climax of God's plans for her. He was bewildered at the temptation of greater joy at the prospect of her presence than gratitude that God should save her soul alive. But he never for one moment doubted she would come to tell him she had found the light."

We are not present at the death-bed, but we know that Mary has not yielded. Yet she had loved John and in her grief all that is left to her for comfort is the possibility of helping others.

John Ward, Preacher is a remarkably mature and sophisticated novel. Margaret Deland was saying, in effect: this old and vexed argument goes too deep to have any easy solution. The convictions felt by John and Mary Ward are too strong and too widely opposed to afford any compromise. In her novel we encounter for the last time among the religious best sellers this especially American theme. She had said the last word—in public and to thousands.[23]

[23] There is an amusing—and also distressing—chapter on the uproar over *John Ward, Preacher* in Mrs. Deland's autobiography, *Golden Yesterdays*, New York, 1941. Many public libraries banned the novel, and the religious press reviled her. A native of Kennebunkport, Maine, refused to sell Mr. De-

As the daughter of a professor at the Andover Theological Seminary, Elizabeth Stuart Phelps (1844–1911) grew up in the midst of talk about the Old Law and the New. Like Mrs. Stowe she was a strong-minded woman and she made her own decisions about religious questions. In her long career as a writer she communicated them to an appreciative public in short stories, juveniles, and an autobiography, *Chapters from a Life* (1897). In her first novel, *The Gates Ajar* (1868), she dealt with a problem which was of so much concern to the thousands upon thousands of women who had lost sons and husbands and lovers in the Civil War that the book was immediately a best seller. The country was dark with sorrowing women. "The regiments came home, but the mourners went about the streets." Could she say something that would comfort the "bereaved wife, mother, sister, and widowed girl" whose drawn faces showed piteously everywhere? [24] The novel which was prompted by this universal sorrow grew so naturally that it seemed to Miss Phelps as if she had no more to do with the writing of it "than the bough through which the wind cries, or the wave by means of which the tide rises." "The angel said unto me, 'Write!' and I wrote."

The first chapters of *The Gates Ajar* are genuinely moving. Mary Cabot has lost her brother Roy in the War. He may be damned (Deacon Quirk thinks this is possible) but even if he is in heaven where she may join him eventually, heaven is a place of disembodied spirits. There will be no love there, no conversation, no warm human life, no joys like earthly joys. The first word of real comfort Mary receives comes from her aunt, Mrs. Forceythe, a widow who has also known the torture of bereavement. Presently she, and her little daughter Faith, come to live with Mary. The rest of the novel shows Mary's slow recovery under her aunt's instruc-

land a house because "the church folks claim your woman has wrote a bad book." When the Delands did settle there three years later, many doors were shut to them.

[24] Ch. v, "The Fall of the Pemberton Mill: The Gates Ajar," in *Chapters from a Life*, Boston, 1897.

tion. She comes at last to believe in the kind of immortality in which she and Roy can live forever in sweet converse. At one point Mary draws back from Mrs. Forceythe's explicit descriptions of the Heavenly Kingdom but is reassured when her aunt gives a name to her version of immortality. It should be called "spiritual materialism." "I do not believe in a *gross* heaven," says Mrs. Forceythe, "but I believe in a reasonable one." There *will* be marrying and giving in marriage —of a kind—in heaven. There will also be books and music—even pictures.

> "All that Art, 'the handmaid of the Lord,' can do for us, I have no doubt will be done. Eternity will never become monotonous. Variety without end, charms unnumbered within charms, will be devised by Infinite ingenuity to minister to our delight. Perhaps,—this is just my fancying,—perhaps there will be whole planets turned into galleries of art, over which we may wander at will; or into orchestral halls where the highest possibilities of music will be realized to singer and hearer. Do you know, I have sometimes had a flitting notion that music would be the language of heaven? It certainly differs in some indescribable manner from the other arts. We have most of us felt it in our different ways. It always seems to me like the cry of a great sad life dragged to use in this world against its will. Pictures and statues and poems fit themselves to their work more contentedly. Symphony and song struggle in fetters. That sense of conflict is not good for me. It is quite as likely to harm as to help. Then perhaps the mysteries of sidereal systems will be spread out like a child's map before us. Perhaps we shall take journeys to Jupiter and to Saturn and to the glittering haze of nebulae, and to the site of ruined worlds whose 'extinct light is yet travelling through space.' Occupation for explorers there, you see!" [25]

[25] Mark Twain was moved to near-ribaldry by *The Gates Ajar*. For years he kept tinkering with a parody of it—"Visit to Heaven." His friend William Dean Howells liked it and suggested—jocosely—that he bring it out in England, with an endorsement from Dean Stanley. But Livy (Mrs. Clemens) disapproved of this kind of irreverent jape and the manuscript was kept locked up. Finally after Livy's death, Twain let Harpers publish *Extract from Captain Stormfield's Visit to Heaven* in book form (1909). By this time, of course, the parody had lost all its steam. But the story can still be enjoyed for its own sake. Miss Phelps had forgotten a number of logical

That Harold Frederic's *The Damnation of Theron Ware* (1896) should have been a best seller is surprising. One guesses that it was not read or at least not enjoyed by the admirers of *The Minister's Wooing* or *The Gates Ajar*. Frederic (1856–1898), a newspaperman who knew his rural up-state New York region well, was one of the first American realists. He does nothing in this novel to spare the sensibilities of pious readers. On the other hand, though this is the story of the lapse from faith and the degradation of a young Methodist minister, Frederic does not scoff at religion. This is no *Elmer Gantry*. Theron's fall is pitiable but not ludicrous.

There are several forces at work to pull Theron down and he has only the weakest of defenses to rally against them. He holds mildly liberal views in theology but one of his trustees tells him what kind of preaching his congregation expects of him.

" 'What we want to hear is the plain, old-fashioned Word of God, without any palaver or 'hems and ha's. They tell me there's some parts where hell's treated as played out—where our ministers don't like to talk much about it, because people don't want to hear about it. Such preachers ought to be put out. They ain't Methodists at all. What we want here, sir, is straight-out, flat-footed hell—the burnin' lake o' fire and brimstone. Pour it into 'em, hot an' strong. We can't have too much of it. Work in them awful deathbeds of Voltaire an' Tom Paine, with the devil right there in the room reachin' for 'em, an' they yellin' for fright—that's what fills the anxious seat an' brings in souls hand over fist!' "

---

necessities and Twain supplies them; the fact, for example, that there are so many famous people in Heaven that to get a glimpse of Adam or Moses one may have to wait many heavenly years. And then there are all those strangers from the other planets, and the unexpected inhabitants.

"Have they really rung in Mahomet and all those other heathens?"

"Yes—they all had their message, and they all get their reward. The man who don't get his reward on earth, needn't bother—he will get it here, sure."

Theron tries, rather feebly, to meet the requirement, to stick "by the Discipline an' the ways of our Fathers of Israel." His next trial—within his church—is the successful preaching of Brother and Sister Soulsby, shrewd and vulgar evangelists who know how to bring good Methodists to the pitch of frenzy required by the old-time religion. He must suffer them, too, good-hearted though they are.

There are enemies without. Theron comes to know—and to marvel at—the local Catholic priest, Father Forbes, a learned and cynical man who "could talk coolly about the 'Christ-myth' without ever ceasing to be a priest, and apparently a very active and effective priest." Father Forbes has a friend, Dr. Ledsmar, who is an agnostic and says the most outrageous things without, it seems, any realization of how terribly he blasphemes. By this time poor Theron has begun to perceive that "there was an intellectual world, a world of culture and grace, of lofty thoughts and the inspiring communion of real knowledge, where creeds were of no importance, and where men asked one another, not 'Is your soul saved?' but 'Is your mind furnished?' Theron had the sensation of having been invited to become a citizen of this world."

He is certain that the invitation has been issued when Celia Madden, the beautiful but pagan daughter of a rich Irish-Catholic immigrant takes him up—or so he thinks. She plays Chopin to him in a magnificent, dimly lighted room. What's more, she gives him Benedictine to drink. This is the end of Theron. Hearing that Celia and Father Forbes have gone to New York, he decides they must be lovers. He follows them to the city and disgraces himself at the Murray Hill Hotel. (They *do* have an errand; it is to rescue Celia's brother from his latest debauch.) In the end it is Sister Soulsby who straightens Theron out and packs him off to Seattle where he will—we hope—grow up with Washington Territory.

Frederic got his hands on a great theme and he did much with it. *The Damnation of Theron Ware* is one of the best of all American novels on a religious subject. What, he was asking, happens to the old-time religion when it is assailed by a strong and subtle Catholicism; the new learning (Dr. Ledsmar), analytical, critical, scientific; and the paganism of a Celia Madden? It goes down, of course. Theron's dallying with the doctrines of the Free Methodists was the beginning of his downfall.

In view of the fact that the warfare between Science and Theology raged in the pulpits and the church press for nearly fifty years, it is surprising that the religious novelists paid so little attention to this controversy. Possibly the issues were considered too complex or too risky for treatment in fiction. So far as I know, the only best seller which makes this debate the center of action is James Lane Allen's *The Reign of Law* (1900). This novel was a digression in the career of a novelist who was well known for such sweet and gentle stories as *A Kentucky Cardinal* and *The Choir Invisible*. But Allen (1849–1925) had been pondering the issues ever since he was a student at Transylvania College (Lexington) during the late 1860's. He risked losing his popularity by publishing so controversial a piece of fiction, but, as things turned out, the consequent notoriety brought him an even larger public.

The Reign of Law is a "conversion novel," only this time the conversion is from sectarian Christianity to an uncompromising belief in science as the answerer. Young David, son of pious parents, and grandson of a pioneer who had built a church open to preachers of every denomination, is determined to get an education at the Bible College in Lexington. To earn his tuition he works for two years in the hemp fields. At first he is delighted with the college, but his inquiring mind soon begins to question the limited theology of his professors. A sermon warning the students against the works of the evolutionists has the effect of sending David to them. He reads Darwin with wonder and acknowledges to himself that "it was the first time in his life that he had encountered outside of the Bible a mind of the highest order." David is presently expelled from college and goes home in disgrace.

With the help of Gabriella, whose religion is not dogmatical but intuitive, he recovers his hope and his life. He is convinced now that Science is the only road for him.

> "Science! Science! There is the fresh path for the faith of the race! For the race henceforth must get its idea of God, and build its religion to Him, from its knowledge of the laws of His universe. A million years from now! Where will our dark theological dogmas be in that radiant time? The Creator of all life, in all life He must be studied! And in the study of science there is least wrangling, least tyranny, least bigotry, no persecution. It teaches charity, it teaches a well-ordered life, it teaches the world to be more kind. It is the great new path of knowledge into the future. All things must follow whither it leads. Our religion will more and more be what our science is, and some day they will be the same."

David will go to a northern college, study physical science, and then teach some branch of it.

Since Allen had taken no pains to disguise the college he had in mind in attacking the dogmas of David's teachers, he was immediately involved in a public quarrel with President McGarvey of Transylvania. The church magazines, from the Episcopal *Church Standard* to the *Catholic News*, took up the hue and cry. But the public did not follow their lead. The novel was a best seller within the year of its publication. When the Macmillan Company issued it in England, as *Increasing Purpose*, it took hold there as well and the sales of Allen's other novels were carried upward with it.[26]

A large reading public was evidently ready for such a novel as *The Reign of Law*. The vexed argument over the

[26] See Grant C. Knight, *James Lane Allen and the Genteel Tradition*, Chapel Hill, 1935, pp. 137–141, for additional information about the reception of *The Reign of Law*.

evolutionary hypothesis as subversive of sound theology was about played out, except in Fundamentalist circles, and Allen's assertion that "the development of Man is itself the great Revelation of Him" suited the temper of the times.

V. In His Steps: The Social Gospel

As the strong sectarianism of the Protestant churches faded in the second half of the nineteenth century, the figure of Jesus loomed larger. On Him and His promises the believer depended for the hope of salvation and personal immortality. Even in the earlier part of the century, as Professor Stow Persons has noted, the moral and spiritual orientation of organized Protestantism was profoundly individualistic. "Religion was an affair of the individual with his Maker. Repentance, salvation, sanctification—all were understood in private, personal terms." [27]

This intensely individualistic character of American religion underwent a great change in the '90's because of the growing concern of thoughtful laymen and clergymen over the social disorganization of American life. The indifference of men of great wealth to the plight of the workers who made their fortunes possible, the alarming increase of slum-poverty in the cities, the degradation of the hordes of immigrants who never moved beyond the ports of entry, prolonged and bitter strikes, destitution among the farmers, the uncontrolled spread of drinking and prostitution, corruption in local and state governments: how could Christians remain indifferent to these social evils? The church would lose its power with the great majority of the people if it did not act.

Several social scientists—notably John Bates Clark and Richard T. Ely—prepared the way for action by their extensive documentation of the evils which needed correcting. But the more liberal and courageous clergymen were not far

[27] Stow Persons, *American Minds. A History of Ideas,* New York, 1958, p. 410.

behind. In many city churches, deserted by their parishioners as the slums closed in, efforts were made to provide the poor with decent recreation, day nurseries, and courses of instruction which would make better jobs possible. The "institutional church" was what the new day demanded. Soon the theological schools were adding courses in sociology and social work. Shailer Mathews, Dean of the Divinity School at the University of Chicago, became one of the leading proponents of the "Social Gospel" and wielded an immense influence. Of the clerical practitioners of the new doctrine the Rev. Washington Gladden, a Congregationalist, was the best known throughout the country, but he had hundreds of followers. A fearless champion of labor's right to organize, he was nevertheless respected as a mediator by capitalists. He spread the new gospel by his active participation in many industrial disputes and by such influential books as *Applied Christianity* (1888) and *Tools and the Man* (1893).

Of the many books which gave impetus to the social gospel movement one of the most powerful was written by the English journalist W. T. Stead—*If Christ Came to Chicago. A Plea for the Union of all who Love in the Service of all who Suffer* (1894). Stead's data about crime, drink, prostitution, and municipal corruption in Chicago were sensational but in the main true. He had taken pains to get them at first hand from saloon-keepers, madames, and officials who were willing to tell all.[28]

Meanwhile the novelists had begun to take a hand in spreading the social gospel. Some took their cue from the title of Part v of Stead's book—"What Would Christ Do in Chicago?"—transforming the question into this form: "What must the Christian minister do in his community if he would follow the example of Christ?" In the year of Stead's book two novels appeared which attempted to answer the

[28] Good brief accounts of the social gospel movement are given in Persons, pp. 409–417; Arthur M. Schlesinger, *The Rise of the City, 1878–1898*, New York, 1933, pp. 338–344; Harold U. Faulkner, *The Quest for Social Justice, 1898–1914*, New York, 1931, pp. 217–224.

question: Elizabeth Stuart Phelps Ward's *A Singular Life* and the Rev. Charles M. Sheldon's *The Crucifixion of Philip Strong*.

Moved by what she had seen of the ravages of drink among the sailors and fishermen in Gloucester, Massachusetts, Mrs. Ward deserted her spiritualistic themes and told the story of a young clergyman whom the Congregational Council refuses to ordain because of his unorthodox views. Unlicensed, he preaches on the waterfront and befriends the drunkards and magdalens of Angel Alley. Just as his Jesus-like behavior is about to win over the theologians, he is killed by a rock thrown from a sullen mob of those who still resent his ministrations.

Sheldon's novel preaches the social gospel more overtly. His hero, Philip Strong, accepts a pulpit in a fashionable church in a "noisy, dirty manufacturing town full of working men, cursed with saloons, and black with coal smoke and unwashed humanity." He attacks the saloons and nearly loses his life in consequence. He tries to persuade his congregation to accept a Negro convert and to let him turn the parsonage into an orphans' home. His efforts to lead the Christ-like life and to persuade his parishioners to do the same bring about his dismissal. While he is preaching his dramatic farewell sermon, standing in front of a large cross painted on the wall, he has a heart attack and dies before his appalled and repentant congregation.

Sheldon (1857–1946) had come to Topeka, Kansas, in 1889 to found the Central Congregational Church. He was a profound believer in the social gospel and knew at first hand the social evils he would soon describe in his religious novels. Hard-pressed, as most ministers were beginning to be, to keep up attendance at the Sunday evening service, he discovered a device for filling the pews which would soon have momentous consequences. Instead of delivering a second sermon he read to his congregation a chapter of a religious novel. He ended each reading with a scene so full of suspense that everyone had to come back for the next installment. (*The Crucifixion of Philip Strong* was the third in this series of Sunday evening novels.) In 1896 Sheldon was reading to his congregation another of his serialized "cliff-hangers," *In His Steps, "What Would Jesus Do?"* Neither he nor any of his parishioners imagined that it would become in time another of the phenomenal best sellers among religious novels.

Sheldon was an amateurish novelist but he knew how to engage the interest of a wide variety of listeners and readers. In this novel no member of society is permitted to escape responsibility for behaving as Jesus would have him do. A seedy man, who is no ordinary tramp, interrupts the Rev. Henry Maxwell's service and demands to be heard. He is homeless and jobless. What will the First Church do for him and others like him? When the man dies in the parsonage, he says to the minister: "You have been good to me. Somehow I feel as if it was what Jesus would do." The die is cast. Maxwell resolves to form a league in his church made up of those who will do what Jesus would do. One by one his parishioners join: a newspaper editor who decides to print no Sunday edition and take no tobacco and liquor ads; a church singer who refuses an offer to sing in comic opera but instead devotes her voice to the cause of Jesus; a railroad superintendent who resigns when he learns that his company is violating the Interstate Commerce Law. Each of these answerers to the great question draws up for himself a list of instructions. Here is "What Jesus would probably do in Milton Wright's place as a business man."

1. He would engage in business for the purpose of glorifying God, and not for the primary purpose of making money.

2. All money that might be made he would never regard as his own, but as trust funds to be used for the good of humanity.

3. His relations with all the persons in his employ would be the most loving and helpful. He could not help thinking of them all in the light of souls to be saved. This thought would always be greater than his thought of making money in business.

4. He would never do a single dishonest or questionable thing

or try in any remotest way to get the advantage of any one else in the same business.

5. The principle of unselfishness and helpfulness in all the details of the business would direct its details.

6. Upon this principle he would shape the entire plan of his relation to his employes, to the people who were his customers, and to the general world with which he was connected.

Of course there is bitter resentment of Maxwell's program. Those who line up on the side of Jesus are ridiculed, ostracised, threatened, dismissed. The going is particularly rough when they make their great effort to purify the "Rectangle," the seed-bed of all the vice in the city. But they win, in the end. The Rectangle is sanctified and becomes an urban Utopia. The movement spreads to Chicago and we are left with the belief that what the First Church of Raymond has done can be accomplished even in Chicago by a bishop and a Doctor of Divinity who have seen the light and the way.

To the end, the Rev. Charles M. Sheldon remained the simple, devout, persistent man of God of the earlier days before he was known the world over. How many copies of his famous novel have been sold baffles the calculations of so astute a historian of American best sellers as Frank Luther Mott.[29] In his autobiography Sheldon estimated that by 1924 8,000,000 copies of *In His Steps* had been printed in America. The total for the world he put down as "over 22,000,000." The nearest Mott could come, in 1947, to a reasonable estimate was an over-all 6,000,000. We know that the novel had a tremendous vogue in England, where it was sold in a penny edition. It has been translated into at least twenty foreign languages. *Books in Print, 1958* lists editions by five different publishing houses.

The typical dispenser of the social gospel, one concludes, must stand his ground, fighting the evils of society where he

[29] In his *Golden Multitudes,* pp. 193–197, Mott does his best to cope with the legend of the popularity of *In His Steps.* To this end he went to Topeka in 1942 to interview Sheldon about the book's fame. The visit was not very rewarding. Mott says: "He simply had no mind for exact statistics, while at the same time he had a strong feeling for the romance of fine round numbers."

finds them—and that usually means in the city—until he wins or goes to his crucifixion. The Rev. Harold Bell Wright (1872–1944) preached a different version in his religious novels. His heroes are as much concerned as any of the social gospelers with the narrowness of creeds, the hypocrisy of deacons and elders, and the subservience of ministers to the wealthy members of their congregations. But to him the answer was escape to the simplicity of life in the hills or among devout and honest country folk.

In a sense Wright was himself a retreater all his life. But how vast were the rewards for castigating the spiritual failure of modern civilization and then walking out! His career is one of those unbelievable American success stories which *Time Magazine* records with delight, week in week out. Born in Rome, New York, he drifted to the West and with little education became a minister in the Church of the Disciples. In twelve years he held pastorates in Pierce City and Lebanon, Missouri, in Kansas City, in Pittsburg, Kansas, and in Redlands, California. When he was thirty, and a minister in Pittsburg, Wright wrote his first novel, *That Printer of Udell's*. By good fortune he had met in Chicago, in the winter of 1902, a mail-order bookseller, Elsbery W. Reynolds, who was as devoutly religious as he. They formed an alliance which soon made them both famous. Wright furnished the novels; Reynolds issued them through his Book Supply Company of Chicago. For the first time the religious novel in America was in the hands of a genius at advertising and promotion. Wright's second novel, *The Shepherd of the Hills* (1907)—the story of a minister who, for personal reasons, abandons his city pastorate and becomes a shepherd in the Ozarks—was so phenomenally successful that the author left the ministry and became a full-time novelist. His decision was justified by what Reynolds accomplished with the third novel, *The Calling of Dan Matthews* (1909). Once again Wright's hero is a man who becomes profoundly dissatisfied with the church as an institution (routine piety, inoperative Christianity, an inert ministry). The Rev. Dan Matthews tries to make his congregation see the peril which threatens their souls and his famous sermon, "The Fellowship of Service," moves many. But he has done all he can, and it is not enough. In his farewell sermon he tells his congregation that he is leaving for another ministry.

"God is as truly in the fields of grain, in the forests, in the mines, and in those laws of Nature by which men convert the product of field and forest and mine into the necessities of life. Therefore these are as truly holy as this institution. Therefore, again, the ministry of farm, and mine, and factory, and shop; of mill, and railroad, and store, and office, and wherever men toil with strength of body or strength of mind for that which makes for the best life of their kind—that ministry is sacred and holy."

The Rev. Dan Matthews will become the manager of a valuable mine located on his family's property. There he may hope to serve as he had never been permitted to do in Corinth's Memorial Church.

A strange novel, with its theme of retreat and abdication, to become a best seller! But Reynolds knew what he was doing. His advertising appropriation for it was $48,000, a sum which was "nothing less than revolutionary." The first printing was 100,000 copies; within eight months a second printing of the same size was announced.[30]

At this point in his career we must drop Harold Bell Wright because *The Calling of Dan Matthews* was the last of his novels on a religious theme. The entire story of his fabulous best-selling success can be read in Mott's *Golden Multitudes*. Wright's popularity dwindled in the 1930's and his last novel, *The Man Who Went Away* (1942), was a failure. But Mott estimates that the grand total for the sales of his nineteen books was over ten million copies.

The last of the impressive social gospel novels was Winston Churchill's *The Inside of the Cup* (1913).[31] A much

[30] Mott, *Golden Multitudes*, p. 229.

[31] The later course of the social gospel movement is ably discussed in Paul

more sophisticated author than Wright, Churchill (1871–1947) also found very early the way to popular success. His first novels were of the variety which has come to be called the "costume romance"—*Richard Carvel* (1899) and *The Crossing* (1904). But Churchill was not a mere chronicler. His idealism and seriousness of purpose are shown in a series of novels written between *Coniston* (1906) and *The Dwelling Place of Light* (1917) which deal with various social, political, and ethical problems of the day. *The Inside of the Cup* takes its place among them. Again we see a young city pastor struggling to bring his wealthy congregation to a realization of what Christ would ask them to do with their money and influence. The central situation—the Rev. John Hodder's own spiritual awakening and his subsequent battle with his rich and worldly parishioners—gives rise to many rousing scenes. But the novel is weighed down with long discussions about theological and social questions. Conceivably this tract-like tone helped its sales. Churchill contrives to weave into his story just about all of the problems which were troubling thoughtful Protestants at that time.[32]

VI. Some Recent Variations

Although religious fiction is as popular today as it was in any period I have described, patterns and trends are difficult to discern.[33] The most persistent of the older themes—The

---

A. Carter's *The Decline and Revival of the Social Gospel: Social and Political Liberalism in American Protestant Churches, 1920–1940*, Ithaca, 1954. I find almost no reflection of the newer issues in the religious best sellers of this period.

[32] Religious questions continued to exercise Churchill's mind. One of his last books, *The Uncharted Way. The Psychology of the Gospel Doctrine*, Philadelphia, 1940, is an attempt to reconcile his ideas of evolution with the Christian message and so discover the dynamic aspect of the gospel and its creative significance.

[33] The best study of recent religious fiction is James D. Hart's "Platitudes of Piety: Religion and the Popular Modern Novel," *American Quarterly*, VI, Winter 1954, pp. 311–322.

Christ Appears—turns up seasonally (Sholem Asch, *The Nazarene*, 1939; Lloyd Douglas, *The Robe*, 1942, and *The Big Fisherman*, 1948). The social gospel novel, much diluted, gives what substance there is to Agnes Sligh Turnbull's *The Bishop's Mantle* (1947). Again we meet the conscientious young (Episcopal) minister in a city church who has to fight his most powerful vestryman. (Inevitably he is the owner of the worst slums in the city.) But the Rev. Hilary Laurens does not spend all his time trying to discover what Christ would do. He has too many personal problems to wrestle with—a wife who drinks, an entanglement with a young widow who tries to have an affair with him, a temporary loss of belief in immortality caused by his brother's death.

This novel illustrates as well as any an extremely important difference between the modern religious novel and the religious best sellers thus far considered. The emphasis now is on behavior rather than belief. The implicit question is: how can I discover and bring into my life the power of religion in order that I may become a better human being?

As a knowledge of the Bible and a reliance on Scriptural authority have diminished, many Protestant ministers have decided to devote their sermons to ethical problems and how they may be solved by getting in tune with the infinite or by the power of positive thinking or by abundant and confident living. An occasional Biblical embellishment adds tone to the discourse and the invocation of the name of Jesus is still useful to provide a dramatic climax.[34]

[34] The Rev. Harry Emerson Fosdick in his autobiography, *The Living of These Days*, New York, 1956, p. 92, describes his efforts to develop a new style of preaching, suited to the needs of his congregation.

"Meanwhile, my struggle to discover how to preach went on with no little perplexity. The stereotyped routine into which old-fashioned expository preaching had fallen was impossible to me. First, elucidation of a Scriptural text, its historic occasion, its logical meaning in the context, its setting in the theology and ethic of the ancient writer; second, application to the auditors of the truth involved; third, exhortation to decide about the truth and act on it—such was the pattern in accordance with which every week multitudes of sermons were manufactured. That a vital preacher could use that model to good effect goes without saying, but there was something the matter

The religious novelists followed this lead, and none more successfully than the Rev. Lloyd C. Douglas (1877–1951), a Lutheran, later a Congregational clergyman turned fiction-writer. (It was impossible for him *not* to write a best seller.) The new formula is abundantly illustrated in his *Green Light* (1935). Dean Harcourt of Trinity Cathedral is an inexhaustible fount of spiritual power. Those who find their way to his study drink and are transformed. Every problem—interpersonal, professional, sexual—is resolved by his healing influence. At one point in the novel Dean Harcourt reveals the secret of his power.

" 'For your comfort, my son, let me tell you that I have laid hold upon a truth powerful enough to sustain me until I die! I know that, in spite of all the painful circumstances I have met, *my course is upward!* I know that the Universe is on my side! It will not let me down! I have been detained at times—but—eventually—*I go on through!*' . . . '*I go on through!*' he repeated earnestly. 'I have suffered—but I know that I am Destiny's darling! . . . *You* have suffered—but *you, too, can carry on through!* . . . Take it from me! I know! In spite of all the little detainments, disappointments, disillusionments—*I get the lucky breaks! I get the signal to*

with the model. To start with a passage from Moses, Jeremiah, Paul or John and spend the first half of the sermon or more on its historic explanation and exposition, presupposed the assumption that the congregation came to church that morning primarily concerned about the meaning of those ancient texts. That certainly was not what my congregation in Montclair was bothered about.

"It was easier, however, to be impatient with the prevailing stereotype than constructively to replace it with a better method. I spent some vexatious years, impatient and floundering. 'Only the preacher,' I petulantly wrote, 'proceeds still upon the idea that folk come to church desperately anxious to discover what happened to the Jebusites.' "

In fairness to Fosdick, I must add that he deprecated the timeliness of the topical preachers who strained after new and intriguing subjects. "One knew that in private they were straining even more strenuously after new intriguing ideas about them." In so doing "they started with their own opinions on some matter of current interest, often much farther away than a good Biblical text would be from the congregation's vital concerns and needs."

go forward! I have been delayed—long—long—long—but—at length—*I get the* GREEN LIGHT!' "

A word is needed about Catholic best sellers or, rather, the lack of them. None of the novels discussed in this chapter were written on Catholic themes. Are there any explanations of this anomalous situation?

It has often been pointed out that the American Catholic writer in the past has not been cherished by members of his faith. For many years, until this century, in fact, the Catholic Church in America was a missionary church, intent on converting non-Catholics, training priests and nuns, building churches, schools, hospitals, and orphanages. It had little time for the arts.[35] Furthermore, because the country was predominantly Protestant, a novel which dealt with religious problems from the Catholic point of view could not possibly have found a large audience. There have been American novelists of the Catholic faith who made regular appearances in the best seller lists, notably Francis Marion Crawford (1854–1909), Kathleen Norris, and Frances Parkinson Keyes, but none of these writers attempted a religious novel.[36]

The situation was bound to change, and it has changed. One can mention at least two recent best sellers which may

[35] John Pick has written an excellent study of the many aspects of the problem of the Catholic writer and his relations with his readers and his Church: "Survey of United States Catholic Letters in the Twentieth Century," *Journal of the Faculty of Arts*, Royal University of Malta, I, 1957, pp. 58–74.

[36] There are, of course, several excellent Catholic novels which did not have phenomenal sales: for example, Harry Sylvester, *Moon Gaffney*, 1947; Brendon Gill, *The Trouble of One House*, 1950; R. O. Bowen, *The Weight of the Cross*, 1951; and Caroline Gordon, *The Malefactors*, 1956. Catholic intellectuals point out that there might have been many more novels of similar stature if a number of excellent novelists who were born into the Church had not left it (F. Scott Fitzgerald, Ernest Hemingway, James T. Farrell, and Katherine Anne Porter). They also observe ruefully that the best religious novel written from the Catholic point of view is Willa Cather's *Death Comes for the Archbishop* (1927). Miss Cather was not a member of the Church.

qualify as Catholic novels: Russell Janney's *The Miracle of the Bells* (1946) and Henry Morton Robinson's *The Cardinal* (1950).[37] Reviewers in the better Catholic journals did not think well of them as novels or as presentations of the Catholic position on the various questions of faith and morals they sparingly deal with.[38] The trouble is, of course, that both novelists had to accommodate themselves to the large audience they were seeking, Protestant as well as Catholic. Religious issues are only incidental to the plots, and the sterner doctrines of the Church are not dwelt on. The Catholic clergy are depicted as solid American types, some of them a little crusty or authoritarian perhaps, but good-hearted and benevolent all the same. Each novel makes use of a gimmick. *The Miracle of the Bells* is a Hollywood spectacular—with Frank Sinatra as the star, it was fabulously successful in the movie version. *The Cardinal* is an American success story, with its Horatio Alger hero robed as a priest who finally has the cardinal's hat bestowed on him. But Janney and Robinson were pioneers. Others will follow the trail they made.

What would those other pioneers—the Rev. William Ware and the Rev. Joseph Holt Ingraham—think of these newest variations on their themes?

[37] Janney lists himself in *Who's Who* as a member of the Society of Friends; Robinson is a Roman Catholic.

[38] The reviewer in *Commonweal* said of *The Miracle of the Bells* that it was "the kind of novel about Catholics and Catholic ways usually described as fit reading for the entire family. No one will come down with sin after reading this book, but quite a few people will come down with nausea and spasms of derisive laughter." Of *The Cardinal* the *Catholic World* observed: "The basic truths of the Faith are open to misinterpretation because they are presented in such elaborately staged dramatics."

THE PLACE OF THE BIBLE IN AMERICAN FICTION *

CARLOS BAKER

THE subject before us is so wide-ranging that, for thorough examination, it would need twenty times the space here devoted to it. Indeed, the further one explores, the larger the domain appears to be. The investigator begins at last to feel like that Norwegian sailor in Milton's *Paradise Lost* who anchored his tiny skiff under the lee of what he took to be an island, only to discover that it was in fact a slumbering whale.[1] Under the bland surface of a veritable ocean of literary endeavor this whale of Biblical influence conceals its mighty dimensions. Sometimes it breaches for long enough to give the awed observer some little idea of its length and breadth before vanishing once more into the whelming deeps. No reader of what follows will be more conscious than the author of these remarks of the fact that they constitute the logbook of a mere temporary encampment on the flanks of Leviathan.

The breeding-ground for this mammoth influence is the King James version of the Bible. Quite apart from its theological implications, it is our greatest English classic. Moreover, as Professor Randall Stewart has asserted, "the Bible has been the greatest single influence on our literature."[2] This is very nearly a truism, whether we are thinking in terms of style or in terms of substance. From the beginnings of American fiction in the early national period, our writers have shown a marked tendency to turn to the Bible either for rhetorical inspiration or for stylistic conditioning. Some-

* Editors' Note: This essay was solicited as the result of a lecture which Professor Baker gave at the Princeton Theological Seminary, Princeton, New Jersey. Its revision for us in essay form has subsequently appeared in the Seminary's periodical, *Theology Today*, XVII, no. 1, April 1960, pp. 53–76.

[1] *Paradise Lost* 1:202–208.

[2] *American Literature and Christian Doctrine*, Baton Rouge, 1958, p. 3.

times this turning has been unconscious or subconscious, sometimes overtly intentional. We learn, for example, that James Fenimore Cooper, our first novelist of any real stature despite his manifest shortcomings, not only helped to found the American Bible Society but also made a fetish of reading a hundred verses of the Bible with his wife every morning before breakfast.[3] Qualitatively speaking, one could wish that the many styles of the Bible had exerted a greater effect than in fact they did on the prose of J. F. Cooper. Yet it is plain that he is only one of many who consciously exposed themselves to the syntax and vocabulary of Biblical utterance. The unconscious or subliminal effect of Biblical poetry and prose has been even more extensive. Hawthorne, for example, speaks with a kind of ironic nostalgia of "the old wooden meeting-house in Salem [Massachusetts] which used, on wintry Sabbaths, to be the frozen purgatory of my childhood."[4] But it is entirely possible that without that purgatorial deep-freeze in his early years, when we may be sure he was obliged to commit to memory dozens of passages from the Bible, Hawthorne's later prose would not have melted into such fluent periods as we find in *The Scarlet Letter* or *The Marble Faun.* Hawthorne the stylist was of course influenced by Spenser and Bunyan and Milton, who in their turn had felt the impact of Biblical literature in their own verse and prose.[5] Yet this is merely to place Hawthorne with his contemporary Melville, and with many others before and

[3] L. E. Nelson, *Our Roving Bible,* New York, 1945, p. 158. See also R. E. Spiller, *Fenimore Cooper,* New York, 1931, p. 68; and H. W. Boynton, *James Fenimore Cooper,* New York, 1931, p. 26.

[4] Hawthorne, *Our Old Home,* ch. XI. Other memoirs of the period allude to the austerity of atmospheric conditions in the meeting-houses. The narrator in Mrs. Stowe's *Oldtown Folks* (ch. V) recalls a local Connecticut tradition that communion was once "administered under a temperature which actually froze the sacred elements while they were being distributed." He goes on to speak of "winter sessions in that old meeting-house" during which "I sat with my poor dangling feet perfectly numb and paralyzed with cold."

[5] This vexing problem in stylistics always requires caution and taste. John Cline's admirable dissertation on *Hawthorne and the Bible* (unpublished, Duke University, 1948) discovers a strong influence of the King James version on Hawthorne's early story "The Gentle Boy," which first appeared in

since whose work betrays both direct and indirect Biblical effects. We hear of Stephen Crane in the late years of the nineteenth century, whose father was a doctor of divinity, a noted preacher, and a rather reluctant Methodist. The young man's version of Hawthorne's *Scarlet Letter* was *The Red Badge of Courage*, written at a time when Crane was in a state of active rebellion against the religion of his youth. Yet we are told what many of his stories plainly reveal, that his early religious training, including much reading of the Bible, provided a "permanent enrichment" of his emotional life.[6]

We have so far been speaking almost exclusively of stylistic matters. The debt to the Bible among our writers of prose fiction is, however, even deeper in the realms of image and idea. Again and again in the history of American letters we find writers using metaphors of Biblical origin. Not least among these is the great synoptic metaphor which so stimulated the imaginations of the American colonists in the seventeenth and eighteenth centuries that they thought and spoke of themselves under the image of the Chosen People, undertaking a task of plantation as the crowning act in God's providential plan. Not only did they call America the Promised Land, but also, as Perry Miller has observed, "they grew to regard themselves as so like the Jews that every anecdote of tribal history seemed like a part of their own recollection."[7] The metaphor has had almost innumerable

The Token in 1832, an early date for American fiction. At one point the boy says: "They drove me forth from the prison when they took my father thence, and I stood afar off watching the crowd of people, and when they were gone I came hither, and found only his grave." Yet to the ear of another reader, the quoted passage seems to ring even more exactly with the accents of Bunyan. See Cline, pp. 222–223.

[6] Vernon Loggins, *I Hear America*, New York, 1937, p. 24. Among Crane's biographers, Thomas Beer, John Berryman, and D. G. Hoffman agree that Crane's father imbued him with the New Testament and his mother with the Old, and that he made literature from the internal quarrel. On Crane's early church attendance, see Berryman, *Stephen Crane*, New York, 1950, p. 14.

[7] See Perry Miller's brilliant essay, "The Garden of Eden and The Deacon's Meadow," *American Heritage*, 7, December 1955, p. 60.

repercussions both in and out of our literature. Thomas Jefferson and Benjamin Franklin, while engaged in the search for a suitable motif for the Great Seal of the new republic, called for a picture of "the children of Israel, led by a cloud by day and a pillar of fire by night." [8] Herman Melville named one of his heroes Israel Potter as a means of signifying that "for more than forty years, poor Potter wandered in the wild wilderness of the world's extremest hardships and ills." [9] In our own day, the same metaphor appears in the new context of John Steinbeck's *Grapes of Wrath*, that memorable novel of the uprooted Okies in their ironic pilgrimage from the arid wilderness of the Dustbowl to California, the Promised Land of milk and honey.[10]

Great metaphors, like this one of the Chosen People, have ways of surviving in imaginative literature, especially when they are constantly reinforced by the authors' return to the book where they originated. It is unfortunate in many respects that we did not produce prose fiction in this country during the colonial period. One finds histories, diaries, biographies, autobiographies, sermons, and a wealth of charming doggerel verse. The Puritan prejudice against prose fiction, and indeed against secular literature of most kinds, is well summarized by a seventeenth-century minister named Thomas Shephard, whose reason for not reading books was that Jesus Christ is "not got with a wet finger." [11] Yet we can be roughly

[8] *Papers of Thomas Jefferson*, ed. Julian P. Boyd et al., Princeton, 1950, Vol. I (1760–1776), pp. 494–495. In 1776 Franklin and Jefferson, though both of deistic inclination, offered designs for the Great Seal of the United States which seemed to suggest their belief in the interposition of God in human history. Their proposals depicted Moses on the Red Sea shore, touched with rays from a pillar of fire in the clouds, and extending his hand over the waves, which are about to overwhelm Pharaoh and his legions. Cf. Exodus 14:8–30 and Numbers 14:14.

[9] Melville, *Israel Potter*, ch. I. Quoted by Nathalia Wright, *Melville's Use of the Bible*, Chapel Hill, 1949, p. 53. See also Reinhold Niebuhr, *The Irony of American History*, New York, 1952, especially pp. 24–25 and 70.

[10] Peter Lisca, *The Wide World of John Steinbeck*, New Brunswick, N.J., 1958, pp. 168–173.

[11] See Kenneth B. Murdock's excellent *Literature and Theology in Colonial New England*, Cambridge, Mass., 1949, p. 62.

certain of the kind of fiction the colonists would have written: homespun, probably realistic, filled with lively imagery drawn about equally from the Bible and the barnyard, strongly moralistic in its aesthetic orientation, and having constant recourse to the metaphor of the Chosen People.

Well into the early national period, when our prose fiction began, the New England mind was saturated with the Old Testament rather than the New. All children were raised on the Bible from the cradle, and writers could assume, as we can no longer do, that the stories of Moses in the bulrushes, or Lot's wife, or Ruth amid the alien corn, or Abraham's sacrifice, were known to them as our children know the complex lore of missiles and moon-conquest. Professor Miller has observed that "there are hundreds of Edens, Josephs, Elijahs for every rare crucifixion or still more rare recreation of the Manger, while Madonnas, are, of course, non-existent" for the very probable reason that these images smacked of popery.[12]

Even after the Second Great Awakening had begun to arouse a fresh interest in the teachings of the New Testament, the Pentateuch and the Old Testament prophets continued to exert a powerful influence on the American literary imagination. One discovers evidence of a not very surprising cultural lag in the transfer of imaginative allegiance from the Old Testament to the New. The children, after all, still played with miniature Noah's arks, still read in their primers about the fall of Adam, who happily came first in the alphabet and therefore in the charming hornbooks of the period, and still spoke of Job's comforters as comfortably as they spoke of the comforters on their own trundle-beds. The literary effects of this kind of upbringing have been well stated by Harriet Beecher Stowe, who grew up in Connecticut in the early nineteenth century, and subsequently became one of our most pertinacious writers of fiction. "I think," wrote Mrs. Stowe, "that no New Englander brought up under the regime

[12] Perry Miller, p. 55.

established by the Puritans could really estimate how much of himself had actually been formed by this constant face-to-face intimacy with Hebrew Literature." As for herself, she said, the "passionate oriental phrases" of the Old Testament, "its quaint pathetic stories, its wild transcendent bursts of imagery, fixed an indelible mark in my imagination." [13]

Mrs. Stowe's remarks are worth a moment's reflection, for they serve to emphasize two major and quite different reasons for the popularity of the Bible with writers of fiction. The first, which is summed up in her phrase "face-to-face intimacy," embodies a certain comfortable and unmysterious familiarity of association, a fund of information held in unison, always available in the common talk of the kitchen and the market-place, springing to mind in the most ordinary situations and shared by rich and poor alike. This intimacy, this warm sense of association with Adam and Eve, Job and Jonah, David and Jonathan, Esau and Jacob, Ruth and Boaz, Isaiah and Ezekiel, and even Sodom and Gomorrah, appears constantly in the so-called "local color" movement in nineteenth-century American fiction.[14] To take only one example, it is reflected in the humorous writing shortly before the Civil War when the Widow Bedott, after long pursuit, has finally succeeded in marrying the Reverend Mr. Sniffles, and sets her heart on redecorating the walls of the parsonage

[13] Harriet Beecher Stowe, *Oldtown Folks,* ch. XXII. That Oldtown folks were Old Testament folks is clear from the narrator's recollection that the Bible was read aloud "twice a day in every family of any pretensions to respectability, and it was read as a reading-book in every common school. . . . I am certain that the constant contact of the Bible with my childish mind was a very great mental stimulant, as it certainly was the cause of a singular and vague pleasure. The wild poetic parts of the prophecies, with their bold figures, vivid exclamations, and strange Oriental names and images, filled me with a quaint and solemn delight. . . . Where Kedar and Tarshish and Pul and Lud, Chittim and the Isles, Dan and Beersheba, were, or what they were, I knew not, but they were fixed stations in my realm of cloudland."

[14] Stowe, *Oldtown Folks,* ch. VI, speaks of a servant girl named Polly who was so "circumstantial about all that took place at the time the angels fell, and where the covenant was made with Adam in the Garden of Eden, that I sometimes question whether she really might not have been there personally." Many a Polly, it is clear, continued the unofficial indoctrination of the children around the evening fire.

parlor.[15] The height of her aspiration is represented by some "Scripter pieces" that hang in the home of her neighbor Sister Myers. They strike her as "wonderful interestin', especially the one that represents Pharoh's daughter a findin' Moses in the bulrushes. Her parasol and the artificials in her bunnit is jest as natral as life. And Moses, he looks so cunnin' a lyin' there asleep, with his little coral necklace and bracelets on." And she also likes another picture that shows "Pharoh a drivin' full tilt into the Red Sea after the Isrelites. How natral his coat-tails flies out," she cries, and it is clear that the Reverend Mr. Sniffles will have no peace until his house can boast Old Testament art-objects to rival those of Sister Myers.

Yet we must not ignore the other side of Mrs. Stowe's observation. For what left an indelible mark on her imagination was the strain of Oriental exoticism which the Biblical stories carried into the deeper recesses of the New England mind. She speaks advisedly of the "passionate oriental phrases" such as one could easily locate in the Song of Solomon. She praises the "wild transcendent bursts of imagery" which punctuate the Psalms, vitalize the prophecies of Isaiah, and bring to a climax the colloquy between Jehovah and Job. It was, no doubt, the continuous exposure to the exotic in thought and language which helped to make the Bible so precious a book to all who were seeking to wrest a richer mode of imaginative life from the stark conditions of daily existence either in New England or along the westward-moving frontier. The Bible, says Mrs. Stowe, and her words are worth our attention, "insensibly wrought a sort of mystical poetry into the otherwise hard and sterile life of New England."

If we turn to the fiction of Nathaniel Hawthorne, Mrs. Stowe's far more eminent contemporary, we need not wonder

[15] Mrs. Bedott, afterwards Mrs. Sniffles, was the creation of Frances M. Whitcher (1811–1852). A sampling of the widow's monologues is conveniently accessible in Walter Blair, *Native American Humor, 1800–1900*, New York, 1937, pp. 271–278.

to find there abundant evidence of the considered use of imagery derived from "exotic" Old Testament sources. His famous complaint about New England, embodied in his preface to *The Marble Faun* in 1859, says that "no author" who has not tried it can imagine the difficulty of writing a fictional romance "about a country where there is no shadow, no antiquity, no mystery, no picturesque and gloomy wrong, nor anything but a commonplace prosperity, in broad and simple daylight." Hawthorne's working knowledge of the Bible, like his interest in demonology and witchcraft among his Puritan ancestors, helped him to infuse a continuous lurking sense of the remotely antique, the exotically oriental, and the far distant in time and place into such localized New England novels as *The Scarlet Letter*, *The House of the Seven Gables*, and *The Blithedale Romance*.

The tendency is especially visible among the dark heroines in Hawthorne's major romances. A rich oriental quality pervades their beauty as if to suggest some distant blending of the black Caucasian and the Semitic. In *The Blithedale Romance*, for example, a young writer named Miles Coverdale, who happens to share the name with a famous sixteenth-century translator of the Bible, arrives at the socialist community of Blithedale on a snowy day in April. He immediately strikes up a playful conversation with the most beautiful woman there, who is mysteriously named Zenobia. It is too bad, says Coverdale, watching Zenobia closely, that the women of the colony must cook and scrub, for in that other paradise "Eve had no dinner-pot, and no clothes to mend, and no washing-day." Zenobia replies that Blithedale is still too wintry to be mistaken for Eden. "No, no, Mr. Coverdale," she says, "the only flower hereabouts is the one in my hair, which I got out of a green-house this morning. As for the garb of Eden," she adds, shivering playfully, "I shall not assume it till after May-day!" Assuredly, says Coverdale, Zenobia could not have been serious. "But these last words, together with something in her manner, irresistibly brought up a picture of that fine, perfectly developed figure, in Eve's earliest garment. . . . We seldom meet with women nowadays, and in this country, who impress us as being women at all. . . . Not so with Zenobia. One felt an influence breathing out of her such as we might suppose to come from Eve, when she was just made, and her Creator brought her to Adam, saying, 'Behold! here is a woman!' Not that I would convey the idea of especial gentleness, grace, modesty, and shyness, but of a certain warm and rich characteristic, which seems, for the most part, to have been refined away out of the feminine system." [16]

This curious passage is only one among the nearly 300 occasions on which Hawthorne invoked the memory of the Bible for purposes of plot or characterization. The strain of oriental exoticism in the portrait of Zenobia is unmistakable, and it belongs to the same order of suggestion with which Hawthorne surrounds another of his dark heroines, the beautiful artist Miriam in *The Marble Faun*. Among the sketches Miriam has made, as preliminary to oil paintings, are no fewer than three on Biblical subjects: one from the Book of Judges showing "Jael driving the nail through the temples of Sisera," another from the Apocrypha, depicting Judith with the head of Holofernes, and a third from the Gospel according to Matthew, representing "the daughter of Herodias receiving the head of John the Baptist in a charger." The context of the novel, and the subsequent development of the character of Miriam herself, make it quite clear that Hawthorne selected these bloody occasions as a means of suggesting to his readers not only the direction which Miriam's life would presently take but also the "passionate and fiery" nature of her inmost character.[17]

But the craft which Hawthorne displays in the manipula-

[16] *The Blithedale Romance*, ch. III.

[17] *The Marble Faun*, ch. V. Dr. Cline's actual count of Biblical allusions in Hawthorne is 287, divided 121 to the Old Testament, 163 to the New Testament, and 3 to the Apocryphal Books. The favored Old Testament books seem to have been Genesis, Psalms, Job, and Proverbs, in that order. New Testament books, also in order, are the Gospels of Matthew, Luke, and Mark, and Revelation. For a comparison with Melville's preferences, see footnote 32, below.

tion of Biblical backgrounds is nowhere better exemplified than in his account of the living-quarters of the Reverend Arthur Dimmesdale in the ninth chapter of *The Scarlet Letter*. For Hawthorne is engaged in a story about the consequences of the adulterous relationship between Dimmesdale and Hester Prynne, with the figure of Dr. Chillingworth, Hester's wronged husband, always present in the reader's consciousness even when he is not actively engaged in the development of the story. Dimmesdale's study in his Boston boarding-house is "rich with parchment-bound folios of the Fathers, and the lore of Rabbis, and monkish erudition" of which, says Hawthorne, the Protestant preachers of New England, though they might decry or vilify both Catholic and Jewish positions, "were yet constrained to avail themselves." What is even more noteworthy, however, is the Gobelin tapestry on the walls of the minister's room. It represents, Hawthorne tells us, "the Scriptural story of David and Bathsheba, and Nathan the Prophet, in colors still unfaded," that is, the ancient story of another adulterous relationship whose consequences were attended with human misery. It does not matter that the story in Second Samuel is by no means a precise analogue for Hawthorne's New England tale. By the artful use of the tapestry at a strategic moment, Hawthorne contrives to hint at as much of the parallel as his story requires. For as the Old Testament makes clear, "the thing that David had done" in pilfering the wife of another was anathema in the eyes of the Lord. And the Scarlet Letter on Hester's bosom, like its counterpart on Dimmesdale's flesh, represents Puritan society's Nathan-like judgment that no man or woman is justified in putting asunder those whom the Lord has joined together.[18]

The method of Hawthorne is instructive for any reader whose religious commitment is deep rather than loud, and whose taste in fiction has been formed by a study of the masters. For it seems to suggest the important aesthetic law

[18] *The Scarlet Letter,* ch. IX.

that the use of Biblical materials should always be made with extreme delicacy if the effect is not to become banal to the point of actual embarrassment. This is not, of course, to say that religious ideas may not be legitimately and movingly dealt with in fiction. Yet it is to insist that a writer who turns to a Biblical episode for any metaphorical or illustrative purpose ought to be content to treat it allusively, to allow it to operate in the realm of suggestion, unless he is willing to vulgarize his source, or to count on windy rhetoric to carry his point.

It may be of some use to illustrate the operation of this law by looking at two contrasting presentations of a Biblical episode in which Hawthorne himself once expressed an interest, though he never chose to give it fictional treatment. This is the episode of the division of the garments of Jesus from the Gospel according to John. "Then the soldiers, when they had crucified Jesus, took his garments and made four parts, to every soldier a part; and also his coat: now the coat was without seam, woven from the top throughout." Hawthorne once recorded in his notebooks that he had been discussing this incident with an artist named Thompson, and that he thought he could "make something" of the story of the robe without a seam and the Roman soldier who won it in the gamble at the foot of the Cross where Jesus hung.[19] Now it happens that Hawthorne never got around to this story, though it is probable that his treatment of it would have been in good taste. At the other end of the scale of taste is the modern handling of the story in *The Robe*, the historical novel by Lloyd C. Douglas, the ex-Congregational minister whose religious fiction virtually dominated the best-selling brackets of the Depression period. The artistic level of *The Robe* is only slightly above that of the late Cecil B. DeMille's most recent version of *The Ten Commandments*, and must share with it the blame for an almost unendurable

[19] John 19:23. See Hawthorne, *American Notebooks*, ed. Randall Stewart, New Haven, 1932, p. 249.

cheapening of the Old and New Testament materials with which Douglas and DeMille respectively concern themselves. The soldiers who cast lots for the raiment of Jesus in the Douglas novel speak in a mixture of modern slang and a pseudo-Biblical patois which can only be the author's own tasteless invention. In the presence of these creatures it is a rare individual who can breathe comfortably while his sensibilities are being assaulted by the nauseous smog of platitudinous piety with which Douglas surrounds his account of the third greatest event in Christian history.[20]

It is quite otherwise when a genuine artist like Sarah Orne Jewett makes illustrative use of the Gospel account of the casting of lots at the foot of the Cross. For she is wise enough to suggest the idea and then to let it accomplish its imaginative effect. The scene comes in a short story called "The Flight of Betsy Lane" which describes an old lady's attempt to run away from the Byfleet Poor Farm in southern New England. It is May and the aged inhabitants are planting corn in the fields. Each year they gently play a little joke, which is to dress up a scarecrow in the "forlorn discarded garments" of one of the old people on the farm. We are given two views of the scene. In the first, two old men have finished their hoeing and are preparing to dress the scarecrow in the clothes they have purloined. "They knelt in the furrows, chuckling," writes the author, as they lifted and examined the cast-off clothes. Our second view of the same scene has taken on a degree of psychic distance. "Behind the men," writes Miss Jewett, "was the foundation for this rustic attempt at statuary—an upright stake and bar in the form of a cross. This stood on the highest part of the field; and as the men knelt near it, and the quaint figures of the corn-planters went and came, the scene gave a curious suggestion of foreign life. It was not like New England; the presence of the rude cross appealed strongly to the imagination." The "for-

20 See the editorial, "Movies: The Bible Against Itself," *Christian Century*, 76, 28 October 1959, pp. 1235–1236.

eign life" which Miss Jewett has in mind is ultimately that of Jerusalem in the first century, A.D. The rude cross and the figures who kneel at its base handling the pieces of clothing catch the imagination precisely because they suggest the gambling scene at the Crucifixion. Miss Jewett might have gone on to belabor her point, which is to hint that the annual scarecrow joke at Byfleet Poor Farm is a pathetic and unintentional shadow of the original event. These aged people, living humbly in the local poorhouse, have in effect been cast off by the society they served. Each one in his turn is vicariously crucified in effigy, in what is essentially a tiny travesty of the event on Calvary. But the author wisely refuses to labor her point. She is content to make the suggestion, and to leave it to do its work.[21]

For every author of Miss Jewett's caliber, American fiction has spawned at least a score of popular novelists who sentimentalize with awesome perseverance at the level of Lloyd Douglas. In a valuable article called "Platitudes of Piety," Professor James D. Hart has recently summarized more than a century of American experience with the popular religious novel.[22] He shows that while the roots of this fiction are often

[21] *The Best Short Stories of Sarah Orne Jewett*, Mayflower Edition, ed. Willa Cather, 2 vols., Boston, 1925, II, 41. The incidence of Biblical themes and allusions in the American short story is, of course, enormous, and is merely touched upon here. See, for example, W. M. Forrest, *Biblical Allusions in Poe*, New York, 1928. Cf. also Sherwood Anderson's *Winesburg, Ohio*, briefly discussed in the present essay. It is of some interest, in connection with the modern emphasis on the Bible as literature, to recall Dean James S. Stevens' choice of the twenty best short stories in the Bible. See James O'Donnell Bennett, *Much Loved Books*, New York, 1927, p. 13. The Dean named the following: the Books of Ruth, Esther, and Jonah; Joseph (Gen. 37–48); Balaam and Balak (Numbers 22–24); Capture of Jericho (Joshua 6); Wars of Gideon (Judges 6–8); Jephthah's daughter (Judges 11); Samson (Judges 14–16); David and Goliath (I Samuel 17); David and Jonathan (I Samuel 18–20); Elijah and the Prophets of Baal (I Kings 18); Naboth's vineyard (I Kings 21); ascension of Elijah (II Kings 2); the three Hebrew children (Daniel 3); Daniel in the lion's den (Daniel 6); Good Samaritan (Luke 10); Prodigal Son (Luke 15); the healing of the lame man at Bethesda (John 5); and the shipwreck of St. Paul (Acts 27).

[22] James D. Hart, "Platitudes of Piety," *American Quarterly*, 6, Winter 1954, pp. 311–322.

in the ground of the New Testament, the bark can generally be seen to ooze with the moral equivalent of sap. The history of this genre begins in Boston in the 1820's with such works as C. R. Gilman's *Memoirs of a New England Village Choir* (1829) and Jacob Abbott's Rollo books, especially one called *The Young Christian*, by which the modern reader will be amused though scarcely edified. This literary undergrowth continues to re-seed itself throughout the next century and a quarter. One notable example is the enormously popular series about the beauties of heaven by Elizabeth Ward. The first of these, called *The Gates Ajar*, tells the story of a New England girl who has lost her brother in the Civil War and is consumed by grief until her Aunt Winifred paints for her a landscape of heaven in such glowing colors and such detailed topography that the bereaved girl gains consolation. The three sequels to *The Gates Ajar* were called *Beyond the Gates*, *The Gates Between*, and *Within The Gates*. The series so enraged Mark Twain, who also attacked Christian Science, that he rejoined with a travesty called "Captain Stormfield's Visit to Heaven," in which he outlined the adventures of a crusty old salt inside a far less sugary supernal domain than that of Mrs. Ward.[23]

[23] Mark Twain regularly adopted a tone of raillery at what he construed to be religious sentimentalism. He was very much aware of the impact of scientific thought on fundamentalist interpretations of the Bible. To the Reverend T. K. Beecher of Elmira, New York, he once made the jocular suggestion that a statue to Adam be erected there, on the grounds that the gradual acceptance of Darwin's teachings on the descent of man would eventually expunge Adam's very name from human memory. He sardonically reports that two bankers in Elmira immediately put up $25,000 in the hope of making Elmira a mecca for Adamite pilgrims and accordingly benefiting local business. See *Works*, New York, Harper, 1917, Vol. 24, p. 296. The same volume closes with two rather sentimental sketches called "Extracts from Adam's Diary" and "Eve's Diary." Twain's final publication, which appeared in the fall of 1909 six months before his death, was called *Extract from Captain Stormfield's Visit to Heaven.* The late Dixon Wecter published the full text for the first time, together with a shorter piece called "Letter from the Recording Angel." See *Report From Paradise*, New York, 1952. Twain's mother joined the Presbyterian Church about 1843, and in boyhood Mark counted himself an "abandoned Presbyterian." Wecter, also Twain's biographer, says that the form Presbyterianism took on the Missouri frontier in the 1840's fostered "morbid preoccupations about sin, the last judgment, and eternal punishment" in the boy's mind, and that "through all

The rather touching popularity of *The Gates Ajar*, which appeared shortly after the Civil War when many people were still reckoning with the recent loss of fathers and sons, has an importance far greater than the novel itself or Mark Twain's none-too-successful parody of it. For the record shows that times of social *Sturm und Drang* in the United States have often called forth novels in which the teachings of the Bible are reinterpreted—and frequently misrepresented—for popular consumption. This is easy enough to explain. Owing to its infinite variety, and therefore its almost infinite adaptability to a variety of situations, the Bible has been used as the ultimate authority for all sorts of actions, whether for the maintenance of the *status quo ante* or as a manifesto of revolutionary doctrine. It is instructive to recall that on the occasion when Franklin and Jefferson were thinking of designs for the Great Seal, they wished to show Moses on the Red Sea shore, touched with the rays from a pillar of fire in the clouds, and extending his hand over the waters where Pharaoh is about to be overwhelmed. The motto they proposed for this representation was "Rebellion to tyrants is obedience to God," a watchword which applied not only to the tyrant of Egypt in his persecution of the Chosen People but also to the tyrant George III in his resistance to the American Revolution.[24]

It is therefore no surprise to find that during the Social Gospel movement of the 1890's, well over a century after the

---

the years of his adult 'emancipation' " Twain felt the afterglow of "hellfire and terror." Dixon Wecter, *Sam Clemens of Hannibal*, Boston, 1952, p. 88. The afterglow is clearly evident in *Tom Sawyer* and *Huckleberry Finn.* Huck's celebrated decision to "go to hell" rather than betray his friend Nigger Jim to the slave-holding community from which both have sprung has been rightly called by Professor Randall Stewart (*American Literature and Christian Doctrine*, p. 121) "a moral choice of the first magnitude." Twain was, in fact, a moral realist who would not have been unhappy in the neo-orthodox religious movement of the twentieth century. *Mark Twain's Autobiography*, New York, 1959, offers much hitherto unpublished evidence on Twain's religious and moral beliefs. One nostalgic passage early in the volume (p. 5) speaks of swimming-holes "which were forbidden to us and therefore much frequented by us. For we were little Christian children and had early been taught the value of forbidden fruit."

[24] See footnote 8.

Great Seal episode, a number of American novels began to propagandize in favor of a special activist version of the Christian ethic. Typical of this special genre, as Professor Willard Thorp has pointed out in his essay in the present volume, was Charles M. Sheldon's *In His Steps,* where a midwestern minister performs a twelve-month experiment in the application of Christ's teachings to the modern American social situation, asking himself at every juncture, "What would Jesus do?" A Canadian minister named Charles W. Gordon (Ralph Connor, pseud.) published a novel called *The Sky Pilot* just before the turn of the century. Gordon's story is likewise informed by virile Christian Socialism, and shows how a muscular and fearless minister of the Gospel wins respect and makes many converts among the cowpokes of the Canadian Rockies.[25] The unfortunate aspect of such works of fiction is their low quality as works of art. Aesthetically speaking, they are one and all dated ruins. The poet W. B. Yeats summed up the problem posed by such amateurish attempts at Christian propaganda when he remarked that "a writer must not write badly, or ignore the examples of the great masters in the . . . service of a cause." [26]

Twenty years after the publication of *The Sky Pilot,* the socio-literary situation had ironically reversed itself. Professor Hart has pointed out that during the decade 1919–1929 "there was no best-selling American novel that could be called religious in theme or attitude." [27] The dates are noteworthy:

[25] For a fuller discussion see Hart, "Platitudes of Piety."

[26] W. B. Yeats, *The Cutting of An Agate,* London, 1919, pp. 53 and 56–57.

[27] Hart, "Platitudes of Piety." This is not to say, of course, that both atheism and strong religious skepticism had not had their innings at an earlier date, notably among writers of fiction. Ambrose Bierce may be singled out because his *The Devil's Dictionary* well summarizes the sardonic strain which became visible in the opening years of the twentieth century. The Devil's definition of *Religion* is "a daughter of Hope and Fear, explaining to Ignorance the nature of the Unknowable." *Flesh* is said to be "the Second Person of the secular Trinity." A *Christian* is defined as "one who follows the teachings of Christ in so far as they are not inconsistent with a life of sin." *Works,* Vol. 7, 1911.

this was the period of the roaring twenties before the great debacle in Wall Street. It is true that Bruce Barton the advertising man sought to stem the anti-Christian tide with his non-fiction best-sellers on Jesus and the Bible, *The Man Nobody Knows* and *The Book Nobody Knows*. But the novelists of the time proved at least that they knew the Bible well enough to use it as a means of "debunking" what they saw as religious pretension and hypocrisy. This ten-year period is ushered in by Sherwood Anderson's *Winesburg, Ohio*. While not strictly typical of the attitudes of the time, it does contain two chapters which reflect on the perils of religious fundamentalism in what H. L. Mencken satirically called the Bible Belt. In one called "The Strength of God," Anderson portrays the struggle of a Presbyterian minister to overcome lustful thoughts. The obvious text is Matthew 5:28, the passage on adulterous concupiscence from the Sermon on the Mount. In the end the minister is delightedly convinced that God has acted to redeem him through the sight of a naked woman at prayer in the bedroom of a house beside his church. Another story from *Winesburg*, called "Terror," appears to combine elements from the episode of Abraham and Isaac with other ideas from the account of David and Goliath. It tells of a grandfather named Jesse Bentley who is so grateful to God for his financial successes that he decides to sacrifice his grandson David. The boy saves himself by hitting the old man with a stone from his slingshot. But Anderson's mild strictures on religious fundamentalism were presently superseded by a number of attacks on Bible-quoting ministers whose left hands neither knew nor cared what their right hands were doing. Middle-aged people today can still recall the scandalous flavor of novels like Robert Keable's *Simon Called Peter* (1922) and Sinclair Lewis' *Elmer Gantry* (1927). Lewis presented a kind of "rake's progress" by an evangelical Baptist preacher, whose reprehensible career was meant to expose American religious hypocrisy during the early years of the century. Such works of fiction, like the Christian Socialist novels of the Nineties, can have today at best a merely historical interest. They acquaint us with attitudes which prevailed in some quarters of the country at the time they were written. But neither *Elmer Gantry* nor *The Sky Pilot*, diametrically opposed as they are in their attitudes towards Christianity, can lay claim to serious literary consideration.[28]

But in rejecting them, we are led directly to a far more important point, namely, that there is a strong tradition of dissent from religious orthodoxy among the best American novelists of the past century. Professor Amos N. Wilder has had much to say about the tradition of dissent in modern poetry. He has repeatedly stressed the obligation of the Protestant community to examine modern works of art for the clues they provide to the operation of the Christian faith in secular thought—a position for which he can find support in the writings of Paul Tillich. Modern poets, novelists, and artists, he points out, may be described as "the outriders of the faith. They continue its explorations, its advance, and its witness at a distance from the main body. If they are heretics we may yet recall the paradoxical thesis that the blood of the heretics is often the seed of the church. We should, indeed, recognize the contribution of those that are well outside the faith."[29] One might add to Professor Wilder's testimony

[28] Lewis the iconoclast, it has been noted, chose as his target-images the American divinity schools, the institution of the ministry, Protestant denominationalism, Catholicism, and Christian beliefs in general—a considerable set of targets for one of Lewis's firepower. A later manifestation of the same motif comes in 1935 with Erskine Caldwell's *Journeyman*, the story of a sex-ridden, gun-toting preacher who conquers a rural community in Georgia, fleecing the men and seducing the women.

[29] Amos N. Wilder, *Modern Poetry and the Christian Tradition*, New York, 1952, pp. 243–244. See also his valuable earlier volume, *The Spiritual Aspects of the New Poetry*, New York, 1940. *Modern Literature and the Religious Frontier*, New York, 1958, includes some consideration of fiction as well as poetry and offers (pp. 129–134) a useful selected bibliographical check-list. This book is by Nathan A. Scott, Jr., who has noted (*Journal of Religion*, 33, October 1953, p. 271) the "steadily increasing impulse of the Protestant community to relate itself imaginatively to the major artistic movements of our time, particularly in the field of literature." Professor

by pointing out that these "outriders" have been at work in American fiction for well over a hundred years now. In one way or another, Hawthorne, Melville, and Mark Twain all stood resolutely opposed to the ethic and metaphysic of orthodox Calvinism. Yet the impressive evidence which they all amassed in their most mature writings about the darker aspects of the human soul indicates clearly that their private vision of the human situation had little in common with contemporaneous pietism. Indeed we may apply to these three romantic novelists a remark once made by T. S. Eliot about three romantic poets. "It is not a wilful paradox," says Eliot, "to assert that the greatness of each of these writers is indissolubly attached to his practice of error, of his specific variation of error. Their place in history, their importance for their own and subsequent generations, is involved in it. . . . They would not have been as great as they were but for the limitations which prevented them from being greater than they were. They belong with the numbers of the great heretics of all time." [30] The Biblical rubric which appears to be most pertinent here is one lately quoted by J. J. Bunting in an article on religious ideas among certain American novelists. It is part of the "Good Shepherd" passage from the tenth chapter of John. "And other sheep I have, which are not of this fold: them also I must bring, and they shall hear my voice." We might make application of this text to our literary heritage in fiction over the past hundred years. Many a seemingly, or actually, rebellious black sheep outside the Christian fold appears to have heard the voice, even though

---

Scott may be overstating the case. But certainly, as he says, the reading of literature in the light of modern theology is a "necessary enterprise of the Christian intelligence." For an admirable reading of Milton and Bunyan from the point of view of classical and modern theology, see Roland Frye, *God, Man, and Satan*, Princeton, 1960. See also N. A. Scott, Jr. *The Tragic Vision and the Christian Faith*, New York, 1957.

[30] T. S. Eliot, *The Use of Poetry and the Use of Criticism*, Cambridge, Mass., 1933, pp. 99–100. The three romantic poets are Goethe, Wordsworth, and Shelley.

he has not chosen to interpret its meaning in the light of received opinion.[31]

It is very likely a considerable overstatement to place Hawthorne, Melville, and Twain among the "great heretics of all time." Yet it is unquestionably true that one finds in each a strain of relentless probing into the darker aspects of human character and motivation, a constant obsessive questioning which suggests that each is somehow dissatisfied with the formulations offered by his predecessors or his contemporaries, whether these formulations are Calvinistic, or Transcendentalist, or connected with the rather saccharine pietism of their day. One might risk the generalization that Hawthorne's preoccupations are mainly ethical while those of Melville are on the whole metaphysical. Melville's choice of the name Ishmael for his narrator in *Moby-Dick* seems, in part at least, to have been founded on the description of his namesake in Genesis: "He will be a wild man; his hand will be against every man, and every man's hand against him." But, as Nathalia Wright has pointed out, the Hebrew meaning of the word Yishmáel is also pertinent: "God shall hear."[32] For

[31] See J. J. Bunting, *Religion in Life*, 24, Spring 1955, pp. 208–218. See also the essay by Harold C. Gardiner, "A Christian Appraisal," in *Fifty Years of the American Novel, 1900–1950*, ed. H. C. Gardiner, New York, 1951.

[32] *Melville's Use of the Bible*, p. 48. Nathalia Wright has located some 650 references to Biblical people, places, and events in Melville's writings. As readers might anticipate, the allusions favor the Old Testament over the New in the proportion of 2 to 1. The order of his chief references to Biblical personages is Jonah, Jesus, Noah, Solomon, Job, Abraham, Moses, and Paul. Like Melville, Jonah and Noah were seafaring men, while Our Lord walked upon the waters, and St. Paul suffered shipwreck. Miss Wright's searching book supersedes earlier work on the subject, but an interesting short article, considering its date (1935) and its place of publication (*The Southern Workman*, Vol. 64, pp. 339–340) is Odell Shepard's "The English Bible and American Men of Letters." Shepard writes in part (p. 340): "Poe knew his Bible well . . . and the supple rhythms of Hawthorne's prose are musical with the chimes and strong with the roll and thunder of the King James version. . . . Thoreau . . . is the Jeremiah of the western world. . . . In Melville's *Moby-Dick* . . . not so much the actual words and tales of the Bible, but its inmost spirit and essence, its grandeurs and its tragedy, have passed into the mind of Melville. His Ahab is a modern Job with Job's huge insoluble problem tormenting heart and brain, and with Job's large utterance.

who shall say that God does not hear the voice of the rebellious questioner, searching in sweat and fury for the answer to the riddle of man's relation to God and to the moral universe? What Hawthorne wrote of Melville, after they had talked together among the sandhills outside Liverpool in 1856, also fits the idea of the artist as rebel: "He can neither believe nor be comfortable in his unbelief; and he is too honest and courageous not to try to do one or the other." [33] The remark underscores the metaphysical worries of Melville, which have their most coherent development in his long masterpiece, *Moby-Dick*, and his short masterpiece, *Billy Budd*. If Hawthorne stresses Melville's metaphysics, Melville in his turn sums up the moral speculations of Hawthorne: "this great power of blackness in him derives its force from its appeal to that Calvinistic sense of Innate Depravity and Original Sin from whose visitations, in some shape or other, no deeply thinking mind is always and wholly free." [34]

Yet it is apparent that Hawthorne's inquiries led him away from Calvinism, and away, too, from the spirit of the Pauline text that "whatsoever a man soweth, that shall he also reap." For as John Cline has suggested, there is a persistent notion in Hawthorne's major writings "that sin could be educational, broadening, and redemptive in effect." In *The Marble Faun*, the artist Miriam wonders whether the story of the Fall of Man is not distantly reflected in her own story. An optimistic

---

That agony of long ago in the land of Uz is lived out again before us on the deck of his New Bedford whaler—and there is something that goes almost beyond Job in the splendid courage of Ahab's final cry: 'Defyingly, I worship thee!'" This essay, written at the bottom of the great depression and published in a workingmen's journal, emphasizes once again the human tendency to read earlier literature in the light of contemporaneous social attitudes.

[33] See Hawthorne, *English Notebooks*, ed. Randall Stewart, New York, 1941, pp. 432–433.

[34] Melville's review of Hawthorne's *Mosses* appeared in *The Literary World* for August 17 and 24, 1850. This long review-essay is conveniently reprinted in Willard Thorp's extremely useful *Melville: Representative Selections*, American Writers Series, New York, 1938, pp. 327–345. See especially pp. 332–333.

thinker might conclude, she says, "that sin, which man chose instead of good, has been so beneficently handled by omniscience and omnipotence that whereas our dark enemy sought to destroy us by it, it has really become an instrument most effective in the education of intellect and soul." Miriam's fellow-artist Kenyon adds that sin may even be a necessary element in human growth, "through which we struggle to a higher and purer state than we could otherwise have attained." Thus in his last novel, as he had also done in his earlier masterpiece *The Scarlet Letter*, Hawthorne engages the ancient paradox of the Fortunate Fall. Through the figure of Donatello, the innocent, Adam-like pagan nobleman who is in effect born into responsible thought as a direct consequence of his sin, Hawthorne succeeds, moreover, in dramatizing the idea that man as responsible moral agent is infinitely preferable to such a prelapsarian innocent as Donatello has been at the outset.[35]

It is a curious coincidence that in the figure of Billy Budd, Hawthorne's friend Melville should likewise have portrayed a primal innocent. Billy's response to the challenge of radical evil in the person of his shipmate Claggart leads directly to a kind of educational experience comparable perhaps to that of Job in the Old Testament—an experience in which he is compelled to face metaphysical problems of which he has hitherto been unaware. The tragic paradox in the case of Billy Budd is that he must be hanged for a crime perpetrated in innocence, which is at the same time the crime by which he has been initiated into an awareness of the nature of evil in the universe. It is probably an error to describe Billy Budd as a Christ-figure, since he is more like Adam at the gates of

[35] This paragraph is much indebted to John Cline's dissertation, *Hawthorne and the Bible*. See *The Marble Faun*, especially the close of ch. XLVII. R. W. B. Lewis, *The American Adam*, Chicago, 1955, p. 151, comments on Hawthorne's realization that the "pristine virtues" would "inevitably encompass their possessor's destruction." For Hawthorne, he says, "the proper denouement was the acquisition through suffering of different and tougher virtues. His version of the fortunate fall found the fortune in the fallen; and it suggested an acceptance of the world and its authority."

paradise. Yet it is a fact that at the moment of his death his compatriots feel emotions comparable to those which are said to have been felt at the original crucifixion. Melville's longer and earlier masterpiece, *Moby-Dick*, poses a quite different kind of problem. Like his Old Testament namesake from the Book of Kings, the heroic Captain Ahab is doomed to die in fulfillment of a prophecy. But as Melville presents him, Ahab is a true romantic rebel, taking arms against that whole *complexus* of metaphysical evils which he masses together, confuses with Godhead, personifies in the white whale, and seeks to destroy in his long pursuit of that probably innocent but certainly enigmatic beast.

The mention of the whale in Melville brings us back to that Leviathan with which we began, the immense—and immensely consequential—influence which the Bible has exerted in American fiction. We may now remind ourselves that the vast question of the Bible's influence in present-day fiction has so far only been touched upon. But in the remaining space it should be possible at least to suggest the dimensions of the problem in our time.

The quickest way to sum the matter up is to say that the tradition of secular exploration, fictional dramatization, and lay exegesis which we have been trying to describe has continued unbroken up to the present moment. It is amusing to recall that as long ago as 1903 an American commentator complained of what he called "The Literary Loss of the Bible." "The old saturation with Biblical phraseology and imagery and illustration," he said, "is a thing of the past. An arid and astounding ignorance has too often succeeded it." [36] Similarly in 1922, Burton Rascoe cast a Menckenesque eye back over the American literary experience with the Biblical

[36] Rollo Ogden, "The Literary Loss of The Bible," *Century*, 65, 1903, pp. 629ff. Views similar to Ogden's seem to have had some currency around the turn of the century. R. P. Utter and Gwendolyn Needham, historians of manners, point to the death of Queen Victoria as the time when the 500-year-old habit of Bible-reading ended and most people "decided that the Bible was a bore." *Pamela's Daughters*, New York, 1936, pp. 470–471.

style and concluded that "the Levantine sonorities of the Old Testament" had too often been invoked to conceal an essential poverty of thought. "The dubious, the false, the untrue, the bombastic, and the commonplace" had leaned upon Biblical rhetoric and thus gained an appearance of profundity. While the grandeur of the original was unassailable, the imitators had often twisted it to pernicious ends, making the Bible a "tool of charlatans" who were intent on shrouding "the debatable in oracular cerements." [37]

It is probably mainly a fact that the stylistic effects of the Bible for which Mrs. Stowe had thanked her stars in the nineteenth century had pretty well dissipated themselves in American fiction by the end of the first quarter of the twentieth. Yet this Lazarus of Biblical influence was soon to revive because he had other powers besides that of style. I shall mention only two. The first may be called the Biblical ethos, and the second the Biblical mythos.

No one who has looked into this subject can help being struck by the fact that in times of social stress in the United States there has been a tendency to turn back for ethical ideals and values to ancient religious literature. Thus in Ludwig Lewisohn's novel, *Stephen Escott*, which appeared in 1930, the first year of the Great Depression, the hero visits the home of a Jew named David Sampson. Sampson and his family, says Lewisohn, "were sustained in the meaningless welter of our modern life by a tradition, a sense of continuity, and the conviction of belonging to a community that stretched across the ages and annihilated time and space." Only nine years later, the distinguished Jewish novelist Sholem Asch inaugurated a series of historical novels beginning with *The Nazarene* on the eve of World War II. In the very year the United States entered that war, Mr. Asch said that he wished "to point to ancient moral values which are charged with the

[37] Burton Rascoe, *New Republic*, 30, 17 May, 1922, pp. 338–339. The date of this essay should be noted, for it falls within the period 1919–1929 when Biblical influence on American fiction probably reached its nadir. It also falls at a time when "debunking" was a fashionable act.

power of salvation for us and for our days."[38] Echoes of these sentiments continue to be audible. A third Jewish novelist, Saul Bellow, writing in the early Fifties, makes his hero Augie March assert that "ancient wisdom is right"—or again, with a shrug and a grin, "Well, given time, we all catch up with the legends, more or less." In his latest novel, *Henderson the Rain King*, which tells of a troubled Yankee millionaire who flies to Africa in search of spiritual regeneration, Mr. Bellow makes significant use of the Old Testament stories about the conversion of Nebuchadnezzar and the story of Daniel in the den of lions.[39]

Similar ideas appear in the work of non-Jewish novelists. Thus Harvey Fergusson's *The Conquest of Don Pedro* employs a moving passage from the Talmud at the climactic point of a historical novel about the American Southwest.[40] Theodore Morrison in *To Make a World* explores some of the modern implications of the Pauline doctrine of charity.[41] In *The Pearl*, John Steinbeck presents an ethical legend about the pearl of great price in a modern Mexican setting. Again in *East of Eden*, he examines the postlapsarian problem of ethical choice in a twentieth-century version of the Cain and Abel story. And though the modern name of the wayward bus in his novel of that title is "Sweetheart," the curious observer, bending close, can see that its former name was "El gran poder de Jesus."[42] It is certainly no accident that James

[38] Sholem Asch, *What I Believe*, New York, 1941.

[39] *The Adventures of Augie March*, New York, 1953, p. 480. This, like its successor, *Henderson the Rain King*, New York, 1959, is essentially a philosophical novel cast in picaresque form. In *Augie March*, p. 260, for example, a dour student named Kayo Obermark remarks that "everyone has bitterness in his chosen thing. . . . That's what Christ was for, that even God had to have bitterness in his chosen thing if he was really going to be man's God, a god who was human. . . . That was Christ. Other gods poured on the success, knocked you down with their splendor."

[40] *The Conquest of Don Pedro*, New York, 1954, p. 241.

[41] *To Make a World*, New York, 1957, is a university novel about the work of a philanthropic foundation, one of the forms "charity" takes in our time.

[42] A good many of Steinbeck's novels are parabolical in intent if not always in visible method. Thus *The Pearl* (1947) tells of a Mexican fisherman who

Gould Cozzens should call one of his novels *The Last Adam* and another, *Men and Brethren,* or that Robert Penn Warren, who has made the most profound use of the doctrine of the Fortunate Fall since the time of Hawthorne, should name his novel-in-verse *Brother to Dragons* from a passage in the Book of Job.[43] Job has, in fact, been a popular figure in our parlous times. He is the hero of Frost's verse-play, *The Masque of Reason,* of Archibald MacLeish's prize-winning verse-play, *J.B.*, and he puts in a spiritual if not an actual appearance in Theodore Morrison's novel, *The Stones of the House.*[44] Mr. Frost's rueful little couplet on God's ways to

---

finds in the sea an enormous pearl, and ends by hurling it back after it has worked him woe. In *East of Eden* (1952), a Chinese named Lee becomes interested in the meaning of the Hebrew word *timshal,* which is variously translated in several versions of the Bible. The word occurs in God's colloquy with Cain after the murder of his brother, and Lee concludes that its proper translation is "Thou mayst"—that is, that man may choose not to sin, but that God has left man the choice. *The Wayward Bus* (1947) is almost if not quite a religious allegory after the model of *The Pilgrim's Progress,* to which it is evidently indebted.

[43] Cozzens' "last Adam" is a Connecticut doctor who defies his community's attempt to impeach him from the Board of Health following an epidemic. As often in Cozzens, religious ideas are considered either centrally or peripherally. The title of this novel is not from the Bible but from John Donne's "Hymne to God My God, in My Sicknesse"—"As the first Adam's sweat surrounds my face,/ May the last Adam's blood my soul embrace." *Men and Brethren* gets its title from St. Peter's Pentecostal sermon (Acts 2:37): "Men and Brethren, what shall we do–" The novel concerns the professional life of a Protestant minister. Robert Penn Warren's *All the King's Men* (1946) emphasizes the theme of good-out-of-evil in an absorbing story related to the rise and fall of the late Huey P. Long of Louisiana. *Brother to Dragons* (1953) derives its title from Job's complaint upon his calamity (Job 30:29): "I am a brother to dragons, and a companion to owls." The story, based on an actual episode in early nineteenth-century Kentucky frontier history, lays emphasis on man's capacity to do evil while convincing himself that he is doing it for good and sufficient reason; and secondly, on the probable fallacy of believing, with such eighteenth-century social philosophers as Thomas Jefferson, who figures in the book, that man's inherent tendency to do evil can ever be extirpated.

[44] Robert Frost, *The Masque of Reason,* 1945. Cf. Frost's second verse-play, *The Masque of Mercy,* which whimsically examines Pauline doctrine, and was published in 1947. Archibald MacLeish's *J.B.* was published in 1959, midway of a successful run on Broadway. Theodore Morrison's *The Stones of the House* is an enthralling academic novel which asks Job's question, "What good does it do to do good?" It appeared in 1953.

man is not strictly in the spirit of the Old Testament, yet is clearly related to one modern reading of the Job story:

> Forgive, O Lord, my little jokes on Thee,
> And I'll forgive your great big joke on me!

In short, on the side of ethos, it is evident that modern American novelists, like their nineteenth-century counterparts, have often transposed Biblical stories into twentieth-century contexts, or have engaged moral and metaphysical themes whose traceable source is the Bible. Nor should we be deceived by their outwardly naturalistic appearances, to say nothing of the rather gamey idiom in which they are sometimes cast, into supposing that they do not seriously concern themselves with problems of Biblical origin.

Turning finally to the side of mythos, the present-day critic can discover a very ample use of Biblical metaphors, symbols, and mythological stories in recent American fiction. In an early review of James Joyce's *Ulysses*, T. S. Eliot provided the classic literary rationale for this kind of operation when he praised Joyce for successfully manipulating "a continuous parallel between contemporaneity and antiquity." For Joyce had located, said Eliot, a useful means of "controlling, ordering, giving shape and significance to the immense panorama of futility and anarchy which is contemporary history." [45]

Among the available examples, the work of William Faulkner stands out most clearly, for as one born and raised in the Bible Belt of northern Mississippi he was continuously exposed from childhood to "Good Book" stories and allusions. Thus his novel *Absalom, Absalom!* immediately suggests his imaginative engagement with the father-son motif from the Book of Samuel. The hero is Colonel Thomas Sutpen, a planter of lower-class origin who is monomaniacally determined to found a personal dynasty. He is clearly based on the figure of King David and, like his spiritual ancestor, he

[45] T. S. Eliot, "Ulysses, Order, and Myth," *Dial*, 75, November 1923, pp. 480–483.

loses two sons in the prime of their lives. But Faulkner is even more deeply concerned with the incestuous triangle which involves King David's children, the girl Tamar, and the young men Absalom and Amnon. In effect, Faulkner combines Freud and the Old Testament, changes the names and motivations of his characters slightly, and transfers the locale from the Middle East to Yoknapatawpha County, Mississippi. In his recently completed trilogy, Faulkner returns to the Genesis story about the Satanic invasion of Eden, embodying the force of evil in a wonderfully complex family named Snopes.[46]

But Faulkner's literary imagination has been even more fully attracted by the life and character of Jesus. The heroic figure of Isaac McCaslin is especially notable because he takes the life of Jesus as a model for his own. He determines on the profession of carpentry because "if the Nazarene had found carpentering good for the life and ends He had assumed and elected to serve, it would be all right too for Isaac McCaslin." [47] The implication here is not infrequent in modern

[46] The title *Absalom, Absalom!*, which echoes David's words on the death of his son (II Samuel 18:33) is slightly deceptive in that while this dynastic novel is very much concerned with Sutpen's desire to perpetuate his name and estate through his son, it also makes use of the story of Amnon's rape of Tamar at II Samuel 13. A good Mississippi touch appears in the Bible when we are told that after the murder of Amnon "all the king's sons arose, and every man gat him upon his mule, and fled." (II Samuel 13:30.) The Snopeses appear in *The Hamlet* (1940), *The Town* (1957), and *The Mansion* (1959). Faulkner has recently explained his views on the Bible. "To me," he says, "the Old Testament is some of the finest, most robust, and most amusing folklore I know. The New Testament is philosophy and ideas, and something of the quality of poetry. I read that, too, but I read the Old Testament for the pleasure of watching what these amazing people did, and they behaved so exactly like people in the nineteenth century behaved. I read that for the fun of watching what people do. The New Testament I would read for the reason that one listens to music, or one would go to a distance to see a piece of sculpture, a piece of architecture. That to me is the difference. One is about people, the other is about the aspiration of man within a more or less rigid pattern. . . ." R. A. Jelliffe, ed., *Faulkner at Nagano*, Tokyo, 1956, pp. 45–46.

[47] In Faulkner's famous story, "The Bear." See R. W. B. Lewis, *Kenyon Review*, 13, Autumn 1951, pp. 641–660. According to Lewis, this story "does as much as literature may with propriety try to do: it enacts for us, by means of human individuals in a local habitation, the miracle of moral

American fiction; any good and simple man is likely to show resemblances to the Savior—a conviction that Ernest Hemingway used notably in his portraits of old Anselmo in *For Whom the Bell Tolls* and of Santiago, the aged fisherman in *The Old Man and the Sea*.[48]

Faulkner has also shown interest in the idea of the Second Coming. In *The Wild Palms*, for example, he makes young Dr. Wilbourne exclaim that "if Jesus returned today we would have to crucify him quick in our defense, to justify and preserve the civilization we have worked and suffered and died shrieking and cursing in rage and impotence and terror for two thousand years to create and perfect in man's own image." [49] In *Light in August* seven years earlier he had presented a kind of tragic travesty of the life and ministry of Jesus through the figure of Joe Christmas, a mulatto outcast who was raised by a fundamentalist farmer, rebelled against his foster-father's legalism, and ended in an awful parody of the Crucifixion. It was perhaps this novel which led R. W. B. Lewis to remark that "the life of Christ is not under any circumstances a subject for fiction: not at all because irreverent, but because within the limits of literature, it would be impossible." [50]

Faulkner nonetheless attempted the impossible in *A Fable*, which won him his first Pulitzer Prize and was instrumental in the award of the Nobel Prize. In this book the Christ-figure is a nameless corporal with a twelve-man squad who foment a passive resistance movement in the French trenches one day in 1918. Faulkner is at great pains to show how the

---

regeneration." See *Portable Faulkner*, ed. M. Cowley, New York, 1949, p. 342.

[48] On this point see the chapters on *For Whom the Bell Tolls* and *The Old Man and the Sea* in Carlos Baker, *Hemingway: The Writer As Artist*, 2nd ed., Princeton, 1956.

[49] *The Wild Palms*, New York, 1939, p. 136.

[50] See "The Doomed and the Damned: Faulkner's Young Rebels," by Carlos Baker in *The Young Rebel in American Literature*, ed. Carl Bode, London, 1959. See also R. W. B. Lewis, *Kenyon Review*, 13, Autumn 1951, p. 660.

ruling powers, intent on justifying and preserving the civilization for which they have worked, suffered, and died, must quickly rid themselves of this radical force for the good. The importance of the novel is not so much in Faulkner's invention of modern parallels for New Testament situations as in the consideration of what happens when an absolute of love invades a world constituted like our own. It may be noticed that this is the same problem to which T. S. Eliot among our poets has often addressed himself. But that is another story.

The late French novelist Albert Camus recently remarked that the American novel is "the novel of men without memory." [51] In the light of our present investigation, this position cannot be fully maintained. For within this nation whose soul, as Thomas Mann once said, "is still close to the Biblical and the monumental," the Old and New Testaments have been a constant force making for remembrance of things past.[52] We may possibly have outgrown the stylistic influence of the Bible, and it is a real question whether or not that has led to the impoverishment of our American prose style. But our best novelists continue to make full use of the Bible as a sourcebook for ideas, images, and mythological frameworks. The American experience in fiction, at any rate, proves once again the truth of the assertion by I. A. Richards: "The saner and greater mythologies are not fancies; they are the utterances of the whole soul of man and, as such, inexhaustible to meditation." [53]

[51] Albert Camus, *The Rebel*, New York, 1958, p. 266.

[52] Thomas Mann, "The Problem of Freedom," an address to the Faculty of Rutgers University at Convocation, 28 April, 1939. I am indebted for this reference to Mr. Niels Barfoed.

[53] I. A. Richards, *Coleridge on Imagination*, New York, 1935, p. 171.

RELIGIOUS POETRY IN THE UNITED STATES

RICHARD P. BLACKMUR

After meditating off and on for three years about American religious verse, I find that it seems to reach in different directions and by different routes than those taken by what is called English or French or Italian religious verse; and it appears to have used, or cultivated, different forces in the Psyche than those within the specific familiar limits of traditional Christian feeling and dogma. It is as if religion itself had reached, or is in the process of reaching, another and different stage in its history than our regular historical sense would have predicted. Some of our Protestant theologians—as Reinhold Niebuhr—say this in their own way when they refer to present times as post-Christian; and they shall have all the rest of the words on this aspect of the subject, which is American religious verse and especially the small amount of it which is also poetry; but I want to keep in mind that unexpected forces of the Psyche are at work in it.

Which is also poetry. Anyone has enough talent to write verse within a body of recognized conventions, but very few have enough talent to make their verse poetry. We are all poets in little, else we could not read it when large; it is a matter, as Croce insisted, of quantity not quality of talent. Most verses written out of love are drivel, and most versifications of the psalms take the poetry out of them and substitute mnemonic rehearsals of doctrine and archetypal images. Hence the morals, like the love, are flagrant, and all the substance of the writer's faith and passion which he would have made public is missing forever. He is not there in front of us, and he has not put his presence into his verse. It is the presence of the human Psyche in words that makes the scandal of poetry as its presence in action makes the scandal of religion.

The distinction is worth insisting on, and I can think of no better language for it than a short passage from George Santayana's preface to *Interpretations of Poetry and Religion* where he outlines the single idea to which his whole book leads. "This idea is that religion and poetry are identical in essence, and differ merely in the way in which they are attached to practical affairs. Poetry is called religion when it intervenes in life, and religion, when it merely supervenes upon life, is seen to be nothing but poetry."[1] It is a matter of choice, chance, and tact or grace, which is which; and religious poetry, I take it, is when the two are taken together. As religion takes new forms and changes the nature and scope of its interventions, so the poetry associated with religion supervenes differently upon our reading lives in manifest presence. There is an area in us where religious poetry at one and the same time both comes among our actions and overcomes them, an ordering together with a ravishing.

The second of the Homeric Hymns to Aphrodite is like that, and the *Pervigilium Veneris*, and perhaps the invocation to Venus in *De Rerum Natura.* They intervene and supervene at once as they persuade us of our occupation. Though the first is a narrative of events, the second an incantation, and the third a part of a philosophical discourse, in each the intervention is religious, the supervention poetic: they touch on behavior fused with aspiration. Reading, we act and breathe and lose the action in our breath. It is the same thing, I think, when we come to the *Cantico delle Creature* of St. Francis where the gap between God and nature is annihilated through the salutation of both in single breath and all our occupation is gone and come at once. Reading St. Francis' Canticle our substance is ravished with all weathers—*onne tempo*—and all the weathers have their own meaning in the being of God. The first three poems we know are not Christian; of the Canticle we know that it is a Christian who wrote it, and one who changed Christianity through the forces that led him to write it. Here are two lines of Iacopone da Todi (of whom it is said that he wrote the *Stabat Mater*) taken from the beginning of his poem on the incarnation of the divine word:

[1] *Interpretations of Poetry and Religion*, New York, 1922, p. v.

Fiorito è Cristo nella carne pura:
or se ralegri l'umana natura

Christ has flowered in pure flesh:
Now let human nature rejoice

and three from the beginning of his poem "That it is the highest wisdom to be thought mad for love of Christ":

Senno me pare è cortesia · empazir per lo bel Messia. . . .
Ello me sa sì gran sapere · a chi per Dio vol empazire,
en Parige non se vidde · ancor si gran filosofia.[2]

Sense and nobleness it seems to me to go mad for the fair Messiah. . . . It seems to me great wisdom in a man if he wish to go mad for God; no philosophy so great as this has yet been seen in Paris.

Iacopone was a Franciscan, too, of the second generation, and a splendid Christian struggle had begun in his poetry, of which St. Francis was free in his simplicity of salutation—the struggle, the wrestling of spirit, to join himself to God. It is a man we know who speaks, as it was in the others a voice we discovered. We hear a voice like this in Donne (in "Batter my heart"), in Crashaw ("The Hymn to St. Teresa"), in George Herbert ("The Pulley"), even in Milton ("Samson Agonistes"). In them all there is a spiritual sensuality behaving like a prodigal mathematics. Religious poetry was for them, as it is somewhat today, a natural technique for the speculative framing and the dramatic solution of the problem of the troubles that beset us when we would play the role of God in our own way. Those who care for the word may say that this was the Baroque spirit at work, and this might be apt from St. John of the Cross to Milton; but it does not help with Iacopone, and helps very little with later poets in the nineteenth and twentieth centuries, like Crane and Eliot and Auden, nor with all those who have read too much St. Augustine and Gerard Manly Hopkins. I would say rather

[2] *The Penguin Book of Italian Verse*, George Kay, ed., Bungay, Suffolk, 1958, pp. 13, 17.

that it is the great wrestling tradition which has inhabited the great majority of religious poets since the Council of Trent, and it makes no difference whether they were Catholic or Protestant or non-juring or simple abstainers. The Reformation and the Counter-Reformation alike put upon us the compulsion to a wrestling (and to an irregular metaphysic to account for the wrestling): a wrestling with God, with the self, with the conscience, and above all in our latter day with our behavior. Pascal stands as a natural monument of one form of this wrestling, Baudelaire as another, and Henry James and James Joyce as a kind of composite for our day. But the mind roams and needs a point of return which is in Genesis (xxxii, 22–32):

> And Jacob was left alone; and there wrestled a man with him until the breaking of the day.
>
> And when he saw that he prevailed not against him, he touched the hollow of his thigh; and the hollow of Jacob's thigh was out of joint, as he wrestled with him.
>
> And he said, Let me go, for the day breaketh. And he said, I will not let thee go, except thou bless me.
>
> And he said unto him, What is thy name? And he said, Jacob.
>
> And he said, Thy name shall be called no more Jacob, but Israel: for as a prince hast thou power with God and with man, and hast prevailed.
>
> And Jacob asked him, and said, Tell me, I pray thee, thy name. And he said, Wherefore is it that thou dost ask after my name? And he blessed him there.
>
> And Jacob called the name of the place Peniel: for I have seen God face to face, and my life is preserved.
>
> And as he passed over Penuel the sun rose upon him, and he halted upon his thigh.
>
> Therefore the children of Israel eat not of the sinew which shrank, which is upon the hollow of the thigh, unto this day: because he touched the hollow of Jacob's thigh in the sinew that shrank.

It is astonishing that we do not have poems called "The Place Peniel" and "The Sinew that Shrank"; for there is in this adventure of Jacob half the subject-matter of modern poetry—which is why we can fill in so well the bareness of this original account with the muscle and nerve of our own wrestling with God, man, or angel, as it may turn out—at any rate a damaging *and* saving confrontation of the self and the "other" self. What seem to be the beginnings of American religious poetry—Anne Bradstreet and Edward Taylor—illustrate the theme in its simple form as the versification of typical experiences and enthusiasms, of doctrine and behavior, where versification is a kind of rehearsal for an act or a role yet to be undertaken. Mrs. Bradstreet, for example, has a dialogue between Flesh and Spirit which precisely fits this description. Her much lovelier, and more sensuous, poem beginning "As weary pilgrim, now at rest" has a feeling in it of a longing, a wooing, of confrontation; but we do not feel either instance or instant. There is no architecture, and the last line ("Then Come, deare bridgrome, Come away!") seems merely pious where it had struggled to be an act of piety. This, at the furthest imaginable reach, I should like to compare to Henry Adams' "A Prayer to the Virgin and the Dynamo," a poem which he carried for many years as a kind of amulet in his wallet, and in which there is present both all the architecture of the cathedral at Chartres and all the space in the Hall of Dynamos at the Paris World's Fair. This is, I think, one of those poems in which the poetry ceases to matter—in which, as in Mrs. Bradstreet, the verse does some damage to the moving thought under the words; but there is a great struggle for the confrontation of a vision gone: the vastation in which one still lives. Here is the last stanza:

> Help me to bear! not my own baby load,
>   But yours; who bore the failure of the light,
> The strength, the knowledge and the thought of God,—
>   The futile folly of the Infinite.[3]

[3] "Prayer to the Virgin of Chartres," in *Letters to a Niece*, Boston and New York, 1920, p. 134.

One thinks of a Pascal of our days: *Le silence éternel de ces éspaces infinis* . . . and there is a regret only for the *words* of the last line. Under them there is a full act of piety to the numinous power, and Jacob's adventure is very near.

It is near perhaps because, not very good poetry itself, it is in the mode of poetry rather than the mode of religion. Herman Melville left a manuscript poem (which is said to have been much rewritten) that may be taken as evidence as to how these modes may cross—how two prayers may be said at the same time—in the special self-consciousness of American imagination. The poem is called "Art" but it deals also with Jacob. Since it is short it is quoted entire.

> In placid hours well-pleased we dream
> Of many a brave unbodied scheme.
> But form to lend, pulsed life create,
> What unlike things must meet and mate:
> A flame to melt—a wind to freeze;
> Sad patience—joyous energies;
> Humility—yet pride and scorn;
> Instinct and study; love and hate;
> Audacity—reverence. These must mate,
> And fuse with Jacob's mystic heart,
> To wrestle with the angel—Art.[4]

The poetry—the art, the Angel Art—at which these lines are aimed, is, it seems to me, one excellent way to describe what has happened to religious poetry in America, and it is possible to religion herself, too. To keep to the poetry, it has simultaneously insisted on the value of what it can itself create and on the pressure (who knows its value) of the numinous power within us, and the relationship between the two is mutinous; as for God—the intervening power—there is discontent, distrust, and dismay for what he has created, but with a lingering addiction of first and last resort. It is Melville again who put this in the final quatrain of an otherwise undistinguished poem about a picture called "The Coming

[4] *Collected Poems of Herman Melville,* Howard P. Vincent, ed., Chicago, 1947, p. 231.

Storm" by Sandford Gifford. For Melville it was the storm in the lull of which we live.

> No utter surprise can come to him
> Who reaches Shakespeare's core;
> That which we seek and shun is there—
> Man's final lore.[5]

Of these lines F. O. Matthiessen observed that they "constitute one of the most profound recognitions of the value of tragedy ever to have been made." I think tragedy an accidental word here, which might have been any other whole word, and especially the word religion; and Shakespeare is another accident. Melville fought the archetypes he sought, and he sought the God he fought. The lines represent many confrontations and many visions, and are therefore always ready to exact from us the details with which to fill them out in what we have done with our own behavior, or in the qualms it has left in us. If it were not so long there is a poem of Melville's called "After the Pleasure Party" which I would quote in illustration at full length; but I content myself with a few lines plus its subtitle, "Lines traced under an Image of Amor Threatening":

> 'Tis Vesta struck with Sappho's smart.
> No fable her delirious leap:
> With more of cause in desperate heart,
> Myself could take it—but to sleep! . . .
>
> Could I remake me! or set free
> This sexless bound in sex, then plunge
> Deeper than Sappho, in a lunge
> Piercing Pan's paramount mystery! [6]

These are matters which had been exorcised by Christianity, but they are none the less the very earth of religious concern, and they have been creeping back into the articulations as well as the blood-stream of Christians. Though the argument (since

[5] *ibid.*, p. 94.
[6] *Poets of the English Language*, W. H. Auden and Norman H. Pearson, eds., New York, 1950, v, 310, 312.

it is the argument of our actual motion) would be worth pursuing for its interest and vitality, for present purposes we can get about as far ahead by thinking of Edward Taylor and Robert Lowell in single context. Both are characteristic New England wrestlers with the spirit. Each has the ghastly sophistication of the Christian Puritan Protestant—a hangnail may be taken as excruciation—and each is aware of the bottomless resources of Enthusiasm and Antinomianism generally. (I remember that T. S. Eliot once in a hot moment reprehended certain addicts of the Inner Voice by saying that it was the eternal voice of Vanity, Fear, and Lust; and he was right.) Lowell wrestles—or behavior wrestles—against the conscience of his faith as revealed to him at the moment. Taylor wrestles against his private conscience. Taylor is full of the *strong lines* of the late metaphysicals, and Lowell writes in strong lines of his own making; each—and I mean the words literally—is obstinate in the spontaneity of his corruption, arrogant in his inadequacy: each is fiercely humble. The chasm between them is like the chasm each saw in himself: upon no razor's edge can this be crossed, and yet one's feet are upon razors. One of Taylor's poems is called "The Souls Groan to Christ for Succour" and it is of such groans that the majority of Lowell's poems are made. Another pair of Taylor's poems make grating accusations of the inner and the outer man where each, so to speak, is stripped into a reversal of role. In each the "other" self confronts the self; and, again, so it is with Lowell, the devil in him wrestles with the man, the angel with the god, in such poems as "To Delmore Schwartz" and "To Speak of Woe that is in Marriage." The difference is that Taylor pushes his sensibility into conceit (almost into formal allegory) and the conceit is the meaning of the sensibility, while Lowell drenches his conceit (the position he has been forced into) with his sensibility and the sensibility, like a road-barrier, is the meaning we are stopped by. Taylor cultivates the numinous or religious force for a purpose already anticipated, Lowell makes the force the purpose itself. For Taylor unity already existed and had to be acknowledged as a mystery that enlightens; for Lowell what unity there is you make yourself and it darkens you forever.

One can imagine Lowell repeating the remark in Gide: God woos us by his calamities, and that is how He shows His love for us; but we cannot imagine Lowell repeating what Taylor heard as "Christ's Reply" to "The Souls Groan to Christ for Succour," for it would have done this latter-day or post-Christian Christian no good. Taylor can write at the end of "Upon a Wasp Chilled with Cold":

Till I enravisht climb into
The Godhead on this ladder doe:
Where all my pipes inspir'de upraise
An Heavenly musick, furr'd with praise.[7]

Lowell writes at the end of his "Memories of West Street and Lepke":

Flabby, bald, lobotomized,
He drifted in a sheepish calm,
where no agonizing reappraisal
jarred his concentration on the electric chair—
hanging like an oasis in his air
of lost connections . . .[8]

The difference is absolute, and we have come again full circle to Iacopone:

Fiorito è Cristo nella carne pura:
or se ralegri l'umana natura.

That is, we can speak of Whitman, for he could have written the Italian lines with only the substitution, to him simple and natural, of himself for Christ: All of me has flowered in my flesh, so let us rejoice in human nature. Indeed it is not in his naïve barbarism (in which the artists and intellectuals of the last century found such companionship) but in his direct and deeply civilized piety, which is precisely where

[7] T. H. Johnson, "Edward Taylor Gleanings," *NEQ*, XVI, June 1943, p. 283.

[8] *Life Studies*, New York, 1959, p. 86.

he resembles Iacopone, that his poetry endures. Since it is more familiar to more people than most of his poems, we can let "When Lilacs Last in the Dooryard Bloom'd" stand for the rest, the more especially because in this poem it is very clear how he met his archetypes—his governing and vitalizing images—the symbols that made him fruitful in words—both in the open road and in the thicket of the Psyche: in what man does and in what he finds doing in himself, in which is included what man has in the past done with his poetry. Whitman, says Northrup Frye in his *Anatomy of Criticism*, was "perfectly right in feeling that the *content* of poetry is normally an immediate and contemporary environment. He was right, being the kind of poet he was, in making the content of his own 'When Lilacs Last in the Dooryard Bloomed' an elegy on Lincoln and not a conventional Adonis lament. Yet his elegy is, in its *form*, as conventional as *Lycidas*, complete with purple flowers thrown on coffins, a great star drooping in the west, imagery of 'ever-returning spring' and all the rest of it. Poetry organizes the content of the world as it passes before the poet, but the forms in which that content is organized come out of the structure of poetry itself." [9]

This is very fine; but I should like to add for present purposes that this is how *religious* poetry operates—when poetry comes nearest to positive intervention in the actions of the soul. As Mr. Frye says, it is not only the Adonis material; there is also the sprig of lilac with its mastering odor, the hidden bird and the secluded swamp, and the "tallying chant" in which all come together: "Lilac and star and bird twined with the chant of my soul." There are two progresses in the poem, of Lincoln's body and of the images, which join in the sacred knowledge of death. Lincoln, Lilac, and Thrush are merged in a full act of piety.

It is a difference of half a century as much as a difference of sensibility in the particular poets that strikes us when we

[9] *Anatomy of Criticism*, Princeton, 1957, p. 102.

look into the thicket of Robert Frost: in which there are obstinate possibilities and obstinate forces, not human themselves, that yet—as they are cultivated into the sensibility—change the human dimension and alter, a little, the reticulation of the elements of the human Psyche. To acknowledge this is a religious action: a momentary conversion. The consuming or purifying fire is always at hand in such acknowledgments, and the more so if, as in Frost, the individual is held on to, nevertheless and because. But one does not wish to exaggerate. Here is an example in the poem "Come In."

As I came to the edge of the woods,
Thrush music—hark!
Now if it was dusk outside,
Inside it was dark.

Too dark in the woods for a bird
By sleight of wing
To better its perch for the night,
Though it still could sing.

The last of the light of the sun
That had died in the west
Still lived for one song more
In a thrush's breast.

Far in the pillared dark
Thrush music went—
Almost like a call to come in
To the dark and lament.

But no, I was out for stars:
I would not come in.
I meant not even if asked;
And I hadn't been.[10]

Frost exposed himself to the thrush in the wood—the *selva oscura*—the thicket where perceptions not one's own become a part of one, and found himself confronted with himself. There is no doctrine here and no dogma, but there is the per-

[10] *A Witness Tree*, New York, 1942, p. 16.

ception out of which many doctrines have sprung and the kind of grasping imagination which has made dogma vital. Those who have need of doctrine and dogma first, before they risk perception, may bring what they will and it will work. Let us say only that there are two remotenesses here: of what is dark and at hand and of what is light (the little that is known of it) and afar; and there is a double invitation to loneliness. Intimations spring from one to the other through the man between, changing and remaining in the graininess of his voice. This is Frost's way, I hazard it, of recording the light in the dark and the dark in the light and the coiling movement between them of the self confronting the self.

It is perhaps unfair to make a foil for Frost's poem of Edwin Markham's "The Man with the Hoe"—once so famous for its perception of man's lot and man's need; but I can think of nothing that shows so well the difference between poetry and good will as to think of the two poems together. Let us put it baldly. Millet's painting was in natural piety to the land and the man with the hoe was very close to being a part of the land which was his life, which it takes deep knowledge to perceive. To my mind Frost's poem and Millet's painting are two versions of the same perception of the human condition, which it is damnation to ignore and a strange redemption to accept. Markham made of the painting a poem of social protest and flagrantly righteous indignation. Out of a false naïveté he saw a false archetype and constructed a faulty iconography. It is the condition in which every perception disappears and hope is thereby hollow. In Frost's poem, not Markham's, the dumb Terror replies to God.

For the other type of foil to Frost, the type that sustains and protects, there is the poetry of Emily Dickinson, which puts the hand upon the quick within her and sings hymns to the actuality of every illusion, and every crowding hope, that struck her. In her, religion supervenes and poetry intervenes upon her secular life without discrimination. Faith, she thought, was the experiment of our Lord.

The auctioneer of parting,
His "Going, going, gone,"
Shouts even from the crucifix
And brings the hammer down.

He only sells the wilderness.
The prices of despair
Range from a single human heart
To two—not any more.[11]

The variety is sufficient, but I should not like to stop lest it be thought I would set up categories into which religious poetry should, or must, fall. I think of Hart Crane's "Voyages," of Wallace Stevens' "Sunday Morning," of Archibald MacLeish's play about Job, and of the new Catholic poets such as Daniel Berrigan, Thomas Merton, and Ned O'Gorman. All of these poets, and no doubt many more, write poetry which can be understood only if it is taken as religious; and yet the variety varies more than the winds. To repeat, since there is no seal upon us in this post-Christian time, our religious like our other emotions come out of Pandora's box; or, to repeat more precisely, as religion takes new forms and changes the nature and scope of its interventions, so the poetry associated with religion supervenes differently upon our reading lives. If there is anything in common not only with itself but with the past, aside from its impulse, I do not know what it is, but it is possible to make a few unaligned suggestions. We are likely to be concerned with the excruciation (as Jacob was not); with Jacob's wrestling with Angel, Man, or God; with the dark night of the soul that never ends since it was a darkness we ourselves made; with the nightmares of the numen or the night-life of the spirit rather than its waking wide safety; and altogether with the great sweep of rival creation since, like Ivan in *The Brothers Karamazov*, we can accept God but not His Creation. We are lost, as Eliot seems to suggest (in his essay on Dante), in our new immersion in

[11] *Poets of the English Language*, W. H. Auden and Norman H. Pearson, eds., New York, 1950, v, 396.

our lower dreams, with the higher dreams gone by the board or unavailing; and indeed only Eliot seems to see the place where the two dreams cross, and it may be only his language that sees that, for he himself calls it "The unread vision in the higher dream" and "the brief transit where the dreams cross." These are the hardships we come by in our daily life, and our poetry reflects them since they are actual.

What is actual, when we would be religious, invades us like a nightmare of our own behavior suddenly seen, and it is our own monsters that keep us from God, and no mere scholarship of the dark will save us, only acknowledgment. We must remove the obstacles, as Pascal saw, that keep us from falling into the abyss; and the obstacles are of our own invention. I think of Allen Tate and his poem "The Wolves," of W. H. Auden and his poem "Petition," and of Eliot's "Little Gidding." Each of these poems, by way of those intrusive monsters anthropology, psychology, and behavior, finds it time for human nature to rejoice, each tries to construct something, as Eliot says, upon which to rejoice, but each is left impaled upon the nature of man. Each therefore is the prayer of what is terrible in human nature (which is nature herself) addressed to the "honor of man," to "a change of heart," and to the "refining fire."

What then are they doing? As one reorganizes one's life one sees that one has been religious all along in the poetry one has made of it. Religious poetry has to do with the modes of power and powerlessness, of glory and misery. These it asserts. With these it wrestles and argues; to them submits; on them rises; in them dies. These are the terms of the poem's relation with the numinous force; the force within the self, other than the self, greater than the self, which, as one cultivates it, moves one beyond the self. Poetry is one of the ways of cultivation; and the harvest is vision. One would see God and die—so Petrarch put it. In any case there is a confrontation, and in the confrontation a flowing of force ending in an access or filling of being, else in a vastation or desolation; and the two are much the same: in calm of mind all passion spent, or *In la sua voluntade è nostra pace.* Who can say which is which?

> And courage never to submit or yield
> And what is else not to be overcome . . .

> O dark, dark, dark, amid the blaze of noon . . .

> *Sunt lacrimae rerum et mentem mortalia tangunt* . . .

> Myself, my Sepulcher, a moving Grave . . .

> *or se ralegri l'umana natura.*

RELIGIOUS MUSIC IN AMERICA

LEONARD ELLINWOOD *

Religious music has occupied an important place in American life from the earliest time. Colonial congregations, which consisted of the major part of the populace, sang hymns with fervor long before there were any secular concerts. Even today, our many symphony orchestras reach far fewer people than do the parish choirs each week. A popular anthem, such as Bach's *Jesu, Joy of Man's Desiring*, is known by far more people than is a Beethoven symphony or overture. In spite of nearly forty years of radio listening, hymns such as "Abide with me," "Onward Christian soldiers," and "I need thee every hour" are known and sung by more Americans than are any popular songs or ballads. Furthermore, the selection of hymns does not change as constantly as do the more ephemeral secular songs. It is fitting that a comprehensive discussion of religion in American life should include this tremendous role that religious music plays.

Native Indian Music

Our forefathers who settled the thirteen colonies along the Atlantic Coast during the seventeenth century had little interest in the music of the primitive aboriginals whom they displaced. With minds closed by the bigotry which for too many persons was a concomitant of their Protestantism, few of those early settlers were concerned about either the native's religion or his music. Unfortunately for the modern ethnomusicologist, even had there been an interest in the

* Editors' note: Professor Otto Kinkeldey was to have been the author of an essay on this subject. After devoting a great deal of time to the project and compiling an extensive file of notes, he found that for reasons of health it was impossible for him to complete the task. His generosity in submitting all his notes to Dr. Ellinwood and in making himself available for consultation is deeply appreciated.

Indian's music, techniques had not been developed at that time which could have recorded the music in a way which would have reproduced it for us today.

Toward the end of the nineteenth century, when serious research began into the musical life of the remaining primitives, it became apparent how completely music was involved in the religious life of those people, in fact with every important aspect of their personal experience. Believing that music was the medium of communication between man and the unseen, the Indians had particular songs for every ceremonial occasion, for every activity of life. These songs were personal, belonging either to a single individual, a family clan, or a tribal organization, depending on the rite or ceremony. They were not common property which could be sung by anyone who liked. Indeed, among the older singers, when attempts were first made to record their songs, there was a strong belief that a song could not be sung except on its proper occasion. One actually had to go buffalo hunting if he were to sing the Buffalo Hunting Song, for the song was by its very nature a prayer for the success of the hunt. Similarly with love songs, visiting songs, war songs, or death songs—none could be used save on their proper occasions.

The music which has been recorded and studied since about 1880 shows this close affinity between the song and the life and activities of the singer.[1] In no case is there any music which existed purely for recreation or impersonal entertainment. White musicians wishing to hear and record the Indian's songs met with real fear and great reluctance at any suggestion that a song be used out of context, lest such sacrilege redound to the singer's harm. Although the Puritans considered the Indian an ignorant heathen, today we know that he was essentially a religious person, with a highly developed culture suited to his own way of life. His music was inherently religious, and to be guarded zealously.

[1] Principal studies are listed in Part Four of the Bibliography. In recent years, the Recording Laboratory of the Library of Congress has made available a series of phonograph records of Indian music, recorded by Frances Densmore, Willard Rhodes, and others.

The Indians' songs were sung as solos or in unison, with little instrumental accompaniment save that of a drum. Flutes and rattles of a simple type were occasionally used, among some western tribes more than others. At no time does there appear to have been a special group of professional musicians who had a monopoly on the tribal music. Only in group ceremonies were the more talented singers given precedence over the others.

The above generalizations can be made about most of the native Indian music of North America as far as it is known today. When one comes to particulars, there is wide divergence between the tribes, since there was little communication between one tribe and another. There is considerable divergence, too, in the subject matter of their songs, reflecting the differing conditions under which the various tribes lived in their respective parts of the country.

Indian Missions

The Spanish, English, and French, each in their own North American colonies, began to teach Christianity to the native Indians as soon as they had learned enough of their languages to be able to communicate with them. The Indians had early shown an interest in the singing of the white men, in marked contrast to the colonists' lack of interest in the Indians' own lore. When Sir Francis Drake's expedition was laid up for repairs in 1579 in what is now called Drake's Bay, just north of San Francisco, his chaplain wrote that the Indians ". . . tooke such pleasure in our singing of Psalmes, that whensoever they resorted to us, their first request was commonly this, Gnaáh, by which they intreated that we would sing."[2]

Compilation of the French or Genevan metrical Psalter had just been completed in the year 1562 when the Hugue-

[2] The Rev. Francis Fletcher, "The World Encompassed by Sir Francis Drake," in H. S. Burrage, ed., *Early English and French Voyages*, New York, 1906, p. 163.

nots brought it to their abortive settlement in Florida. But after only three years, the result was that ". . . long after the breaking up of Laudonnière's colony, the European, cruising along the coast or landing upon the shore, would be saluted with some snatch of a French Psalm uncouthly rendered by Indian voices, in strains caught from the Calvinists." [3]

In New England, John Eliot, the "Apostle to the Indians," set the Psalms to verse in the Algonquin language in 1661 and bound them with his famous Indian Bible. Here again the natives took to Psalm-singing so well that over twenty years later, in 1687, Increase Mather wrote that "the whole congregation of Indians praise God with singing, and some of them are excellent singers."

The Spanish *conquistadores* to the south attempted to transplant as much of their Old World culture as possible. In fact, of the three main colonizing races, the Spanish were the only ones who brought over singers and organists in order to set up musical establishments using the same polyphonic repertory as did their cathedrals at home. As early as 1524, Fray Pedro de Gante (Brother Peter from Ghent), a Franciscan from Louvain University, established a school at Texcoco, Mexico, for the training of Indian musicians.[4] With his fellow Franciscans, Fray Pedro not only taught the natives to sing plainsong and polyphony but also to play and build organs and other musical instruments. All together, there are records of twenty-five music schools in the missions of New Spain during the seventeenth century. Whereas, in the English colonies, any teaching of the Indians was purely for the salvation of their souls, the Spanish had the further ulterior motive of training choristers for service in their newly established cathedrals.

The first of these mission schools within the present limits of the United States of America was at the Mission of San Felipe in New Mexico, where Fray Cristóbal de Quinones

[3] Charles W. Baird, *History of the Huguenot Emigration to America*, New York, 1885, I, 68.

[4] Lota M. Spell, "The First Teacher of European Music in North America," *Catholic Historical Review*, New Series, II, 1922–23, pp. 372–378.

installed a small organ and began teaching the San Felipe Indians to sing the Roman liturgy sometime between 1598 and 1604.[5] During the following century and a half, the many Franciscan missions laid a love of the Church and its music, especially the music of a folk character, in the hearts of their Indian converts that even the extensive deprivations and betrayals of the nineteenth century failed to erase.

Among the Indian musicians there developed, entirely apart from the music of the liturgy which they had learned, three aspects of Christian folklore and music which were peculiarly their own: the *alabados*, *Penitentes* processions, and *Los pastores* pageants.

The *alabados* (songs of praise) were simple folk hymns in the form of the old Spanish *romance* which could be used on all occasions. Their texts were summaries of the basic teachings of the Church so that they were a valued means of spreading the faith among illiterate natives, either composed in, or translated into the different Indian languages. In more recent times, many have been preserved and sung in the Spanish tongue. They have not been noted in the early records of sixteenth-century New Spain, but from the late seventeenth and early eighteenth centuries there are many references to them. A leader in their diffusion was Fray Antonio Margil de Jesús (1657–1726), who walked—since he was physically unable to ride a horse—and taught all the way from Costa Rica to Louisiana.[6]

A number of *alabados* have been recorded from communities along the Rio Grande between Alamosa, Colorado, and Santa Fé, New Mexico, as sung by the flagellants during Holy Week processions.[7] Until recent years these members of the Penitent Brothers of the Third Order of Saint Francis

[5] Dorothy L. Pillsbury, "Christmas at San Felipe," *The Cathedral Age*, XXVI, 4, Christmas 1951, pp. 22–23.

[6] José de J. Núñez y Dominguez, "The Alabado and Alabanzes," *Mexican Folkways*, II, 5, December 1926, pp. 12–22, reproduces a broadside with the original Spanish text and an Aztec version by Fray Margil. The latter's biography has been compiled by Eduardo Enrique Ríos, México, 1941.

[7] Juan Bautista Rael, *The New Mexican Alabado; with Transcription of Music by Eleanor Hague*, Stanford, 1951.

annually made their way through village streets, black-hooded and stripped to the waist, while bearing heavy wooden crosses, whipping themselves and each other until the blood ran. Today the flagellation has been largely suppressed, but the *Penitentes* still wend their way during Holy Week singing *alabados.*

Another phase of the mission music which has survived among the Indians of the Southwest is found in the pageants, descendants of the medieval liturgical dramas and the Spanish *autos.* Of these, the Christmas pageant, *Los pastores* (The Shepherds) has remained the most popular. Apart from staged performances in folk festivals, it is still given at Christmas-tide in isolated villages back in the mountains beyond Santa Fé. As traditionally performed, many homely details of village life are woven into the Nativity story, with music which is a curious medley of Latin plainsong, Spanish air, and native Indian melody.[8]

Much later and far less enduring was the work of the twenty-one Franciscan missions in California which Fray Junípero Serra began at San Diego in 1769. Fray Serra was an ardent musician and it was not long before the Indians of the West Coast were likewise being taught so that native choirs and orchestras flourished for a time. Indeed some of the Franciscan fathers, especially Fray Narciso Durán, composed masses as well as compiled service books for their Indian musicians.[9] But in 1822 the revolution in Mexico put a stop to the financial support of the missions and in 1834 the territorial legislature of California passed an abortive act secularizing the missions. American confirmation of mission property rights in 1855 came too late to preserve more

[8] Details of one such performance are given by Dorothy Pillsbury, "Ancient Christmas Customs in the New World," *The Cathedral Age,* XXIV, 4, Christmas 1949, pp. 12–13. Several versions of the pageant have been published in recent years. Songs from a production at Cotulla, Texas, were recorded in 1934 by John Lomax; they are obtainable from the Recording Laboratory of the Library of Congress.

[9] Owen Francis da Silva, *Mission Music of California,* Los Angeles, 1941. Some of this music is available on recordings.

than a few remnants of the labors of two generations of Franciscans. Yet the Indians' love and knowledge of the music of the liturgy remained, without further teaching, for another full generation. Robert Louis Stevenson has described the music led in 1879 by an aged, blind Indian in one of the isolated chapels where the *padre* came but once a year.[10]

The Jesuits, working in the French areas in the north, similarly taught Christianity to the Indians through their singing. At Green Bay, Wisconsin, in 1761, Father Louis André told how he was able to reach the adult Indians by teaching their children to sing.[11] In Maine, Father Sébastian Râle trained a vested choir of forty young Abnakis for his chapel at Norridgewock around 1700.[12] The Iroquois Indians are unique in American religious life in that they received a Papal Indult in 1668 which permitted them to have their services, including the Mass, in the Iroquois tongue rather than in the Latin required in all other Roman Catholic churches in America. This privilege is still observed at the mission in St. Regis, Quebec.[13]

Beginning in Georgia in 1735, the Moravians worked with the Indians for several generations in the Appalachian region, teaching them to sing translations of Moravian hymns. In 1745, at a love feast in Bethlehem, Pennsylvania, the old German carol, *In dulci jubilo*, was sung in thirteen different languages, with Mohawk and Mohican Indians participating.[14]

Traces of all this early music of the Christianized Indians has disappeared today in most parts of the country just as the Indian himself has vanished, and for the same reason. A few, such as Elias Boudinot and Thomas Commuck, pub-

[10] "Monterey" in Stevenson's *Across the Plains*. First published in *Fraser's Magazine*, CII (N.S. 22), November 1880, p. 647.

[11] *Jesuit Relations*, LVI, 133, Reuben G. Thwaites, ed.; Cleveland, 1899.

[12] George Thornton Edwards, *Music and Musicians of Maine*, Portland, 1928, pp. 6–8.

[13] J. Vincent Higginson, *Hymnody in the American Indian Missions*, in *Papers of the Hymn Society*, XVIII, New York, 1954, p. 13.

[14] Rufus A. Grider, *Historical Notes on Music in Bethlehem, Pennsylvania, from 1741 to 1871*, Philadelphia, 1873.

lished hymn- and tune-books of their own during the early nineteenth century. As the Indian was forced westward and into crowded reservations, new missionary work continued in his own languages and in the English he gradually acquired. Some of the Indian hymns can still be heard when they gather for special occasions such as the famous Niobrara Convocation held annually in South Dakota.

Colonial Psalmody

The English colonists settled along the coast of North America without any royal subsidies to assist them in transplanting the cultural and religious establishments of their homeland. In fact, the New England colonists wanted none of the Established Church as they had known it in England. The stern business of grubbing a livelihood from the soil discouraged the immigration of any musicians for nearly a century. Consequently, the only music the colonists could have was that with which they were most familiar in the old country, the congregational singing of metrical Psalms.

At Jamestown in 1607, they sang from the Old Version of Sternhold and Hopkins, using the musical settings of Thomas Est, 1592. When the Massachusetts Bay Colony was founded, 1628–30, the Old Version with the Ravenscroft tune-book of 1621 was used. The Separatists who landed at Plymouth in 1620 used the Ainsworth Psalter of 1612 which had been especially edited to accommodate the Genevan or Bourgeois tunes which the Pilgrim congregation had learned during their years in the Netherlands. Here was a phenomenon which was to become characteristic of church life in America: the Anglican or Episcopal colonists in Virginia, no matter what their differences in theology or church government, sang the same hymns from the same metrical Psalters that were used by the Congregationalists in New England. In New Amsterdam, the Dutch Reformed congregations sang the Genevan tunes to the metrical Psalms in Dutch verse by

Peter Datheen until 1767, when, after the introduction of English preaching, Francis Hopkinson was commissioned to adapt English words to their traditional tunes.

The Old Version had many critics on both sides of the Atlantic. It was considerably easier to make changes in a young, theocratic colony than in the conservative homeland, especially since the court circles were interested in listening to cathedral music rather than the congregational singing which was so popular in the nonconformist chapels. Consequently a committee of New England clergymen began to prepare a revision of the metrical Psalter soon after they settled in the colony. This appeared in 1640 as *The Bay Psalm Book,* published by Stephen Daye in Cambridge—the first book of any sort to be published in the British colonies of North America. In England, the New Version of Tate and Brady was published in 1698, but so popular had *The Bay Psalm Book* become that it went through twenty-seven editions in New England, and approximately twenty more in England, before 1762. There was so little demand for new music during the years which Millar Patrick called "The Great Eclipse" [15] that no music editions of *The Bay Psalm Book* were published until 1698, and then only the following familiar tunes were included: *Litchfield, Canterbury, York, Windsor, Cambridge, St. David's, Martyrs, St. Mary's (Hackney), Old 100th, 115th, 119th,* and *148th.*

It is difficult for us to realize how extremely narrow-minded our Puritan forebears were towards church music.[16] The verses of the metrical Psalms were by some considered so sacrosanct that they could not be rehearsed—special practice verses, examples of which are given by Millar Patrick, must be used in learning the tunes. Other men held the tunes themselves so holy that they would "put off their hats and put on a great show of devotion and gravity, whenever Psalm-

[15] Millar Patrick, *Four Centuries of Scottish Psalmody,* London, 1949, ch. x.

[16] This does not apply to their attitude toward secular music. *Cf.* Percy Scholes, *The Puritans and Music,* London, 1934.

tunes were sung, though there were not one word of a Psalm."[17]

Books were scarce in colonial times, and literacy was by no means as universal as today. Consequently there developed at an early date, on both sides of the Atlantic, the practice of lining-out the metrical Psalms or hymns. The parish clerk, precentor, chorister, or deacon, as he was variously designated, used a desk which was raised one step above the floor of the church, beneath the minister's reading desk and/or the pulpit.[18] After the minister had announced and usually read the entire hymn through out loud, the clerk rose, announced the tune to be sung by name, for example, *Litchfield*, and then proceeded to sing the first line of the hymn. The congregation repeated the line after the clerk who then continued with the second line, and so on to the end of the hymn, each line being sung first by the clerk and then repeated by the congregation. As was only natural, some of the congregation could not hear or remember the full line accurately, with resultant bedlam many times. Even more confusion arose when the clerk gave out a tune whose metre did not fit that of the text! Although pitch pipes were used, clerks who could line the Psalm and stay on pitch, to say nothing of taking a pitch suitable to the range of the tune, were in great demand but too seldom obtainable. Yet in spite of such lapses, untrained voices, and lack of all instrumental support in many churches, congregations sang heartily and meaningfully.

By the mid-eighteenth century the device was no longer needed. So conservative and slow to accept change were many congregations, especially in rural communities, that in many places in both America and Scotland lining-out was not fully discontinued until about 1850. Foote[19] describes several of

[17] Thomas Symmes, *The Reasonableness of Regular Singing, or Singing by Note*, Boston, 1720.

[18] In many Episcopal churches there were three-deckers containing clerk's desk, lectern, and pulpit, one above the other. Elsewhere, two-deckers were the rule.

[19] Henry Wilder Foote, *Three Centuries of American Hymnody*, Cambridge, Mass., 1940, Appendix A.

what must have been many pathetic scenes when an elderly clerk led the singing for the last time. As a rule, churches did not make a complete break at first but rather proceeded as did the church in Brimfield, Massachusetts, which voted on August 31, 1781, "that the Psalm to be sung be read, line by line, in the forenoon, but not in the afternoon." After eight years of transition, they voted on October 19, 1789, that "the singers for the future shall sing without reading." [20]

Singing Schools and Early Choirs

Throughout the seventeenth century there had been a basic lack of music education. Psalmody had relied on oral tradition, had avoided the use of professional musicians, had found its musical level at the lowest common denominator of each congregation. Consequently, congregations of 1720 were actually able to sing far fewer tunes than those of 1620. Nothing specific is known of singing schools before 1720, but by that date there was a considerable demand for them, especially on the part of the young people. The need was given printed expression in a pamphlet entitled *The Reasonableness of Regular Singing: or Singing by Note*, published in 1720 by the Rev. Thomas Symmes of Bradford, Massachusetts. Fifteen similar pamphlets were published during the following decade by various of the more liberal Massachusetts clergy. Material for these singing schools was provided by a brief manual called *A Very Plain and Easy Introduction to the Singing of Psalm Tunes*, first published around 1712 by the Rev. John Tufts of Newbury, Massachusetts. This went through eleven editions, many copies of which were bound together with *The Bay Psalm Book*. Tuft's manual was followed by a more detailed text, *The Grounds and Rules of Musick Explained*, by the Rev. Thomas Walter of Roxbury, Massachusetts. This second work was published at Boston in

[20] Jason Morse, *Annals of the Church in Brimfield*, Springfield, Mass., 1856.

1721 on the press of James Franklin, whose younger brother, Benjamin, was then an apprentice in the shop.

The social change which took place throughout the colonies as a result of this movement for "regular singing" was not slight, for it wrought fundamental changes in the worship habits of each community. During the previous century, when the Psalms were lined-out, everybody sang them, no matter how poorly. In the mid-nineteenth century, when the use of a piano at rehearsals had become commonplace, Lowell Mason was to remark about what a crutch it was for lazy singers. The lack of all instrumental support during the lining-out era may have helped give people more courage to lift their voices, no matter how ineptly, in following the leadership of the parish clerk. But as soon as the various communities had groups of young people who had learned the rules of music [21] and could read music for singing purposes, these same groups had little patience with the rest of the congregation who did not know the new tunes and therefore relegated them to silent listening. By 1800, the music undoubtedly sounded better on the ears of the listener, but it had lost the spiritual power which had come from entire congregations lifting their voices together in worship. Another century elapsed before serious efforts were made to restore congregational singing.

The transition began in each parish when conditions under the lining-out system had become so bad that the community was willing to appropriate from their limited funds to pay for a singing teacher. According to Gould,[22] the singing school frequently had to be held in the village tavern lest the church be profaned. Singers were expected to buy their own music books and to come with their own candles and a board to hold both book and candle. Instruction consisted of the simple elements of musical notation, followed by basic voice-placement exercises, sung by rote. As soon as possible, the

21 Hence "regular singing"—music according to rule.

22 Nathaniel Duren Gould, *Church Music in America*, Boston, 1853.

class would learn some new tunes. Since financial support was nearly always limited, few schools ran for more than twenty-four evenings. Records of the First Church of Christ (Congregational) at New London, Connecticut, for 1797 show:

"To one Quarter's Tuition of Singing School beginning 17th of July and ending 17th of October as per agreement with the Singing Committee £3-5-0."

After such a series of lessons, the group was expected to be ready to take its place in the choir loft on the Sabbath, either with the older members or as the nucleus of a new choir where none had previously existed.

An interesting description of what must have been typical of eighteenth-century choirs is given by the Rev. Samuel Gilman, author of "Fair Harvard," in his *Memoirs of a New England Village Choir; with Occasional Reflections, by a Member.*[23] Although fictitious names are used, the scene is supposedly laid in Atkinson, New Hampshire, during the author's youth, immediately after the year 1800. The *Memoirs* describe the petty jealousies and rivalries over the leadership of the choir, the duties of which consisted in giving out the pitch and singing lustily but accurately to encourage the less talented members. At one point, when the choir was making a fresh start after a period of decline, singing meetings were held in private houses on two or three evenings of each week "for practice and improvement."

During the eighteenth century, there are frequent references to singing classes in various city churches. In the first half of the nineteenth century, they continued to be a vital factor in community musical and social life in the smaller towns and rural areas, gradually moving westward with the newly opened areas.[24]

Not all teachers were tune-book compilers, but all of the

[23] Boston, 1829.

[24] Cf. Jean Lincoln, *Music in Michigan before 1860*, Master's thesis, Michigan State University, 1939.

compilers were active teachers. The flood of tune-books began with *Urania: Or a choice collection of Psalm Tunes, Anthems, or Hymns, from the most approved authors, with some entirely new . . .* , published at Philadelphia in 1762 by James Lyon, a recent graduate of Princeton who subsequently became a Presbyterian minister in Nova Scotia. This was followed a year later by *A Collection of Psalm Tunes* prepared for two Episcopal churches of Philadelphia by Francis Hopkinson, later a signer of the Declaration of Independence and the first Secretary of the Navy in Washington's Cabinet. Still another year later, in 1764, Josiah Flagg brought out in Boston *A Collection of the best Psalm Tunes . . . to which are added some Hymns and Anthems; the greater part of them never before printed in America* from plates engraved by Paul Revere. By the turn of the century, over one hundred and thirty such collections had been published in various cities and towns up and down the coast.[25] Most of these tune-books had a section on the "Rudiments of Music" bound in the front of the book, embodying in written form the elements of theory which were taught orally in the singing-schools.[26] Then followed the body of the work consisting of old and new tunes, usually with but a single stanza of the hymn text given, concluding with a few anthems. The air, usually sung by tenors because of lack of women capable of carrying their own part in this early period, was placed on the line above the bass part. Gould[27] tells of the reluctance of the tenors to give up the air as more women singers became available; they felt it was wrong for women to sing the governing part, as it was proper for men only to lead in song as in other aspects of life! Many of the

[25] Unpublished *Bibliography of Early Sacred American Music*, comp. Allen P. Britton and Irving Lowens, School of Music, University of Michigan.

[26] Summarized in Allen Perdue Britton, *Theoretical Introductions in American Tune-books to 1800*, Ann Arbor, *University Microfilms*, 1949, no. 1505. Abstracted in *Microfilm Abstracts*, x, 1, 1950, p. 97.

[27] p. 122.

earlier collections had only three-part harmony provided, due to the scarcity of women singers.

After 1800, the number of collections published grew enormously. Best known are the many collections edited by Lowell Mason (1792–1872) who began the teaching of music in the public schools. One of the most famous of his tune-books was the *Carmina Sacra* which went through thirteen editions between 1841 and 1860 and is estimated to have sold over 500,000 copies. Another collection, well known in the South, was Joseph Funk's *Genuine Church Music*, later called *Harmonia Sacra*, of which twenty editions and 80,000 copies were sold from Singer's Glen, Virginia, between 1832 and 1860.

It is interesting to compare the contents of many of these early tune-books. Starting with the older, familiar Psalm tunes from England and Scotland, there were gradually added newer original tunes by the compilers and by other English and American composers. Editorial accuracy was by no means high, with the result that one finds tunes falsely attributed to G. F. Handle [Handel] and *Old Hundredth* to Luther. On the other hand, it is remarkable how fast tunes like *Adeste fideles*, *Sicilian Mariners*, *Pleyel's Hymn*, *Home* [*sweet home*] and *Spanish Chant* (*Spanish Hymn*) spread after their first introduction in this country.

Britton,[28] in analyzing the contents of the eighteenth-century collections, has noted that the tunes by native American composers are readily distinguished by their close alliance with folk music, their irregularity of phrase, use of the natural minor scale, and strong rhythmic pulse. There are also a far greater number of what appear to be harmonic ineptitudes—contrapuntally derived dissonances and the hollow fifths of incomplete chords. This was particularly true of a group of tunes which closely resemble the old English folk melodies of the southern mountain regions. The first

[28] *The Musical Idiom in Early American Tunebooks*, abstracted in the *Journal of the American Musicological Society*, III, 1950, p. 286.

collection to contain these quasi-folk tunes was the second part of John Wyeth's *Repository of Sacred Music* (Harrisburg, Pennsylvania, 1813). This was soon followed by a group of tune-books containing still more folk tunes published between 1815 and 1832 in the Shenandoah Valley of Virginia by Ananias Davisson, James M. Boyd, James F. Carrell, and Joseph Funk.

Reference was made earlier to the social change which resulted from the segregation of the choirs from the congregation. This was augmented by the use of the new repeat or fuging-tunes which made their appearance around 1761. Although some had appeared earlier in England, the ones used in American tune-books until well past 1850 were almost entirely by native American composers. They were tunes which, set in either three- or four-part harmony, have an opening homophonic phrase followed by a polyphonic section using either strict or free imitation in at least three parts. This section is then followed by a concluding homophonic phrase. Frequently, all save the opening phrase is repeated. Such a tune, still in popular use although frequently disguised with superfluous harmonies, is John Francis Wade's *Adeste fideles*. These fuging-tunes were exactly the sort of stimulus needed for ambitious village choirs, but they served to take still more of the music away from the congregation as a whole. At Brimfield, Massachusetts, in 1781 at the same vote taken on lining-out the Psalms,[29] the church voted "that no repeating tune be sung in the forenoon but may be in the afternoon," when regular singing was also permitted. Before their popularity waned, there were close to a thousand such tunes composed, many, such as Lewis Edson's *Greenfield* and *Greenwich,* also Jeremiah Ingalls' *New Jerusalem,* were published in a number of collections. Occasionally a conservative compiler, such as the Mennonite Joseph Funk, would include a popular tune but conceal its fuging character by supplying full harmonies, through the central part of the

[29] Cf. p. 299 above.

tune. Although their use had largely died out in the North by 1850,[30] the fuging-tunes continued to be sung in the rural South throughout the nineteenth century from such popular collections as William Walker's *Southern Harmony* and Benjamin White's *Sacred Harp*.

Most of the tune-books also contained a few short anthems. At first these were by English composers, taken from two popular tune-books published in England, Tans'ur's *Royal Melody Complete* and Aaron Williams' *Universal Psalmodist*, but after the Revolution the English anthems were gradually replaced by native American works based on the English models.[31] All were relatively short pieces, of four to five minutes' duration, for unaccompanied chorus, with short solo passages for any or all of the various parts. Occasionally there was an instrumental continuo part, usually accompanying the solos. However, the lack of all instruments in so many localities prompted American compilers to omit the instrumental introductions, interludes, and accompaniments in most instances where they had occurred in the English editions. Rhythmically and harmonically, they are very simple when compared with anthems from the English cathedral repertory of the same period, but they are several steps ahead of the Psalm and fuging-tunes in those same respects and so must have been popular incentives for nascent choirs.

Musical Instruments

The problem of setting the correct pitch in lining-out the Psalms was mentioned earlier. When singing schools had introduced singing in parts, this problem became acute and involved. At first, various types of pitch pipes or forks were used, the most common of which was shaped like a small

[30] As a boy, the author sang several, including *New Jerusalem*, from a gospel song-book published in 1916 at an Adventist campmeeting at Alton Bay, New Hampshire.

[31] Ralph T. Daniel, "English Models for the First American Anthems," *Journal of the American Musicological Society*, XII, 1959, pp. 49–58.

wooden organ pipe with an adjustable tuner. For each hymn, the choir leader had first to find the keynote of the tune selected, then to sound out the different opening notes for the bass, tenor, and alto parts, as well as the air. Except with the relatively few highly skilled leaders, this was a slow, laborious process which must have been disconcerting for worshipers in the congregation.[32]

Consequently, earlier prejudice against the use of musical instruments on the part of the non-liturgical colonial churches (Congregational, Baptist, Methodist, and Presbyterian) gave way to their acceptance as supports for the several parts in the choir. Clarinet and "bass viol," meaning the violoncello, are the instruments most commonly named. They, with the occasional addition of flute, oboe, bassoon, serpent or ophicleide, and trombone, as available, supported the gallery singers for two or three generations. This was true not only in the East but also in the Middle West, in church after church, until reed or pipe organs gradually supplanted them during the first half of the nineteenth century. One of the earliest references to their use is in Christ Church, Cambridge, Massachusetts. This church had acquired a small pipe organ in 1764, but most of the lead pipes had been melted up for bullets used at the Battle of Bunker Hill. A contemporary letter describes a service attended by General George Washington and his officers on New Year's Day, 1776:

"Unfortunately the organ could not be used. Some of the leaden pipes had been taken out to furnish ammunition for our men at the fight in Charlestown last June, and it was quite out of order, but a bass viola and clarionet played by some musical soldiers led the singing which was very good. The strong voices of the many men who thronged the Church made fine music for my [feminine] ears. . . ."[33]

[32] One collection, the *Federal Harmony*, 1794, gave "Directions for pitching a tune by a concert pitch pipe."

[33] Gardiner M. Day, *The Biography of a Church*, Cambridge, Mass., 1951, p. 30.

In some communities, the bass viol was public property, acquired by vote of the town meeting and called the "church fiddle"—in contradistinction to the "devil's fiddle" or violin, so called because of its use by the dancing-masters. Eventually, even the violin was admitted to the musicians' gallery; an Athol, Massachusetts, record states that in 1868 a pipe organ was placed in the singers' gallery of the Evangelical Congregational Church, "taking the place of the violins, bass-viols, trombone, flute, and seraphine that had for many years pealed forth their music for the singers." [34]

The first pipe organs were imported shortly after 1700, but their use was strictly limited to Episcopal, Lutheran, and Moravian churches. Within a few years, organ builders were active in several of the colonies, but by 1800 there were still no more than twenty organs throughout New England. The lone "dissenting" organ among these was in the First Congregational Church at Providence, Rhode Island, which acquired it in 1770 after considerable hesitation and debate.[35] Even after the prejudice against pipe organs had waned, there was still the economic factor which has always kept smaller churches from using them. Reed organs, melodeons, or harmoniums, as they were variously called, began to be manufactured in this country about 1818. By mid-century, the larger "cabinet organs" had been developed, some of which contained as many as twenty-four sets of reeds on two or three manuals, with full sets of pedals. The perfected reed organ effectively displaced the last of the gallery instrumentalists, only to be displaced in turn by electronic organs after 1935.

Quartet Choirs

With the growth of mixed choirs as a result of the singing schools, the clerk or the choir leader was the first person to

[34] Lilley B. Caswell, *Athol*, Athol, Mass., 1899, p. 56.

[35] Details of these early organs will be found in Leonard Ellinwood, *History of American Church Music*, New York, 1953, chs. VII, XIV.

receive remuneration for his services, especially where a congregation wished to retain the services of a particularly competent leader. As interest grew in having still better music in the churches, there was a growing tendency in the early nineteenth century to hire other skilled singers until a full quartet was achieved. It was believed that this would assure a dependable background on which the full choir could lean. Unfortunately, the use of these paid singers led to much solo singing in order to display their voices. This in turn led to a lack of interest on the part of the volunteer singers. Scanning local church histories, one is confronted again and again with instances where gallery choirs and orchestral instruments were used until around 1840 when the installation of a pipe organ, in the front of the church where it could be admired, was a common incentive to eliminate the volunteers and have "finer" music from a professional quartet. Sad to relate, the conduct of various members of the choirs in those rear galleries was a frequent argument given for making the change. The organs were replaced or enlarged each generation, but the quartet choirs persisted in the majority of churches until after 1920. Yet as early as 1845, objections were raised, as in the following resolution passed at the American Musical Convention held in the Broadway Tabernacle, New York City, on October 8–10, 1845:

> "Resolved: that all the advantages derivable from Quartette Choirs in churches can be combined in larger choirs, and that when larger choirs can be obtained it is not advisable to limit the number to four persons."

The trend toward such limited numbers and professionalism certainly removed the music still further from congregational participation; there was not enough choir left to lead the congregation in singing the hymns.

The professional singers were frequently more concerned with personal vainglory and competition than with the worship of Almighty God. This fault was all the more apparent in liturgical churches, for the quartets could seldom achieve that impersonal union of music and liturgy which is the essence of true worship. Curiously, the Oxford Movement, which led the way for the revival of liturgical worship in many denominations, developed during the same years as did the quartet choir.

Hymns

Increased congregational participation in the church service was one of the ideals of the Oxford Movement. This was given its first boost, after a century of steady decline, in the 1860's with a sweeping change in the publishing of hymnals. Prior to that time, singers had to contend with separate books of tunes and words, "bobbing the head like a shuttlecock between the tune-book and the hymn."[36] For the Episcopal Church, *Songs of the Church*, compiled by George C. Davies (Cincinnati, 1858) was the first of the newer hymnals which included all of the words of each hymn on the same page with the four-part harmonization of each tune. Coupled with the growth of public school music, making it possible for anyone who could "carry a tune" to read music, these new hymnals again made it possible for the entire congregation to join together in sacred song.

The late Canon Charles Winfred Douglas used to refer to the hymnal as "the layman's manual of theology." This became increasingly true as denominational lines became more acute during the late eighteenth century. The first significant breaking away from the metrical Psalms came with the revival movement known as "The Great Awakening" which began with the preaching of the Rev. Jonathan Edwards at Northampton, Massachusetts, in 1734. It was spread throughout the colonies by the preaching tour of George Whitefield

[36] Erastus Wentworth, "Methodism and Music," *Methodist Quarterly Review*, XLVII, 1865, pp. 359–372.

in the years from 1739 to 1741. Whitefield played an active part in promoting the use of Isaac Watts's new *Hymns and Psalms*. "The Great Awakening" from the first was accompanied by enthusiasm for singing. As Edwards expressed it: "It has been observable, that there has been scarcely any part of Divine worship, wherein good men amongst us have had grace so drawn forth, and their hearts so uplifted in the ways of God, as in singing his praises." [37]

Whitefield also brought with him from England copies of John and Charles Wesley's *Hymns and Sacred Poems*, just off the press in London. It was not however until two decades later, after the first Methodist societies were organized in the colonies, that the Wesleyan hymns began to be used extensively. In 1784, a Methodist Conference meeting in Baltimore answered the question, "How shall we reform our singing?" with the ruling: "Let all our preachers who have any knowledge in the notes, improve it by learning to sing true themselves, and keeping close to Mr. Wesley's tunes and hymns." [38]

Although Watts wrote as a Congregationalist, his hymns soon became popular with certain factions in the Presbyterian churches from Massachusetts to Virginia. The resultant "Great Psalmody Controversy" raged for nearly a century, frequently splitting congregations asunder.

The following quotations show the varied treatment which successive authors gave to a specific passage of Holy Scripture. Six verses of Psalm 137 are quoted, first from the prose of the Authorized Version of the Bible, then from the three metrical Psalters in common use, and finally the hymns of Isaac Watts and the American author Timothy Dwight, based on the same passage:

[37] Quoted in Foote, p. 148.

[38] Cited in Louis F. Benson, *The English Hymn*, New York, 1915, p. 285.

AUTHORIZED VERSION (1611)

1. By the rivers of Babylon, there we sat down, yea, we wept, when we remembered Sion.
2. We hanged our harps upon the willows in the midst thereof.
3. For there they that carried us away captive required of us a song; and they that wasted us required of us mirth, saying, Sing us one of the songs of Sion.
4. How shall we sing the Lord's song in a strange land?
5. If I forget thee, O Jerusalem, let my right hand forget her cunning.
6. If I do not remember thee, let my tongue cleave to the roof of my mouth; if I prefer not Jerusalem above my chief joy.

OLD VERSION (1562)

1. When we did sit in Babylon
The rivers round about,
Then in remembrance of Sion
The tears for grief burst out.

2. We hang'd our harps and instruments
The willow-trees upon:
For in that place men for their use
Had planted many one.

3. Then they to whom we pris'ners were
Said to us tauntingly,
Now let us hear your Hebrew songs
And pleasant melody.

4. Alas! said we, who can once frame
His heavy heart to sing
The praises of our loving God,
Thus under a strange king?

5. But yet if I Jerusalem
Out of my heart let slide;
Then let my fingers quite forget
The warbling harp to guide:

6. And let my tongue within my mouth
Be ty'd for ever fast,
If I rejoice before I see
Thy full deliv'rance past.

BAY PSALM BOOK (*1640*)

1. The rivers on of Babilon
There when wee did sit downe:
Yea even then wee mourned, when
Wee remembred Sion.

2. Our Harps wee did hang it amid,
Upon the willow tree.
Because there they that us away
Led in captivitee,

3. Requir'd of us a song, & thus
Askt mirth: us waste who laid,
Sing us among a Sions song,
Unto us then they said.

4. The lords song sing can wee? being
In strangers land. Then let
Loose her skill my right hand, if I
Jerusalem forget.

5. Let cleave my tongue my pallate on,
If minde thee doe not I:
If chiefe joyes or'e I prize not more.
Jerusalem my joy.

NEW VERSION (*1696*)

1. When we our weary limbs to rest,
Sat down by proud Euphrates' stream,
We wept, with doleful thoughts opprest,
And Sion was our mournful theme.

2. Our harps, that, when with joy we sung,
Were wont their tuneful parts to bear,
With silent strings neglected hung
On willow trees, that wither'd there.

3. Mean while our foes, who all conspir'd
To triumph in our slavish wrongs,
Music and mirth of us requir'd,
"Come, sing us one of Sion's songs."

4. How shall we tune our voice to sing?
Or touch our harps with skilful hands?
Shall hymns of joy to God, our King,
Be sung by slaves in foreign lands?

5. O Salem, our once happy seat!
When I of thee forgetful prove,
Let then my trembling hand forget
The speaking strings with art to move!

6. If I to mention thee forbear,
Eternal silence seize my tongue;
Or if I sing one cheerful air,
Till thy deliv'rance is my song!

ISAAC WATTS (1719)

1. Along the banks where Babel's current flows,
Our captive bands in deep despondence stray'd,
While Sion's fall in sad remembrance rose,
Her friends, her children mingled with the dead.

2. The tuneless harp, that once with joy we strung,
When praise employ'd and mirth inspir'd the lay,
In mournful silence on the willows hung;
And growing grief prolong'd the tedious day.

3. The barbarous tyrants, to increase the woe,
With taunting smiles a song of Sion claim;
Bid sacred praise in strains melodious flow,
While they blaspheme the great Jehovah's name:

4. But how, in heathen chains and lands unknown,
Shall Israel's sons, a song of Sion raise?
O hapless Salem, God's terrestrial throne,
Thou land of glory, sacred mount of praise!

5. If e'er my memory lose thy lovely name,
If my cold heart neglect my kindred race,
Let dire destruction seize this guilty frame;
My hand shall perish and my voice shall cease.

6. Yet shall the Lord, who hears when Sion calls,
O'ertake her foes with terror and dismay,
His arm avenge her desolated walls,
And raise her children to eternal day.

TIMOTHY DWIGHT (*1800*)

1. I love thy kingdom, Lord,
The house of thine abode,
The Church our blest Redeemer saved
With his own precious blood.

2. For her my tears shall fall;
For her my prayers ascend;
To her my cares and toils be giv'n,
Till toils and cares shall end.

3. Beyond my highest joy
I prize her heav'nly ways,
Her sweet communion, solemn vows,
Her hymns of love and praise.

4. Jesus, thou friend divine,
Our Saviour and our King,
Thy hand from every snare and foe
Shall great deliv'rance bring.

5. Sure as thy truth shall last,
To Sion shall be giv'n
The brightest glories earth can yield,
And brighter bliss of heav'n.

The Baptists, with theological tenets not expressed in either metrical Psalm or Watts, began at an early date to write their own hymns, singing them to popular melodies with refrains, in some of which are the earliest traces of folk hymnody. One of the first of these unfettered American writers was the Freewill Baptist evangelist Henry Alline (1748–1784). Another prolific writer was Elder John Leland (1754–1841), an itinerant preacher of western Massachusetts and Virginia. One of his hymns, written to encourage the faint-hearted to undergo immersion in spite of wintry weather, read:

Christians, if your hearts are warm,
Ice and snow can do no harm.

His evening hymn, beginning:

The day is past and gone,
The evening shades appear;
O may we all remember well
The night of death draws near.

is still found in many hymnals, the oldest text by an American author in current use.

The Episcopal Church, in its first official *Hymnal* adopted in 1789, retained the New Version of the metrical Psalms and also included twenty-seven hymns taken not only from Watts and Wesley but also from Doddridge, Addison, Dryden, and Maxwell. Not until 1808 was a text by an American author added: Clement Clarke Moore's "Lord of life all praise excelling." The revision of the *Hymnal* in 1826, stimulated by William Augustus Muhlenberg's *Church Poetry*, 1823, moved still further in the direction of higher literary quality and permanent value. Notable among the new hymns were five by Muhlenberg and others by George Washington Doane, later Bishop of New Jersey, and the layman, Francis Scott Key.

By 1800, the Unitarian hymn writers in New England had begun to turn out lyrics of equal significance. William Cullen Bryant, John Pierpont, Henry Ware, and Frederic Henry Hedge during the first quarter of the new century wrote a number of texts which have since been used by many denominations.

Once the confining chains of metrical psalmody had been released, each new generation began to express its own current problems in the phrasing of new hymns. Religious movements such as the campmeetings and revivals, and the rise of particular sects, each gave birth to a hymnody which will be discussed later. Of wider impact were the hymns which came into existence as a result of social and political forces.

An important group of hymns, largely but not exclusively by Unitarian writers and dating from the 1840's, gave expression to the concern which Christian men began to feel for some of the problems consequent upon the social upheaval wrought by the industrial revolution in New England. This was reflected in Edmund Hamilton Sears's Christmas hymn, "It came upon the midnight clear," written in 1849, whose third and fourth stanzas (too often omitted in popular singing) read:

Yet with the woes of sin and strife
The world has suffered long;
Beneath the heav'nly strain have rolled
Two thousand years of wrong;
And man, at war with man, hears not
The tidings which they bring;
O hush the noise, ye men of strife,
And hear the angels sing!

O ye, beneath life's crushing load,
Whose forms are bending low,
Who toil along the climbing way
With painful steps and slow,
Look now! for glad and golden hours
Come swiftly on the wing;
O rest beside the weary road
And hear the angels sing!

The agonies of the American Civil War found expression in Julia Ward Howe's "Mine eyes have seen the glory of the coming of the Lord," which lifted the earlier ballad "John Brown's body" above the passions of the immediate conflict to an exhortation toward true humanity and freedom. George Duffield's "Stand up, stand up for Jesus" (1858), although written for a different purpose, also did noble duty during the Civil War.

James Russell Lowell's poem "The present crisis" was written in protest against the War with Mexico in 1845. Fifty years later, an English editor saw further possibilities in the now familiar lines beginning "Once to every man and nation." This hymn expressed Christian ideals on both sides of the Atlantic during World War I.

At the end of the nineteenth century, as America became more aware of the problems of urban life, a new group of hymns marked the Church's concern. Among these were Frank Mason North's "Where cross the crowded ways of life," and William Pierson Merrill's "Not alone for mighty empire" whose fourth stanza reads:[39]

> God of justice, save the people
> From the clash of race and creed,
> From the strife of class and faction,
> Make our nation free indeed;
> Keep her faith in simple manhood
> Strong as when her life began,
> Till it find its full fruition
> In the brotherhood of man!

Subsequent decades saw an increasing number of hymns reflecting social problems, notable among which were Walter Russell Bowie's "Lord Christ, when first thou cam'st to men," and Harry Emerson Fosdick's "God of grace and God of glory."

At mid-twentieth century, social problems became no less complex and to meet them there arose still another group of hymns with such divergent emphases as Francis Bland Tucker's:

> Our Father, by whose Name
> All fatherhood is known,
> Who dost in love proclaim
> Each family thine own,
> Bless thou all parents, guarding well,
> With constant love as sentinel,
> The homes in which thy people dwell.

Bates Gilbert Burt's:

> O God of youth, whose Spirit in our hearts is stirring
> Hope and desire for noble lives and true,
> Keep us, we pray thee, steadfast and unerring;
> With light and love divine our souls endue.

or:

[39] The full text of this and the following partial citations may be found in the Episcopal *Hymnal 1940*.

God, deigning man to be,
Who in thy manhood strong
Summoned to walk with thee
Twelve from the common throng;
As thou didst call them from their ways,
Lord, call us too, who sing their praise!

by Frank Damrosch, Jr.

As early as 1931, Howard Chandler Robbins anticipated man's current interest in outer space:

And have the bright immensities
Received our risen Lord,
Where light-years frame the Pleiades
And point Orion's sword?
Do flaming suns his footsteps trace
Through corridors sublime,
The Lord of interstellar space
And Conqueror of time?

During the quartet-choir era, most of the new hymns were set to tunes with full part-writing of a sort which made them sound like miniature anthems. These so-called "choir-tunes" gradually gave way after 1900 to broad, sweeping, unisonal tunes which helped greatly in restoring strong congregational singing. At the same time, there was a widespread interest on the part of many denominations in the melodies as well as some texts of the older German hymns or chorales. The revival of these melodies, frequently with the richly contrapuntal harmonizations of Johann Sebastian Bach, has given added encouragement to congregational singing.

Campmeeting Songs

Life in many parts of the American colonies, by 1750, had settled into an urban-village culture which had developed a comfortable and relatively large middle class of persons who encouraged the new hymn singing, choirs, and growing concert life. But after the Revolution, when the western frontiers began to open up and established churches were being suppressed as royalist, the backwoods teemed with people who worked and played hard in their efforts to cut out of the forest a better life for themselves. There were neither ministers nor funds sufficient to build churches as fast as they were needed in the newly settled areas. The era was one of isolated cabins and farms, rather than of clustered homes in villages on the pattern of those in the original colonies. Consequently, the churches had to develop special frontier techniques.

Many early Methodist meetings, "field meetings" as they were called, had been held out-of-doors. In back-country Pennsylvania, German-speaking Lutheran and Methodist groups held "Grosse Versammlungen," some of which lasted ten or twelve days. The earliest use of the term "campmeeting" comes from the rules which the Baptist preacher, John Waller, published about 1775 for his protracted outdoor gatherings in the South.[40] All of these meetings anticipated the campmeeting characteristics of high emotional fervor and rowdy opposition.

What has been termed the Second Great Awakening, the revival fervor of Cumberland, Kentucky, Presbyterians under the McGee brothers and James McGready, began in June, 1800. The immediate wave of frontier campmeetings, the more notable because their emotionalism was such a sudden and radical change from the customary conservative Presbyterian love of order, found Presbyterian, Methodist, and Baptist ministers working side by side in the same meetings. In the larger gatherings, several groups would be singing and preaching simultaneously in adjacent portions of the same grove. From the first, attendance ran high. It is said that the Cane Ridge meetings from August 6 to 12, 1801, had over 10,000 in attendance constantly, and that the shouting and singing could be heard for miles.

Tents were used for sleeping, but all the meetings as well

[40] Charles Albert Johnson, *The Frontier Camp Meeting; Religion's Harvest Time*, Dallas, 1955, Appendix IV-A.

as the eating facilities were out in the open so that favorable weather was anxiously sought. Gradually, as the institution matured, the campmeetings became annual affairs with a permanent location. By 1840 on many grounds, wooden auditoriums and simple cottages came into use. By going indoors, the meetings sobered up considerably, but at the same time lost much of the earlier camper hospitality.

At first the meetings depended largely on the Watts and Wesley hymns of inspiration. Jeremiah Ingalls' *Christian Harmony*, published in 1805 at Exeter, New Hampshire, may have been the earliest special collection or songster. One of the best known, going through many editions, was Thomas Hinde's *Pilgrim Songster*, first published at Cincinnati in 1810. This contained 120 hymns, nearly half of which are by unknown authors. A few others are by the Wesleys and John Newton. More than forty are by two Methodist circuit riders, John A. Granade and Caleb Jarvis Taylor.

A shortage of books kept up the older practice of lining-out the hymns. It also encouraged, in keeping with the spirit of the campmeetings, a basic simplification of the texts of the hymns. Verses were shortened, repetitious expressions and ejaculations were added. Older hymns had seldom used refrains, but popular ballads had always found them useful. The new campmeeting songs found them a primary requisite, for the great mass of people could quickly learn and sing a refrain while a more limited group sang the successive verses; in fact it soon became common practice to sing the refrain several times for each verse of the song—and even sometimes to use several repetitions of the refrain without any verses. Typical of the process of building refrains where none had previously existed is the treatment of the following text from William Cowper's *Olney Hymns*, 1779. Cowper wrote:

There is a fountain filled with blood
Drawn from Immanuel's veins,
And sinners, plunged beneath that flood,
Lose all their guilty stains.

By repetition of the last two lines, the campmeeting singers built a refrain, reading:

Lose all their guilty stains,
Lose all their guilty stains.
And sinners, plunged beneath that flood,
Lose all their guilty stains.

Similarly, the second stanza would be sung:

The dying thief rejoiced to see
That fountain in his day:
And there may I, though vile as he,
Wash all my sins away.
        Wash all my sins away,
        Wash all my sins away.
        And there may I, though vile as he,
        Wash all my sins away.

The repetition of lines in the refrain is typical of a large percentage of these songs, for it drove home the basic point which the authors wished to convey. Such repetition also occurs in the following stanza from a hymn by Samuel Stennett, 1787, although here it is built with fresh lines:

On Jordan's stormy bank I stand
And cast a wishful eye
To Canaan's fair and happy land
Where my possessions lie.
        I'm bound for the promised land,
        I'm bound for the promised land.
        Oh, who will come and go with me?
        I'm bound for the promised land.

The larger number of texts used in the campmeetings were religious ballads similar to the two quoted above. The idiom was not entirely new, as is witnessed by the familiar Elizabethan ballad:

Jerusalem, my happy home,
When shall I come to thee?
When shall my sorrows have an end?
Thy joys when shall I see?

with its vivid picture of the heavenly Jerusalem, as in the eighth stanza:

Thy turrets and thy pinnacles
With carbuncles do shine:
Thy very streets are paved with gold,
Surpassing clear and fine.

This was too far removed from pioneering mentality, so that the typical American ballad was more like the following, attributed to Oliver Holden:

When Jèsus stood before the bar
Of Pilate's judgement seat,
The Roman prince a question ask'd,
A question most discreet;

What, Sir, is truth? (if thou canst tell)
But silent he remain'd;
For Jesus knew his heart full well,
His pride was never stain'd.

Had he desired the truth to know,
He would have ask'd again;
But many ask as Pilate did,
Who never seek t'obtain.

O may I never, never ask,
Without a wish to have;
And may I never cease to pray,
Till Jesus deign to save.

A second type of text was the "experience song" such as the following by John Newton (*Olney Hymns*, 1779):

In evil long I took delight,
Unaw'd by shame and fear;
Till a new object struck my sight,
And stopped my wild career.

The "mourners' songs" were similar if not identical in type:

Stop, poor sinners, stop and think
Before you further go, . . .

These differed little from the funeral section in denominational hymnals of the period.

Quite distinct, but not so plentiful, were the martial songs:

> I've 'listed in the Holy War,
> To fight for life and endless joy; . . .

Lastly, there were the farewell songs which voiced the sadness of the campers at the final service and breaking up of the campmeeting, as they went through the closing ritual of handshaking:

> Lord! when together here we meet,
> And taste thy heav'nly grace,
> Smiles are so divinely sweet
> We're loath to leave the place.

Best known today of this category is "God be with you till we meet again," written in 1882 by Jeremiah Eames Rankin while minister of the First Congregational Church of Washington, D.C.

Hymns of these four types, drawn from the works of English writers named above and from early American writers such as Holden and Leland, were literally sung to pieces. Their lines altered and simplified, with added refrains, by the 1820's many had become true folksongs both in text and in the modal melodies to which they were sung. Many of the fuging-tunes, mentioned earlier, had also been written in the minor mode. As collections began to be published for the campmeetings, many were retained and to them were added new minor tunes, so that at first the New England books were predominantly minor. One such was *The Young Convert's Companion: being a Collection of Hymns for the Use of Conference Meetings* (Boston, 1806), which is believed to have been compiled by Holden. This pocket-sized collection of one hundred and forty-three texts has eighteen tunes printed separately at the end, all of which are in the minor mode. Northern publications soon became more sophisticated, in the Lowell Mason idiom, but in the Shenandoah Valley of Virginia and from thence further South and West the minor, folk style of tunes continued to be published until mid-century. George Pullen Jackson has traced some 550 of these folk hymns and their tunes through a number of collections.[41]

A related, interesting phenomenon was the development of rural singing-meetings in the South, where hundreds of people all through the late nineteenth century would gather for an all-day sing in school, court, or meeting-house. These were not religious gatherings, but were the outgrowth of singing schools. Two collections which were mentioned earlier predominated: William Walker's *Southern Harmony*, first published in 1835, and *The Sacred Harp*, first compiled in 1844 by Benjamin F. White and E. J. King. Both collections went through many editions. Jackson's *The Story of the Sacred Harp* (1944), in connection with a centennial edition of this famous collection, gives an excellent picture of these singing-meetings which were so popular until modern transportation and radio brought their demise.[42]

Fresh impetus to the singing of campmeeting songs came, especially in the northern states, with the Millennialist movement of William Miller in 1842 and 1843. These Adventist preachers drew large crowds in both cities and towns, with meetings held each evening until the fateful February 15, 1843, when Miller had predicted the end of the world. Since their emphasis had been on being "ready to meet the Lord," a large portion of the older and familiar campmeeting repertory was still appropriate, but a few new lyrics were written for special collections such as *The Songs of Canaan, or the Millennial Harmonist* (Boston, 1842) and *Second Advent Hymns* (Exeter, N.H., 1843).

41 Cf. his *Spiritual Folk-Songs of Early America*, New York, 1937, and *Down-East Spirituals*, New York, 1943.

42 An album called "Sacred Harp Singing" is obtainable from the Recording Laboratory of the Library of Congress. It was recorded by Jackson and Allan Lomax at the thirty-seventh annual session of the Alabama Sacred Harp Singing Convention at Birmingham in August, 1942.

Negro Spirituals

At first there was no segregation of races in the southern campmeetings, but gradually the colored preachers began to hold forth in separate portions of the campgrounds. How large the colored groups were in proportion to the white congregations is difficult to determine, but a brief summary of their background may be in order.

The slave trade to the United States began in 1619 with the arrival of the first shipload of Negroes at Jamestown. By 1650, there were still not more than 300 slaves in the colonies, but by 1775 they had grown to a half-million. Forbidden by federal law in 1807, the importation of additional slaves from Africa began to taper off, although smuggling continued until around 1840. A basic policy of the African traders was to mix native tribal groups thoroughly before shipping the slaves, in order to prevent ready communication between them. Thus there could be little or no preservation of native culture on the part of the slaves after arrival in America. Indeed, few were able to become literate during the first generation on these shores. By 1800, however, many of the house servants had acquired much of the cultural background of their masters; many of the latter had paid especial attention to the teaching of their Christian faith to their slaves as a matter of principle. The coming of the campmeetings found the Negro ready to enter fully into its emotional excitement.

Jackson [43] has shown that the early spirituals were close adaptations of campmeeting songs, or "white spirituals," as he calls the folk hymns of the time. Almost nothing was recorded of the Negroes' music during the early nineteenth century, but it is clear that the spirituals, as distinct from the work songs, had their origins in these folk hymns of the campmeeting. Several which today appear to be among the earliest are: "All my sins done taken away," "Dere's no one lak

[43] George Pullen Jackson, *White and Negro Spirituals*, New York, 1944.

Jesus," "Death is dis Lawd," and "Glad I got religion." [44]

As they spread among the slave population, the spirituals became a veritable "oral Bible" for the illiterate. There were the same ballad, "experience," martial, and farewell types of songs as in the campmeeting hymns, but frequently with an otherworldliness which gave expression to the longing for freedom. This may be seen in spirituals such as "Look away in de heaven, Lord," "Heaven, heaven, everybody talkin' 'bout heaven ain't goin' there," "I got shoes," and "Dere's a great camp meeting in de promised land."

The first collecting of these spirituals was begun in the decade immediately following the Civil War. They were exploited by the Fiske University Jubilee Singers and others, beginning in 1871, for the purpose of raising money for the support of Negro educational institutions. Over the subsequent years this resulted in the curious circumstance that the Negro spirituals became better known in cultured musical circles of the North than were the white folk songs of America. Like many other racial groups, as the Negroes became urbanized they abandoned their folk music, so that with the twentieth century the spirituals became known more and more only in the concert hall. With the modern revival of interest in folk song in general, some of the spirituals are being added to various hymnals so that once more large congregations can lift their voices in subjective intensity over the thought:

> Were you there when they crucified my Lord?
> Oh! Sometimes it causes me to tremble,
> Were you there . . .

In the best "oral Bible" tradition, this spiritual goes on to query the listener as to the rest of the Passion scene and on to the triumphant scenes that followed:

> Were you there when they nailed him to the tree?
> Were you there when they pierced him in the side?
> Were you there when the sun refused to shine?

[44] Howard Washington Odum and Guy B. Johnson, *The Negro and His Songs*, Chapel Hill, 1925, pp. 301–302.

Were you there when they laid him in the tomb?
Were you there when he rose up from the dead?
Were you there when he ascended on high?

The Negro artist Allan Rohan Crite has published a series of brush drawings illustrative of this and several other spirituals which have a deeply moving sense of reality.

Gospel Songs

The term "Gospel song" or "Gospel hymn" became part of English vocabulary as a result of the six collections of *Gospel Hymns and Sacred Songs* issued between the years 1875 and 1891 by Ira D. Sankey and his collaborators, although the term had already been used as title of several earlier collections such as the *Gospel Melodies* dating from 1821. By mid-century, the fuging-tunes had dropped out of use, as had most of the minor-mode melodies. Otherwise, the bulk of the campmeeting hymns, especially their texts, formed a large part of the earlier gospel song repertory. The refrain continued to be a distinguishing feature. The newer major-mode melodies, following the style of the popular songs of the Civil War era, lent themselves to simple repetitive harmonies so that the songs could be sung either in unison or in four parts. Rhythmically too, the songs had little variety until twentieth-century ragtime and jazz introduced syncopated rhythms into some of the melodies.

The simplicity of melody, harmony, and rhythm played a significant role. This can be readily observed by contrasting melodies used with a single hymn such as Charles Wesley's "Jesus, Lover of my soul." The broad minor Welsh melody *Aberystwyth*, by Joseph Parry, and the richly harmonized Victorian setting *Hollingside*, by J. B. Dykes, give an entirely different atmosphere to the text from that of the simple American singing-school tune *Martyn*, by Simeon B. Marsh.[45]

[45] The three tunes are given together at no. 415 in the Episcopal *Hymnal 1940*.

Throughout their history, gospel songs have remained extremely subjective. Seldom does one find anything approaching the objectivity of the Ambrosian medieval office hymn "O splendor of God's glory bright." Personal pronouns are almost always in the first person singular: "I love to tell the story," "He leadeth me," "I need thee every hour." How strange it would sound to hear "Jesus loves us, this we know," or what would be even stranger but better theology:

> We love Jesus; this we do
> For the Bible tells us to.

Similarly, just the dropping of the refrain in a song like "I need thee every hour" tends to give it more seriousness.

Ira D. Sankey (1840–1908) was Dwight L. Moody's musical assistant or song leader from the early days in Chicago until Moody's death, that is, from 1870 to 1899. The success of his singing was phenomenal; his voice was not perfect, but it had exceptional volume, purity, and richness of tone. It is not easy to understand how in city after city, both in England and America, he could sit behind a small reed organ and sing effectively to 20,000 people at a time, without the use of amplifiers. Yet William Lyons Phelps, who heard him while a student at Yale, wrote: "An audience of thousands in absolute stillness heard him sing 'The Ninety and Nine,' or 'What shall the Harvest be?' or the terrifying 'Almost persuaded,' and no one ever forgot him."[46] Sankey's success lay in his complete dedication to singing the Gospel in such a way that people were won to Christ. His songs were simple but they filled a real need in the lives of the congregations. In the religious field, they did what the secular songs of Stephen Foster did for folk singing. At the beginning of a revival service they set the atmosphere for the preaching of the evangelist. At the close of the service, with their songs of pleading, they made the mood still more intense for his

[46] Quoted by William M. Runyan, "A Century of Sankey," *Moody Monthly*, XL, August 1940, p. 653.

exhortations. In most revival services from the early campmeeting days down to the present day, from twenty-five to fifty per cent of the total time has traditionally been taken up by singing, largely the massed singing of the congregation.

Other important composers, leaders, and compilers of gospel songbooks, whose names are still found in current collections, were Philip Paul Bliss (1838–1876), Robert Lowry (1826–1899), George Coles Stebbins (1846–1945), Charles McCallon Alexander (1867–1920), and Homer Alvan Rodeheaver (1880–1955). Alexander and Rodeheaver were more like masters of ceremonies or leaders of community songfests than was Sankey. They used massed choirs and orchestral instruments to help encourage the congregation to join in the singing. Rodeheaver, Billy Sunday's song leader, was famous for his occasional playing of a song as a trombone solo. They would begin their song services as soon as the hall was well filled, sometimes an hour before the scheduled time, recapturing for their urban congregations something of the social significance of the frontier campmeeting life.

It may be too early to evaluate with any degree of accuracy the singing in the Billy Graham meetings, although the song leader, Cliff Barrows, has set a fresh pattern. Ever since the decline of the Billy Sunday services after World War I, gospel songs have suffered from a lack of inspiration, both in leadership and in composition. Their publication has been commercialized more than ever, with new compilations of the same older songs augmented by stereotyped additions in a veritable Tin Pan Alley fashion. Consequently, and perhaps abetted by the increased passive listening engendered by radio and television, the modern revivalist's congregation tends to let the chorus do most of its singing. Reflecting this change, the *Billy Graham Crusade Songs* used in his New York meetings during 1957 contained only seventy-one hymns as against the average of three hundred hymns in the older song books. It is interesting to note the spread of the authors: Martin Luther's great Reformation hymn, "A mighty fortress is our God," is the only one written before 1700. Nine come from the eighteenth century, forty (or over one-half) from the nineteenth century, and fifteen from the period 1900 to 1930. Only six were written during the generation since 1930. This is strong evidence of decadence, for during all previous generations, as far back as the first Great Awakening in eighteenth-century New England, each fresh revival movement found its own expression in new gospel songs. Of the older hymn-writers represented more than once, there are Isaac Watts, Charles Wesley, P. P. Bliss, and the two prolific gospel song-writers, Fanny Crosby (1820–1915) and Charles Hutchinson Gabriel (1856–1932). The use of refrains in frontier campmeetings, where few could read and perhaps fewer owned song books, was noted earlier. Now, 150 years later, in this *Billy Graham Crusade Songs* collection, the six contemporary songs consist of refrains only. Have we again become musically illiterate to such a degree?

During the quartet choir era, which coincided with the years in which Moody and Sunday held their large revivals, congregational singing had been greatly discouraged in most churches. As Louis F. Benson expressed it: "Seated between a pulpit asserting its supremacy in everything but song and a choir loft monopolizing the song, the people were no longer a band of common worshipers but merely an audience attending a performance of worship."[47] But since World War II, congregations in churches throughout the country have again found their voices and are joining whole-heartedly in the singing of the hymns. Entirely apart from personal talents, perhaps Sankey and his immediate followers were successful in their congregational singing because it filled such a need; has Barrows been less successful because there is no longer that need?[48]

47 *The Hymnody of the Christian Church*, New York, 1927, pp. 259–260.

48 Cf. also Marvin McKissick, "The Function of Music in American Revivals since 1875," *The Hymn*, IX, 4, October 1958, pp. 107–117.

Carols

The basic church calendar, the cycle of festivals observed by Christian churches throughout the year, has changed very little during the centuries except for the addition of local observances and, on the part of the Roman Catholic Church, of newly canonized saints. Excessive observances caused the sixteenth-century Reformers to reduce the number of feast days to a bare minimum. The American colonists, especially in New England, paid relatively little attention to even the two basic festivals, Christmas and Easter. In the last hundred years, however, these two days have become major American folk-festivals, entirely apart from their religious meanings.

The days of Lent immediately preceding Easter are an occasion for great choral productions by choirs and choral societies. More than at any other time in the year, this is the period during which there are special concerts of religious music. Easter itself is celebrated musically by choirs with augmenting instruments on the most lavish scale of the year. In sharp contrast, Christmas has attracted much less activity on the part of choirs and professional musicians; it has rather become almost wholly an occasion for music of a folk nature.

The Middle Ages knew many religious folk songs, a number of which had macaronic texts, combining the more familiar phrases of the Latin liturgy with vernacular verse. The very term "carol" is thought to be a derivation from the cry *Kyrie eleison.* The many carols of the fifteenth and sixteenth centuries were characterized by a refrain or burden which was sung before and after each stanza. There were carols for all of the church and secular festivals, the seasons of the year, and even a few describing political or historical events, such as the famous carol on the Battle of Agincourt, 1415. A large part of their use was suppressed in Puritan England, just as the carol singing and maypole dancing was suppressed in 1628 at Merrymount in Puritan New England. After the Restoration, carol singing gradually returned in England so that Washington Irving in his *Sketch Book* was able to describe the singing of Yorkshire village waits in 1820.

By the mid-nineteenth century in both England and America, the popular singing of Christmas songs had become widespread. A very few of the older songs and hymns of Christmas of varied racial sources, such as the German carol "In dulci jubilo," have retained their earlier popularity, but most of the carols that are sung today date from the eighteenth or early nineteenth centuries. "God rest you merry, gentlemen" is eighteenth-century English, "Angels we have heard on high (Les anges dans nos campagnes)" is eighteenth-century French, "Here betwixt ass and oxen mild (Entre le boeuf et l'âne gris)" is nineteenth-century French. "The first Nowell the angel did say" has not been recorded in England before 1820. "Silent night, holy night" was composed in Austria in 1818, while "Away in a manger" was written in America about 1883.

Several Christmas hymns by American authors such as Edmund Hamilton Sears and Phillips Brooks, as well as older hymns like Charles Wesley's "Hark the herald angels sing," 1739, John Francis Wade's "Adeste fideles," about 1740, and even Martin Luther's "Vom Himmel hoch," 1534, have joined anonymous ones in that broad grouping of Christmas songs which the average person today thinks of as carols. Even those written less than a hundred years ago, such as John Henry Hopkins' "We three kings of Orient are," are fast becoming folk songs through their broad acceptance and oral transfer by all sorts of people.

In recent years, the early promotion of Christmas shopping by the retail trade has resulted in the playing of recorded carols in department stores from early November until late December. During the final weeks, they are heard in restaurants and on public transportation vehicles almost *ad nauseam*. Yet such is the appeal of the carol that on Christmas Eve, in offices, legislatures, schools, and out-door community gatherings, non-Christians join Christians of all creeds in singing these simple songs which tell of One who once "came upon the midnight clear"—the only form of community singing which survives in modern America.

Modern Choirs

In the larger parish churches, once having broken away from the quartet choir tradition, the music program has become truly involved. Where a professionally trained organist is employed and equipped with an adequate instrument, there are either regular or seasonal organ recitals by both the resident and guest organists. Sunday School orchestras are also popular in many Protestant churches. Taking advantage of the instrumental music program of the public schools, these orchestras permit the young people to use their instrumental talents in the services of the church. Several hymnals have been published with separate parts arranged for full orchestra, so that the latter may be used in Sunday School, evening worship services, or special massed gatherings. They also accompany the choirs upon occasion.

Out of the large volunteer choirs has grown a system of multiple choirs. Here, the church musicians have found it necessary to supply a modern gap in the public school music curriculum, that of basic vocal training. The work begins with a children's choir, sometimes called the Cherub Choir. This is composed of boys and girls between the ages of five and nine who rehearse one afternoon each week, learning simple chorales and unison anthems, largely by rote. By age nine, they are beginning to read music and are advanced into a youth choir which sings music in two or three parts. In some larger churches, boys are taken separately at this point for a traditional boys' choir, the girls continuing to sing by themselves. All of these groups participate regularly in the church school services, singing special numbers as they are prepared.

Around the age of fourteen, the young people again combine for a so-called Chapel Choir, capable of modest four-part singing. They furnish the special music each Sunday for the nine o'clock service, called in many parishes the Family Service. During or after college years, they move into the senior or adult choir, sometimes called the Chancel Choir, which furnishes music for the eleven o'clock services. Where this multiple-choir organization has been in effect over a period of years, the result is a steady flow of trained singers for the choral music of the church, singers who have good vocal training, reading ability, and a knowledge and appreciation of the musical heritage of the church. For festival occasions, several of the youth choirs augment the adult choir, making possible either antiphonal singing or the performance of larger choral works.

Choral Music

The anonymous writer in 1849 of *An Essay on Camp-Meetings,* in justifying their existence, wrote: "It is a conceded fact, that every association of men, whatever its object, must have great occasions, when friends may meet at some central point, and animate each other in their common enterprise."

The campmeeting admirably filled such a need for frontier society. In an Old World society, and in twentieth-century America, cathedrals have been erected where people from the smaller parish churches could come on festivals for the inspiration which is gained by worshiping together in a large assemblage. This same need is felt by choir members.

As singing schools flourished in the eighteenth century, there arose an institution called the musical convention, which brought together people from a number of choirs in nearby communities. New music would be learned, and at the final exercise of the convention a larger work would be sung, either an anthem which was beyond the abilities of the individual choirs, or a simple cantata. In some cases, a single singing school would expand into a more permanent form. The best example of this is the famous Stoughton (Massachusetts) Musical Society which began as one of the many singing schools conducted by William Billings and is today the oldest musical organization in continuous existence.

Early groups in other communities gave notable performances of great music at an early date, although their organization was less permanent. In New York, on January 9, 1770, the clerk of Trinity Church directed the first performance of seventeen numbers from Handel's *Messiah* to be given in this country. Charleston, South Carolina, long had a Saint Cecilia Society, founded in 1762 and generally considered to have been the first musical society formed in America. At Providence, Rhode Island, Oliver Shaw, Thomas Webb, and others founded the Psallonian Society in 1809 "for the purpose of improving themselves in the knowledge and practice of sacred music and inculcating a more correct taste in the choice and performance of it." [49]

In Boston, Johann Christian Gottlieb Graupner, Asa Peabody, and Thomas Webb issued an invitation in March, 1815, for a meeting to consider "the expediency of forming a society for cultivating and improving a correct taste in the performance of sacred music, and also to introduce into more general practice the works of Handel, Haydn, and other eminent composers." Sixteen persons responded and the following month the group organized as the Handel and Haydn Society, by 1900 one of the largest and finest oratorio societies in the world.[50] Similar, but less durable, societies have been formed in almost every city in America. In 1929, Pierre

[49] Quoted by John Tasker Howard, *Our American Music*, New York, 1931, p. 141.

[50] Some years ago, the author purchased in a second-hand bookstore on Boston's Corn Hill a vocal score of *The Messiah* in which a former member of the Handel and Haydn Society had carefully listed the conductor and soloists of the Society's annual performances of this work over a period of more than thirty years.

Key's *International Music Year Book* listed a total of 576 American choral societies.

For over a century, most of these organizations, consisting of from one to two hundred members, have given an average of three or four concerts a year with orchestral accompaniment. They have performed all of the great religious oratorios, many within a few months of their composition. They have commissioned new works from famous European composers and from rising young American composers. In contrast with the symphony orchestras whose members are almost exclusively paid professional musicians, the choral societies work entirely on a volunteer basis. None but trained singers may participate, and these not only give their time for weekly rehearsals but also pay dues toward the expenses of hall and orchestra for their performances.

Although seldom if ever strictly limited to the performance of religious music, most of the choral societies find that their repertory is largely religious owing to the available literature. In the case of the annual music festivals, such as those held at Worcester, Massachusetts, since 1858, and at Cincinnati since 1873, the choral works also continue to be largely religious, but paralleled with secular operatic and symphonic works. The choral repertories began with Handel oratorios and Haydn oratorios and masses. Mozart and Beethoven works were added toward mid-century, then Gounod and Mendelssohn. At the beginning of the twentieth century, works by the American composers, John Knowles Paine, George Whitefield Chadwick, Horatio Parker, Edgar Stillman Kelley, and Henry Hadley found a place of nearly equal footing with the European masterpieces. During the second quarter of the century, the great choral music of Bach, after nearly two centuries of neglect, became as popular in America as abroad. Today the repertory is broader than ever before, with older works sharing programs with new compositions.

The few anthems included at the back of the tune-books were discussed earlier in this chapter. During the first half of the nineteenth century, several collections of short anthems by both native and foreign composers were published for the use of particular churches. With the rise of choral societies and increased knowledge of the oratorios which they sang, arias and individual chorus movements from more popular works like *The Messiah* or Rossini's *Stabat Mater* became pap for the quartet choirs. In the bigger churches, orchestral instruments augmented the organs with a louder and more colorful volume of sound in a manner calculated to attract larger audiences—audiences which seldom resembled singing, worshiping congregations. The practice survives in the mid-twentieth century, in the brass and tympani that some churches add on Easter Sunday.

During the latter half of the nineteenth century, there was an enormous volume of anthems turned out by American composers for the quartet choirs. The so-called organ parts of these anthems are all so pianistic in style as to make one suspect that the piano was much more frequently used for accompaniments, as indeed it must have been in many smaller churches throughout the country. Most of these anthems were for solo voice with concluding quartet. Climax in the quartet style came with the compositions of Dudley Buck (1839–1909) and Harry Rowe Shelley (1858–1947), whose works remained in choir repertories for over two generations. Buck's works were so highly regarded in his own lifetime that each new anthem was reviewed in *The Atlantic Monthly* by the distinguished music critic William F. Apthorp. His *Te Deum* in B Minor and the Easter anthem "As it began to dawn" were sincerely believed by many to be the highest expression of religious music at that time. Today musicians realize that, although his sympathetic treatment of the texts is worthy of the finest art-song, they are simply too expressive for the meditative needs of most church services. Actually the same can be said for much of the music composed during this romantic era on both sides of the Atlantic.

Radical change in the repertory came during the second

decade of this century, brought on by several divergent factors. Interest in Johann Sebastian Bach's organ works had grown fairly steadily from the mid-nineteenth century, but relatively little was known of his choral music until J. F. Wolle inaugurated the annual Bach Festivals in 1912 with his now famous Bethlehem Bach Choir. From his pioneering, the Bach cult in America has grown until today Bach harmonizations are found in most hymnals and there are but few choirs which do not sing Bach chorales, choruses, or cantatas. Similarly, a Palestrina cult was advanced considerably by the work of Nicola A. Montani's Palestrina Choir in Philadelphia. This was broadened to include the entire rich field of sixteenth-century polyphony by the work of Archibald T. Davison with the Harvard and Radcliffe Glee Clubs. Many works which he first edited and published for these college groups a generation ago are now enriching the repertory of better choirs throughout the country.

After World War I, American knowledge of and interest in Russian church music were enhanced by the concerts of Serge Jaroff's Don Cossack Choir. Much of this literature was made available for church choirs through the editions of Lindsay Norden, Kurt Schindler, and Winfred Douglas. As interest in the polyphonic era grew, a number of Spanish works were edited by Schindler and Walter Williams. Editions of the Tudor musicians, Byrd, Gibbons, Tallis, and others, prepared in England by Fellowes and Terry, have become equally popular. The exploitation of this great literature from the past by school and college choral groups, following the example of the Harvard Glee Club, has aided church music in two ways: it has trained young people to sing these varied styles of music, and it has taught congregations to appreciate and understand their beauty.

Until this revival of Renaissance polyphony, American choirs used a much higher percentage of works by native composers than did the American symphony orchestras. Today the balance is more even in the choral literature. The preponderance of American compositions among contemporary works is offset by the interest in European works from the sixteenth, seventeenth, and eighteenth centuries.[51] While the symphony orchestras no longer boycott young American composers, the latters' greatest opportunities to have their works performed still come from the choirs and choral societies of the country.

Special Denominations

Much of the hymnody and choral music which have been described above constitutes the entire musical activity in many denominations. In each there has been progression from seventeenth- and eighteenth-century Psalm-singing to the use of the great body of hymnody in which individualistic tendencies are submerged and almost all denominations are joined together in an ecumenicity of song to a degree unattainable at the conference tables. Each denomination varies, however, in the degree to which it vacillates in its music between the use made of the more legitimate hymnody and the gospel songs. They vary, too, in the extent to which their church school and youth fellowship music falls a victim to what one writer has called "Billy Sunday jazz"—a style of performance to which all shades of hymnody can succumb. These denominations also vary greatly in their use of choirs as a social activity, as attendance builders.

In the more liturgical churches, there are certain individual characteristics which should be discussed. Although each of these developed originally in the music of a particular denomination, here again they are no longer the exclusive property of that denomination but are frequently used today in individual churches of other denominations.

The Church of England, later to become the Protestant Episcopal Church in the United States of America, was well

[51] Statistics may be found in Ellinwood, *History of American Church Music*, ch. XVI.

established in Virginia early in the seventeenth century. The metrical Psalter used at Jamestown was mentioned earlier. During the interregnum Commonwealth in England, use of the *Book of Common Prayer* was suppressed, but with the Restoration in 1660 the Episcopal Church began a period of vigorous growth in many of the colonies. There have been, during the three hundred years since that time, two distinct features which have characterized much of the musical life in this Church: the boy choir and the Anglican chanting.

Boys have been used for the treble part in cathedral choirs all over Europe for hundreds of years. They had also been used in some of the Indian missions earlier in America. In the colonies, the rural agricultural nature of the economy at first was such that there were no sizable communities where boys could be recruited for this service. In 1709, Trinity Church, New York, founded a charity school for boys from which singers were drawn. During the following century there are frequent references in the vestry minutes which indicate that a boy choir was being maintained.[52] In mid-century, Francis Hopkinson was training boys to sing for Christ Church, Philadelphia. His *Anthem from the 114th Psalm*, preserved in manuscript at the Library of Congress, is scored for two treble parts and bass, a pattern common to boy choir music during this period. In 1791, the establishment of a municipal orphanage in Charleston, South Carolina, prompted the rector and English-trained organist of St. Michael's Church to teach selected boys for their choir.[53] None of the colonial boy choirs gained permanency, perhaps because of the suspect nature of the Episcopal Church during and immediately following the American Revolution.

The Oxford Movement of the 1830's and 1840's exerted a great influence on church music and especially the music of the liturgy in the Episcopal Church; it initiated the restora-

[52] Arthur H. Messiter, *A History of the Choir and Music of Trinity Church*, New York, 1906.

[53] George W. Williams, *St. Michael's, Charleston, 1751–1951*, Columbia, South Carolina, 1951.

tion of the medieval plainsong, and focused anew the aims and ideals of worship through music. Many of the innovations met with stiff opposition within the Church, but today most of them are being used not only there but with appropriate modification by many other Protestant churches. By 1900 boy choirs had become so popular that in many communities there were not sufficient boys to meet the demand and they were augmented by women, carefully hidden behind screens in some churches. Modern athletic and music activities in the public schools have competed successfully for the time and interest of boys in many communities so that there are not as many boy choirs today as there were two generations ago. They continue to be popular in the larger communities, especially where a private school can provide their academic education. Sentimentalists adore the sight of the youngsters in their Eton collars and vestments, but this is hardly a reason for their retention. The chief advantage of the boy choir is its clear, ethereal tone quality, so accurate in pitch and so impersonal in character. No other form of choral music has been able to achieve that perfection of tone and ensemble which the blending of men's and boys' voices gives. Consequently, for liturgical worship, which directs the attention of the congregation Godward, it has proven ideal. While most commonly associated with the Episcopal Church in this country, the boy choir has been occasionally found in individual Roman Catholic, Lutheran, and a few Methodist churches.

Almost all choirs were kept in the rear gallery until the nineteenth century; due to the careful seniority system worked out in each community to accommodate the town fathers, the rear gallery was the only unrestricted seating available. The Oxford Movement led many churches to install vested choirs, seated like the English cathedral choirs in two sections facing each other on opposite sides of the chancel. When well handled architecturally, a trained, balanced choir sounds better in this position. For many volunteer choirs of mixed men's and women's voices, the gallery position is to be preferred; postwar trends in church architecture have aided a return to the gallery in many cases.

Until choirs were well established, there could be little or no chanting of prose Psalms and canticles in services using *The Book of Common Prayer.* Until after the Revolution, there is no evidence of chanting in America. The first printed examples of Anglican Chant, that is, the recitation of prose texts on a single pitch or reciting tone with a concluding cadence, all in four-part harmony, to be found in this country were published in Andrew Law's *Rudiments of Music,* 1783. Two years later, Francis Hopkinson included some with the hymn-tunes bound in the back of the Proposed Prayer Book of 1785. Episcopal churches must have been among the best purchasers of tune-books, for by the end of the century almost all new publications included a section of Anglican Chants. So familiar is this chanting today that most congregations of the Episcopal Church join in singing the chanted canticles as readily as they sing the hymns. Until the recent revival of plainsong, there has been some Anglican chanting in the English language services of the Lutheran churches. In other Protestant churches, it has been used occasionally when choirs have wanted to chant responses in quasi-liturgical portions of their services.

Choir vestments and processional crosses, which were also introduced into this country by the Oxford Movement, are no longer characteristics of Episcopal choirs alone. Like the organ a century earlier, they have been accepted and used by many other churches in recent years as their advantages have been recognized and older prejudices have been overcome by reason.

Maryland was originally founded as a refuge for Roman Catholics from England, but nothing is known of early church music there. Although several chapels were started in southern Pennsylvania too, there is no record of music until during the Revolution. The reason for this lies in the small and scattered membership, and the lack of any well known body of congregational hymnody in their traditions. Whereas the small Episcopal congregations in rural chapels could sing familiar metrical Psalms, even though their liturgy was spoken, the Roman Catholic congregations had to limit themselves to low mass and vesper offices which were entirely spoken. Missionaries to the Indians had been able to train native choirs with varying degrees of success, but the European settlers lacked the leisure time required for such training.

The first record of the use of music in any Roman Catholic services in the colonies is found in the *Pennsylvania Packet* for July 10, 1779. St. Mary's Church, Philadelphia, was used by the French and other Roman Catholics connected with the Continental Congress; there at noon on Sunday, the Fourth of July, was held a service commemorative of the signing of the Declaration of Independence three years earlier. The service was attended by the President and members of Congress who heard a "*Te Deum* solemnly sung by a number of very good voices, accompanied by the organ and other kinds of music."

The first music published for the use of the Roman Catholic Church in this country, John Aitken's *Compilation of the Litanies, Vespers, Hymns and Anthems As they are Sung in the Catholic Church*, 1787, is indicative of the sort of music which was in use in those churches having musicians. Other editions were published in 1791 and 1814, giving evidence to the fact that by the end of the century these churches were beginning to have music of sorts. These last editions had music in three parts. The original edition had only single melodies, with certain sections like the *Holy Mass of the Blessed Trinity* in two parts. The texts for the various hymns and anthems were largely in English; a few had both English and Latin, while still fewer were only in Latin. Two were in German.[54] Other collections which appeared in the early nineteenth century continue to give evidence that, save for the texts of the hymns and the excerpts of the liturgy which were sung, Roman Catholic music differed little in general style, harmony, and character from other church music of the day. In quality, it dragged behind much of the rest. Bishop Fenwick of Boston stated in 1840 that in two-thirds of the Roman Catholic churches in America there was no singing at all.[55] The glorious heritage of medieval and Renaissance music was entirely unknown, due in large measure to the background of both clergy and congregations which were composed principally of poor German, Irish, and Italian immigrants who had known little better music in their homelands.

Improvement began with the formation of the Caecilian Society in 1873 by John Baptist Singenberger (1848–1924). The latter had been a pupil of Franz Xavier Witt, the founder of the society in Germany and an editor of the Ratisbon edition of the Church's plainsong. In this country, working largely with the German-American congregations of the Middle West, Singenberger's Caecilian Society within a few years achieved a membership of over three thousand musicians. Through annual conventions, lectures, and the pages of its magazine, *Caecilia,* the Society strove to purge Roman Catholic services of cheap, sentimental music, and to cultivate the use of plainsong and polyphony. Some of the religious houses and seminaries, notably St. John's (Benedictine) Abbey, Collegeville, Minnesota, also tried to concentrate their music on the traditional heritage of their Church during these same years. Nonetheless, in 1900 there were still more Lutheran and Episcopal than Roman Catholic churches using plainsong in their services.

Since the promulgation of the famous *Motu Proprio* of

54 Its contents are listed in Ellinwood, *History of American Church Music,* pp. 38–40. A facsimile edition of Aitken's *Compilation* appeared in 1954.

55 Robert H. Lord, *History of the Archdiocese of Boston,* New York, 1944, II, 376.

Pius X in 1903, there has been constant emphasis, especially in the parochial schools and seminaries, on the use of the plainsong in the Vatican-Solesmes edition. Schools such as the Pius X School of Liturgical Music, founded in 1918, and the Gregorian Institute of America, founded in 1941, have trained teachers in the best Solesmes tradition so that the music in the schools has improved greatly. In spite of all this, there is still little or no congregational singing in the average parish church, and the lay members of the Church have no share in their own musical heritage. In the lives of the many who attend masses each Sunday, there is even today almost no religious music.

Roman Catholic Church music has suffered greatly in this country from a lack of financial support. Almost all choirs have had to function on a purely volunteer basis, and organists have seldom been well paid. The only boy choirs to achieve distinction have been those of the Rev. John B. Young, S.J., at the Church of St. Francis Xavier, New York, around 1885, and the Paulist Choristers of the Rev. William Joseph Finn, C.S.P., in Chicago and New York.

The first Moravians came to this country for missionary work among the Indians. Their principal center, at Bethlehem, Pennsylvania, was begun in 1740. Sixteen years later, a report to the colonial governor stated that the community consisted of 188 married persons and 322 children, with 225 additional single men, 67 single women, and 96 other children who were orphans or boarding pupils in their schools. Forty-eight were absent at the time, engaged in missionary work among the Indians, 54 were preaching or teaching school in other parts of the American colonies, 62 were tutors or attendants in their local schools.

Wherever the Moravians were, they used music in their daily life. They sang at meals, in the fields, in the work shops, and while traveling. Hymns helped speed the completion of arduous tasks.

A distinctive feature of their music, preserved to the present time, is the trombone choir. Trombones were brought with the first Moravian missionaries to Georgia in 1735 and have continued in use ever since. The quartet or choir[56] consists of treble, alto, tenor, and bass trombones, permitting the chorales to be played in four-part harmony. A schedule of tunes was worked out which provided special chorales for each occasion in the life and worship of the community. Thus the *Passion Chorale* by Hans Leo Hassler was used to announce from the church belfry the death of a member of the community. Special announcement tunes welcomed distinguished visitors, such as General George Washington and his retinue. Playing in the trombone choir was an honored, albeit rigorous service, and the trombonists put in long years of daily devotion to their duties.[57]

The Moravian Collegium Musicum was established soon after they settled in Bethlehem to perform sacred choral works, also symphonic and chamber music. Research in recent years has disclosed evidence of performances and manuscript copies of works by leading contemporary European composers, especially those of the Mannheim group, many of which were not heard elsewhere in America for over a century. There were several significant local composers who wrote for symphony orchestra as well as choral works. A few of their chorale melodies found their way into the tune-books of other denominations.

Their music was not buried in the community, as is evidenced by Benjamin Franklin's account of his visit of 1756, recorded in his *Autobiography:* "I was at their Church, where I was entertain'd with good Musick, the Organ being accompanied with Violins, Hautboys, Flutes, Clarinets, &c."

[56] In recent years at Bethlehem it has numbered over twenty-five trombones, and at Winston-Salem, North Carolina, has been a full brass band.

[57] Rufus A. Grider, *Historical Notes on Music in Bethlehem, Pennsylvania, from 1741 to 1871*, Philadelphia, 1873, records the names of these players. Cf. also Joseph A. Maurer, "The Moravian Trombone Choir," *The Historical Review of Berks County*, Reading, Pa., October–December 1954, pp. 2–8.

The Bethlehem Seminary enjoyed a high reputation for the quality of its teaching. One twelve-year-old girl wrote a letter describing her life there which was published in the New Haven, Connecticut, *Gazette* for April 17, 1788.[58] Among other things she wrote:

"On Sundays divine service is performed in the great chapel, where the whole society, men, women, and children meet. Their preaching is sometimes in English and sometimes in German. They sing enchantingly, in which they are joined with the bass-viols, violins and an organ. To call the people into the chapel four French horns [trombones!] are blown, with which you would be delighted. . . ."

Testifying to the caliber of the Seminary is the fact that Washington wrote in 1796 seeking admission for two of his grandnieces.

Another Moravian contribution was in the making of musical instruments. The organs built by Mons Gustavus Hesselius, Johann Gottlob Klemm, and David Tannenberg were used by Moravian, Lutheran, Roman Catholic, and Episcopal congregations for many years; some of them are still preserved in museums or incorporated into their successors. Less known, but still important, were the orchestral instruments made by Moravian craftsmen during the hundred-year period before 1850.

Since the mid-nineteenth century, the name Bethlehem, Pennsylvania, has become synonymous with that of Johann Sebastian Bach, due to the traditions of Moravian choral music and the talents of the Moravian Church organist, John Frederick Wolle. Born and bred in the local musical atmosphere, after study in Munich Wolle returned to lead the Bethlehem Choral Union and to begin the Bach tradition

[58] Quoted at length in Donald M. McCorkle, "The Moravian Contribution to American Music," *Music Library Association Notes*, Second Series, XIII, September 1956, pp. 597–606.

which led in 1900 to the first complete performance in America of Bach's *B Minor Mass.* The annual Bach Festivals since 1912 have made Bethlehem a musical Oberammergau in America. Among the two hundred or more participants each year have been farmers and city dwellers, steel workers, carpenters, professors, women from the mills, homes, schools, and offices. Almost all of the singers are still church members, and their devotion permeates the Festival, giving the music a spiritual glory in keeping with its heritage.[59]

Mention was made earlier of the tunes developed for use with the metrical Psalms in the French or Genevan Psalter. In English-language hymnody, save for their use during the seventeenth century in the Plymouth colony, most of them were dropped until the late nineteenth century because of their more complicated meter. The Reformation in Germany, led by Martin Luther, developed a larger, comparable body of hymn-tunes known today as chorales. These were so closely allied with the Lutheran services[60] that they remained the characteristic element of Lutheran church music in subsequent centuries. Composers developed organ preludes based on the chorale melodies. They used them as the basis of cantatas and motets for the choir. So intensive was their use that J. S. Bach included a total of fourteen chorales in his setting of *The Passion According to Saint Matthew,* 1729.

Many of these chorales were brought to America by the Moravians and other groups of German Protestants. Swedish and other Scandinavian Lutheran bodies brought their own linguistic variants of this repertory. By the end of the eighteenth century, there were many congregations, especially in Pennsylvania, where the chorales were well known and sung by devoted congregations. So well known were they by the Lutheran congregations that there is no suggestion of the

[59] Joseph A. Maurer, "Central Moravian Church: Center of Moravian Music," *The American Organist,* XLI, November 1958, pp. 407–412.

[60] Luther had even versified the Creed and other parts of the liturgy so that all of the people could better sing them to these melodies.

chorales ever needing to be "lined-out" as were the Psalm-tunes. Perhaps one should not paint too rosy a picture of colonial Lutheran singing, however, for several contemporary writers complain about its quality.[61]

Like the Episcopal Church, there was never any reluctance to use organs on the part of the Lutheran Church, so that each one acquired an instrument as soon as it could be afforded. During the period from 1841 to 1860, newly arrived Swedish Lutheran congregations in the Middle West used their native Psalmodikons until they could afford reed or pipe organs. This Psalmodikon was an improved form of the medieval monochord, tromba marina, or nun's fiddle, about forty inches long, which was played with a bow. It was used both to sound the pitch and to play the melody of the chorale in support of the congregational singing.[62]

With a perversity typical of the descendants of many immigrant groups in America, by the end of the nineteenth century there was a strong tendency among Lutheran congregations to abandon the great chorales which were their own peculiar heritage and to substitute the hymns used in churches of English or Scottish background. Unfortunately, this was often accompanied by the use of inferior tunes of the Lowell Mason variety. Interestingly enough, this trend came just at a time when other English and American congregations were becoming aware of the musical riches in the chorales and were introducing many of them into their own hymnals.

During the second quarter of the twentieth century, there has been a marked revival of musical interest and activity in the Lutheran churches. There has been a return to chanting

[61] e.g., Henry Melchior Muhlenberg, *Journals*, Philadelphia, 1942– , I, 297.

[62] Carl Leonard Nelson, *The Sacred and Secular Music of the Swedish Settlers of the Midwest, 1841–1917*, Ph. D. dissertation, New York University, School of Education, 1950. Available on *University Microfilms*, no. 2190.

appropriate parts of the liturgy in both plainsong and Anglican Chant. New organs and better choirs have combined to perform the splendid literature based on the German chorales, both in the church services and in special sacred concerts.

Over the nearly two thousand years of the Diaspora, melodies from many divers civilizations have entered the synagogue. Wherever Jews have lived in the course of their wanderings, elements of the national musical idiom have entered into the oral tradition which was Jewish music until modern times. In recent centuries newly composed music has reflected the national background of each composer, in Jewish sacred music as much as in Lutheran or Anglican music. Unfortunately the musical tradition of the European synagogues was at its lowest ebb at the beginning of the nineteenth century, the date when American synagogue music had its beginnings.[63]

The few congregations which were organized in the colonial period of American history followed the Sephardic ritual with its predominantly Hispanic, Oriental background. During the nineteenth century, as immigration from eastern Europe grew, the newer synagogues followed the Ashkenazic ritual with its different historical background. Initial contrasts in the music of Sephardic and Ashkenazic congregations reflected this diversity of background, but during the course of the nineteenth century they became less sharp as modern denominational lines developed in Judaism.

Originally, each congregation in America had to depend on the cantor (Ḥazan) to conduct its services; the first ordained rabbi did not settle in America until 1840. Unfortunately, neither the Sephardic nor the Ashkenazic cantors were proficient musicians, and there was no opportunity for the training of the cantorate in this country. After the arrival of ordained rabbis, preaching assumed primary importance, as was the situation in so many Protestant churches, and Ortho-

[63] Eric Werner, *In the Choir Loft*, New York, 1957.

dox Jewish congregations came to prefer to do their own chanting without the services of a cantor, except for the High Holy Days. As a result, there is today more congregational participation in the singing at the Orthodox synagogues than at any others.

The only musical instrument permitted in the Orthodox services is the Shofar, or ram's horn. This sounds its solitary note on the two High Holy Days, (1) reminding God and Israel of the covenant between God and Abraham as a result of the latter's readiness to sacrifice his son Isaac,[64] and (2) in commemoration of the liberation of slaves in the Jubilee Year.[65]

Conservative congregations use the same traditional chants as do the Orthodox, but they depend almost entirely on cantors and professional choirs, with little congregational participation. In a few instances, organs have been installed for the better use of modern choral services.

The Reform Movement in America, led by Rabbi Isaac M. Wise (1819–1900), introduced English prayers and hymns into its services. To support these new hymns, Reform synagogues installed organs and hired choirs whose musical training was almost entirely in the hands of Christian organists. During the anti-traditionalist generation, from 1880 to 1915, most cantors were dismissed from Reform synagogues. These congregations believed that they could best become Americanized by cultivating the manners and practices of the Protestant churches. Leaders of the Reform Movement thus adopted the vernacular hymn or chorale as their main musical form. They made extensive borrowings of both texts and melodies from Protestant hymnody, intermixed with new hymn texts and Jewish folk-tunes. Best known of this new hymnody is the metrical paraphrase of the *Yigdal* made jointly in 1884–1885 by Rabbi Max Landsberg and the Rev.

[64] Cf. Genesis 22.
[65] Cf. Leviticus 25.

Newton Mann in order to have a hymn in which both Jewish and Christian congregations could join together in singing, to the traditional tune *Leoni*,

Praise to the living God!
All praised be His Name
Who was, and is, and is to be,
For aye the same.
The one eternal God
Ere aught that now appears:
The First, the Last, beyond all thought
His timeless years!

Unfortunately, Reform attempts at congregational hymnody came during the era when the quartet choir dominated church music throughout this country to the general detriment of congregational singing. Conditions in the Reform synagogues were no better, for in spite of expensive organs and choirs there is even today very little congregational singing in their services.

The anti-traditionalist trend was checked musically by the research and teaching of Professor Abraham Z. Idelsohn of Hebrew Union College. The Zionist Movement, with its emphasis on Jewish culture, also played a strong although less direct role. Idelsohn's research brought a renewed interest and respect for the Oriental elements in traditional Jewish music. By 1920, men like A. W. Binder, J. Weinberg, and Lazare Saminsky were editing, composing, and performing music for Conservative synagogues which, while modern, still returned to the traditional spirit and roots.

By 1935, the cantorate had again taken its traditional place in the Reform synagogues. Considerable portions of their *Union Prayerbook* have been set to choral music, some of it with orchestral accompaniments, by Ernest Bloch, Schoenberg, Milhaud, and other distinguished modern composers.

During the twentieth century, immigrants and refugees from Greece, the Levant, and Russia have come to this country in sufficient quantities to have their own Eastern Orthodox

Church services in many cities. While the basic liturgy is identical in all Eastern Orthodox services, differing only in the language used, the people remain in small, separate congregations, each trying to preserve something of the memories of worship as they knew it in their respective native lands, whether Albanian, Armenian, Greek, Russian, Serbian, Syrian, or Ukrainian. In these churches, one may hear some fine chanting of the medieval Byzantine liturgy by the cantors. A few also have small choirs which sing the more modern unaccompanied works very well. In almost none of these Orthodox churches is there any congregational singing in the sense that it is known in Protestant churches. On the other hand, there is a great love for their liturgy which in many ways compensates for any lack of active participation on the part of the laity.

Religious Communities

The monastic, communistic life has often aided the cultivation of special types of music. Canon Charles Winfred Douglas did most of his work in adapting the medieval plainsongs to English texts in connection with the Community of Saint Mary at Peekskill, New York.[66] Roman Catholic religious houses have at various times been noted for their singing of the Latin plainsongs. The basic nature of the cloistered life keeps much of this music within itself, but visitors do hear it from time to time and the monastic choirs occasionally sing under more public conditions. At all times, they afford models of rendition of the style of music which they cultivate.

In colonial and nineteenth-century America, there were several religious communities, living apart from the secular world, which cultivated their own peculiar style of music, thereby attracting considerable attention from the very world from which they sought exclusion. The first of these were the

[66] Leonard Ellinwood and Anne W. Douglas, *To Praise God, the Life and Work of Charles Winfred Douglas*, New York, 1958.

Hermits, or Mystics, of the Wissahickon. This was a small group of men, German Pietists, under the leadership of Johannes Kelpius, who settled in 1694 for a few years on a site now included in Fairmount Park, in the Roxborough section of Philadelphia. Their morning and evening devotional services attracted many visitors. Their choir and instrumentalists (viol, oboe, trumpets, organ, and tympani) furnished the music at the (Swedish) Gloria Dei Church in Wicacoa, Philadelphia, for an ordination in 1703, at a time when such instrumental music was hardly available anywhere else in the colonies.[67]

Another monastic group, but one distinctly different in character, was the Ephrata Community near Lancaster, Pennsylvania, which was founded in 1720 by Conrad Beissel. This was a mixed community which numbered three hundred persons by 1770. They had their own printing press which turned out Continental money during 1777 and 1778. Their schools attracted pupils from many of the leading Pennsylvania families. Beissel was an outstanding director, composer, and teacher, so that music became a distinctive feature of the community's life. The women were organized into four-part choirs, taking the lower as well as the higher parts. Similarly, the men sang in parts so that when combined the mixed ensemble was in as many as seven different parts, all unaccompanied, for their leader permitted no musical instruments. Much of the music consisted of original compositions by Beissel, homophonic in style but sung in a falsetto voice with a free rhythm governed by the accent of the words. Contemporary accounts speak of the striking impression the sound made on listeners' ears, it being compared to soft instrumental music. Beissel's theories on music were published in two products of the Ephrata press; they were minutely detailed even to the extent of particular diets for high and low voices. The community's manuscript choral books were deco-

[67] *Church Music and Musical Life in Pennsylvania*, I, Pennsylvania Society of the Colonial Dames of America, 1926.

rated with elaborate illuminations based on the mystical tulip, pomegranate, lilies, and doves. Several of these are now preserved in historical collections.[68]

Members of the eighteenth-century United Society of Believers in Christ's Second Coming are today better known as Shakers. Their music went through several changes during the history of the movement, as it was never dominated by a single strong personality as was that of the Ephrata Community. The Shakers' early songs were individualistic, personal entities in much the same sense as were those of the American Indian. They were largely wordless or in "tongues." The New Light and Free Will converts to Shakerism brought into the various communities their first hymns of a corporate nature. After the Kentucky Revival, or Second Great Awakening, other converts brought some of the campmeeting songs with them. Few of these songs remained as part of the Shaker hymnody, but their style was adopted and developed into what, by 1830, was a characteristic idiom. The very nature of Shakerism made their songs and ritual dances a folk art. During the Shakers' own revival period, 1837 to 1850, in their communities there was a strong creative surge which found expression in "gift songs" or "vision songs." These were received during a trance and then sung as gifts or messages for the person indicated in the trance. During this same period, their dances—squares, rings, and marches—became more elaborate than hitherto. Andrews [69] reproduces a number of contemporary drawings of their dances and many of their songs. In their dances, they often acted out the words of the songs, as at "stamp" and "grin" in the following:

I love my faithful brethren more
Than any souls I've seen before;

. . . .

I love to see them stamp and grin . . .

[68] ibid., II; also Ellinwood, *History of American Church Music*, facing p. 34.

[69] Edward D. Andrews, *The Gift to be Simple; Songs, Dances, and Rituals of the American Shakers*, New York, 1940.

The movement of the ring dance is depicted in the following song from about 1840:

'Tis the gift to be simple,
'Tis the gift to be free,
'Tis the gift to come down
where we ought to be.
And when we find ourselves
in the place just right,
'Twill be in the valley of love and delight.
When true simplicity is gain'd,
To bow and to bend we shan't be ashamed.
To turn, turn will be our delight,
'Till by turning, turning we come 'round right.

While far from being the monastic type of community the Shakers were, the Church of Jesus Christ of Latter Day Saints, more popularly known as the Mormons, had many elements in common with the Shakers, especially during their first half-century of development. Like almost all new sects, with the notable exception of the Quakers, the Mormons found both choral and instrumental music helpful in developing the corporate spirit of the group. Their first hymnal, compiled by Emma Smith, the wife of the founder, appeared in 1835. It contained ninety hymns which were adaptations of well known hymns and popular songs made to fit the new doctrines. As the group made their successive moves farther and farther West, under bitter persecution even to the extent of arson and murder on the part of other settlers, numerous editions of their hymnal added fresh references in song to the exciting events of their history and the chronology of their wanderings, as in the following:

Although in woods and tents we dwell,
Shout! Shout! O camp of Israel:
No "Christian" mobs on earth can bind
Our thoughts, or steal our peace of mind.

Their hymns also made clear their unique beliefs:

A Church without a Prophet
Is not the Church for me!
It has not head to lead it;
In it I would not be.

Later conflicts with the Federal government over polygamy were also reflected in their songs.[70]

Once settled in Utah, the Mormon Church encouraged all forms of music. The Saints had used bands from the first days at Nauvoo, Illinois; in Utah they found frequent use for them in the social and political life which was but another aspect of their faith. Dancing, especially square dancing, was another prominent feature in both social recreation and religious expression.

The first Tabernacle organ was built in Australia by Joseph Ridges, who brought it with him to Salt Lake City in 1857 after his conversion. It was rebuilt by him for the permanent Tabernacle in 1866, and has since been rebuilt and enlarged several times. Some of the original pipes still remain in use. The Tabernacle Choir began to achieve musical stature after 1862 under C. J. Thomas, a convert who had been an orchestral conductor in London. Since 1929 it has become nationally known through its radio broadcasts.

Social Strata

Just as all American musical life is by no means limited to the concert halls, so, too, its religious music is diversified. On the secular plane, there are perhaps three fundamental music levels: that of the symphony hall, the popular concert hall, and the night club. Equally distinct are the large city or cathedral choirs, the more modest church choirs, and the gospel mission musical groups. On the one hand there are repertories of Piston symphonies, Grand Canyon Suites, and

[70] Howard Swan, *Music in the Southwest, 1825–1950,* San Marino, California, 1952.

hillbilly songs; in religious music there are works like Sowerby's *Forsaken of Man*, smaller anthems deliberately composed for modest choirs, and an average of fifty gospel-song collections published annually.

It would be difficult to generalize, without considerably more research than has yet been made, on the reasons, aside from family tradition, which make different people prefer more or less involved liturgies. It is equally difficult to determine why some individuals desire a larger or smaller amount of personal participation in the church services.

When it comes to the psychological factors which condition the various social strata attuned to the three musical levels just described, more is known. If an individual moves from interest in secular music to religious music, his tastes do not automatically remain at the same relative level. On the other hand, there is a close correlation between the individual's tastes in literature, the visual arts, and music. One seldom finds a person whose reading is limited to a few headlines and the cartoon strips, whose radio-television interests are soap operas or sport broadcasts, who is also a Bach enthusiast. Most such people prefer gospel songs. At the same time, there are many persons whose cultural background is considerable in all fields save music. These prefer the romantic era of music: Victorian hymn-tunes and anthems by Gounod or Shelley. Thus, while one can generalize that all persons who are musical snobs are devotees of Bach and Sowerby, not all others are addicted to gospel songs. The development of musical taste is fascinating to watch, especially in the field of religious music. The changes outlined in this chapter, through which American musical life has passed, can all be traced in a few adolescent years of many individuals.

From time to time, brash statements have been made intimating that certain denominations in America find their members solely from a particular social level. Such statements can so easily be disproven that they would not be worth mentioning except that certain types of music and certain musical traditions have been consistently associated with particular denominations. This is not so much a social phenomenon as it is a matter of theology. Thus, those fundamentalist bodies which emphasize a personal salvation care relatively little for great religious art, architecture, or music, but prefer simple buildings with little adornment and music which is direct and personal—hence the gospel song idiom. Denominations which stress corporate worship by the group, whose primary concern is not themselves as individuals but rather the worship of Almighty God as a fundamental duty, these embellish the House of God with the finest art and craft they can afford, both visually and aurally; they stress congregational participation through liturgical responses and singing. Between these two extremes lies a group of denominations where the principal emphasis is on preaching. Congregations in these churches are basically listeners, and their music reflects this fact.

RELIGIOUS EXPRESSION IN AMERICAN ARCHITECTURE

DONALD DREW EGBERT

With the assistance of Charles W. Moore *

WINSTON CHURCHILL once declared, "We shape our dwellings, and afterwards our dwellings shape us." [1] It is true that he was referring, not to dwellings of the spirit but to a specific secular edifice, the recently bombed-out House of Commons, which he insisted must be reconstructed exactly as it had been before the bombing in order that its architectural arrangement might continue to foster the British parliamentary system. Nevertheless, his statement has meaning for other kinds of buildings, including religious buildings. For temples, churches, meeting houses and synagogues, if architecturally adequate, all reflect in some way and to some degree religious beliefs of their specific denomination or sect. These buildings, in turn, may also affect the very nature of the religious services held in them, so that an individual architect or a prevailing architectural style may actually foster a new interpretation of some of the doctrines and beliefs of the given religious group.

The purpose of this essay, then, is to seek to show how the architecture of American churches, meeting houses, and synagogues has tended to exemplify, in highly tangible form, important aspects of prevailing American religious beliefs and practices. To begin, we must go back to the original forms of Christian church architecture, as they evolved during the first centuries of Christianity. At the risk of oversimplification one can say that there are two chief types. The first of these is the basilical type—essentially a long rectangle, usually divided along the long axis into three aisles, with the chief

* This essay was in large part written by Professor Moore from a recorded lecture by Professor Egbert, and then jointly revised.

[1] Speech of October 28, 1944.

door in the center of one short end, and at the other end a sanctuary. The sanctuary is often in an apse (a kind of large niche) projecting from the end of the building. Sometimes there are transepts extending out from the long sides of the rectangle, producing a Latin cross plan. Beginning relatively early in the Middle Ages, there were frequently towers (the bell tower was a Benedictine addition that originated in the eighth or ninth century). By the very nature of the basilical plan, attention is focused down the long axis of the structure, at the end of which lies the sanctuary in which the axis culminates.

The second traditional Christian church type has a plan in which attention is focused into the center of the building—even though often the sanctuary is not located at this point. This central type may be circular or polygonal, or it may have a Greek cross plan, that is, one with four equal arms.

Early Protestant churches in Europe often continued these traditional plan types, especially the basilical type with bell tower. The traditional basilica particularly tended to persist where a state Protestant church took over existing Catholic buildings, as was done, for example, by the Anglican church in England, or by the Lutheran church in north Germany and Scandinavia. The continuation of a traditional type was likely to occur, too, where the reaction against the Catholic liturgy and hierarchy was relatively weak, again as in the case of the Anglican church in England. Moreover, the traditional type customarily survived wherever the church edifice was looked upon as a holy building, as the house of God.

Some Protestant groups, however, especially those who —in sharply rejecting hierarchical religious government—were religiously on the far left, added a new kind of church building, the meeting house, to the traditional types mentioned above. Most meeting houses, as their name implies, were derived from the house (with perhaps some influence also from simple, aisleless, rectangular medieval churches), although, as we shall see, there was one important meeting house type that apparently did not stem at all from domestic architecture. As one might expect, meeting houses were most likely to occur where dissenting Protestant groups were frowned upon by the state church, as was the case, for example, in seventeenth-century England, except during the Civil War and the Commonwealth or after the Toleration Act of 1689. As one might expect, also, some type of meeting house was generally found wherever the reaction against the old liturgy and hierarchy was particularly strong. Emphasis was placed then on the priesthood of all believers, on preaching, or—usually—on both. And the meeting house was most likely to be found wherever the building was not regarded as a holy place, but as suitable for all group meetings, secular as well as religious. This was to be the case, of course, in New England, where the town meeting was held in the same edifice that was used for religious services.

Thus meeting houses were built especially by dissenting groups made up of religiously left-wing Protestants. All of these groups emphasized a preaching space, a simple rectangular or, more rarely, polygonal room; and as might be expected, the emphasis was on simplicity, whether from fear of popery, or from fear of persecution, or both. For even more than other Protestants, these groups emphasized what is known as the Protestant plain style.[2]

Such is the general background of the chief types of religious architecture to be found in the American colonies during the seventeenth and early eighteenth centuries. As regards the churches of the Spanish colonies, suffice it to say that they were essentially provincial versions of the traditional basilicas of the mother country. In the other colonies, however, there was more variety—in some the traditional church types prevailed; in others, the meeting house types were

[2] See Anthony Garvan, "The Protestant Plain Style before 1630," *Journal of the Society of Architectural Historians*, Vol. 9, no. 3, October 1950, pp. 5–13.

dominant; while in still others, both were to be found side by side—variations depending on the particular colony and the denominations or sects that prevailed there. The basilical type, for instance, was especially to be found in colonies where the Anglicans were strong, and in colonies where Lutheranism was important.

The beginnings of Anglicanism, it will be recalled, lay in the refusal of the English church under Henry VIII to acknowledge the Pope's supremacy over any other bishop: Henry VIII's promulgation in 1534 of his Act of Supremacy followed the Pope's refusal to grant him a divorce from his wife, Catherine of Aragon, so he could marry Anne Boleyn. As a result, when the Anglican church broke with Rome, it simply took over existing buildings. However, under Henry VIII's successors, especially Edward VI and Queen Elizabeth, an increasingly Protestant tendency developed: under Elizabeth's government were promulgated the Thirty-nine Articles which showed strong Calvinistic and Lutheran influences. During this period, the parish church type of the Middle Ages continued to be built in England, although the type was somewhat modified to contain a more Protestant service.[3]

In the American colonies of Virginia and South Carolina, where the Anglican church was established by law, the basilical type also prevailed. The church building believed to be the oldest in this country is St. Luke's Church near Smithfield, Virginia (Fig. 1), apparently built in 1632. Typically English, this is an Anglican parish church of the medieval type, only slightly modified by Protestantism and by Renaissance classicism. The layout of the building, with its tower at the center of the façade, is of a sort frequently encountered in English parish churches of the medieval period. The Gothic tracery in the windows, the little Gothic pin-

[3] See George W. O. Addleshaw and Frederick Etchells, *The Architectural Setting of Anglican Worship*, London, 1948, one of the few first-rate books on the relation of religious architecture to religious doctrine.

nacles still surviving on the edges of the gables (particularly the rear gable), Gothic buttresses, all are parts of what remains essentially a medieval parish church, but with some new and more classical elements beginning to assert themselves under a fashion then developing in England. Over the door is a triangular pediment, more or less classical, and on the corners of the tower are quoins, both probably somewhat later in date than the body of the building. The look of a medieval parish church is even more pronounced on the interior (Fig. 2)—the Gothic tracery shows in the sanctuary window, and the structure of the roof is exposed in the medieval fashion, rather than concealed as customary later under the influence of the Renaissance and post-Renaissance. The church has a choir screen, also Gothic in spirit but classical in detail: this, with the exposed roof structure, has very recently been restored. Notice that in this church the altar occupies a place of major importance. As a consequence, the pulpit is placed off to one side, although it is nonetheless in a very important position, given prominence by the Protestant emphasis on preaching.

Like Anglican churches, the Lutheran examples of the colonial period also tended to adhere to the basilical type. German Lutherans began to come into the colonies in the late seventeenth century; like the Anglicans, they claimed that their church was catholic and not sectarian, although the colonial American Lutheran leaders, such as Muhlenberg, were in close touch with pietistic left-wing Protestants in Germany. As a consequence, one could expect the architecture of the early Lutheran churches of the Pennsylvania German country to be based on a basilical plan, but with considerable emphasis on the ultra-simplicity characteristic of the architecture of left-wing Protestant groups. One of the most famous examples of the period is Muhlenberg's own church at Trappe, Pennsylvania, known as the Augustus Lutheran Church, built in 1743 (Figs. 3 and 4). The type is basilical, but the church is very simple. Its towerless exterior is not wholly unlike a meeting house; nevertheless it is not a meeting house type because the main door is in the short side and the sanctuary is located at the end of the long axis opposite the main entrance. The interior (Fig. 5) shows the simplicity of the church; the pulpit, as at St. Luke's, is placed off the axis of the church, and the sanctuary is then reserved for communion. A gallery, built to allow more people to get closer to hear the services, underlines the importance of preaching in Protestant churches.

In considerable contrast to the basilical church are the meeting houses, two chief varieties of which occur in the American colonies. These two types—built by those colonial groups regarded in England as dissenters—are quite similar on the inside but different on the exterior, and overlap confusingly. Among the dissenting groups who made use of them, the Calvinists figured with particular importance, and in the American colonies included, of course, the Congregationalists of New England, the Dutch Reformed of New Netherlands (later New York and New Jersey), the Presbyterians in New Jersey and the Piedmont, the German Reformed of Pennsylvania, and the Huguenots of South Carolina and New York.

The first type of Calvinist meeting house to be discussed was often employed by the Congregationalists and also by some Dutch Reformed congregations. The only example of its type remaining from the more than 200 meeting houses known to have been built in New England in the seventeenth century is the famous Old Ship Meeting House at Hingham, Massachusetts (Figs. 6 and 7). This, the second meeting house at Hingham, was built by Congregationalists in 1681 but successively enlarged in 1730 and 1755, so that it is only partly a seventeenth-century meeting house. One might note here that since the New England meeting house served for town meetings as well as for religious services, it became the prototype for many early American town halls—including those of the Western Reserve which was settled by Congregationalists from New England.

Even in its present form, the Old Ship Meeting House shows various survivals from medieval architecture,[4] and in this respect is not unlike most other seventeenth-century colonial buildings, including St. Luke's Church in Virginia. The high pyramidal roof, for instance, reflects medieval antecedents in its steepness, although a Renaissance type of cupola has been placed on the deck at the top of the pyramid.

The earliest meeting house in Connecticut, built in Hartford in 1636, was of the same type except that the high pyramidal roof came to a point, so that the deck and cupola, essentially Renaissance features, were lacking. Other meeting houses had the roof deck, but not the cupola and bell, and in such cases the congregations were usually called together by a drummer standing on the deck.[5] The New Haven meeting house of 1639 already had a cupola, but New Haven was established by relatively wealthy and aristocratic founders whose architecture, therefore, was more likely to be up-to-date in style.

On the interior of all these early meeting houses, the structure was exposed in the medieval fashion: its resemblance to the timberwork of a ship gave the Old Ship Meeting House in Hingham its name. In plan these New England buildings were rectangular, but with reduced emphasis on a long axis; in fact the main entrance at Hingham is on the long side of the building, with the pulpit placed directly opposite the entrance door. On the short axis, it is true, there is a side entrance, but the main axis runs the other way from that of the basilical plan, and the building itself is more nearly a square. Thus, in its interior, which is typical of meeting houses of early type, attention is focused on the pulpit, placed on the long side of the room. Also typically, the men were separated

[4] A conjectural restoration drawing to show the original design of the exterior of this meeting house is published in Marian C. Donnelly, "New England Meetinghouses in the Seventeenth Century," *Old-Time New England*, Vol. 7, no. 4, April–June 1957, p. 87.

[5] A more medieval kind of roof also sometimes used on this squarish type of meeting house was the cross-gable, or four-gable, roof.

from the women, who sat on the right while the men sat on the left. The earliest seats were simply crude benches; as the desire for comfort increased backs were placed on the benches; and then, with increasing wealth, box pews were put in for the aristocracy.

In summary, what was the character of the meeting house as seen here? First, great emphasis was placed on simplicity in the architecture, harmonizing with the primitive simplicity of the service, as these Protestant groups sought to reestablish the simple purity of early Christian services. Secondly, emphasis was placed on the direct connection of the individual worshiper with God, through God's word, for God was regarded as incarnate in the Bible. The belief in the priesthood of all believers, though strong, was less emphasized than among the Quakers, for example, because in Congregationalist New England, the Word was interpreted by the minister as the spiritual shepherd of the flock, whereas the Quakers, on the contrary, have had no clergy until quite recently. Yet for Congregationalist and Quaker alike, as for most other Protestant groups, the individual does not approach God through a priestly hierarchy as in Roman Catholicism. The New England meeting house, far from being a place for the celebration of the Mass, is a preaching house, designed for hearing the word of God expounded. Galleries are included if necessary so that all the congregation can hear, but they are not ordinarily present in the meeting house because the New England town, and the congregation that made up the population of the town, were restricted in size. As soon as the town grew so big that it became difficult for the members of the congregation to get into meeting, another town was established. Not only was the meeting house small in scale, but into its simplicity nothing was allowed to intrude which might distract from the direct connection of the individual member of the congregation with the word of God: no crosses, no images, no altar with the relics of the saints. A pulpit placed close to a communion table marked what was regarded as a return to the spirit and usages of primitive, and true, Christianity.

What is the origin of the Hingham type of meeting house, characterized by a relatively square plan, by an entrance and pulpit on the longer sides, and by a roof of more or less pyramidal shape usually with a deck on top and often a cupola for a bell? It is difficult to say. Interestingly enough, England contains no early meeting houses of exactly this type. It becomes useful, therefore, to interrupt our consideration of this Congregationalist type of building to examine two examples which illustrate the kind of meeting houses used by Congregationalists and similar groups in England, so as to see how they differ from the Hingham Meeting House. The first of these examples is at Horningsham in Wiltshire (Fig. 8). It was built in 1566, and is the oldest Congregational chapel in England (the meeting places of English dissenters are called chapels), although it was originally erected for a group of Scottish Presbyterian masons who were working on a great house, "Longleat," nearby. This meeting house is clearly different from that at Hingham; on the exterior it resembles much more closely a simple house. This could be expected, since the Separatist movement in England, except under the Commonwealth in the middle of the seventeenth century, had to remain to a considerable degree underground, until the expulsion of the Catholic James II by William III of Orange in the Glorious Revolution of 1688 was followed the next year by William's Toleration Act, which gave greater freedom of worship to the dissenters in England.

Yet even when the dissenters had been briefly dominant in England in the mid-seventeenth century, such meeting houses as were built had exteriors of the house type, and so did not resemble the New England meeting houses of the kind found at Hingham. This can be seen in our second English example (Figs. 9 and 10), which was built during the Civil War shortly before the establishment of the Commonwealth. It is a Congregational chapel at Walpole in Suffolk. The original building, constructed in 1647 in the midst of the Civil War, was enlarged about 1690; and the peculiar double gable probably resulted from the enlargement. It has been suggested that this meeting house may originally have been formed by joining two cottages together side by side. Whether or not this is the case, the Walpole meeting house was erected at a time when the Congregationalists who built it were at least locally dominant, yet the exterior of the building is still of the simple house type so characteristic, also, of earlier and later meeting houses in England and so different from the typical New England Congregational meeting houses of the period. The interior, however, is quite similar to that at Hingham, though with galleries and with a flat ceiling covering the upper part of the timbers of the roof.

We are left still with the problem of the origin of the Hingham type of meeting house. Some authorities have suggested that influences from Holland largely determined its form. It indeed seems likely that the Hingham type originated at least partly under Dutch influence, and that it is a modified form of Dutch Reformed, or Dutch Calvinist, church building.[6] The Congregationalists could, of course, have received this Dutch influence while the Pilgrim Fathers were in Holland before embarking for New England. Certainly, similar pyramidal roofs are to be found in Dutch Calvinist churches. One example, the Dutch Reformed Church built in Albany, New York (Fig. 11) in 1715, and seen here in a view of 1805, seems to be of much the same type as the Old Ship Meeting House at Hingham; and the Huguenots in New York had an early meeting house of a similar kind

[6] The problem is complicated by the fact that there is a Presbyterian church at Burntisland, Fife, in Scotland, built in 1592, which has a square plan, pyramidal roof, and belfry (finished in 1749)—though here the belfry is a tower that rests on four piers in the center of the church. Interestingly enough, local tradition has it that this church was copied from the Noorderkerk at Amsterdam, which, however, is some thirty years later in date. See George Hay, *The Architecture of Scottish Post-Reformation Churches*, Oxford, 1957, pp. 32–34.

which likewise resembled the Hingham meeting house except in the absence of the balustraded roof deck. However, it should be noted that by no means all of the Dutch Reformed churches were of this relatively square type: many of them were octagonal, such as the church in Bergen, New Jersey, built in 1680 (Fig. 12), or that erected in New Brunswick in 1767.

Obvious prototypes for this octagonal form, at least, existed in Dutch Reformed churches in Holland. An example at Willemstad, Holland—erected in 1586 (Fig. 13) and the oldest Dutch Protestant church built as such—is a clear forerunner of the octagonal church in Bergen. The ancestry of the Willemstad church form lies in the traditional central type of Christian church, adapted to the Protestant service by the Dutch Reformed Church, the state church in Holland. Again a state church had taken over a traditional type, in this case the central type, one especially adapted to the Calvinistic emphasis on preaching. The source of the form, for the Dutch, may actually have been from French émigrés who were Huguenots. It is possible that the octagonal shape came from a design by the Italian architect Serlio for a "temple" in classic style, first published in 1547 at Paris. On the other hand, ever since the early Middle Ages there had existed not far away at Aachen, in the Rhineland, the palace chapel of Charlemagne, which is polygonal, and which suggests that the form used at Willemstad may have been a local regional type. The roof at Willemstad, an octagonal pyramid surmounted by a Renaissance cupola, is not unlike that at Hingham. If it is necessary to account for the shift from building polygonal churches to building rectangular ones, an answer might be that it is easier to roof a rectangular structure. It may be tentatively suggested, then, that the New England meeting house of the Hingham type originated, at least partly, in Holland, and that the polygonal form became rectangular—as also in the Dutch Reformed church at Albany—for greater simplicity of framing and roofing. One might add here that the interior of the church at Willemstad (Fig. 14) shows the characteristic Protestant simplicity, with the pulpit directly opposite the door and the church arranged for easy hearing.

Since the New England meeting house, such as that at Hingham, also served for town meeting, the possibility should be mentioned that this kind of meeting house may reflect the influence of a town hall type (much as later—in reverse—the town halls of the Western Reserve were to reflect the influence of New England meeting houses). For example, a typical English town hall at Abingdon in Berkshire (Fig. 15), built in 1677 and including an open market, has a similar squarish shape, with high roof, cupola, and roof deck.[7] It is true that this generally squarish type of building, which thus appears both in some meeting houses and in some town halls, seems to be characteristic of many types of English and Dutch buildings of the seventeenth century. The Governor's Palace at Williamsburg, for instance—which of course is neither a meeting house nor a town hall—has the same general type of composition, one that in its compact clarity of form probably reflects the increasing influence of the Renaissance and post-Renaissance from Italy, whatever the specific sources of the type may be.

Unlike the Congregationalists in New England and the Dutch Reformed in New York, the other Calvinist groups in the American colonies, particularly the Presbyterians, were especially likely to use the house type of meeting house. And this was also true of such extreme left-wing sects as the Quakers and the Baptists. In other words, the more ultra-Protestant the group, the more likely would be its use of the house type found in England. It must be remembered that meeting houses of this kind presumably originated partly in an effort to avoid attracting undue attention in places where dissent was forbidden or frowned upon, much as is the case

[7] Donnelly, p. 95, draws a somewhat similar parallel with a market hall at Amersham, Buckinghamshire.

in Roman Catholic Spain today. The early meetings of dissenting congregations were thought of, too, as parallels to early Christian meetings, which had often taken place in private houses. Thus there were special reasons for such religiously radical groups as the Quakers and the Baptists to have a building that looked like a house. Although the house type is usually somewhat less square, more elongated than the Congregational meeting house of the Hingham variety, the form differs sharply from the basilical type in that the entrance is on the longer side, and this side is ordinarily placed parallel to the street in front of the building.

A famous Quaker example in England itself, the Quaker Meeting House at Jordans, in Buckinghamshire, built in 1688 (Fig. 16), is fairly early and very typical. Because of its close association with the Penn family, this is of particular interest to American Quakers. Turning to American examples: at Stony Brook, near Princeton, New Jersey, is a charming little Quaker meeting house (Fig. 17) built in 1760, which likewise obviously resembles a private house. (The porch seen in the illustration was added later.) The interior of this, as of many other Quaker meeting houses, is not large enough to allow for a very descriptive photograph; therefore a relatively late and relatively large example, the meeting house at 4th and Green Streets, Philadelphia, is shown (Fig. 18). This was built in 1812, and is a characteristic Quaker meeting house in that it does not have a pulpit, because—as mentioned above—the Quakers until recently have had no ministers. Instead, a group of elders sat in a row facing the rest of the congregation, and, like other members, prayed or preached whenever individually moved to do so by the spirit, the Inner Light. This Quaker meeting house has galleries, because it serves a large city congregation.

An interesting left-wing Baptist example is the Elder Ballou meeting house at Cumberland, Rhode Island (Fig. 19), which was built about 1740 for a group of unorthodox

Baptists known as Free-Will Baptists, and is clearly of the house type. On the interior, it would differ from a Quaker meeting house especially in having a pulpit.

There are exceptions to be noted to the general statement that the Anglicans used a church type with tower and steeple, while dissenters used some kind of meeting house. One exception was this: in the colonial regions where dissent from Anglicanism was dominant, even Anglicans at times felt it necessary to adopt a local meeting house type. This can be seen in St. Paul's Church in Wickford, Rhode Island (Fig. 20), an Anglican church built in 1707 in Narragansett, and moved to Wickford in 1800. (The famous Dean Berkeley preached in it in 1729.) Even though this is an Anglican, or Episcopal, church, it is basically a house type of meeting house, and as such has its long side parallel to the street. On the interior, the pulpit is placed on a long side opposite the main door as in the meeting houses. Although the plan (Fig. 21) does show elements of the basilical type in having a secondary entrance on a short side with the altar opposite it on the other short side, no axis leads from one to the other as it would in a true basilica.

It should be noted, also, that even in colonies where Anglicanism was the established religion, as in South Carolina, local functional considerations might modify the standard basilical scheme. Country churches, for instance, might omit the towers and steeples when they were in areas where the plantations were so widely separated that a bell could not be heard, for there a belfry would be relatively useless. Thus the church of St. James at Goose Creek, South Carolina (Figs. 22, 23, and 24), built in 1711 in plantation country, has no bell tower, although its entrance is on the short side and it has a long axis leading to the sanctuary, as in a typical basilical plan. Here, however, in a period when Anglicanism still tended to reflect some relatively strong Calvinistic influences, the pulpit is placed on the axis, and the communion table a little to one side though still within the sanctuary. At this time, even Anglican churches such as this one were still likely to demonstrate a kind of Protestant simplicity, reinforced at St. James's by the fact that this is a small country church.

As the eighteenth century wore on, however, not only did Anglican churches become less severely Protestant, but under the leadership of Anglicanism the basilica type tended to replace the meeting house type for practically all American religious groups with the notable exception of the Quakers. Moreover, architectural fashion greatly aided the eventual triumph of the basilica type: the increasing use of classic forms, for stylistic reasons, acted in the basilica's favor, because increasing classicism meant greater admiration for the classic temple form. And in the classic temple the entrance was customarily placed on a short side of the building, which, with its pedimented gable, was the side of the building likely to be located—in Roman classic fashion—toward the street. The use of classical forms, in short, greatly encouraged placing a long axis perpendicular to the street, as in the basilical type.

The classic temple composition, which came from the revival of classic architecture in the Renaissance and post-Renaissance, had been introduced into Anglican church architecture in England by a great seventeenth-century architect, Inigo Jones, on the east façade of St. Paul's, Covent Garden, in London. The use of various classical elements was to become customary in Anglican architecture after they had been widely, and freely, employed by Sir Christopher Wren, and especially by Wren's great eighteenth-century successor, James Gibbs.

The transformation of Anglican church building in England at the hands of Sir Christopher Wren and James Gibbs is worth our further attention because of its profound effect on American architecture. Wren, who was born in 1632, lived well into the eighteenth century: he died in 1723. It was, however, soon after the great fire of London in 1666 that he had built a great number of churches in London, and had given a new expression to the Anglican church. Basically Gothic tower and steeple forms were usually retained at the entrance end of the long axis as in so many English medieval parish churches, but now were treated with superimposed classical colonnettes and other decoration, apparently in part under the influence of the towers of some Dutch Protestant churches. Wren used many varieties of both basilical and central plans, but the basilical type, with the pulpit somewhat off the axis, tended to become dominant under the widening classicism of the eighteenth century, especially in the form popularized after Wren by James Gibbs (1682–1754), who had studied in Italy. It was Gibbs whose influence on colonial builders was most direct, largely through the widely popular book that he had published in 1728 entitled *A Book of Architecture*. A typical example of Gibbs's work is the Church of St. Martin-in-the-Fields in London, built 1721–1726. The exterior view (Fig. 25) shows a basilica-type church whose tower, instead of rising from the ground as Wren's ordinarily did, visually rests on the roof so as not to interfere with the classic pediment and portico on the front of the church. For reasons of architectural composition, it is obviously essential to place a pedimented and porticoed edifice of this kind with its short side to the street, as the Anglican church for a long time had often done for other reasons. The interior of the church is not unlike many of Wren's, except that there is a greater degree of elaboration in the chancel, which is given further architectural emphasis in plan (Fig. 26) as well as detail. This tendency toward more elaborate architecture was destined to increase as reaction set in among Anglicans against the Calvinistic simplicity which had so often prevailed in the seventeenth century. Nevertheless, some emphasis on preaching continued, as the galleries here demonstrate, although the pulpit, unlike the arrangement in St. James's at Goose Creek, is off to one side while the sanctuary is reserved for the altar. The position of the pulpit placed to the side of the sanctuary indicates that Calvinist influence is not so strong even as it had been in South Carolina, when St. James's at Goose Creek was built.

An eighteenth-century Anglican church in the American colonies, which may be compared with Gibbs's St. Martin-in-the-Fields, is Christ Church in Philadelphia, built between 1727 and 1754 (Figs. 27, 28, and 29). The interior is not so very different from that of St. Martin-in-the-Fields, but, as could be expected, is simpler and more provincial. Yet for a colonial church of its time, it shows a most unusual degree of elaboration in the chancel end. For this was a church in a big city, the church of wealthy and fashionable people, who, like most wealthy colonials everywhere, were seeking to keep up to date with the latest architectural fashions in the mother country; moreover, at this time it was fashionable for cultivated gentlemen to design buildings in collaboration with experienced craftsmen, and this was the case with Christ Church. Here also, as at St. Martin-in-the-Fields, the pulpit is set off to one side with the altar placed on the axis. The exterior, although lagging behind St. Martin's in having a Wren-type projecting tower, and therefore no portico at the entrance end, otherwise shows the increasing elaboration which had become possible in the colonies as they grew richer—especially in Philadelphia, the most populous city. It shows, too, the increasing prevalence of classical forms even on the sanctuary end of the church. In this case, a classical pediment, although on the end opposite the entrance, nonetheless suggests the long axis of the basilical plan. This is the type of building, then, which was eventually to prevail even for most non-Anglican religious edifices. For in competition with the Anglicans, who had become increasingly fashionable even in non-Anglican colonies largely because Anglicanism was the official religion of the mother country, non-Anglicans gradually found it necessary to adopt the tower and steeple. As classicism increased, they also adopted the pediment with, often, a front portico, which, in accordance with the classic principles of composition of the Renaissance and post-Renaissance, meant—as we have noted in English churches—that the tower would no longer be carried down to the ground in front of the church, like so many of Wren's towers, but would spring from the main roof as in Gibbs's St. Martin-in-the-Fields.

Thus, in seeking to compete with the Anglicans, and to be up-to-date in style, the Calvinists and most other dissenting groups not only took over the tower and steeple, but eventually, also, often combined these with a portico as well as a pediment. At first the dissenting groups merely placed the tower and steeple on the short, or minor, side of a house type of meeting house—the tower and steeple meant that the Hingham variety of meeting house, with pyramidal roof and cupola, had to be abandoned. Now an entrance in the tower could serve for reaching stairs to the galleries, even though the main entrance was still on the long side. Eventually, however, the whole basilical plan was adopted, and, in still later examples, was often combined with a classical entrance portico. It might be noted here that only after the desire for a classic effect had become very strong was the whole edifice likely to be painted white: the pre-Revolutionary churches and meeting houses were generally far more colorful than is usually realized today. For example, New Haven had a meeting house which, when rebuilt in 1764, became known from the color of its paint as the Blue Meeting House, while another Connecticut meeting house, this one at Pomfret, was described in 1762 as painted a deep orange, with doors and bottom boards chocolate, and only a few relatively minor details painted white.

Probably the first Calvinistic example of a meeting house constructed with a tower and steeple placed on the short side of a house-type meeting house was the Second Congregational Meeting House in Boston, known as the New Brick Meeting House, which was built in 1721 and destroyed in 1884. A famous example still standing of such a meeting house with

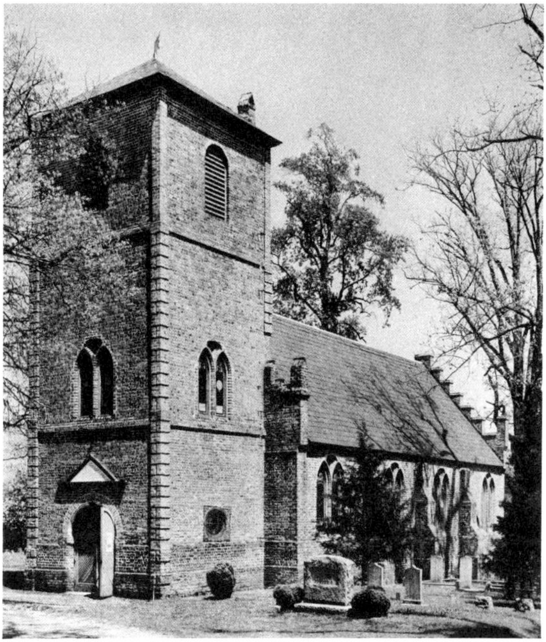

Figure 1. St. Luke's Church, near Smithfield, Virginia (Anglican, 1632, etc.)

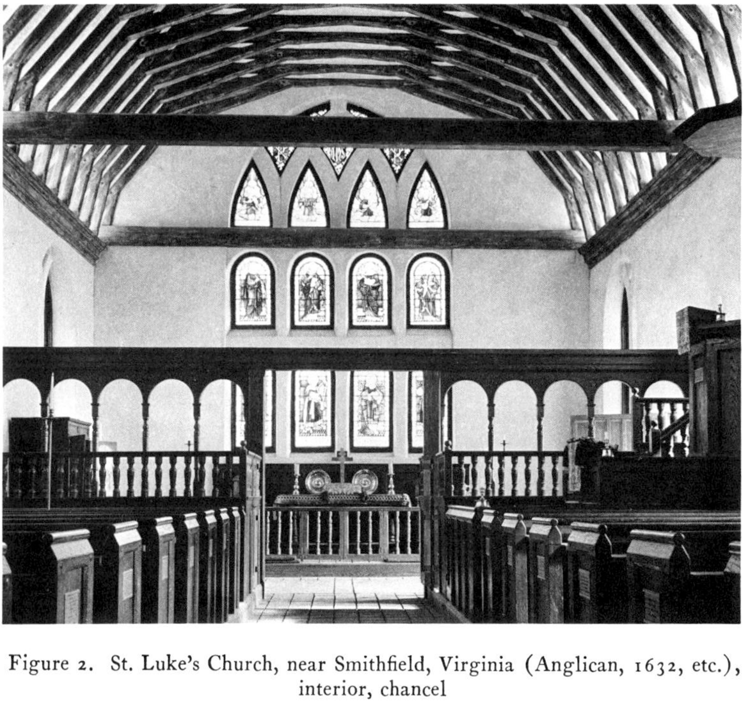

Figure 2. St. Luke's Church, near Smithfield, Virginia (Anglican, 1632, etc.), interior, chancel

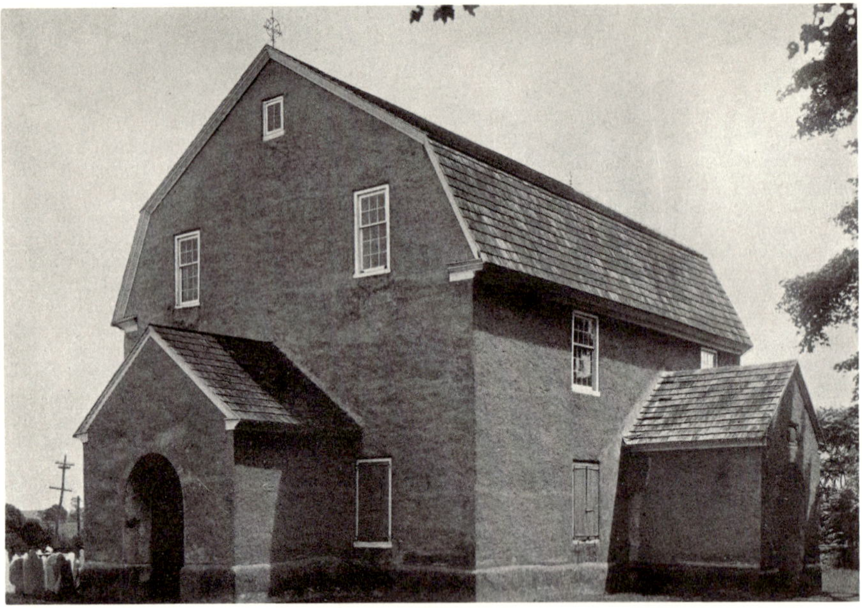

Figure 3. Augustus Lutheran Church, Trappe, Pennsylvania (1743), exterior showing entrances

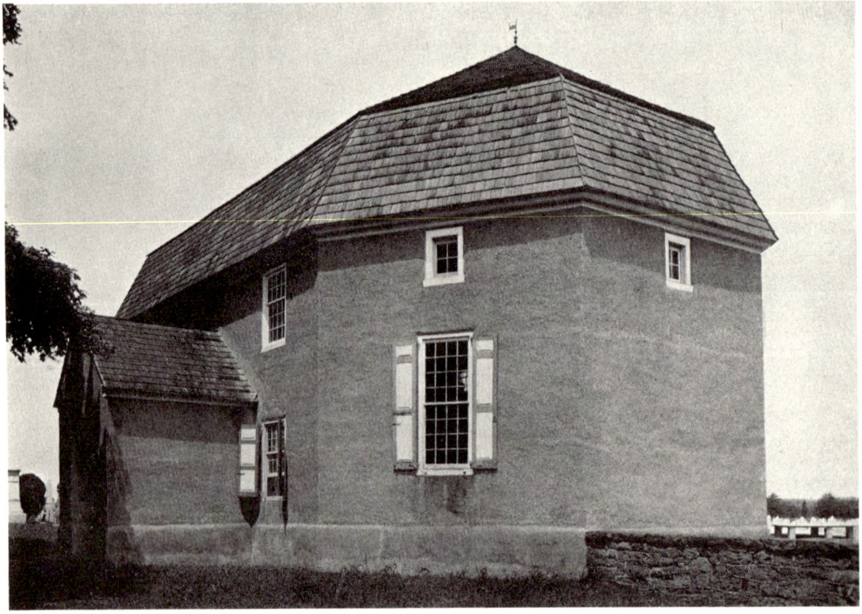

Figure 4. Augustus Lutheran Church, Trappe, Pennsylvania (1743), exterior, sanctuary

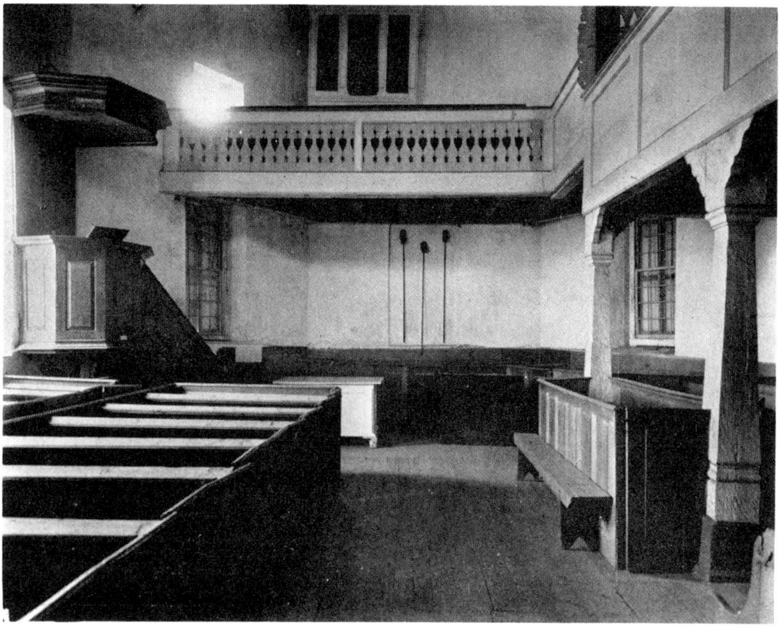

Figure 5. Augustus Lutheran Church, Trappe, Pennsylvania (1743), interior

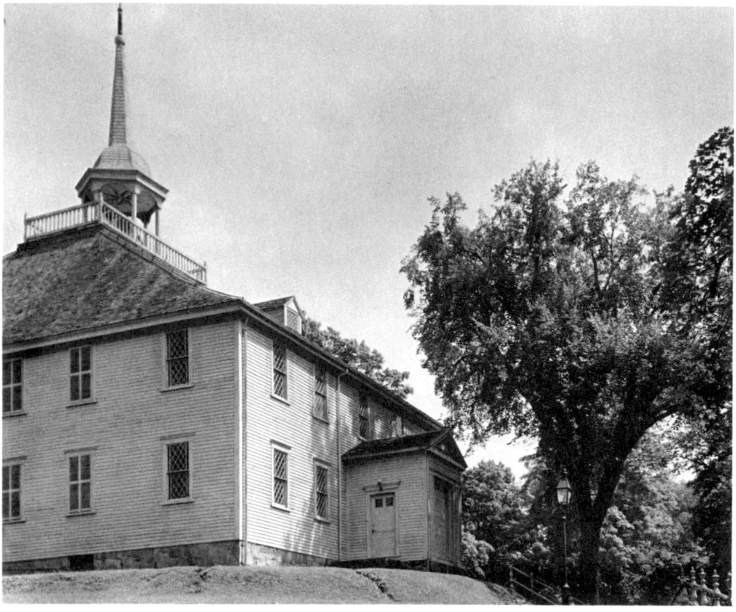

Figure 6. Old Ship Meeting House, Hingham, Massachusetts (Congregational, 1681, enlarged 1730 and 1755)

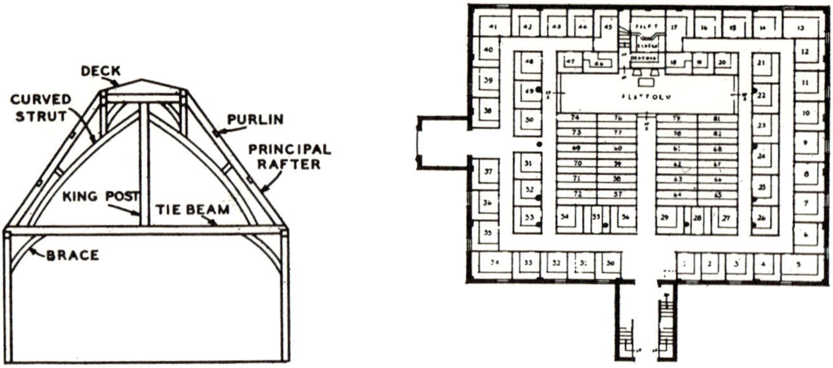

Figure 7. Old Ship Meeting House, Hingham, Massachusetts (Congregational, 1681, etc.), section and plan

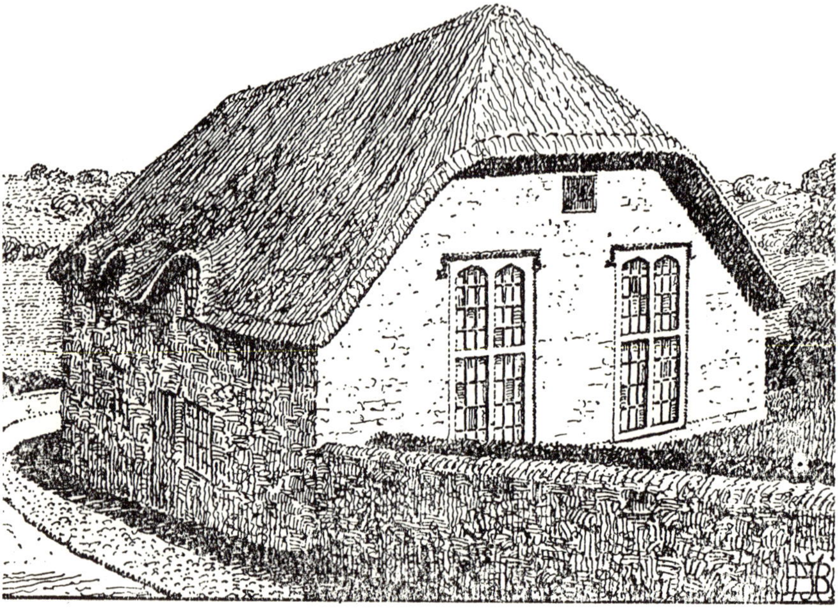

Figure 8. Congregational Chapel, Horningsham, Wiltshire, England (1566)

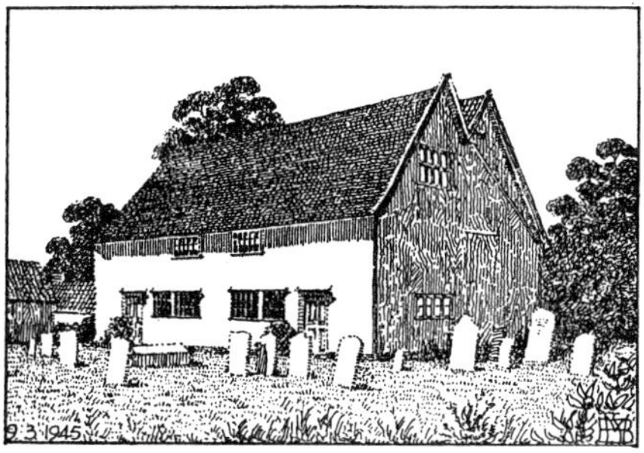

Figure 9. Congregational Chapel, Walpole, Suffolk, England (1647, etc.), exterior

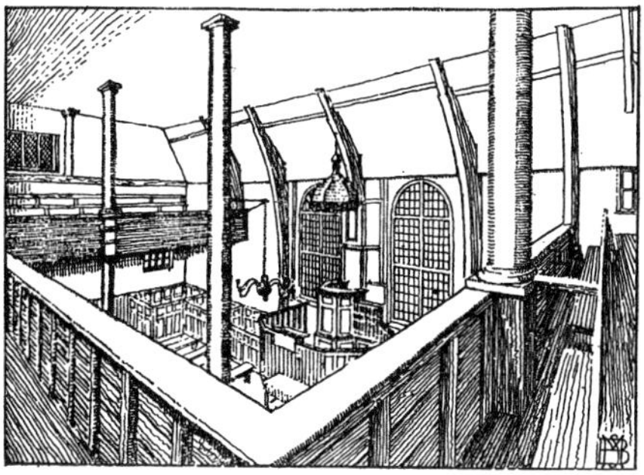

Figure 10. Congregational Chapel, Walpole, Suffolk, England (1647, etc.), interior

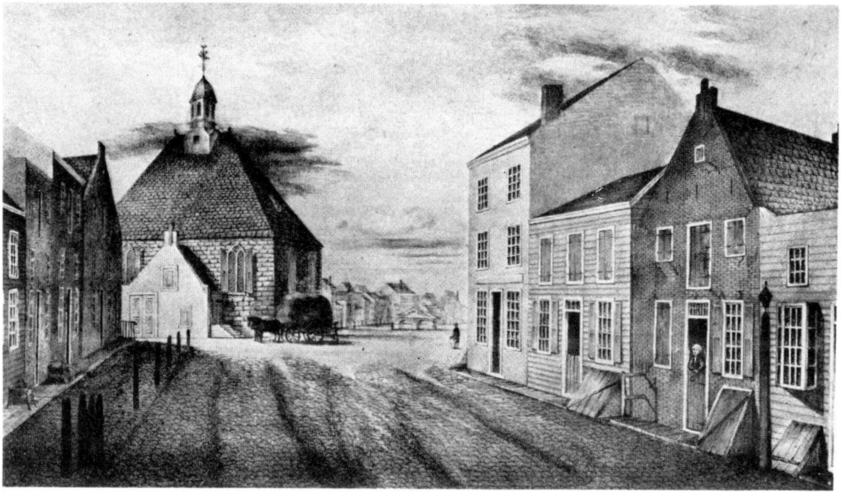

Figure 11. Dutch Reformed Church, Albany, New York (1715)

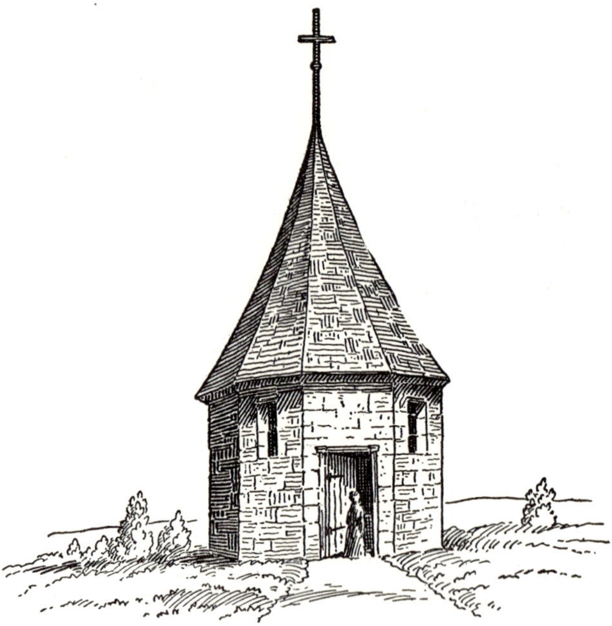

Figure 12. Dutch Reformed Meeting House, Bergen, New Jersey (1680)

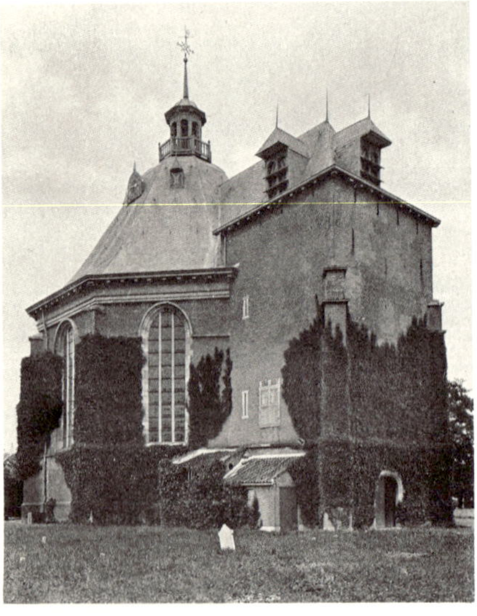

Figure 13. Dutch Reformed Church, Willemstad, Holland (1586), exterior

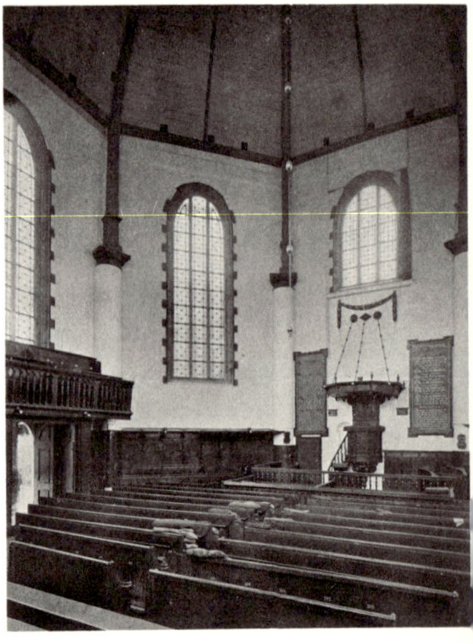

Figure 14. Dutch Reformed Church, Willemstad, Holland (1586), interior

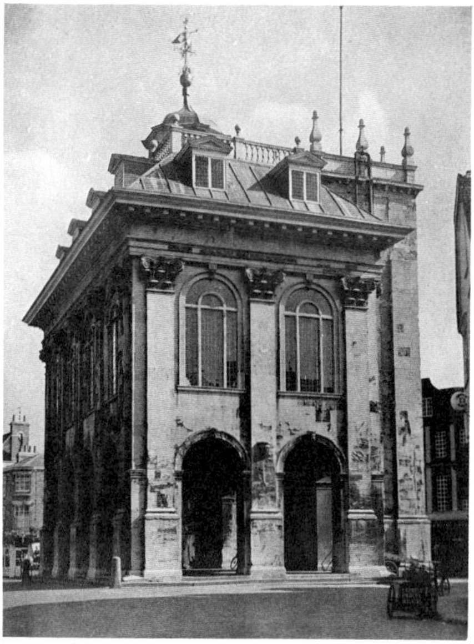

Figure 15. Town Hall, Abingdon, Berkshire, England (1677)

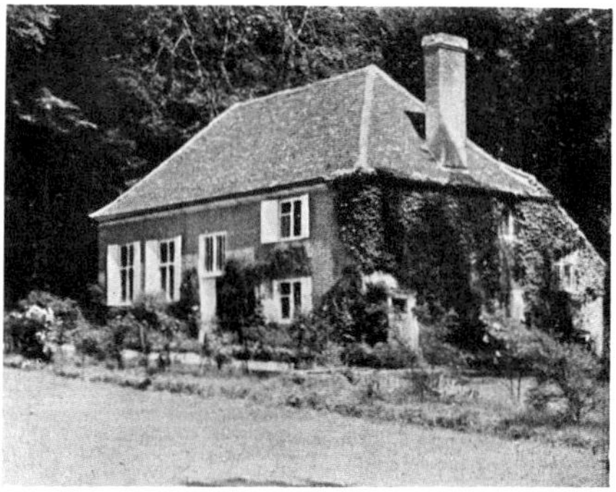

Figure 16. Quaker Meeting House, Jordans, Buckinghamshire, England (1688)

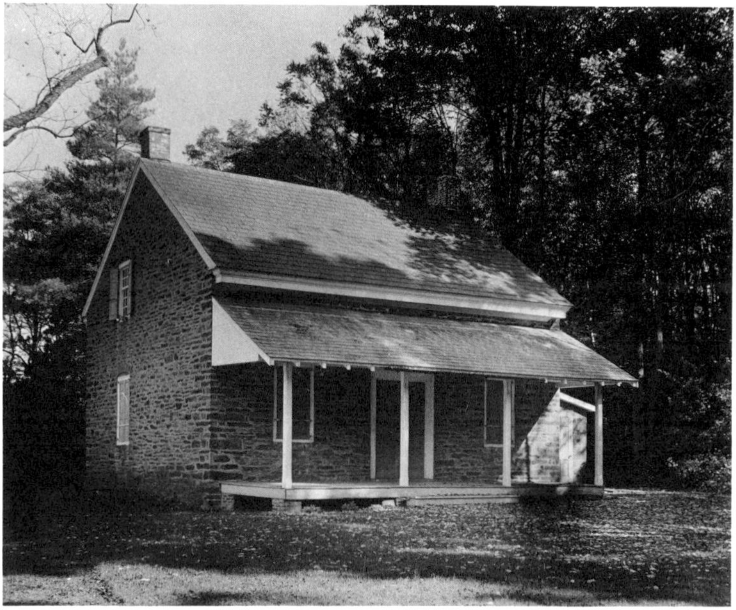

Figure 17. Quaker Meeting House, Stony Brook, near Princeton, New Jersey (1760)

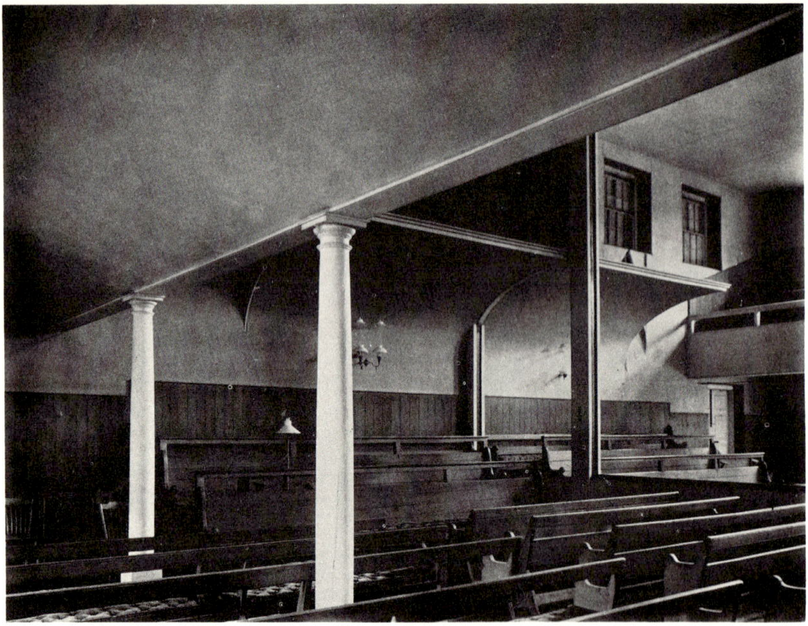

Figure 18. Quaker Meeting House, 4th and Green Streets, Philadelphia (1812), interior

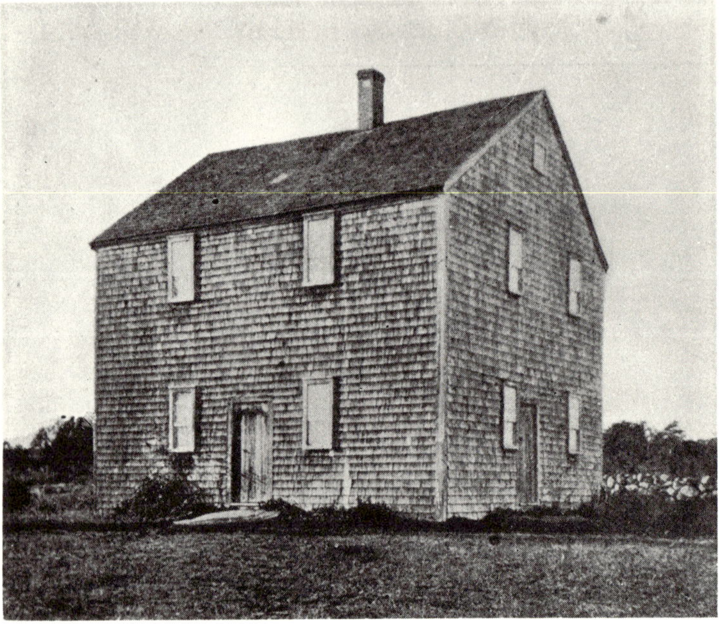

Figure 19. Elder Ballou Meeting House, Cumberland, Rhode Island (Free-Will Baptist, 1740)

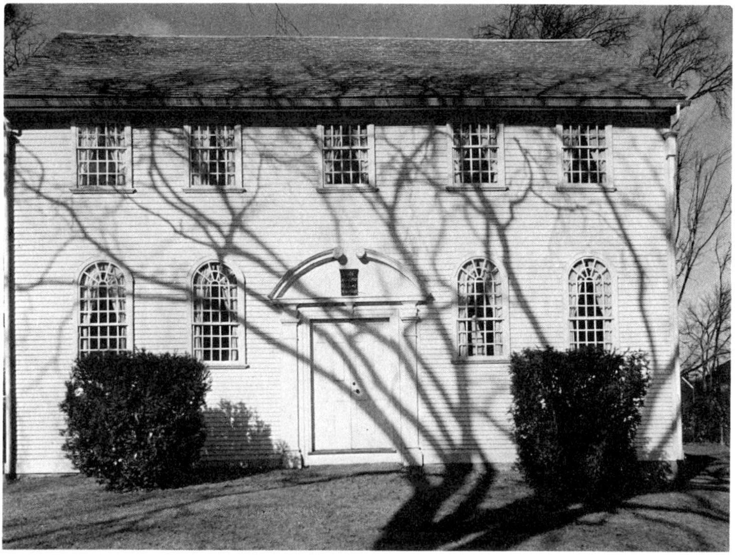

Figure 20. St. Paul's Church, Wickford, Rhode Island (Anglican; built in Narragansett, Rhode Island, 1707), exterior

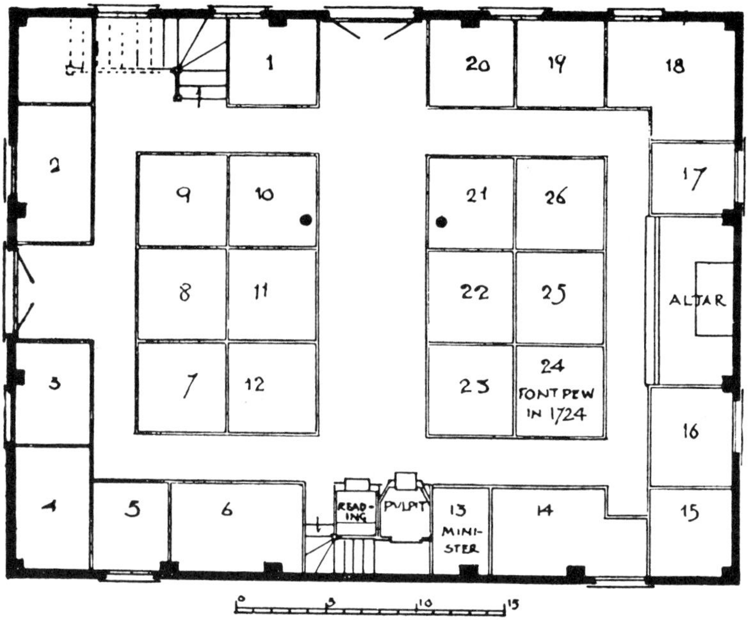

Figure 21. St. Paul's Church, Wickford, Rhode Island (Anglican, 1707), plan

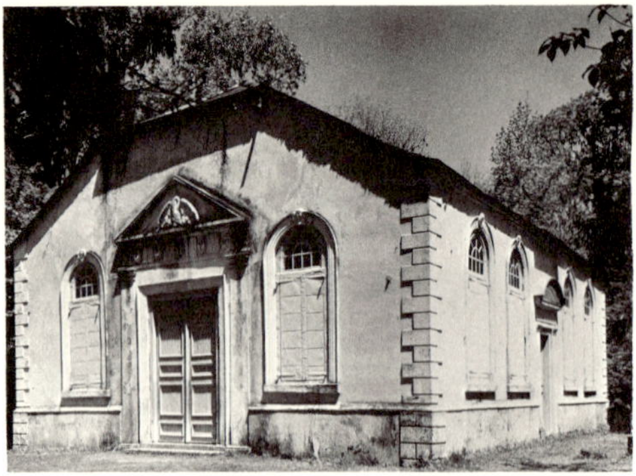

Figure 22. St. James's Church, Goose Creek, South Carolina (Anglican, 1711), exterior

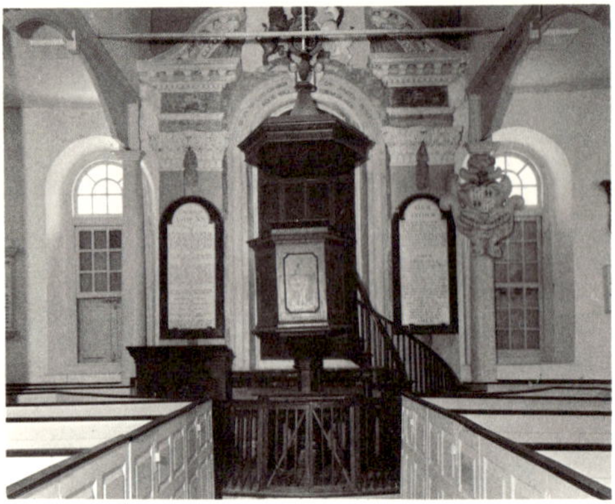

Figure 23. St. James's Church, Goose Creek, South Carolina (Anglican, 1711), interior

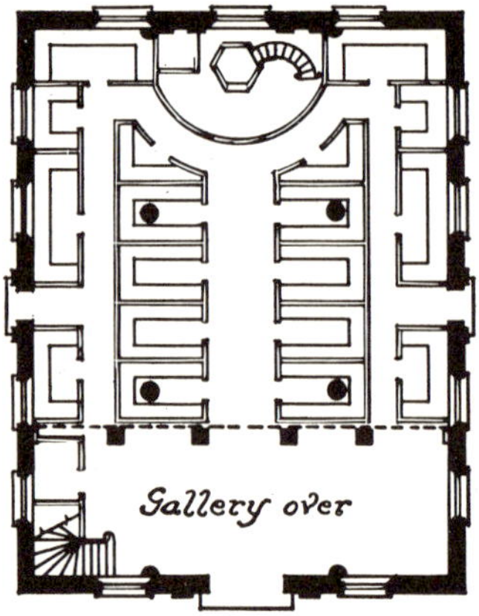

Figure 24. St. James's Church, Goose Creek, South Carolina (Anglican, 1711), plan

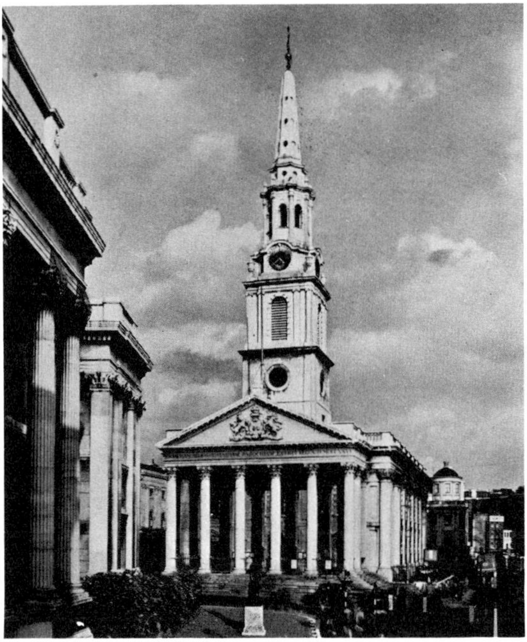

Figure 25. St. Martin-in-the-Fields, London (Anglican, 1721-1726), exterior

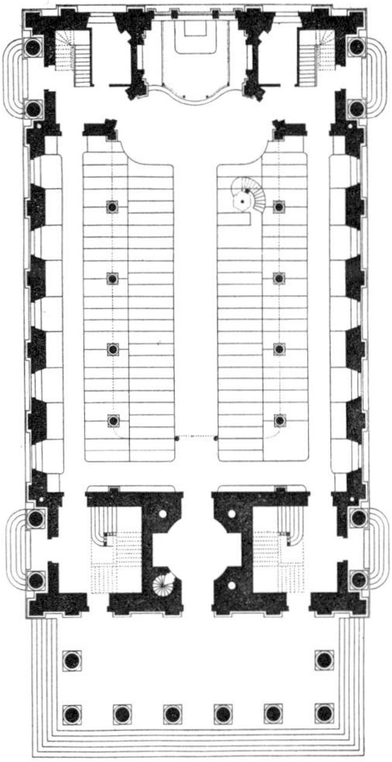

Figure 26. St. Martin-in-the-Fields, London (Anglican, 1721-1726), plan

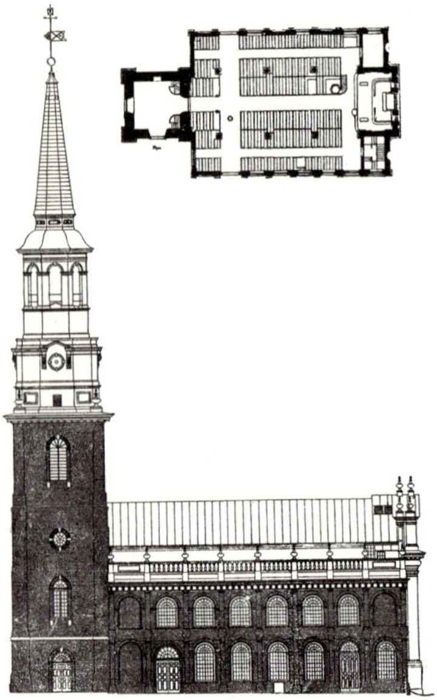

Figure 27. Christ Church, Philadelphia, Pennsylvania (Anglican, 1727-1754), side elevation and plan

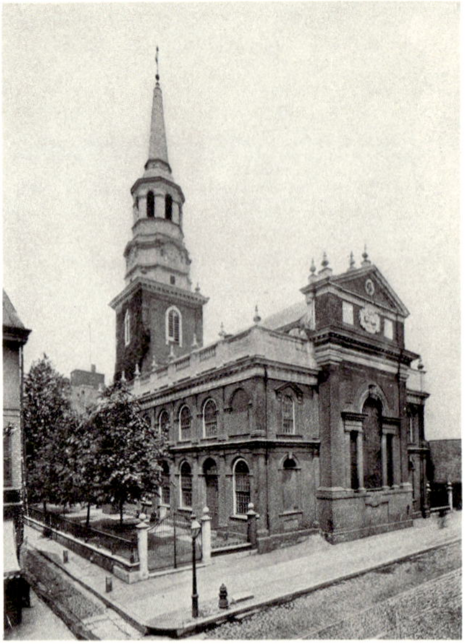

Figure 28. Christ Church, Philadelphia, Pennsylvania (Anglican, 1727-1754), exterior

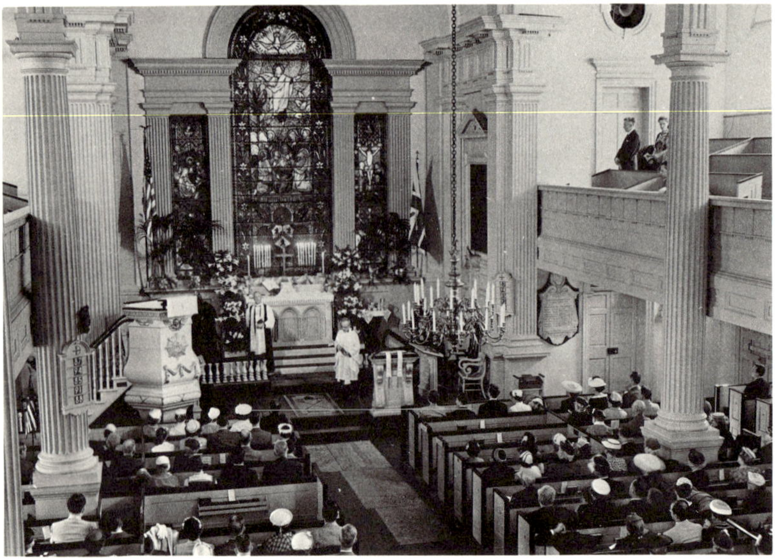

Figure 29. Christ Church, Philadelphia, Pennsylvania (Anglican, 1727-1754), chancel

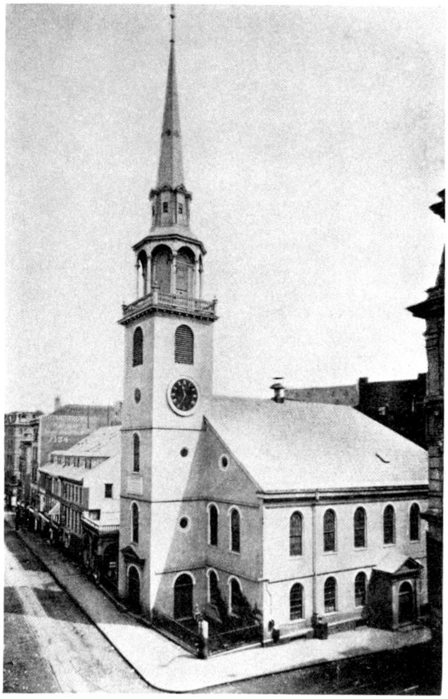

Figure 30. Old South Meeting House, Boston, Massachusetts (Congregational, 1730), old view

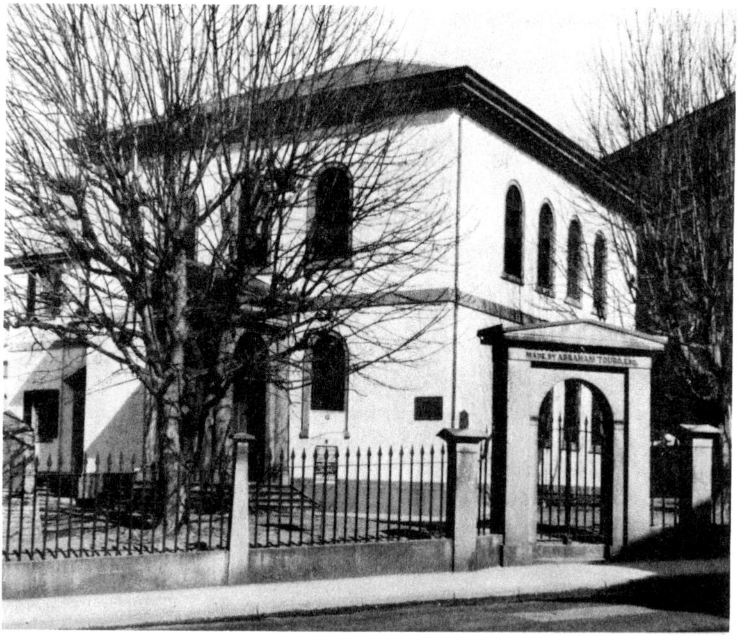

Figure 31. Touro Synagogue, Newport, Rhode Island (1763), exterior

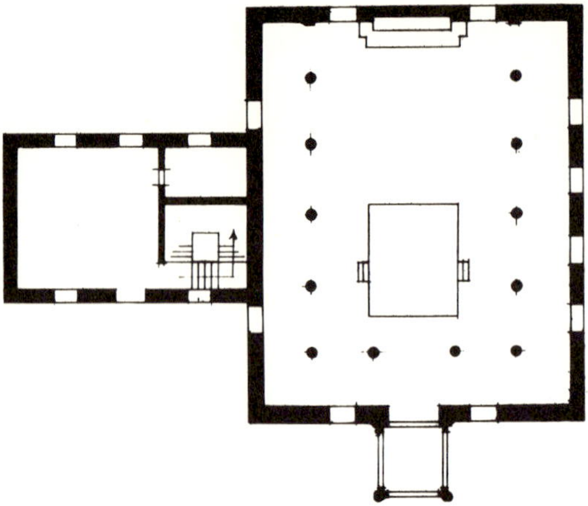

Figure 32. Touro Synagogue, Newport, Rhode Island (1763), plan

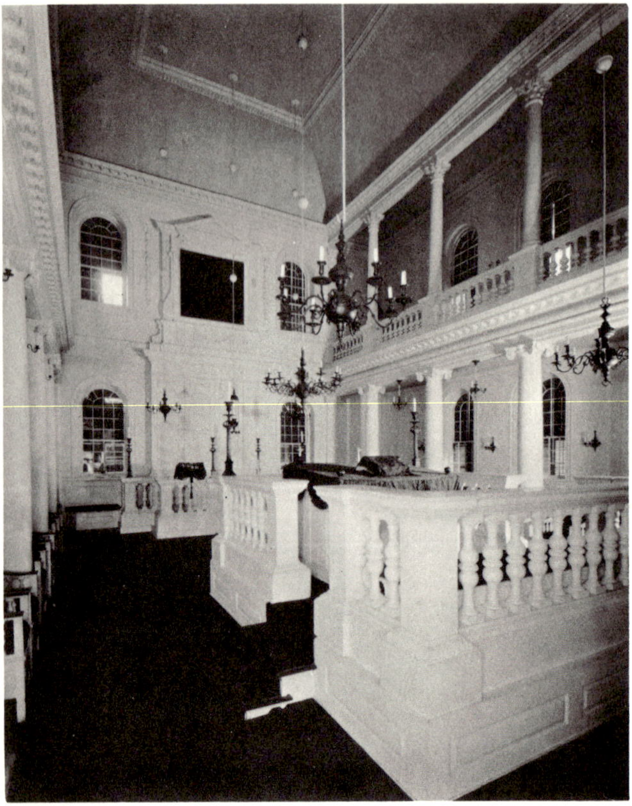

Figure 33. Touro Synagogue, Newport, Rhode Island (1763), interior

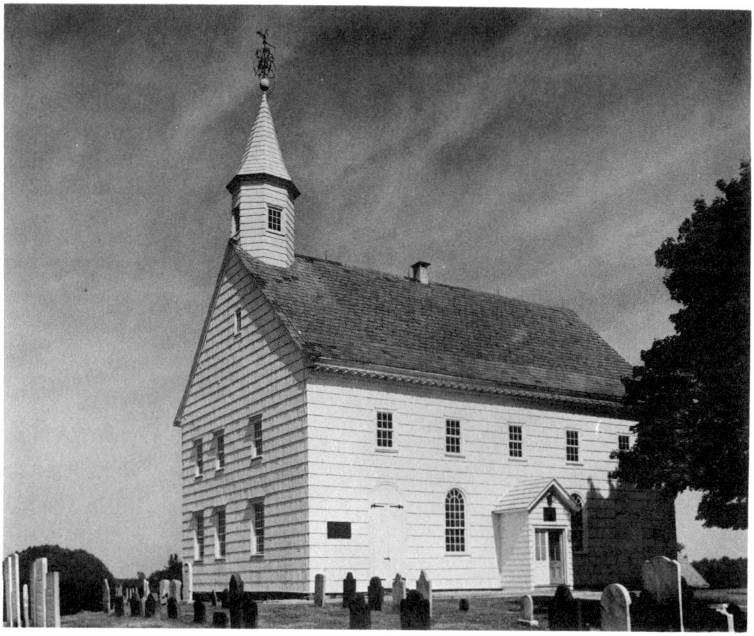

Figure 34. Old Tennent Church, Tennent, New Jersey (Presbyterian, 1731, enlarged 1751)

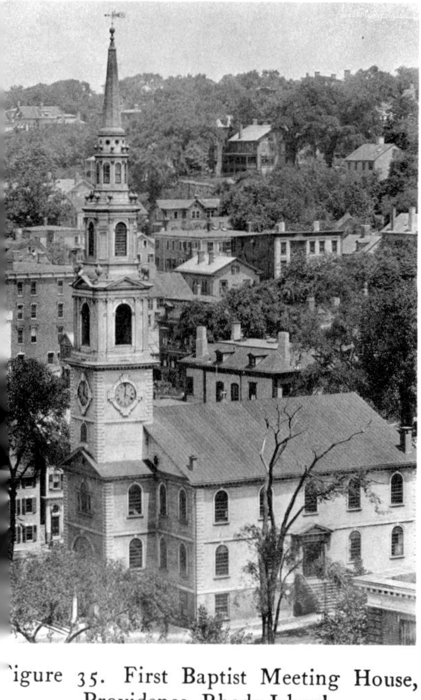

igure 35. First Baptist Meeting House, Providence, Rhode Island (1775)

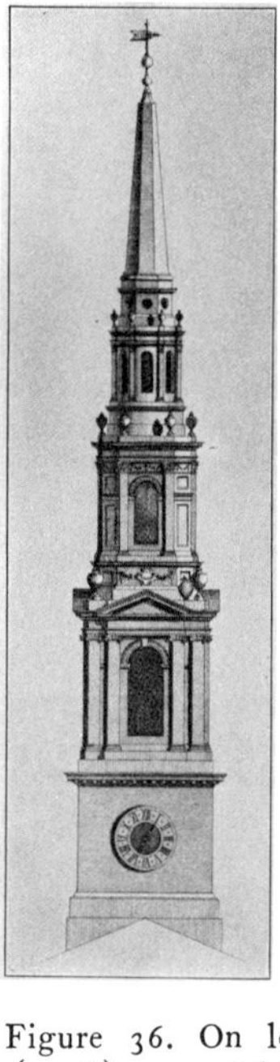

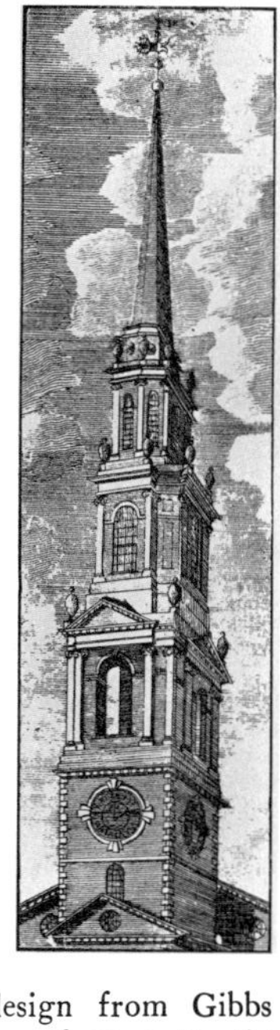

Figure 36. On left, design from Gibbs (1728); on right, spire of First Baptist Meeting House, Providence, Rhode Island

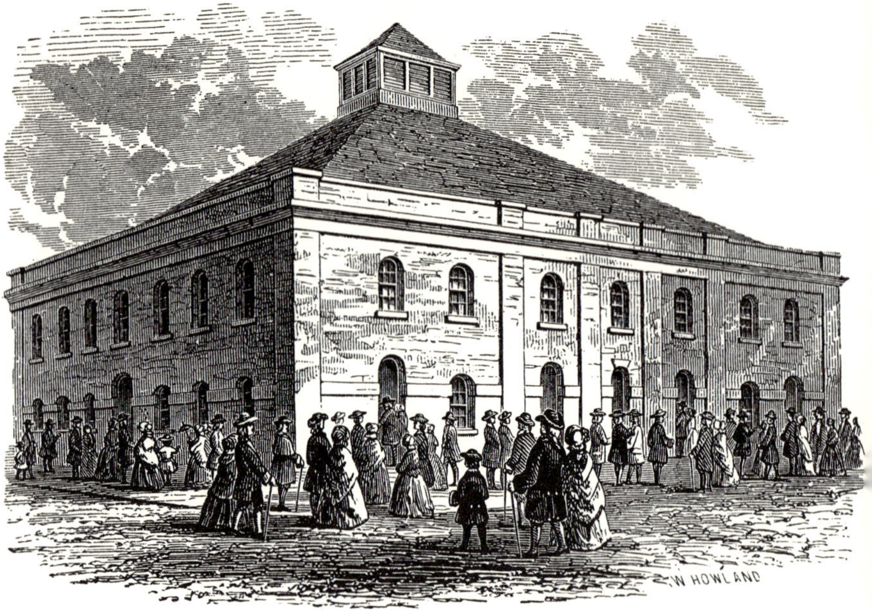

Figure 37. George Whitefield's Tabernacle, London, England (1753)

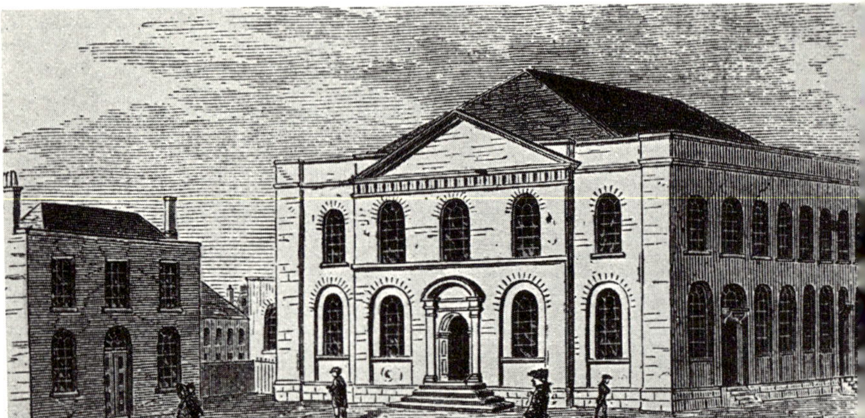

Figure 38. John Wesley's City Road Chapel, London, England (1778)

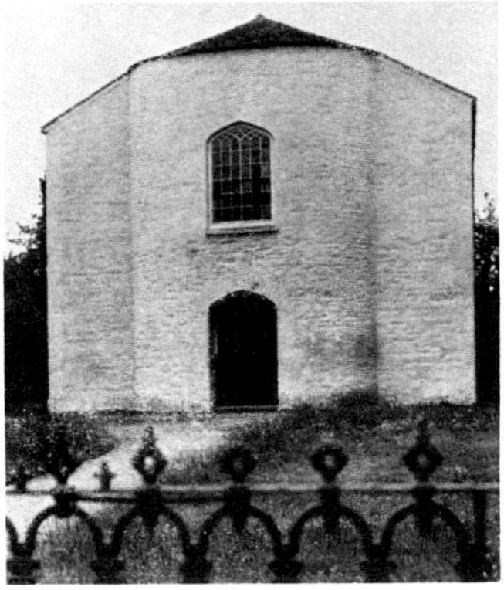

Figure 39. Methodist Chapel, Mawgan-in-Meneage, Cornwall, England (c. 1830)

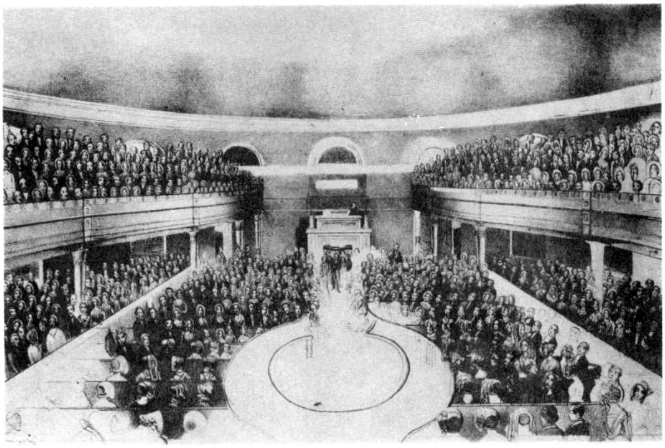

Figure 40. Sansom Street Baptist Church, Philadelphia, Pennsylvania (1808-1809)

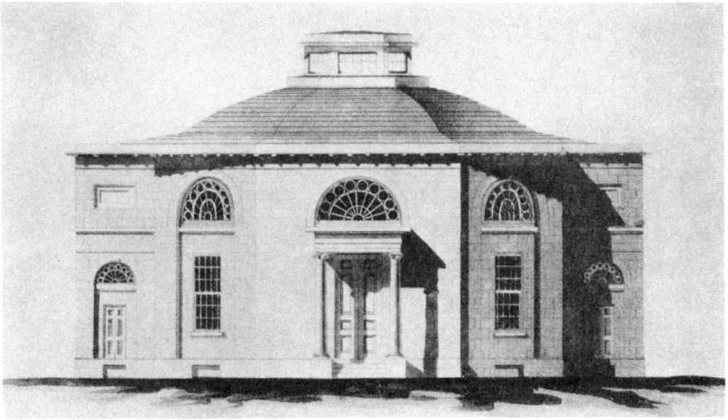

Figure 41. Octagon Unitarian Church, Philadelphia, Pennsylvania (1813)

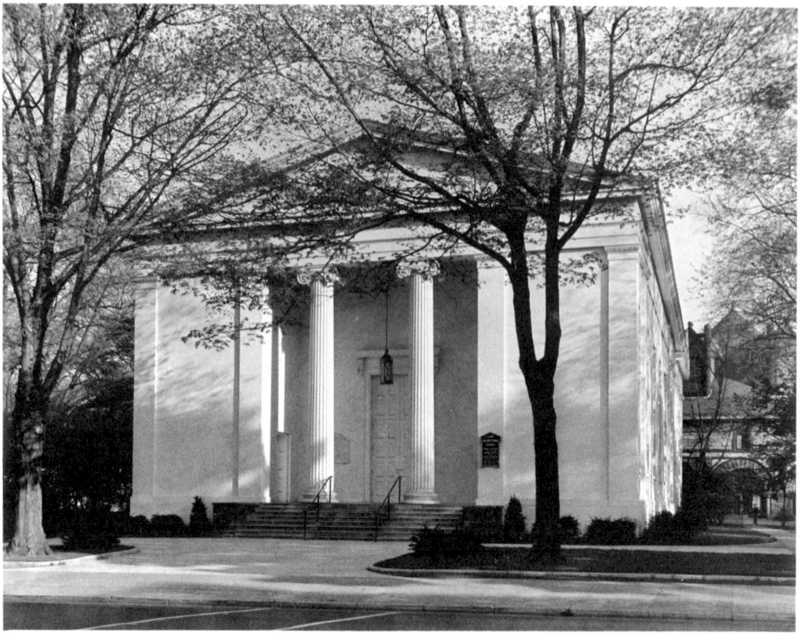

Figure 42. First Presbyterian Church, Princeton, New Jersey, before addition (1836-1837)

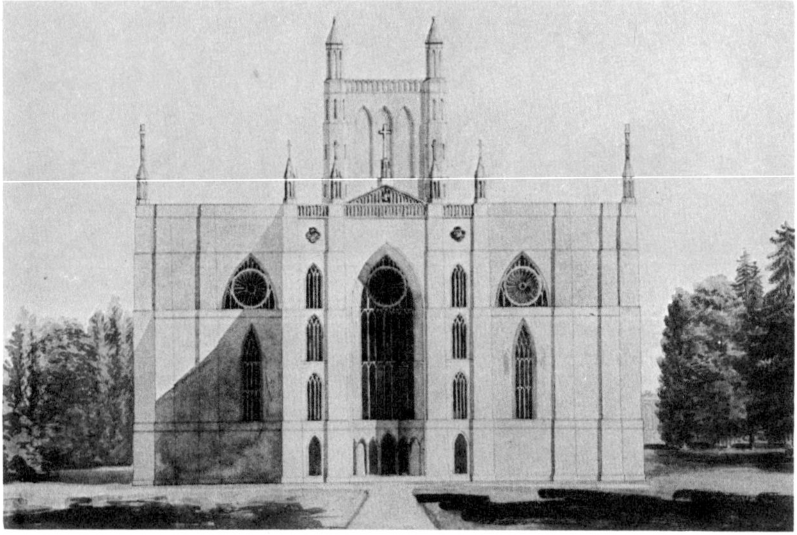

Figure 43. Cathedral of the Assumption, Baltimore, Maryland (Roman Catholic, 1805), alternative design in Gothic Revival style

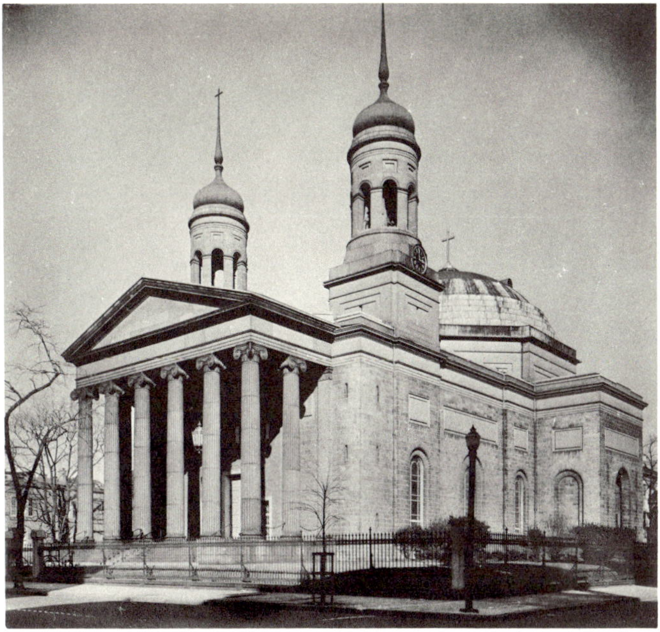

Figure 44. Cathedral of the Assumption, Baltimore, Maryland (Roman Catholic, 1806), exterior

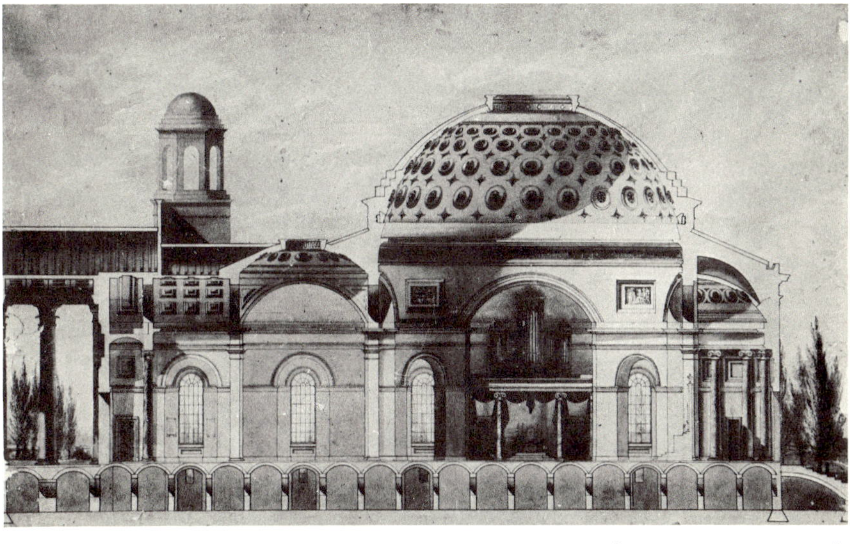

Figure 45. Cathedral of the Assumption, Baltimore, Maryland (Roman Catholic, 1806), section as originally designed

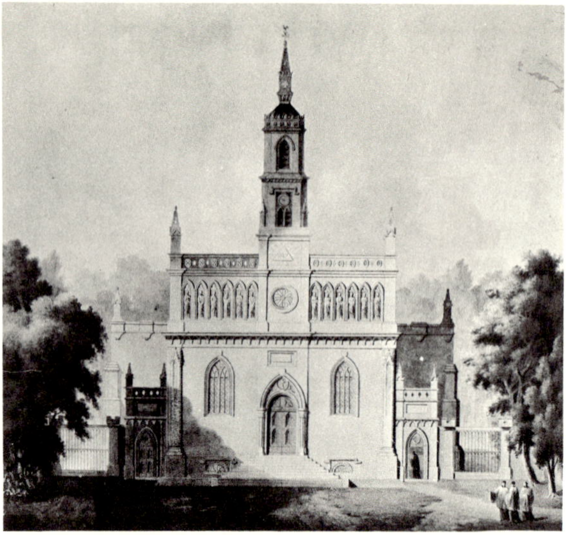

Figure 46. Chapel of St. Mary's Seminary, Baltimore, Maryland (Roman Catholic, 1806)

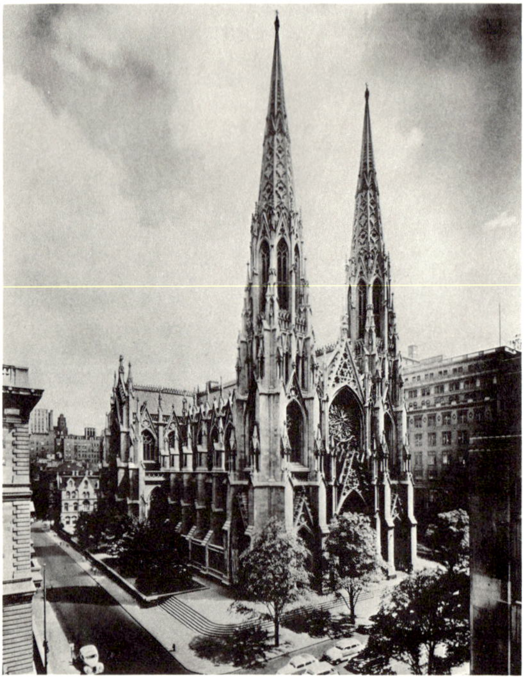

Figure 47. St. Patrick's Cathedral, New York, New York (Roman Catholic, 1850-1879)

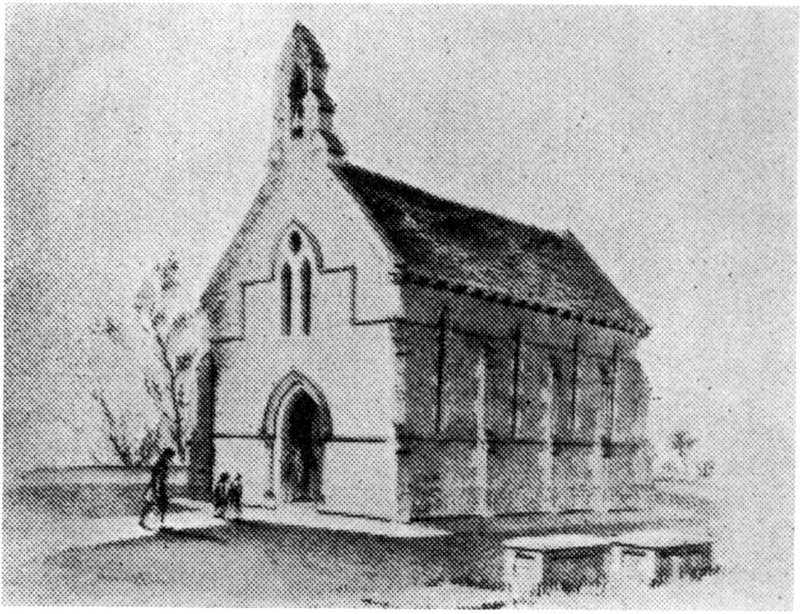

Figure 48. Anglican Church, Littlemore, England (1835-1836), exterior

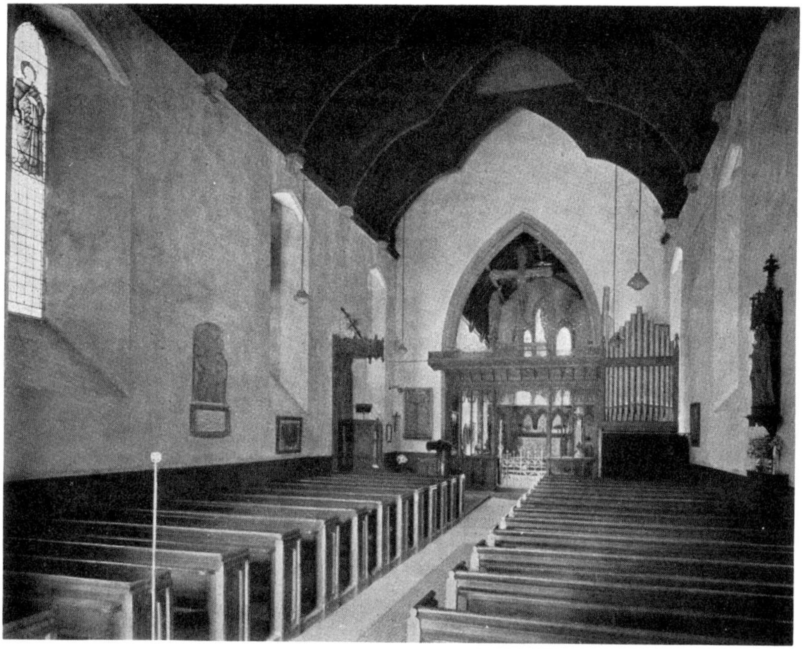

Figure 49. Anglican Church, Littlemore, England (1835-1836), interior

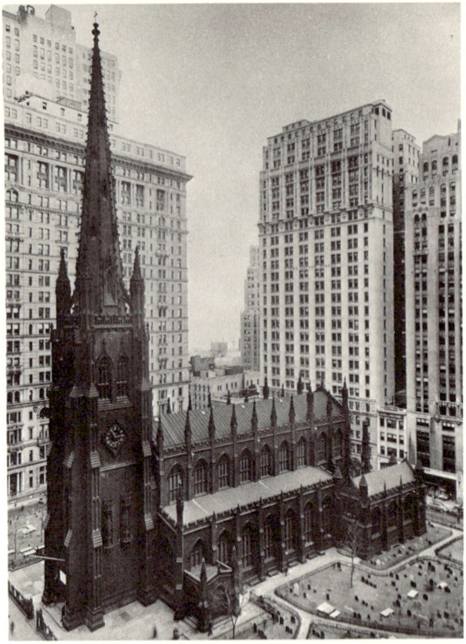

Figure 50. Trinity Church, New York, New York (Episcopal, 1839-1846), exterior

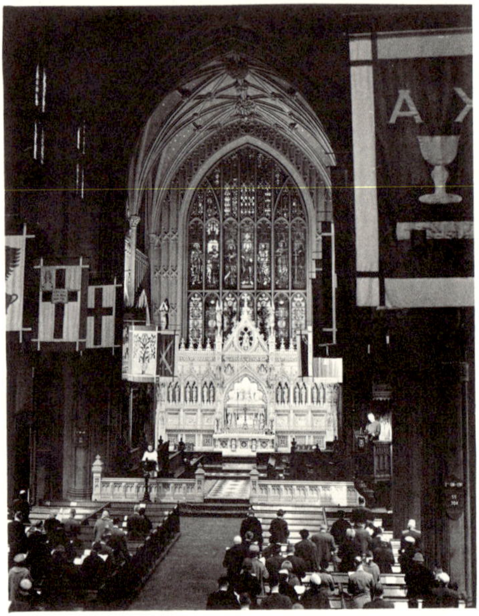

Figure 51. Trinity Church, New York, New York (Episcopal, 1839-1846), interior

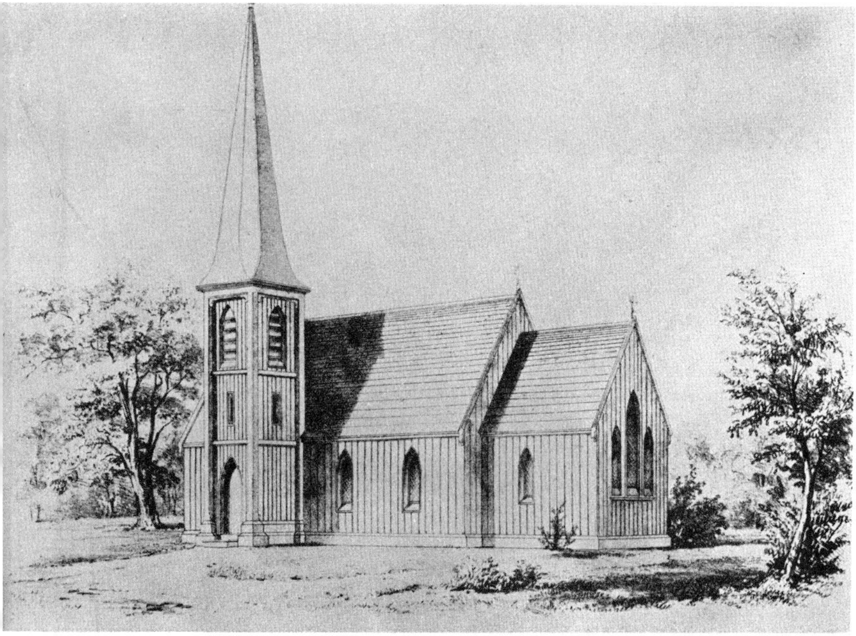

Figure 52. Country Church Design, from *Upjohn's Rural Architecture* (1852)

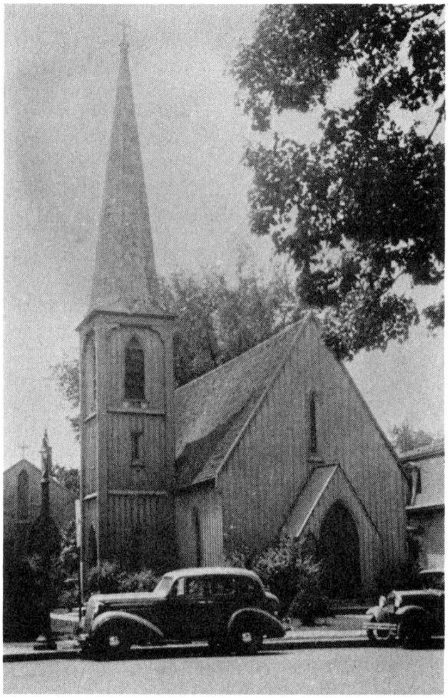

Figure 53. Trinity Church, Warsaw, New York (Episcopal, 1854)

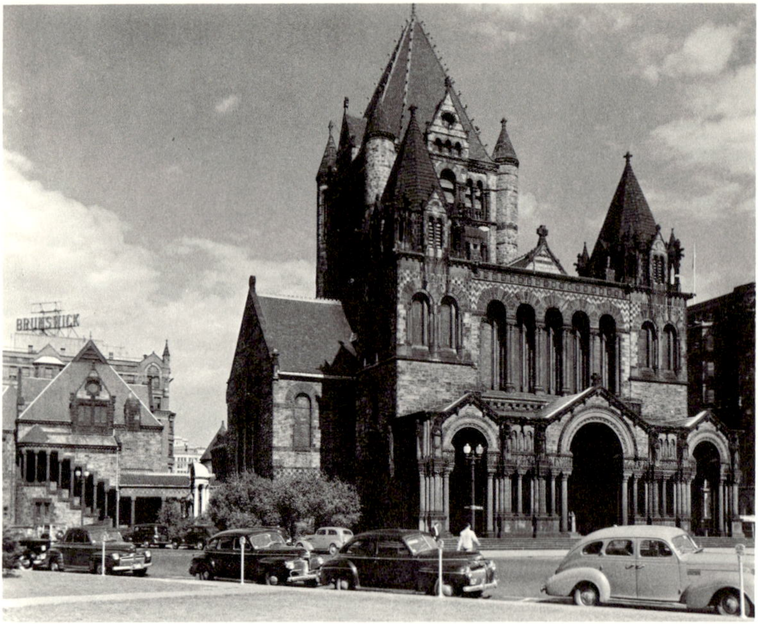

Figure 54. Trinity Church, Boston, Massachusetts (Episcopal, 1873-1877)

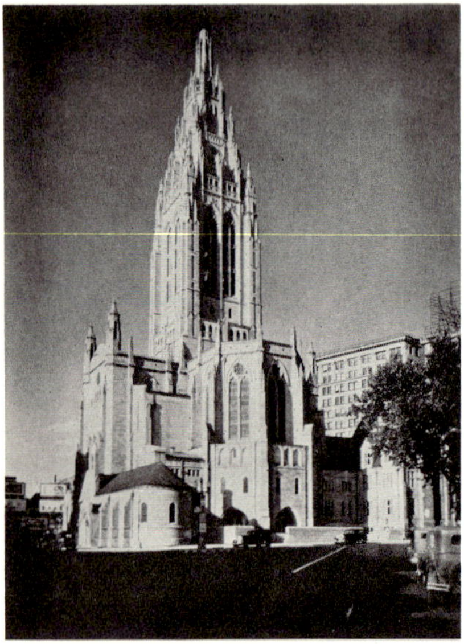

Figure 55. East Liberty Presbyterian Church, Pittsburgh, Pennsylvania (c. 1935), exterior

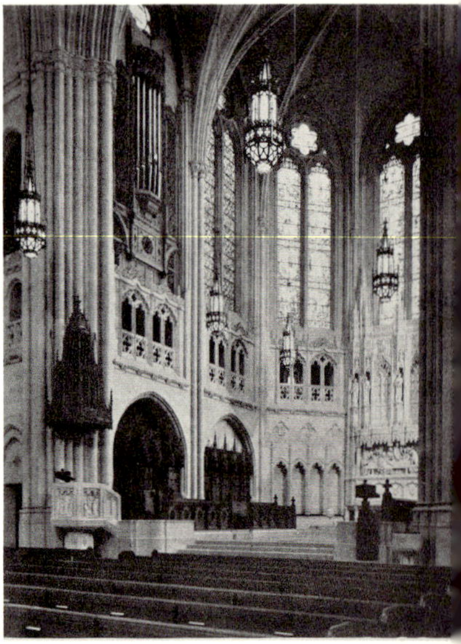

Figure 56. East Liberty Presbyterian Church, Pittsburgh, Pennsylvania (c. 1935), interior

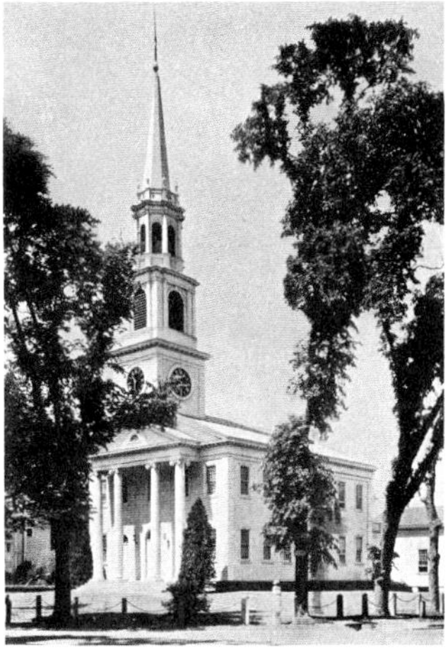

Figure 57. Congregational Church, Lyme, Connecticut (1815-1817)

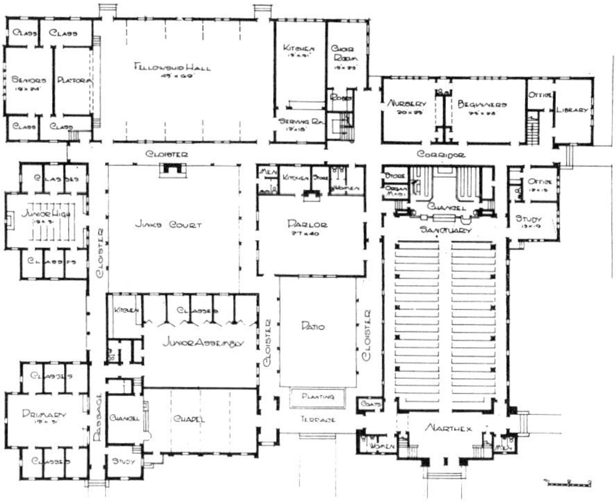

Figure 58. First Presbyterian Church, North Hollywood, California, unexecuted plan (c. 1940)

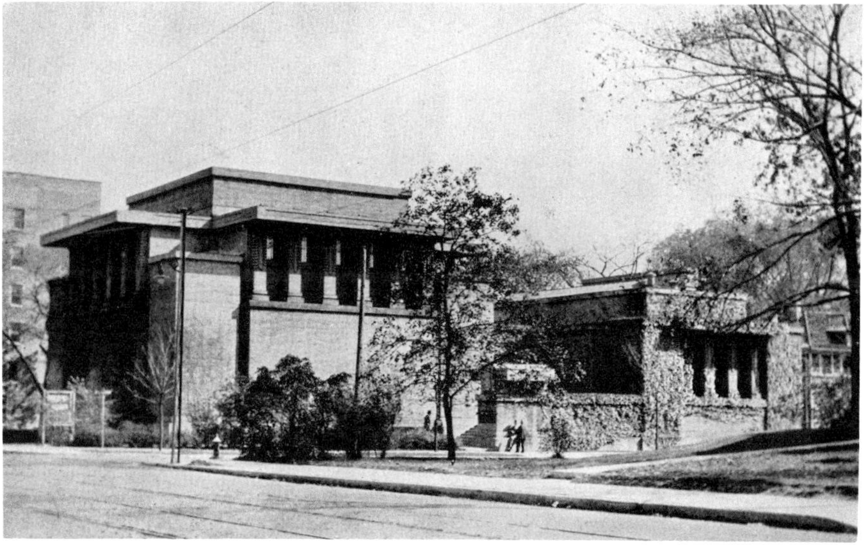

Figure 59. Unity Temple, Oak Park, Illinois (Unitarian-Universalist, 1905-1906), exterior

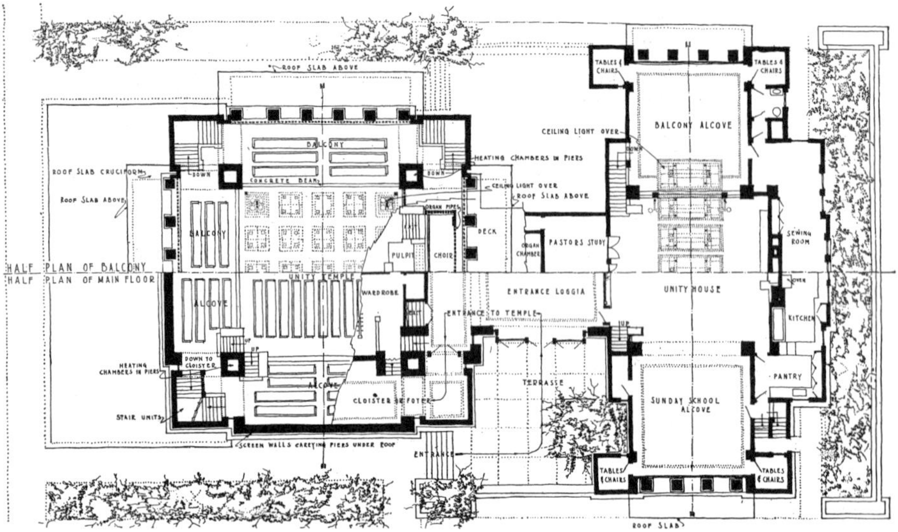

Figure 60. Unity Temple, Oak Park, Illinois (Unitarian-Universalist, 1905-1906), plan

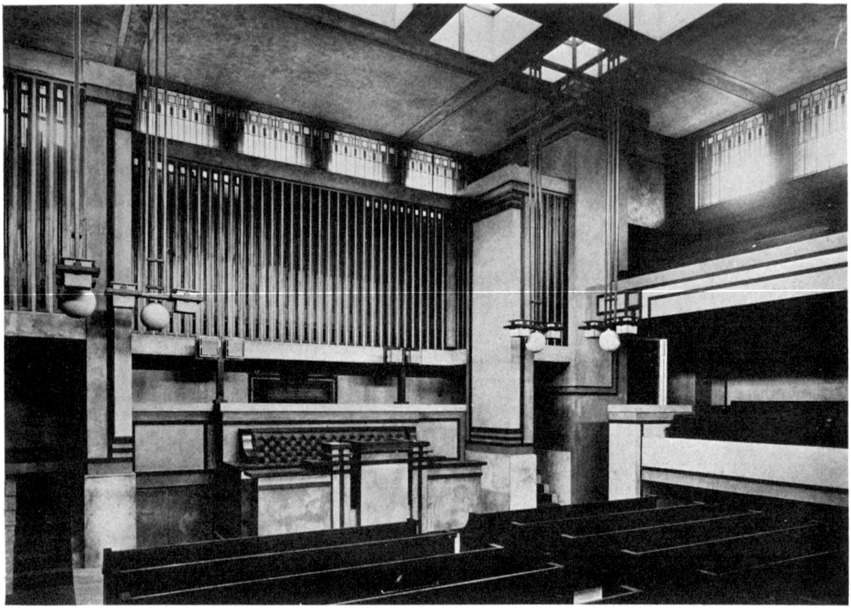

Figure 61. Unity Temple, Oak Park, Illinois (Unitarian-Universalist, 1905-1906), interior

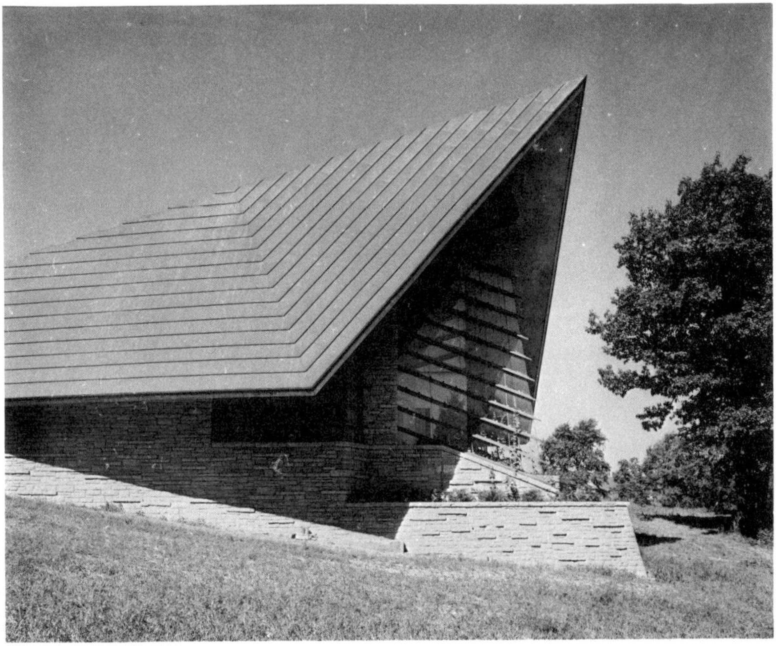

Figure 62. First Unitarian Meeting House, Madison, Wisconsin (1951), exterior

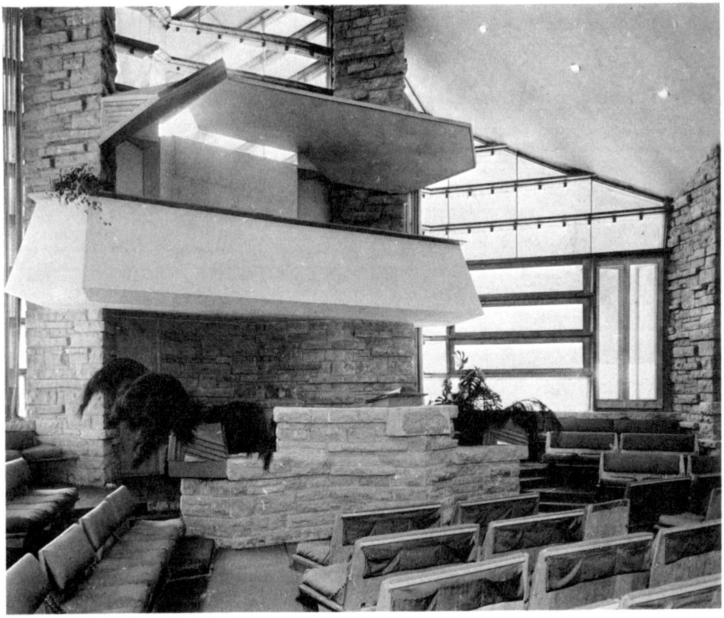

Figure 63. First Unitarian Meeting House, Madison, Wisconsin (1951), interior

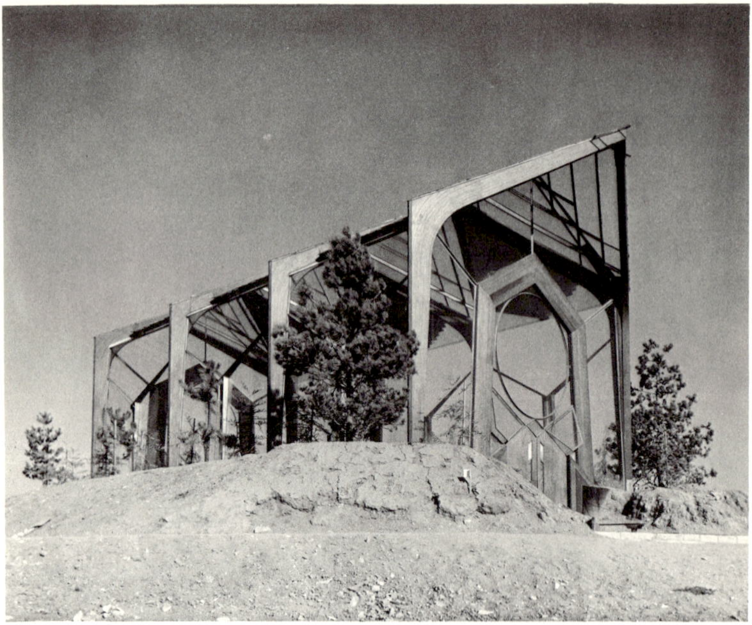

Figure 64. Wayfarers' Chapel, Palos Verdes, California (Swedenborgian, 1951)

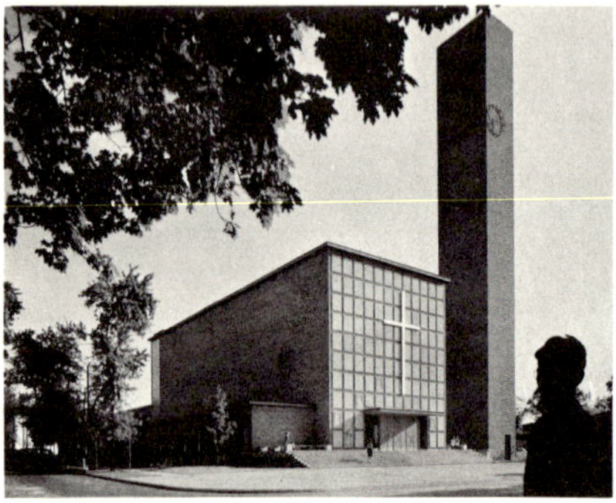

Figure 65. Tabernacle Church of Christ, Columbus, Indiana (Church of Christ, 1940), exterior

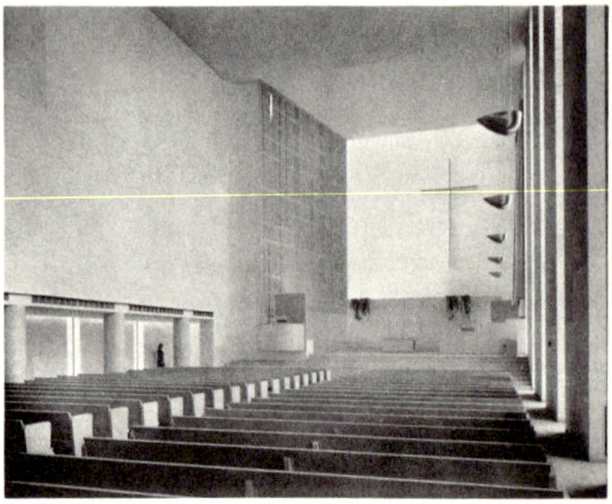

Figure 66. Tabernacle Church of Christ, Columbus, Indiana (Church of Christ, 1940), interior

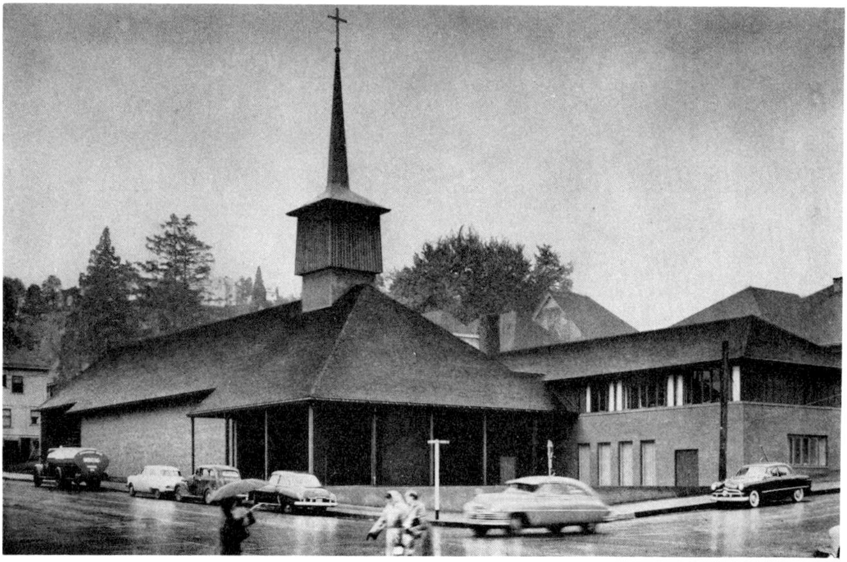

Figure 67. Zion Lutheran Church, Portland, Oregon (1950), exterior

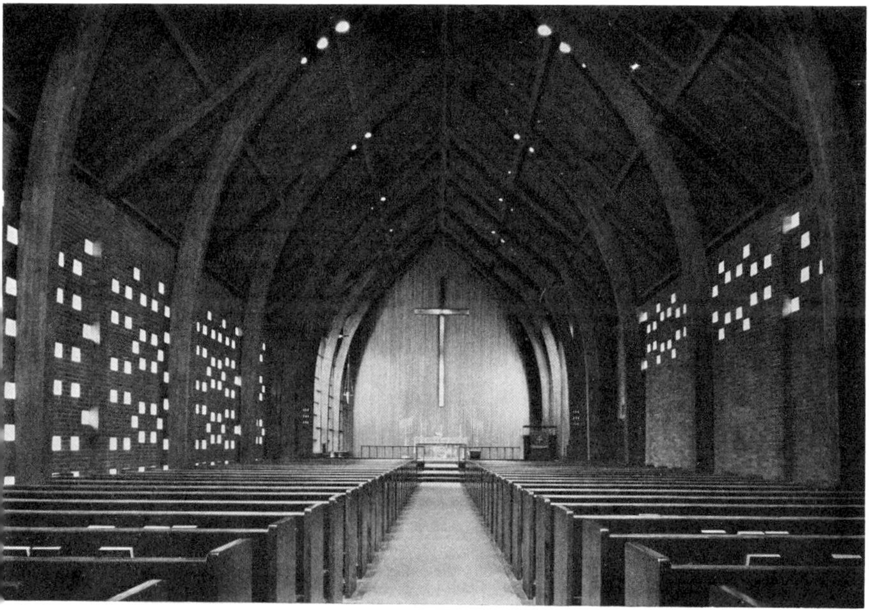

Figure 68. Zion Lutheran Church, Portland, Oregon (1950), interior

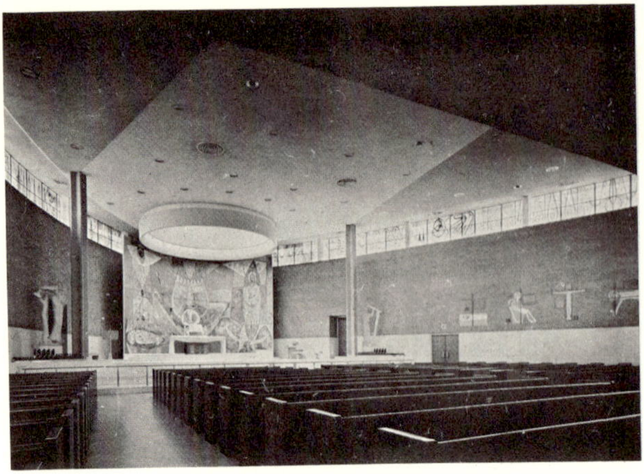

Figure 69. Church of the Resurrection, St. Louis, Missouri (Roman Catholic, 1954)

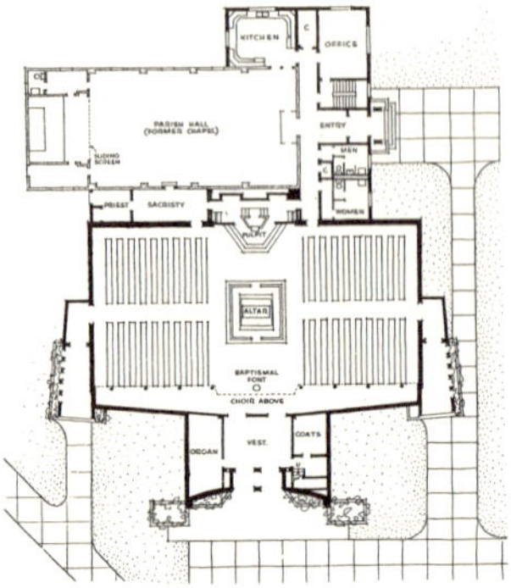

Figure 70. St. Clement's, Alexandria, Virginia (Episcopal, 1949), plan

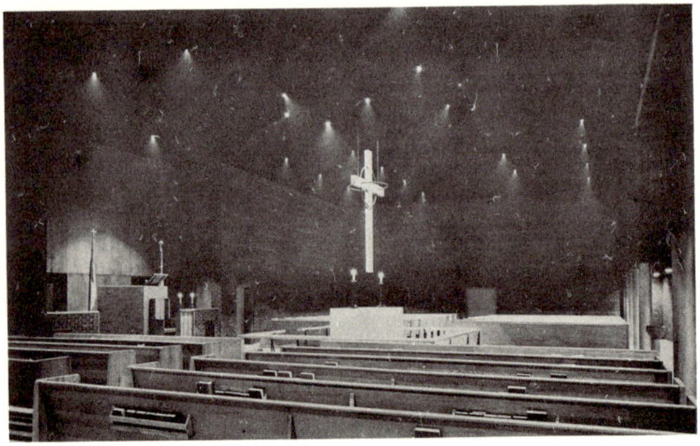

Figure 71. St. Clement's, Alexandria, Virginia (Episcopal, 1949), interior

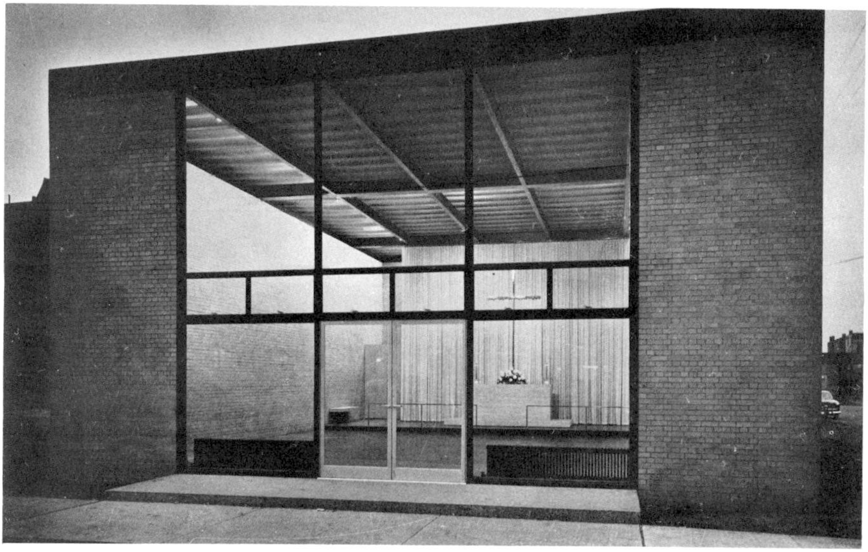

Figure 72. Chapel of St. Saviour, Illinois Institute of Technology, Chicago (Episcopal, 1952)

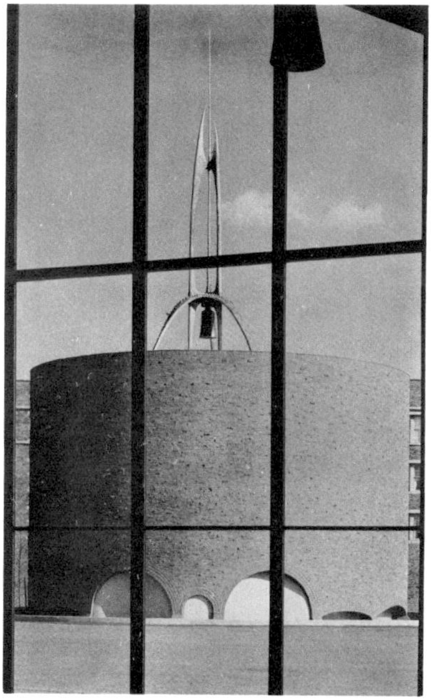

Figure 73. Chapel, Massachusetts Institute of Technology, Cambridge, Massachusetts (non-sectarian, 1955), exterior

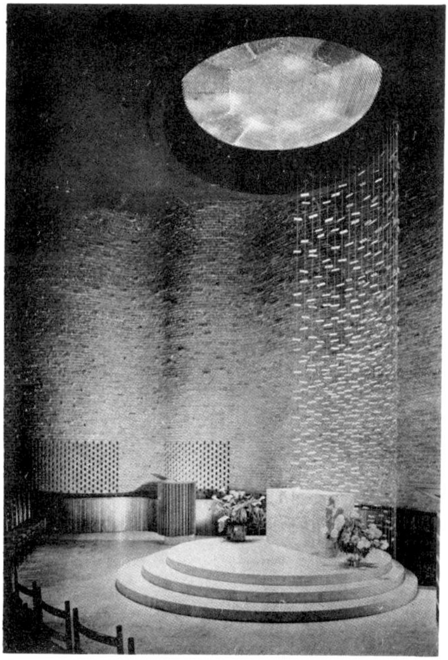

Figure 74. Chapel, Massachusetts Institute of Technology, Cambridge, Massachusetts (non-sectarian, 1955), interior

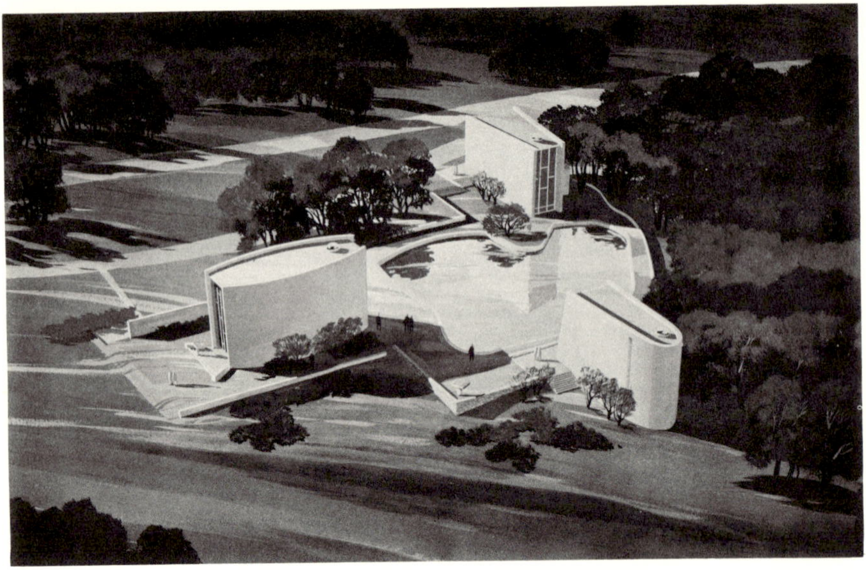

Figure 75. Brandeis University Chapels, Waltham, Massachusetts (Jewish, Protestant, Catholic, 1954-1956)

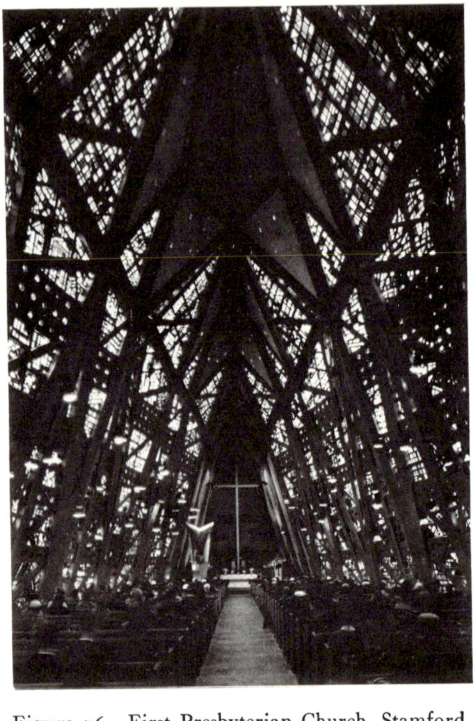

Figure 76. First Presbyterian Church, Stamford, Connecticut (1958)

tower and steeple is the Old South Church in Boston, built in 1730 (Fig. 30). Actually, this is a Congregational meeting house of the house type with which a tower and spire have been combined. The design was unquestionably influenced by Christ Church in Boston, the Old North Church, built by the Anglicans seven years before, in 1723. Because the Old South Church (notice it is now called church; the name meeting house was eventually replaced) had a corner location, two entrances could each be almost equally important. In the meeting house tradition, the main entrance for the congregation was placed on the long side, while the tower entrance now could lead directly to stairways serving the galleries.

A famous Jewish synagogue dating from the colonial period shows many of the same general tendencies that we have seen in Christian architecture of the time. This is the Touro Synagogue in Newport, Rhode Island, designed by a Gentile, the well-known architect Peter Harrison, and built in 1763 for a Sephardic congregation. In being without a tower and simple in other respects, its exterior is not unlike that of a meeting house; yet at the same time the building was not uninfluenced by the trend away from the meeting house toward the basilica type. The synagogue's strict orientation in accordance with specifically Jewish doctrine places it at an angle to the street, and the entrance is through a modest one-story portico (Fig. 31). The plan (Fig. 32) indicates, however, that the still rather squarish building nonetheless has a quite strong longitudinal axis, with the entrance at one end and the Ark at the other, the reading platform being placed midway along the axis. Even the gallery, supported on twelve columns in the Jewish tradition, contributes to this basilical arrangement. A view of the interior (Fig. 33) shows the richness and delicacy of the detail, which is apparently original except that the Ark was remodeled early in the nineteenth century. One might note here that, as Touro Synagogue already indicates, Jewish religious architecture in

America has, on the whole, been subject to the same general stylistic influences as Christian architecture.[8]

Nearly half a century had to pass after the building of the Old South Church before a Puritan church was erected which not only had a tower and steeple like Old South, but an entire basilical plan. This was the Brattle Street Church in Boston, erected in 1772–1773, just before the outbreak of the American Revolution. The main entrance here was at the tower, which was placed at the end of the long axis, with the communion table and the pulpit at the other end in the basilical way. The fact should now be added that in the years following many old meeting houses were to be brought more or less up-to-date by simply adding a tower and spire to them; this was done, for instance, to the meeting house at Cohasset, Massachusetts.

A Presbyterian church that somewhat similarly reflects the tendency away from the meeting house toward a more basilical type is the Old Tennent Church, built in 1731 but enlarged in 1751, at Tennent, New Jersey, near Freehold (Fig. 34), which has a rudimentary steeple on the short side of what is otherwise a meeting house. However, such little steeples were to be found on some Presbyterian meeting houses in Scotland, and so may indicate a Scottish, rather than an Anglican, influence on the Old Tennent Church, the original name of which was Old Scots Meeting House. Notice that the entrances here are still on the long side, as in a meeting house, and that originally there were two, while the pulpit is located in the center of the opposite long side.

The same general development away from a meeting house type toward the basilical plan with tower and steeple took place in the meeting houses of practically all left-wing Protestant sects. Even the Quakers, who have customarily continued to build the traditional type of meeting house, in rela-

[8] This has been made clear by Rachel Wischnitzer in her excellent book, *Synagogue Architecture in the United States: History and Interpretation*, Philadelphia, 1955.

tively recent times have built a few with tower and steeple, especially in the Middle West.

The addition of tower and steeple to the meeting house also became customary in Baptist buildings. The First Baptist Meeting House at Providence, Rhode Island (Fig. 35), erected in 1775, said to be the oldest orthodox Baptist church edifice that still stands in this country, was built with a tower and spire which were directly copied from Gibbs's *A Book of Architecture*, from an alternate design made by Gibbs for St. Martin-in-the-Fields in London (Fig. 36). Yet this Baptist building is still called a meeting house, and it preserves a meeting house type of plan in being squarish, with the main entrance on the long side. The pulpit, however, is placed opposite the tower, and thus in the position it would have in a basilical plan; and the style of the whole interior, too, bears a great resemblance to such famous Anglican churches by Gibbs as St. Martin-in-the-Fields.

Thus, as such examples as the Old South Church in Boston or the First Baptist Meeting House in Providence so clearly show, even before the Revolution the Anglican church type was winning out among non-Anglican denominations and sects, particularly among the wealthy and fashionable congregations of the larger cities. And during the same years, not only were the latest architectural modes of the mother country being increasingly adopted, but at the same time Anglicanism was becoming increasingly fashionable even in regions, such as New England, where formerly it had hardly existed at all or had played a very secondary role. It is true that in the Revolution most of the American Anglicans, especially in the cities, remained loyal to the mother country, and thus were Tories—with the result that Anglicanism (or Episcopalianism, as it was called after the Revolution) was for many years hard hit in the United States. Nevertheless, the shift to the basilical plan with tower and steeple on the front that the influence of the Anglicans had so largely instigated among other American religious groups continued rapidly. Soon the meeting house type was no longer being built except by the Quakers and a few other religiously left-wing groups such as the Shakers. For we shall see that important architectural influences in addition to those coming from Anglicanism strongly encouraged church, rather than meeting house, types.

In various ways, then, the Revolution constituted a kind of architectural boundary or watershed. When it ended, various currents already endemic but secondary in American life were to become much more pronounced. For one thing, the American tendencies toward individualism and anti-traditionalism became much stronger, and helped to encourage the eclecticism in architecture that for a variety of reasons was now developing throughout the Western world. The term eclecticism comes from a Greek verb meaning to choose or pick out, and simply refers to choosing whatever style or styles of present or past may be desired, and even to combining various styles in a single building. The process is, as it were, an expression of architectural *laissez faire*—each individual freely selects the architectural elements and forms that he wishes.

A second current of growing importance for American religious architecture after the Revolution was revivalism. It is true that revivalism, with its emphasis on evangelical Christianity, had begun before the Revolution, especially in the Great Awakening of 1740 which was particularly fostered by an evangelistic tour made by the Reverend George Whitefield, friend of the Wesleys. Like Whitefield, John Wesley, the chief founder of Methodism, regarded himself as an Anglican. However, the evangelicism of the Methodists and their tendency toward revivalism eventually led to their departure from the Anglican church. In 1784, almost immediately after the Revolution, Methodism was officially established in this country, with the result that the Methodists—along with the Baptists—had a profound influence on the spread of revivalism, especially in the back-country and on the frontier.

A glance at the background of English Methodism should include reference to George Whitefield's Tabernacle in St. Luke's Parish, London, built in 1753 (Fig. 37). The name Tabernacle clearly implies the influence of the Old Testament on Christianity. The architectural form itself places an emphasis on revivalistic preaching by providing a preaching room not unlike that of the New England Congregational meeting houses, although on a far larger scale and with huge galleries. In contrast to the small meeting houses of New England, this tabernacle held 4,000 people. And where most earlier New England preaching had been based on a primarily intellectual approach to a theologically trained congregation, Whitefield's preaching was intended to have an emotional appeal. Moreover, this appeal was not restricted here to a congregation made up merely of the population of a small village, but was directed to great masses of people from all over a great city. In this case, then, the emphasis was more on the common man, and on arousing him emotionally, not only by means of emotional preaching but also by the wholehearted congregational singing of revival hymns, rather than of Psalms alone, which is so stressed by Methodists to this day.

Another building important for the background of Methodism in England was Wesley's City Road Chapel in London (Fig. 38), built in 1778. This tabernacle, now also destroyed, likewise was a kind of simplified meeting house for preaching. Although this too was a squarish building, it did have a long axis running away from the entrance somewhat more like a basilica. Interestingly enough, however, this chapel was originally subsidiary to, though separate from, a neighboring Anglican church where the sacraments were administered, while the chapel itself was used simply for a preaching house. In spite of the shape of this building, Wesley once said that he preferred to preach in octagonal structures. He was probably influenced in this by a well-known Presbyterian octagonal meeting house at Norwich, England, which had apparently been inspired by octagonal churches in Holland, so that here again the influence of Dutch Protestant architecture seems to have affected the architecture of an English Protestant group. Furthermore, in accordance with Wesley's preference, many later British Methodist chapels were octagonal: a typical example is that built about 1830 at Mawgan-in-Meneage, in Cornwall (Fig. 39). The simplicity characteristic of the buildings of left-wing Protestants is also evident here, although some of the details show a prevailing architectural fashion of the time, for Gothic Revival touches, such as tracery in the windows, are present.

While in the early nineteenth century revivalism, with its need for a centralized space for preaching and hymn singing, fostered the popularity of the central type of plan, this was by no means the only reason for the type's popularity. Even more important was the fact that this peak of revivalism happened to coincide with the rise to fashion of an architectural style which particularly lent itself to producing such a centralized space. This style was the Roman Revival. And the particular Roman prototype that now especially encouraged central type churches was the great circular temple in Rome known as the Pantheon, erected under Hadrian in the second century A.D. In addition to the Methodists, many of the other American Protestant denominations and sects had their own specific requirements which in some way especially encouraged them to make use of Roman Revival architecture. This was true, for example, of the Baptists. Like the Methodists, they too could make good use of a centralized temple form for revivalistic preaching. However, there was another reason why this type of building was especially suited to the needs of Baptists, as can be seen in an old view of the Sansom Street Baptist Church in Philadelphia (Fig. 40), designed by Robert Mills in 1808–1809. For this kind of building was well fitted to housing and emphasizing the baptismal pool which the Baptists require in accordance with their belief in the baptism, not of children, but of adults old enough to realize the significance of the rite, and by total immersion.

This central type, which as here could be covered with a dome more or less like that of the Roman Pantheon, could serve still other tendencies in American religion. Inasmuch as it possessed a clear rational shape, for instance, it could be attractive to groups like the Unitarians who, far from being revivalists, were strongly rationalistic, and so at an opposite pole of Protestantism. An example is the Octagon Unitarian Church of Philadelphia (Fig. 41), designed in 1813 by the same Robert Mills, in which much the same architectural form was used as in the Sansom Street Baptist Church but for a religion rationalistic rather than enthusiastic, though nonetheless a religion in which preaching is important. Thus in this case the revival of classic architecture went hand in hand with intellectualism and rational simplicity, a third powerful tendency within American religion of the period.

This intellectualism grew out of the eighteenth-century rationalism of the Enlightenment which itself had helped to encourage the revival of Roman and, later, Greek classical forms as an expression of a rational spirit in architecture. Yet these forms, if they were accurately archaeological, could produce many other connotations and associations—some of them far from purely rational. They could symbolize, for one thing, the republican spirit by creating a romantic association with the republics of ancient Rome and Greece, an association which lent a special importance to the classic revivals in the new American republic. Their luster in this respect was even further enhanced for Americans in the 1820's and later because of American sympathy for the modern Greeks who had revolted against the tyranny of the Turks to achieve their own independence in the romantic aura which attended the death of Byron in Greece. For many Americans, the Greek and Roman forms also effectively connoted the primitive virtues and rational simplicity of classic man, as a more natural man than his modern counterpart. This harmonized, of course, rather with the views of Rousseau and of his followers than with Christian belief, but nonetheless had an indirect effect even on religious architecture.

Largely as a result of such Classic Revival fashion, paradoxically a fashion peculiarly suited both to the emotional spirit of evangelical revivalism and to the new rationalism, many religious buildings once more lacked towers and steeples simply because classical temples lacked them. And this Revival imitated not only the form of circular temples, such as the Pantheon, but also that of rectangular temples, Greek as well as Roman. The rectangular form, with its especially clear and easily comprehensible shape, in particular lent itself to the expression of the religious values of the more rationalistic nonconformist groups, Unitarian or Calvinistic. However, the imitation of the rectangular classic temple form meant that the main entrance would have to be placed on the short side beneath the pedimented gable, as it had been in the temples themselves; and to be truly classic there could be no tower or steeple. This was the case with the present building of the First Presbyterian Church at Princeton (Fig. 42), which was designed and built in 1836–1837 by a local architect, and is clearly inspired by a classic temple even though with a façade apparently more or less based on a widely known design made and published by the American architect, Asher Benjamin. This Princeton church stands on the site of two earlier edifices, both of which had burned, and both of which had been meeting houses of the house type, placed, therefore, with the long side parallel to the street. In that long side was the main entrance, directly opposite the pulpit. It was especially the prevalence of classic fashion at the time when the present church was erected, then, that produced a major compositional change. Yet the severely rational form of the present temple-like edifice could also serve here as a clear expression of the rationalistic and antirevivalistic old school Calvinism for which Princeton had come to stand in the nineteenth century. This was a kind of Calvinism in sharp contrast to the Whitefieldian revivalism that the eighteenth-century builders of the original meeting house on this site (and also the founders of Princeton College, which used that meeting house for its Sabbath services and graduating exercises) had once so whole-heartedly accepted.

Even more rationalistic than old school Calvinism, of course, was Unitarianism, whose growth in New England could directly parallel the spread of classical revivalism in architecture. Much later, the Christian Scientists, too, were to use for their mother church in Boston a domical structure not unlike some Renaissance versions of the Pantheon. Even though today the Christian Scientists have no one standard type for their churches, nevertheless the rationally clear form of their building in Boston does seem harmonious with their belief that mind is a fundamental principle of the universe. This doctrine is seemingly also reflected in the fact that they have in their churches no pulpit. In place of the minister there are two readers, one of whom reads from the Bible, the other from the writings of their founder, Mary Baker Eddy. It may be significant that, like Unitarianism, Christian Science was partly an outgrowth from rational Calvinism, and that Mrs. Eddy's own parents were Congregationalists.

The existence side by side in American life, and especially in American Protestantism, of such widely different tendencies as extreme individualism, emotional revivalism, and intellectualism could only be expected ultimately to give rise to a reaction against such confusion—to emphasis on strong central church organization and hierarchy, traditionalism, and an elaborate liturgy. As could be expected, also, this kind of reaction developed especially among groups that had always been more likely to emphasize hierarchy and a richly liturgical service. It therefore was led by Roman Catholics and by Anglo-Catholics. And the architectural style to which both of these groups turned as the best expression of their needs was the Gothic Revival (which, however, like the Classic Revival, was by no means restricted solely to church architecture).

The Gothic Revival, like the Classic Revival also, was encouraged by the romantic love for the remote in space and time; and this, among other things, could encourage a belief that the past was superior to the present—more natural, less spoiled by the development of civilization. In religious architecture this could stimulate a preference for some earlier style regarded as being closer to the original—therefore purer—doctrines of the particular religious group. Both the Roman Catholics and the Anglo-Catholics eventually emphasized a revival of the Gothic style for their church buildings because it was a style that preceded the Renaissance and the Reformation, which for them had sullied the stream of pure Christian doctrine.

Significantly, what is usually called the first Gothic Revival church design in the United States was made for Roman Catholics in Maryland, the only British colony originally settled by Catholics. It was a design prepared in 1805 by the architect Benjamin Latrobe for the Roman Catholic Cathedral at Baltimore (Fig. 43). However, in this design Latrobe—who had recently come from abroad with a most up-to-date Continental and British training in architecture—was ahead of his time. Offered as an alternative solution, this Gothic design was rejected in favor of one in a Roman Classic style clearly inspired by the Pantheon in Rome (Figs. 44 and 45).[9] But although Latrobe's alternative Gothic design was rejected, only a year later Roman Catholics in Baltimore were to build a Gothic Revival chapel for St. Mary's Seminary, designed by the architect Maximilien Godefroy, who had recently arrived from France (Fig. 46). Thereafter, the Gothic Revival, which exponents could regard as exemplifying a revival of the spirit of St. Thomas Aquinas, was to be used with increasing

[9] In execution, Latrobe's design for the cupolas and portico was somewhat modified.

frequency for Catholic churches, as it has been almost to the present. Perhaps the best known example of a Gothic Revival Catholic church in this country is St. Patrick's Cathedral in New York, designed by the architect James Renwick and built between 1850 and 1879 (Fig. 47).

Like the Roman Catholics, and partly under their influence, the Anglo-Catholics—or High Church Episcopalians—reacted against individualism, emotional revivalism, and the over-intellectualism of the Enlightenment, and likewise embraced the Gothic Revival. Anglo-Catholicism really began in England in 1833 with the foundation of what became known as the Oxford Movement. This was led especially by John Henry Newman, who wrote its first tract, but who eventually became a convert to Roman Catholicism and finally was made a Cardinal. A little church built for Newman at Littlemore (Figs. 48 and 49), not far from Oxford, in 1835–1836 is, significantly, in the Gothic Revival style. Its close resemblance to an English parish church of the Middle Ages indicates that the spirit of actual Gothic architecture has been very well understood by the Gothic Revival designer.

The first American publication devoted wholly to Gothic architecture appeared in 1836, three years after the Oxford Movement began in England. This was an *Essay on Gothic Architecture*, written by John Henry Hopkins, the Episcopal bishop of Vermont. While it is true that Episcopal churches with Gothic Revival details had been built before this time, now many Episcopal churches were to be designed in a well-understood Gothic style. The vogue for Gothic Revival church architecture gained particular impetus with the completion of Trinity Church in New York (Fig. 50), which was designed by the architect Richard Upjohn, and built between 1839 and 1846. Upjohn was a devoted and persuasive follower of the High Church movement. As such, he finally succeeded in winning the building committee over not only to having a Gothic church, but a Gothic church with a deep and elaborate chancel. However, he was unable to persuade the vestry of the need for a cross at the top of the steeple—the vestry preferred a weathervane as less redolent of popery. According to a story which has come down in the Upjohn family, Upjohn then secretly put a cross in place on the steeple just before the scaffolding was taken down. With the scaffolding gone, the vestry was reluctant to pay to have it put up all over again; and so the cross is there to this day. The interior (Fig. 51) of the church, as well as its exterior, shows an extensive knowledge and understanding of Gothic architecture. The Gothic detail is highly elaborated, especially in the chancel, where the pulpit's location to one side also helps to indicate the reaction against earlier Calvinist influence on Episcopalianism. Upjohn's own influence extended to country areas with a book, *Upjohn's Rural Architecture*, which was published in 1852, and contained designs for wooden "carpenter" Gothic churches (Fig. 52) of a kind that Upjohn had begun to design about 1845. Innumerable rural churches, especially for Episcopal congregations, were built from the designs in his book by carpenters who, however, usually altered the design somewhat to meet local conditions (Fig. 53).

At the height of the popularity of Gothic Revival, a Romanesque Revival was also flourishing in the United States. The original Romanesque style had preceded the Gothic in western Europe, and—being nearer in time to Roman architecture—tended to retain such Roman characteristics as the rounded arch and a considerable massiveness. In the mid-nineteenth century, the Romanesque Revival was also sometimes called Byzantine (from that style found in the eastern Mediterranean contemporary with the actual Romanesque in western Europe), or sometimes Lombard (from the variety of Romanesque which had occurred in north Italy). However, the role of this Romanesque-Byzantine-Lombard style in the general medieval revival of the nineteenth century was a secondary one until, with the advent of one great architect in the second half of the century, it became immensely popular. This architect was Henry Hobson Richardson. The most famous and most influential example of Richardsonian Romanesque is Trinity Episcopal Church in Boston (Fig. 54), built between 1873 and 1877. Although this building is called Romanesque, it is actually a kind of Victorian free eclecticism in which elements of some diversity are welded by a superlatively skillful architect into one composition. For Richardson's inspiration derived from a variety of sources: the tower was inspired by that of a Spanish Romanesque cathedral; the ornament comes largely from a French Romanesque style, that of the region of central France called Auvergne; while other elements are borrowed from the Romanesque school of Provence. Nor was Richardson inspired only by the Romanesque: on parts of Trinity Church, some Gothic tracery can be found, as well as Gothic colonnettes and ornament. Only an architect of Richardson's immense ability could transform this variety of sources into a personal style which in many ways transcended his models.

Trinity Church in Boston is Low Church. The fact that some earlier Low Church Episcopalian churches—such as St. George's, Stuyvesant Square, in New York—also used a kind of Romanesque style, may indicate a tendency among Low Church Episcopalians to wish to employ a medieval style other than the Gothic Revival in order to distinguish themselves from High Church Episcopalianism. Indeed, their own revival of an earlier medieval style may even have been regarded by them as a revival of a "purer" architecture.

In addition to his characteristically massive stone architecture, so well illustrated by Trinity Church, Richardson also developed a shingle style which likewise had a profound influence, and which was used for many small churches of various denominations by some of his numerous imitators. In his stone and shingle architecture alike, Richardson increasingly gave a direct and natural expression to each specific material. In other words, unlike the average architect of the Victorian period who so often loved to make things look like what they were not, Richardson took expressive advantage of inherent characteristics of the particular material. In this respect, and also in often emphasizing the fundamental geometric forms of his buildings, Richardson was a direct forerunner of major twentieth-century tendencies in architecture.

After his early death in the middle 1880's, however, his style continued to be imitated by lesser architects unable to achieve such creative results, with the consequence that the tendency in Episcopal churches soon was to return to a Gothic Revival style now directly based on the careful use of "good" medieval models. The practitioners of this kind of eclecticism usually did not seek either to copy an original model in full detail, or to develop a very free version of "modern" Gothic as the Victorians had done largely under the influence of John Ruskin. Instead, they devoted painstaking care to evoking the spirit of the actual Gothic of the Middle Ages, and did so with an emphasis on good craftsmanship which often reflected the influence of the artistic beliefs of William Morris, and at times of his social beliefs as well.

The first example in the United States of a Gothic Revival building carefully based on the spirit of good models in this way is said to have been the chapel of a great Episcopalian private school, St. Paul's School at Concord, New Hampshire, designed by an imported English architect named Henry Vaughan, and mostly built in 1888. Other architects, many of them likewise devoted Episcopalians, took over this style: the American architect, Ralph Adams Cram, was notable among these. Cram, who was born in 1863 and died in 1942, was the son of a Unitarian minister; but Unitarianism never satisfied him and he became a convert to Anglo-Catholicism. As a member of the firm of Cram, Goodhue and Ferguson, he developed a large practice, becoming especially known as a highly fashionable church architect, not only for Episcopal churches but for those of other fashionable forms of relatively right-wing Protestantism. One of his most famous works is the Episcopal Cathedral of St. John the Divine, which had been begun by other architects in a Richardsonian Romanesque style. Cram took it over, revising it as far as possible into a Gothic building. An example by Cram that shows how right-wing Protestant congregations who were not Episcopalians might take over this style, is the East Liberty Presbyterian Church in Pittsburgh (Figs. 55 and 56), commissioned by a member of the wealthy Mellon family as a Mellon memorial church and completed about 1935. Of this Cram said in his autobiography: ". . . it is a simple fact that in half an hour, by the addition of a Crucifix and six candles on the Communion table, the church could be prepared for a pontifical High Mass either of the Roman or the Anglican Rite." [10] And privately Cram said much the same of the Princeton University Chapel, completed in 1928. (The fact that in 1907 Cram had become supervising architect of Princeton University—so long a great Presbyterian stronghold even though it has always been technically non-sectarian—is significant for the period.)

Many of those who have disagreed with the point of view represented by Cram have objected to the Gothic Revival in this country on the ground that it is not a national American style, and therefore is necessarily a false expression of American tradition. Nonetheless, various upholders of the Medieval Revival have long sought to glorify it as a national style. To cite a famous secular example—in 1847 Robert Dale Owen, son of the great utopian socialist, Robert Owen, had become the chairman of the building committee for the Smithsonian Institution in Washington. As such he wrote a book telling in detail how his committee had selected a kind of late Romanesque-early Gothic style for the Smithsonian Institution as the best expression of a truly national American style.[11]

Thus we turn to the question of nationalism, which in religious architecture has been most likely to encourage, not the Gothic Revival, but a revival of what is regarded as American colonial style. The revival of the colonial began especially

[10] Ralph Adams Cram, *My Life in Architecture*, Boston, 1936, p. 255.

[11] Robert Dale Owen, *Hints on Public Architecture*, New York, 1849.

after the Centennial Exposition at Philadelphia in 1876, which of course took its name from the fact that it celebrated a century of American independence. At that exposition one of the buildings was supposed to represent a colonial log cabin (although we now know that the original settlers in New England customarily did not live in log cabins); and in it were displayed such examples of colonial furniture as the cradle of Peregrine White, the first white child born in New England, and the desk of John Alden.

Largely out of the Centennial Exposition, then, grew the colonial revival. Yet many of the favorite old examples imitated in the colonial revival actually were works of the federal period, and so did not date from pre-Revolutionary, and therefore colonial, times. As might be expected, it is a revival particularly popular for churches of those Protestant groups, such as the Congregationalists, whose days of greatest influence had been in the colonial period. A beautiful example of the type of Congregational church which was imitated in this supposedly colonial revival is the church at Lyme, Connecticut (Fig. 57). As this was built in 1815–1817, it dates well into the republic, and thus is not colonial at all; yet it is this style that many if not most Americans like to think of as being typically colonial. The church at Lyme has been copied several times in the twentieth century, usually for Congregational churches such as those at Williamstown, Massachusetts, and Norwalk, Connecticut. Interestingly enough, however, the Congregational church at Lyme was also imitated in the private chapel of the late Roman Catholic Cardinal Mundelein, built at his seat near Chicago. In this case, the architecture apparently reflected a desire, conscious or unconscious, to have the Roman Catholic church accepted as traditionally American, in order to meet the criticism of those non-Catholics who—for example, in the Hoover-Smith campaign of 1928—have held that simultaneous allegiance to the United States and the Pope is impossible.

Another tendency that must now be mentioned as affecting

church architecture, particularly Protestant church architecture, ever since the eighteenth century, is the humanitarianism on which the whole Social Gospel movement has been based. It is true that some of the seeds of that movement had long been present in the left-wing Protestant emphasis on the common man, but it was brought to flower by the romantic humanitarianism of the late eighteenth and nineteenth centuries, and was especially fostered by Ruskin's social doctrines. The effect of humanitarianism and the Social Gospel on religious architecture can especially be seen in the increasing tendency for the church edifice and related buildings, particularly of Protestant groups, to develop into a social and educational center. This tendency really began with the Sunday school movement, founded by Robert Raikes in 1780 with Wesley's approval, which originated as an effort to get working-class children off the streets on Sunday, and thus originally involved secular as well as religious education. In view of its outgrowth from Methodism, it is worth mentioning that the Sunday school was later given special importance by an American Methodist bishop, John Heyl Vincent, whose friend, Louis Miller, a Methodist Sunday school superintendent, invented what was known as the Akron plan. This took its name from its demonstration in the Methodist church in Akron, Ohio, built in 1868, and was strongly supported by Bishop Vincent. His motto was "Togetherness and Separateness," and the basic concept of the Akron plan was to have all the members of a Sunday school gather together in one large room for joint activities, then at a signal to break up into separate groups in small classrooms divided from the big room by folding doors. As part of the element of togetherness, singing was stressed, as is usual in Methodism. Adopted by many other Protestant groups, only about 1910 did the Akron plan tend to be abandoned in favor of the departmentalized Sunday school and large parish house. One might add here that the Akron plan had connections with the widely popular Chautauqua movement, of which Louis Miller and

Bishop Vincent were two of the founders. The headquarters of the movement grew out of a center for training Sunday school teachers founded in 1871, and were established at Fair Point on Lake Chautauqua three years later.

Today, of course, the elaborate kind of parish house which, with the decline of the Akron plan, became so popular, often occupies an area far larger than that of the church itself. As everyone knows, its layout is often very complex, with spaces for men's groups, women's societies, boy scouts, bowling alleys, basketball courts, and the like. A good example to illustrate this complexity is a plan of the early 1940's for the First Presbyterian church of North Hollywood, California. Here the total plan (Fig. 58) is so elaborate (even including in the Sunday school area a "Jinks Court," presumably for high jinks) that on paper it is difficult to find the church proper. Notice, also, that in the church building itself, there is a large and elaborate chancel, even though this is a Presbyterian church. As in the period before the Revolution, the influence of Episcopalianism has tended to lead other Protestant groups toward a more elaborate service—again partly, perhaps, because of the fashionableness of Episcopalianism in American society.

When the North Hollywood Presbyterian Church was finally built in 1945 on a different plan, it was in a Spanish style. Yet only fifteen years later it was being altered to a style described by the minister as "contemporary."

This suggests another tendency which since the eighteenth century has increasingly affected much church architecture: an emphasis on progress and modernism. In the nineteenth century when the Gothic Revival was the dominant style for Roman Catholic churches, so also did Popes Pius IX and Leo XIII attack liberalism and modernism. Meanwhile, within the various Protestant denominations and sects there was going on a constant struggle between belief in tradition as good and belief in progress as good. Naturally enough, those liberalistic groups which—under the influence both of scientific and technological progress and of a romantic optimism—have upheld the idea of progress, were more likely than religiously conservative groups to make early use of "modern" architectural forms with little or no reminiscence of the past. However, today the problem is not so simple; and we shall find that some of the most traditionalistic and also some of the most fundamentalist groups have likewise made much use of modern architecture. This paradox we must now try to account for.

Unity Temple, or Church, at Oak Park, Illinois, designed and built by Frank Lloyd Wright in 1905–1906 (Figs. 59, 60, 61), exemplifies a church built by a religiously radical Protestant group subscribing to an optimistic liberal theology in which belief in secular progress is implicit. The building itself was highly radical and progressive for its time in being built of poured concrete, a new material here frankly expressed with no reminiscence of historical style. Significantly, the congregation that built Unity Temple—of which Wright's family had long been members—had originally been Unitarian but had largely become Universalist. In so doing, they had accepted not only Unitarian rationalism but the basic Universalist—and non-Calvinist—doctrine that because of God's love for man, the probability exists that all will be saved, an optimistic liberal theology which had first come to America in 1770. In this building rationalism has combined with theological optimism to encourage a progressive spirit in architecture, and therefore a building was achieved in a technique and style extraordinarily modern for its time. Not only is this true of the materials, the structure, and the architectural form, but of the plan as well (Fig. 60); for Unity Temple was the first church to have the entrance not directly on the street, but opening off a terrace between the church and the parish house so that it might serve them both. This plan has exerted a very wide influence, not only on churches of many different denominations—including Bernard Maybeck's unique Christian Science Church (1912) at Berkeley, California—

but also on many synagogues. The interior of Unity Temple (Fig. 61) shows not merely a lack of historical reminiscence but a deliberate avoidance of it. Nevertheless, the building is still in the Protestant tradition of a preaching room, in which, since the eighteenth century, the singing of hymns has also been important.

Over thirty-five years after Frank Lloyd Wright designed Unity Temple, he was to design a Unitarian meeting house in Madison, Wisconsin (Fig. 62). Looking at this from the exterior of the sanctuary, we can see why Wright has called it "the church in the attitude of prayer," for the treatment has the spirit of hands placed together in supplication. In this symbolic way the architect has conveyed the idea of religious edifice, yet has avoided imitating churches of the past. The interior of the building, however (Fig. 63), which again suggests the Protestant preaching room, shows how Frank Lloyd Wright in his recent churches and chapels often liked to have natural daylight behind the pulpit, and even in some cases to have the congregation look out through a window behind the pulpit into nature. This could suggest the Christian view that nature is good because created by God and because it is the earthly dwelling of man. But in being carried so far, this actually is a reflection of that kind of romantic pantheism which is often implicit in Wright's buildings or in such statements by him as "Buildings like trees are brothers to the man, buildings trees and man are all out of the ground into the light." [12] Nevertheless, it will be noted that in this building Wright—unlike many other modern architects who have used the same device—has distinguished the architectural space of the interior from the natural space out of doors by means of horizontal bars placed across the great windows behind the pulpit.

Wright's son, Lloyd Wright, has gone much further than

[12] Frank Lloyd Wright, *Modern Architecture,* Princeton, 1931, front fly-leaf.

his father toward a kind of romantic pantheism in the Wayfarers' Chapel that he designed in Palos Verdes, California, in 1951 (Fig. 64). Since the photograph used for illustration was taken, trees have grown up around the glass walls, still further erasing any division between architectural space and natural space outside. Moreover, the laminated-wood framework, largely for structural efficiency, has shapes which not only recall Gothic arches but are themselves not unlike forms in nature—in this case the trunks and arching branches of trees—so that this building illustrates almost literally the elder Wright's statement quoted above that "Buildings like trees are brothers to the man." It is probably significant that the Wayfarers' Chapel is a Swedenborgian church, for the mystical side of Emanuel Swedenborg was not unaffected by that Neo-Platonism with pantheistic overtones which so largely gave life to romantic pantheism. Thus Swedenborg himself spoke of "God as the spiritual sun from which proceeds the sun of the natural world; because the world of nature and spirit, while distinct, are intimately related." Lloyd Wright's chapel reflects this intimate relationship between nature and spirit, rather than a distinction between them.

As already mentioned, among the more radical Protestant groups not only the groups of liberal, optimistic, "progressive" theology, but some groups of fundamentalist theology, were led to use highly modern architectural forms. A case in point is the Tabernacle Church of Christ at Columbus, Indiana (Fig. 65), designed in 1940 by Eliel and Eero Saarinen. The members of the Churches of Christ are Campbellite fundamentalists as distinguished from the Disciples of Christ, the Campbellite liberals. The Churches of Christ believe that "where the Scriptures speak we speak, where the Scriptures are silent we are silent," so that they subscribe to a fundamentalist Bible Christianity. It is significant that the church is called "Tabernacle," and that the building committee of the congregation declared, "We attach much importance to our effort to preach and practice primitive Christianity and nothing else. . . ."[13] Primitive Christianity is the clue here: the return to primitive Christianity clearly implies a break with all intervening traditions, including intervening architectural traditions. Thus the bald, cubistic simplicity of the stripped-down forms of much modern architecture can be used, as here, to express a kind of "primitive" simplicity, with the result that the general effect is not unlike that of an Early Christian church. Note, however, that the romantic pantheism characteristic of so many modern architects, including Eliel Saarinen, is here seen in the inclusion of growing nature on the interior (Fig. 66) in the form of actual foliage that grows over the screen at the sanctuary end.

Turning from the more radical Protestant groups today toward Protestant groups with more traditional theology: as one might expect they are especially likely to retain a traditional plan and some associations also with a traditional style, even if, for some reason, they use architectural forms that are otherwise highly modern. This may be illustrated by a Lutheran church, Zion Lutheran Church at Portland, Oregon, built by the architect Pietro Belluschi in 1950 (Figs. 67 and 68). Here, although the structure is modern insofar as the architect has used roof supports made of laminated wood and has replaced windows by glass block, nevertheless by means of his laminated-wood supports in the shape of arches he has suggested the pointed arches of Gothic architecture, and by means of the glass block scattered through the walls he has achieved an effect not entirely unlike that of Gothic stained glass even though color is not actually used here. And then, of course, the cross on the sanctuary wall further connotes church, while the plan is that of a traditional basilica.

In recent years the Roman Catholics, too, have not hesitated to build many modern churches under the influence of what is known as the Liturgical Movement. In part stimu-

[13] *Architectural Forum,* Vol. 77, October 1942, p. 36.

lated by the Gothic Revival, this developed in Germany particularly after World War I, and its major doctrine is that the Church is the local incarnation of the Body of Christ, and so must carry on His redemptive work. It therefore sees the need for impact on a secularized society, not primarily by means of large-scale organized religion, but through small communities of engaged Christians who at various levels take on themselves the task of representing Christ to our secularized society, as well as of representing that society to God in the eucharist. In architecture, then, the Liturgical Movement has given rise to a kind of small church so designed that each person can see and hear, and thus better participate in the Mass. It has also led to the saying of the Mass in people's houses, and thus often to the minimizing of churches altogether. As the Liturgical Movement is itself a modern movement, it has fostered the use of modern forms in Roman Catholic architecture, especially as the traditional long-aisled Gothic and Gothic Revival church plan could not give the kind of space desired. Nevertheless, for so strongly traditional a religion as Roman Catholicism it was only to be expected that even ultra-modern churches would retain associations with traditional Catholic architectural forms. The combination of a basically traditional Catholic spirit in the arts with a truly modern treatment has been especially fostered by the magazine *Liturgical Arts*, founded in 1931, the influence of which has even affected Protestant religious architecture.

Both the influence of the Liturgical Movement and continuing associations with tradition are well illustrated by such a modern Roman Catholic church as the Church of the Resurrection in St. Louis, Missouri, designed by Murphy and Mackey in 1954 (Fig. 69). In its use of modern forms and structure to produce a space so designed that all can see and hear the Mass, this clearly reflects the influence of the Liturgical Movement. Although in these respects this church is a thoroughly modern one, nevertheless there are reminiscences here of past styles closely associated with Catholicism. The effect is still largely that of the traditional basilica plan with a long axis culminating in the sanctuary. The windows high up in the side walls recall the clerestories of Gothic churches, while the oculus that focuses light directly and dramatically upon the altar is a device that recalls similar lighting in various baroque churches of the Catholic Counter-Reformation.

The Catholic Liturgical Movement—itself not wholly unaffected by certain developments within Protestantism—has spread into many Protestant groups in various countries, especially affecting numerous Anglicans, Episcopalians, and Lutherans, but also some Calvinists, particularly in Scotland and France.[14] In American architecture, an Episcopalian example that apparently reflects the influence of the movement is the Church of St. Clement at Alexandria, Virginia, designed by J. S. Saunders in 1949 (Fig. 70), and built so that the service at the altar can be clearly seen and heard from three sides. This ultra-modern church has no windows, and the artificial light is so handled as to enhance the focus on the altar and on the cross that rises from it, on the pulpit and prayer desk, and on the font, while also creating a sense of mystery and awe (Fig. 71). Interestingly enough, St. Clement's, Alexandria, is somewhat Low Church. One would gather that its emphasis on having each member of the congregation equally able to see and spiritually participate in the service, consciously or unconsciously reflects a kind of democratic approach to religion which contrasts with the more hierarchical and conservative point of view of High Church Episcopalians even if they abandon the Gothic Revival, as the more advanced High Church circles have been doing. And it is an approach which, if adopted by Calvinists, could foster a return to a kind of meeting house plan.[15]

[14] See Alfred R. Shands, *The Liturgical Movement and the Local Church*, London, 1959.

[15] See the proposed design for Calvin Presbyterian Church, Long Lake, Minn., published in *Progressive Architecture*, Vol. 40, Part 1, January 1959, p. 134. This has a rectangular plan with the pulpit placed against the middle of a long wall, opposite the entrance.

At St. Clement's, apart from the cross on the altar and the atmosphere of awe created by the lighting, there is almost nothing that traditionally bespeaks "church." And this leads us to a dilemma that commonly faces those modern architects who would hold that a building cannot be good architecture unless it is wholly of its own time, and who therefore are likely to reject traditional forms and traditional symbolism to such a degree that they have great difficulty in achieving a suitable religious expression. It is said that the great German-American architect, Walter Gropius, refuses to accept commissions to design churches because the problem is foreign to his talents and sympathies as a modern architect. Few critics have felt that Mies van der Rohe—Gropius' equally noted friend and former colleague in Germany—has adequately expressed the spirit of Episcopalianism in the Chapel of St. Saviour that he built for Illinois Institute of Technology in 1952 (Fig. 72). Apart from the simple cross on the sanctuary wall, Mies' concern with modern materials and with the modern forms which stem so largely from that modern movement in painting and sculpture known as cubism, has resulted in too completely eliminating the traditional forms and symbols by which the Episcopalian tradition can most directly be expressed.

One particularly difficult kind of problem involving suitable expression for religious buildings became especially acute in World War II. This was the problem of designing chapels for American troops which could be used equally for Catholic, Protestant, and Jewish services. Despite the enormous difficulties that this requirement imposes on a designer, following the war various non-denominational educational institutions have similarly sought to have their chapels designed in a style that could somehow convey the spirit of religion to members of all the chief religious groups in America. An example of this is the chapel designed by Eero Saarinen for the Massachusetts Institute of Technology (Figs. 73 and 74), and built in 1955. We know that the architect consciously sought to express a general image of religious content, non-sectarian by nature; and he made clear to the sculptor for the interior, Harry Bertoia, that he too must respect the non-denominational character of the building. Interestingly enough, Bertoia has told [16] how this restriction led him to design the sanctuary screen as he did. First of all, as he said, "All [specific] images had to be forgotten." In his mind, instead, were vague forms of the primordial cosmos; and he noted that "What was actually evolved . . . was closest to my ideas of the stars." In sum, he sought to achieve a religious effect without recourse to any customary religious symbols, which inevitably tend to connote some specific religion. Therefore, in a most generalized way, he designed his screen to connote the stars and the cosmos as expressive of the handiwork of a God Who transcends earthbound man, and therefore transcends any specific religious group.

As the exterior of this chapel especially shows, however, it is not without faint reminiscences of past styles of religious architecture. The general form, with its heavy walls and round arches, has something in common with Romanesque churches. The spire, by the ultra-modern sculptor, Theodore Roszak, nonetheless recalls the *flèche* of a Gothic cathedral, while the light reflected into the interior from the surrounding pool produces an effect of flickering light and color that suggests an otherworldliness by a kind of dematerialization of the natural world in somewhat the same way as does the stained glass of Gothic architecture.

In contrast to M.I.T., some other educational institutions have sought to solve the problem of suitable religious expression in architecture by deliberately rejecting the non-denominational chapel in favor of separate chapels for the major religious groups. Thus for Brandeis University in Waltham, Massachusetts, the architectural firm of Harrison and Abramovitz erected in 1954–1956 three chapels—respectively Jewish,

[16] In *The Graham Foundation's First Year: 1957*, mimeographed; Chicago, 1957, p. 26.

Protestant, and Catholic—to form an Interfaith Center (Fig. 75). Significantly, unlike the Protestant and Jewish chapels which have windows behind the sanctuary looking directly out into nature in the manner popularized by Frank Lloyd Wright, the Catholic chapel does not, but instead has a definitely enclosed sanctuary. For modern Catholic church architecture has in general rejected the other solution, with its pantheistic overtones, which has become a cliché of modern religious architecture among non-Catholics.

From this rapid survey of American religious architecture since the seventeenth century, what general conclusions can be drawn? For one thing, the fact emerges that any successful religious building must express qualities which are in harmony with the doctrines of the group for whom it is built. Indeed, the finest religious edifices by their qualities in some way enhance and develop the expression of those doctrines, whether through the interpretation given to them by a great individual architect or through new expressive means made possible by developments in architectural style.

Our chronological study has indicated a further fact: that even for the groups with the longest and most orthodox traditions, religious expression in architecture has never remained unchanged for any length of time. Thus the styles of the buildings of even the most conservative Catholics and Episcopalians demonstrate almost constant change, while nearly all the other American denominations and sects have by this time completely abandoned their original architectural expression—derived from, or at least affected by, some form of meeting house—in favor of some other kind of building.

This also can be said: twentieth-century architecture has placed especially strong emphasis on the expression of the physical function of the religious building, so that solutions have been sought which will be particularly well suited physically to seeing, hearing, and participating in the service. Consequently, in recent years there has been a concentration on functional directness and simplicity which in some respects recalls the spirit of the early meeting houses. Paradoxically, however, this new simplicity and functionalism—far from distinguishing the left-wing Protestants, for whom so many of the meeting houses were built, from more completely orthodox denominations—have been almost simultaneously fostered by some liberal Protestant groups, by some fundamentalist Protestants, and even by Roman Catholics under the influence of the Liturgical Movement as it spread from Germany after World War I.

Another tendency characteristic of twentieth-century religious architecture places the modern architect on the horns of a dilemma. On the one hand, the architectural spirit of this century has emphasized progress in the use of new materials and techniques, and of new and therefore untraditional forms. It is not easy to employ these untraditional materials and forms so as to express traditional religious values. Therefore, in the effort to overcome this limitation on the expression of religious content, the modern architect has felt the need to retain some historical reminiscences by making use of at least some qualities and accessories that for Christians have traditionally connoted "church." These accessories (bell tower, cross, and the like), which have mostly been borrowed from the Episcopalians or the Roman Catholics, often have a tendency—in the face of a modern desire for simple, clear, unadorned "abstract" forms—to be mere stripped-down parodies of their historic selves, so that the modern architect has also felt the need to avoid them about as strongly as he has felt the need to use them. But even when he has made use of them, his approach has been sharply different from the eclecticism of the architects of the nineteenth century. For their kind of eclecticism sought the expression of religious values by imitating specific styles of the past regarded as particularly evocative of a whole set of such values—whether those implicit in the Romanesque, the Gothic, the "colonial," or some other style. Such historical eclecticism has now largely vanished in favor of a non-historical kind which has rejected the styles of the past, but has followed closely behind such individual innovators of forms as Frank Lloyd Wright, Eliel Saarinen, or even Mies van der Rohe. The work of any of these men, or of the other leaders of modern architecture, cannot, by its very nature, be particularly rich in forms with specific traditional religious connotations. The church architect, therefore, faced with this dilemma, finds himself adopting even for left-wing Protestant sects, readily comprehensible symbols, such as the cross or a modern version of stained glass, which were once anathema to most Protestant groups as being expressions of "popery."

An example in point is the First Presbyterian Church at Stamford, Connecticut (Fig. 76), completed in 1958 by Wallace Harrison of the firm of Harrison and Abramovitz. On the interior, this shows an imaginative use of techniques and materials, notably pre-cast concrete, that are clearly of the twentieth century, as well as a kind of dynamic architectural expressionism that first appeared in works by German expressionists of the 1920's. At the same time, however, in order to express "church" to the beholder, there are obvious reminiscences of the Gothic style in the plan, the structural forms, the large cross, and especially in the atmosphere created by a kind of modern stained glass actually made at Chartres—forms and qualities that any Presbyterian of the seventeenth or eighteenth century would surely have denounced as "popery." It is true that the exterior does not recall the Gothic, but, as so many who have written about this church have pointed out, its vaguely fish-like form recalls the fish symbol of the Early Christians, which originated chiefly from the fact that the five Greek letters which express the word "fish" form an anagram of the name of Jesus Christ. While it is also true that the early Presbyterians, like other Protestants, in many ways sought to return to the doctrines of early Christianity, this kind of symbolism, applied to architecture, again would surely have been frowned upon by them.

Therefore, with perhaps the exception of the Roman Catholics for whom traditional values are so particularly important, religious groups today are unlikely to express architecturally their own *specific* traditional beliefs and values. However, it should now be noted that this architectural situation does find its counterpart in the ecumenical tendencies which are so strong today within American Protestantism, at least, and which have led and are leading to so many mergers among Protestant groups in the twentieth century. For that matter, even among the Roman Catholics, the strong influence of the Liturgical Movement since World War I reflects certain socio-religious values not so directly expressed in earlier Catholic architecture.

Thus even under present-day conditions, different as they are from those of earlier periods in American religious history, we still see interactions between architectural expression on the one hand and religious situations on the other. In other words, today, as earlier in American history, Winston Churchill's dictum that "We shape our dwellings, and afterwards our dwellings shape us" continues to have meaning not only for the kind of secular architecture to which he was immediately referring, but also—and especially—for the dwellings of the spirit.

ACKNOWLEDGMENTS

The author wishes to thank the publishers, institutions, and individuals who gave permission to reproduce the illustrations used in this chapter. The sources of the illustrations are as follows: Fig. 1, from S. P. Dorsey, *Early English Churches in America* (New York: Oxford University Press, 1952), Pl. 15; Fig. 2, Nina Tracy Mann photo.; Fig. 3, courtesy of the Philadelphia Museum of Art, but reproduced from *Architectural Forum*, Vol. 57 (April 1929), p. 522; Fig. 4, *Architectural Forum*, *loc. cit.*; Fig. 5, courtesy of the Philadelphia Museum of Art, but reproduced from Fiske Kimball, *American Architecture* (Indianapolis: Bobbs-Merrill Co. Inc., 1928), p. 29; Fig. 6, Wayne Andrews photo.; Fig. 7, from Hugh Morrison, *Early American Architecture* (New York: Oxford University Press, 1952), p. 81; Figs. 8, 9, 10, from drawings made by Martin S. Briggs and published in his *Puritan Architecture* (London: Lutterworth Press, 1946), pp. 14, 17; Fig. 11, courtesy of the New-York Historical Society, but reproduced from T. J. Wertenbaker, *Founding of American Civilization* (New York: Charles Scribner's Sons, 1938), Pl. 7; Fig. 12, from *ibid.*, p. 78; Fig. 13, from M. D. Ozinga, *De Protestantsche Kerkenbouw in Nederland* (Amsterdam: H. J. Paris, 1929), Pl. 1; Fig. 14, from *ibid.*, Pl. 3; Fig. 15, Herbert Felton photo., courtesy of the Radio Times Hulton Picture Library, London, but reproduced from Ralph Dutton, *The Age of Wren* (London: B. T. Batsford, Ltd., 1951), Pl. 48; Fig. 16, H. Lidbetter photo., but reproduced from *Architectural Review* [London], Vol. 99 (April 1946), p. 106; Fig. 17, Elizabeth G. C. Menzies photo.; Fig. 18, from P. B. Wallace and W. A. Dunn, *Colonial Churches and Meeting Houses* (New York: Architectural Book Publishing Company, 1931), p. 164; Fig. 19, courtesy of The Society for the Preservation of New England Antiquities, and reproduced from *Old-Time New England,* Vol. 13 (1923), p. 75; Fig. 20, Wayne Andrews photo.; Fig. 21, courtesy of Rhode Island School of Design, but reproduced from H.-R. Hitchcock, *Rhode Island Architecture* (Providence: Rhode Island Museum Press, 1939), p. 18; Figs. 22, 23, Wayne Andrews photos.; Fig. 24, from S. G. Stoney, *Plantations of the Carolina Low Country* (Charleston, S.C.: Carolina Art Association, 1939), p. 48; Fig. 25, A. F. Kersting photo., but reproduced from Bryan Little, *The Life and Work of James Gibbs* (London: B. T. Batsford, Ltd., 1955), Pl. 10; Fig. 26, courtesy of The National Buildings Record, but reproduced from Little, Pl. 2; Fig. 27, from W. R. Ware, *The Georgian Period* (New York: U.P.C. Book Co., 1923), Vol. 6, Pl. 375;

Fig. 28, from Aymar Embury, *Early American Churches* (Garden City, N.Y.: Doubleday, Page, 1914), opp. p. 86; Fig. 29, Jules Schick photo., supplied by Rev. E. A. Harding, D.D., Rector of Christ Church, Philadelphia; Fig. 30, courtesy of The Society for the Preservation of New England Antiquities, and reproduced from *Old-Time New England,* Vol. 13 (1923), p. 110; Fig. 31, Kerschner photo., but reproduced from Rachel Wischnitzer, *Synagogue Architecture in the United States* (Philadelphia: Jewish Publication Society of America, 1955), Pl. 4; Fig. 32, from *ibid.*, Pl. 6; Fig. 33, Kerschner photo., but reproduced from *ibid.*, frontispiece; Fig. 34, Wayne Andrews photo.; Fig. 35, courtesy of Rhode Island School of Design, but reproduced from H.-R. Hitchcock, Pl. 15; Fig. 36, courtesy of The Society for the Preservation of New England Antiquities, and reproduced from *Old-Time New England,* Vol. 13 (1923), p. 158; Fig. 37, from Joseph Belcher, *George Whitefield: A Biography* (New York: American Tract Society, 1857), opp. p. 83; Fig. 38, from W. J. Townsend, *A New History of Methodism* (London: Hodder and Stoughton, 1909), Vol. 1, Pl. 17; Fig. 39, from *Architectural Review* [London], Vol. 88 (Dec. 1940), Pl. 18; Figs. 40, 41, from H. M. P. Gallagher, *Robert Mills* (New York: Columbia University Press, 1935), opp. p. 78; Fig. 42, Elizabeth G. C. Menzies photo.; Fig. 43, from R. H. Howland and E. P. Spencer, *The Architecture of Baltimore: A Pictorial History* (Baltimore: The Johns Hopkins Press, 1953), Pl. 35; Fig. 44, from *ibid.*, Pl. 37; Fig. 45, from *ibid.*, Pl. 36; Fig. 46, from *ibid.*, Pl. 27; Fig. 47, photo. supplied by Archbishopric of New York; Figs. 48, 49, from *Architectural Review* [London], Vol. 48 (Dec. 1945), p. 177; Figs. 50, 51, photos. supplied by the Rev. John Heuss, D.D., Rector of Trinity Church, New York; Fig. 52, from *Upjohn's Rural Architecture,* but reproduced from E. M. Upjohn, *Richard Upjohn, Architect and Churchman* (New York: Columbia University Press, 1939), fig. 68; Fig. 53, from *ibid.*, fig. 69; Fig. 54, Wayne Andrews photo.; Figs. 55, 56, courtesy of Hoyle, Doran and Berry, but reproduced from R. A. Cram, *My Life in Architecture* (Boston: Little, Brown and Co., 1936), opp. p. 254; Fig. 57, from A. L. Drummond, *Church Architecture of Protestantism* (Edinburgh: T. and T. Clark, 1934), opp. p. 80; Fig. 58, reproduced from *Planning Church Buildings*, Copyright 1945 by the Bureau of Church Building, National Council of Churches. Used with permission; Fig. 59, from H.-R. Hitchcock, *In the Nature of Materials* (New York: Duell, Sloan and Pearce, 1942), fig. 118; Fig. 60, from *ibid.*, fig. 119; Fig. 61, from *ibid.*, fig. 120; Figs. 62, 63, 64, Wayne Andrews photos.; Fig. 65, from Albert Christ-Janer, *Eliel Saarinen* (Chicago: Copyright 1948 by the University of Chicago Press), fig. 121; Fig. 66, from *ibid.*, fig. 124; Figs. 67, 68, Roger Sturtevant photos., but reproduced from *Architectural Forum*, Vol. 94 (Jan. 1951), pp. 143, 145; Fig. 69, from *L'Architecture d'Aujourd'hui*, No. 71, Pl. 3; Fig. 70, from *Architectural Record*, Vol. 103 (June 1948), p. 131; Fig. 71, Gottscho-Schleisner photo., but reproduced from *ibid.*, p. 129; Fig. 72, from *L'Architecture d'Aujourd'hui*, No. 24 (Dec. 1953), p. 26; Fig. 73, from *ibid.*, No. 71, Pl. 1; Fig. 74, from *ibid.*, Pl. 3; Fig. 75, from Rachel Wischnitzer, Pl. 149; Fig. 76, Ezra Stoller photo., but reproduced from *Architectural Forum*, Vol. 108 (April 1958), p. 104.

Particular thanks must also be given to Mrs. Helen Wright for securing the above permissions, and to Professor John Schnorrenberg for reading the essay in proof and making various helpful suggestions.

INDEX